Today's TBB

C++ Parallel Programming with Threading Building Blocks

Second Edition

Michael J. Voss
James R. Reinders

Today's TBB: C++ Parallel Programming with Threading Building Blocks, **Second Edition**

Michael J. Voss
Austin, TX, USA

James R. Reinders
Portland, OR, USA

ISBN-13 (pbk): 979-8-8688-1269-9
https://doi.org/10.1007/979-8-8688-1270-5

ISBN-13 (electronic): 979-8-8688-1270-5

Managing Director, Apress Media LLC: Welmoed Spahr
Acquisitions Editor: Susan McDermott
Development Editor: Laura Berendson
Project Manager: Jessica Vakili

Distributed to the book trade worldwide by Springer Science+Business Media New York, 1 New York Plaza, New York, NY 10004. Phone 1-800-SPRINGER, fax (201) 348-4505, e-mail orders-ny@springer-sbm.com, or visit www.springeronline.com. Apress Media, LLC is a California LLC and the sole member (owner) is Springer Science + Business Media Finance Inc (SSBM Finance Inc). SSBM Finance Inc is a **Delaware** corporation.

For information on translations, please e-mail booktranslations@springernature.com; for reprint, paperback, or audio rights, please e-mail bookpermissions@springernature.com.

Apress titles may be purchased in bulk for academic, corporate, or promotional use. eBook versions and licenses are also available for most titles. For more information, reference our Print and eBook Bulk Sales web page at http://www.apress.com/bulk-sales.

If disposing of this product, please recycle the paper

We dedicate this book to the memory of our esteemed colleague, Rafael Asenjo. His wisdom, teaching excellence, and remarkable sense of humor are profoundly missed.

Table of Contents

About the Authors

Michael J. Voss is a Senior Principal Engineer of Middleware Architecture at Intel. He has been a key member of the TBB development team since before its 1.0 release in 2006. Michael has coauthored over 40 published papers and articles on parallel programming and frequently consults with customers across diverse domains to help them effectively utilize parallelism in their applications. He is a member of the ISO C++ committee (WG21), participating in discussions around libraries and concurrency. Before joining Intel in 2006, Michael was an assistant professor in the Edward S. Rogers Sr. Department of Electrical and Computer Engineering at the University of Toronto. He earned his PhD from the School of Electrical and Computer Engineering at Purdue University.

James R. Reinders enjoyed a distinguished career at Intel Corporation that spanned over four decades. With extensive experience in parallel computing, James has authored, coauthored, or edited 12 technical books on parallel programming and contributed to numerous others. A proud graduate of the University of Michigan's engineering programs, he has a deep passion for system optimization and teaching. James has had the privilege of contributing to two of the world's fastest computers, both achieving the #1 spot on the TOP500 list, as well as many other supercomputers and software development tools. With the completion of this book, James has retired from Intel and is now enjoying a well-deserved life of relaxation in Oregon.

Acknowledgments

Mike wishes to express his heartfelt gratitude to his wife, Natalie, and their children, Nick, Luke, and Alexandra (and her husband Royce), for their unwavering support.

James extends his deep appreciation to his wife, Susan Meredith, whose invaluable insights and support have been instrumental in bringing this work to fruition.

We would also like to acknowledge everyone who has contributed to TBB over the years, particularly the many developers at Intel whose significant efforts have enriched the library. Our reviewers, an exceptional group of TBB users and key developers, have provided invaluable feedback that has greatly enhanced this work. We are grateful for the significant advice and insights offered by many, including Ruslan Arutyunyan, Raja Bala, Piotr Balcer, Karolina Bober, Konstantin Boyarinov, Jake Chuang, Chunyang Dai, Lukasz Dorau, Mikhail Dvorskiy, Alexandra Epanchinzeva, Andrey Fedorov, Aleksei Fedotov, Elvis G. Fefey, Adam Fidel, J. Daniel Garcia, Wenju He, Dan Hoeflinger, Ilya Isaev, Shweta Jha, Seung-Woo Kim, Kyle Knoepfel, Alexandr Konovalov, Sergey Kopienko, Alexey Kukanov, Pavel Kumbrasev, Mark Lubin, Olga Malysheva, Matthew Michel, Dmitri Mokhov, Rob Mueller-Albrecht, Sarath Nandu R., Eric L. Palmer, Arun Parkugan, Marc F. Paterno, Lukasz Plewa, Pablo Reble, Ekaterina Semenova, Deepanshi Sharma, Pawel Skowron, Timmie Smith, Tobias Weinzierl, Anuya Welling, Alex M. Wells, and Marek Wyszumirski. We sincerely thank all those who contributed, and we apologize for any omissions.

We thank Tim Mattson for his encouragement and advice regarding parallel patterns and their role in explaining how to be most effective as a programmer writing parallel code.

Our ongoing appreciation goes to Sanjiv Shah, Joe Curley, Cristina Belidica, and Herb Hinstorff for their steadfast support and occasional gentle nudges over the years.

Finally, we would like to recognize the dedicated efforts of the entire Apress team in guiding this book through contracting, editing, and production. Thank you, all.

Mike Voss and James Reinders

Preface

In this Preface, we review essential parallel programming concepts to keep in mind as we begin our journey into teaching Threading Building Blocks (TBB) in Chapter 1.

Think Parallel! This book is designed to be valuable for both newcomers to parallel programming and seasoned experts alike. Whether you are comfortable with only C programming or fluent in modern C++, this book is accessible and relevant.

To address our diverse audience without oversimplifying the content, we have crafted this Preface to help level the playing field. We strongly encourage every reader to review it before diving into the chapters ahead.

BOOKMARK THESE

TBB has been around long enough that a significant amount of outdated material exists online, including two previous books on TBB. While older resources are largely accurate, subtle differences can lead to frustration, particularly as they may reflect changes needed to align with the evolving C++ standard. Since TBB's debut in 2006, when C++03 was the standard, the language has undergone considerable development, making it important to reference up-to-date materials.

Once you are well-versed in TBB and parallel programming, the best online resources for detailed interface information and advanced controls are `https://tinyurl.com/tbbdoc` and `https://tinyurl.com/tbbspec`. No other online resources are as comprehensive or up-to-date. We recommend bookmarking them to supplement your learning from this book.

When teaching TBB, we will use a notation [X . Y] (e.g., [algorithms.parallel_for]) to refer to the specification (`https://tinyurl.com/tbbspec`) page where the relevant online specification can be found. The title X (e.g., algorithms) will be under either oneTBB Interfaces or oneTBB Auxiliary Interfaces, and that will take you to the page where the link for Y (e.g., parallel_for) exists.

Additionally, be sure to bookmark `https://tinyurl.com/tbbBOOKexamples` for access to the source code used in the figures throughout this book. The code is provided exactly as it appears in the book, along with resources to find updates if any examples are revised in the future. All code is available for download.

What Is TBB and oneTBB?

TBB is a powerful solution for writing parallel programs in C++, offering the most popular and comprehensive support of parallel programming for the language. When TBB was first introduced, it provided core functionality – including a task-stealing scheduler, parallelism-aware memory management, and highly concurrent containers – along with features that were absent in C++ at the time such as portable atomics. From its earliest documentation, TBB has the stated goal to see these capabilities make their way into the C++ standard.

In 2019, TBB made a bold decision to streamline its offerings by shedding support for features that had since been incorporated into the evolving C++ standard. This initiative, known as can be seen as an adaptation of TBB to complement "today's C++," focusing on its core strengths: scheduling, memory management, and containers for scalable parallel programming. Despite the rebranding to oneTBB, there is no fundamental difference between it and the original TBB, other than its reliance on modern C++ foundations rather than competing with them. Even with the name change, we still commonly refer to it as TBB, as the interface names and namespace remain `tbb` with `oneapi::tbb` defined as an alias to `tbb`. Using either is fine; similarly, header file paths remain unchanged, but there is also a set of redirection headers that allows `oneapi/` to be added to the path if we prefer. TBB documents and specifications will often show interfaces inside of a new top-level `oneapi` namespace, but as section `[configuration.namespaces]` of the oneTBB specification states, "The `oneapi::tbb` namespace can be considered as an alias for the `tbb` namespace." In this book, we just use the `tbb` namespace directly, and we use just the `tbb` name in the path for include files.

oneAPI is a community managed by the UXL (Unified Acceleration) Foundation. There are multiple oneAPI projects, including oneTBB, that benefit from UXL.

We believe that TBB is the most effective way to write parallel programs in C++, enabling you to fully harness the power of the host CPU – even when offloading some computations to accelerators. Our goal is to help you become highly productive in using TBB.

Organization of the Book and Preface

This book is organized into the following sections:

- Preface: This section provides the background and fundamentals necessary to understand the rest of the book. It includes motivations for the TBB parallel programming model, an introduction to parallel programming, an overview of locality and caches, an introduction to vectorization (Single Instruction Multiple Data, SIMD), and a discussion of C++ features (beyond those in C) that are supported or utilized by TBB.

- Chapters 1–9: These chapters offer a comprehensive introduction to TBB, equipping us with the knowledge needed to perform highly effective parallel programming.

- Chapters 10–11: These chapters provide practical advice, tips, and tricks for writing parallel applications using TBB. Chapter 10 covers the out-of-the-box performance provided by TBB (pillars of composability), discussing TBB arenas and interoperability with other programming models. Chapter 11 delves into performance tuning beyond the default TBB settings.

- Chapter 12: This chapter focuses on migrating from the original TBB (2006–2019) to today's TBB (oneTBB; 2020–present). It serves as a valuable reference for updating older applications and includes advice on transitioning to today's TBB and utilizing modern C++ for parallel programming.

- Appendix A: A tradition since the first TBB book, this appendix offers a historical perspective on the inspirations behind TBB. It highlights how today's TBB benefits from the pioneering research in parallel programming that preceded it.

Think Parallel

For those new to parallel programming, this Preface provides a solid foundation to make the rest of the book more useful, approachable, and self-contained. We've designed it with the assumption that you have a basic understanding of C++ programming, but we introduce the key C++ elements that TBB relies on and supports. Our approach to parallel programming is practical, emphasizing the strategies that make parallel programs most effective. For experienced parallel programmers, we hope this Preface serves as a brief refresher on the essential vocabulary and concepts that enable optimal use of parallel computer hardware.

Three key principles enable parallel programming to be productive and effective:

(1) Program using tasks, not threads.

(2) Parallel programming models need not be messy.

(3) Achieving scalability, performance, and performance portability requires portable, low-overhead, parallel programming models.

TBB is so effective, and popular, because it satisfies all three.

After reading this Preface, you should be able to articulate what it means to "Think Parallel" in terms of decomposition, scaling, correctness, abstraction, and patterns. You'll also gain an appreciation for the importance of locality in parallel programming. Additionally, you'll understand the philosophy behind task-based programming vs. thread-based programming – a revolutionary approach in parallel programming championed by TBB. Finally, you'll grasp the C++ programming elements that go beyond basic C/C++ knowledge, necessary for effective TBB usage.

Effective parallel programming necessitates a clear separation of concerns: the programmer should focus on exposing parallelism through tasks, while the programming model implementation (TBB) handles the mapping of these tasks to hardware threads.

Role of Offloading to Accelerators

TBB provides the most effective methods for managing the full parallelism available on a host CPU. In modern systems, accelerators like GPUs offer additional parallel computational capabilities. These offloading techniques are explored through various C++ extensions, such as Parallel STL (PSTL), CUDA, SYCL, HIP, and OpenCL. However, successful offloading is best achieved within a well-engineered parallel host application that leverages the robust parallelism made possible with TBB.

To maximize performance in parallel programming, it is essential to keep the entire system – both the CPU and accelerators – fully utilized. Accelerators excel at handling highly regular parallel tasks, while the CPU is uniquely efficient at processing irregular parallelism. These differences highlight the importance of thoroughly understanding the available tools and using them optimally based on your specific needs.

Motivations Behind Threading Building Blocks (TBB)

TBB first appeared in 2006. It was the product of experts in parallel programming at Intel, many of whom had decades of experience in parallel programming models including OpenMP. Many members of the TBB team had previously spent years helping drive OpenMP to the great success it enjoys by developing and supporting OpenMP implementations. Appendix A is dedicated to a deeper dive into the history of TBB and the core concepts that go into it, including the breakthrough concept of task-stealing schedulers.

Born in the early days of multicore processors, TBB quickly emerged as the most popular parallel programming model for C++ programmers. TBB evolved to incorporate a rich set of additions that have made it an obvious choice for parallel programming for novices and experts alike. As an open source project, TBB has enjoyed feedback and contributions from around the world.

TBB promotes a revolutionary idea: programmers should be able to expose opportunities for parallelism without hesitation, leaving the underlying programming model (TBB) to map these opportunities to the hardware at runtime.

To fully appreciate the importance and value of TBB, it's essential to understand three key principles: (1) program using tasks, not threads; (2) parallel programming models do not need to be messy; and (3) achieving scalability, performance, and performance portability requires portable, low-overhead parallel programming models like TBB. We'll explore each of these principles in detail, as they are crucial to mastering effective and structured parallel programming. It's fair to say that these concepts were underestimated for a long time before becoming fundamental to our understanding of parallel programming.

Program Using Tasks, Not Threads

Parallel programming should always be conceptualized in terms of *tasks* rather than *threads.* Edward Lee provides an authoritative and comprehensive exploration of this topic, noting in 2006 that "For concurrent programming to become mainstream, we must discard threads as a programming model."

If we express parallel programming through threads, we unfortunately engage in the challenging task of mapping our application to the specific number of parallel execution threads available on the machine at hand. Conversely, when we frame parallel programming around tasks, we focus on identifying opportunities for parallelism. This allows a runtime environment – such as the Threading Building Blocks (TBB) runtime – to efficiently allocate tasks to the available hardware without complicating our application logic.

Threads represent discrete execution streams that run on hardware threads for a limited time, potentially shifting to different hardware threads in subsequent time slices. This thread-centric approach often leads to a misguided one-to-one mapping between execution threads and hardware threads (e.g., processor cores). However, hardware threads are physical resources that vary across machines, and their implementations can differ subtly. We will come back to defining/discussing threads a little later in the section "What Is a Thread?"

In contrast, *tasks* represent *opportunities* for parallelism. The ability to subdivide tasks can be exploited, as needed, to fill available threads when needed.

With these definitions in mind, a program written in terms of threads would have to map each algorithm onto specific systems of hardware and software. This is not only a distraction, but it also causes a whole host of issues that make parallel programming more difficult, less effective, and far less portable.

When a program is written in terms of tasks, the runtime – such as the TBB runtime – can dynamically map those tasks onto the available hardware at runtime. This approach eliminates the need to worry about the number of actual hardware threads present in a system. More importantly, it is the only practical method for effectively enabling nested parallelism. Given its significance, we will revisit and emphasize the importance of nested parallelism throughout this book.

Composability: Parallel Programming Does Not Have to Be Messy

TBB offers *composability* for parallel programming, and that changes everything. Composability means we can mix and match features of TBB without restriction. Most notably, this includes nesting. Therefore, it makes perfect sense to have a `parallel_for` inside a `parallel_for` loop. It is also okay for a `parallel_for` to call a function, which then has a `parallel_for` within it.

Supporting composable nested parallelism turns out to be highly desirable because it exposes more opportunities for parallelism, and that results in more scalable applications. OpenMP, for instance, is not composable with respect to nesting because each level of nesting can easily cause significant overhead and consumption of resources leading to exhaustion and program termination. This is a huge problem when you consider that a library routine may contain parallel code, so we may experience issues using a non-composable technique if we call the library while already doing parallelism. No such problem exists with TBB, because it is composable. TBB solves this, in part, by letting us expose opportunities for parallelism (tasks) while TBB decides at runtime how to map them to hardware (threads).

This is the key benefit to coding in terms of tasks (potential parallelism) instead of threads (mandatory parallelism). If a `parallel_for` was considered mandatory, nesting would cause an explosion of threads, which causes a whole host of resource issues that can easily (and often do) crash programs when not controlled. When `parallel_for` exposes available nonmandatory parallelism, the runtime is free to use that information to match the capabilities of the machine in the most effective manner.

We have come to expect composability in our programming languages, but most parallel programming models have failed to preserve it (fortunately, TBB does preserve composability!). Consider "`if`" and "`while`" statements. The C and C++ languages allow them to freely mix and nest as we desire. Imagine this was not so, and we lived in a world where a function called from within an `if`-statement was forbidden to contain a `while` statement! Hopefully, any suggestion of such a restriction seems almost silly. TBB brings this type of composability to *parallel programming* by allowing parallel constructs to be freely mixed and nested without restrictions and without causing issues.

Scaling, Performance, and Quest for Performance Portability

Perhaps the most important benefit of programming with TBB is that it helps us create a performance-portable application. We define *performance portability* as the characteristic that allows a program to maintain a similar "percentage of peak performance" across a variety of machines (different hardware, different operating systems, or both). We would like to achieve a high percentage of peak performance on many different machines without the need to change our code.

We would also like to see a 16× gain in performance on a 64-core machine vs. a quad-core machine. For a variety of reasons, we will almost never see ideal speedup (never say never: sometimes, due to an increase in aggregate cache size, we can see more than ideal speedup – a condition we call superlinear speedup).

What Is Speedup?

Speedup is formally defined to be the time to run sequentially (not in parallel) divided by the time to run in parallel. If my program runs in 3 seconds normally, but in only 1 second on a quad-core processor, we say it has a speedup of 3×. Sometimes, we might speak of efficiency, which is speedup divided by the number of processing cores. Our 3× would be 75% efficient at using the parallelism.

The ideal goal of a 16× gain in performance when moving from a quad-core machine to one with 64 cores is called *linear scaling* or *perfect scaling*.

To accomplish this, we need to keep all the cores busy as we grow their numbers – something that requires considerable available parallelism. We will dive more into this concept of "available parallelism" when we discuss Amdahl's Law and its implications later in this Preface.

For now, it is important to know that TBB supports high-performance programming and helps significantly with performance portability. The high-performance support comes because TBB introduces very low overhead, which allows scaling to proceed without issue. Performance portability lets our application automatically harness available parallelism as new machines offer more capabilities.

In our confident claims here, we are assuming a world where the slight additional overhead of dynamic task scheduling is the most effective at exposing the parallelism and exploiting it. This assumption has one fault: if we can program an application to perfectly match the hardware, without any dynamic adjustments, we may find a few percentage points gain in performance. Traditional High-Performance Computing (HPC) programming, the name given to programming the world's largest computers for intense computations, has long had this characteristic in highly parallel scientific computations. HPC developers who utilize OpenMP with static scheduling, and find it does well with their performance, may find the dynamic nature of TBB to be a slight reduction in performance. However, the occasional advantages of static scheduling are disappearing (becoming more rare each day) for a variety of reasons. All programming, including HPC programming, is increasing in complexity in a way that demands support for nested and dynamic parallelism. We see these effects in all aspects of HPC programming as well, including growth to multiphysics models, introduction of AI (artificial intelligence), and use of ML (machine learning) methods. One key driver of additional complexity is the increasing diversity of hardware, leading to heterogeneous compute capabilities within a single machine. TBB gives us powerful options for dealing with these complexities, including its flow graph features, which we will dive into in Chapters 4 and 5.

Effective parallel programming necessitates a clear separation of concerns: the programmer should focus on exposing parallelism through tasks, while the programming model implementation (TBB) handles the mapping of these tasks to hardware threads.

What Is Scaling?

Ultimately, parallel programming aims to achieve speedup by using the benefits of parallel computations available in a computer system. Scaling refers to the quality whereby an application is able to take advantage of more and more available parallelism. It is easy writing a program that simply divides a problem into two parallel computations. Such a program should show speedup on a dual-core system (scaling nicely as we move from one to two cores), but will fail to show continued scaling on four, eight, or more processing cores. Both speedup and scalability are important objectives in parallel programming, and it is absolutely critical we understand them well. In a later section titled "How Much Parallelism Is There in an Application," we push to cement these important concepts in our minds.

Introduction to Parallel Programming

Before we delve into the terminology and key concepts of parallel programming, let's make a bold claim: parallel programming is more intuitive than sequential programming. Parallelism is a fundamental part of our daily lives, where performing tasks step-by-step is a luxury we rarely experience or expect. Given that parallelism is so familiar to us, it should naturally extend to our approach to programming.

Parallelism Is All Around Us

In everyday life, we find ourselves thinking about parallelism. Here are a few examples:

Long lines: When faced with a lengthy line, you've likely wished for multiple shorter, faster lines or more attendants at the front to serve customers more efficiently. Examples include grocery store checkout lines, ticket queues at train stations, and lines for buying coffee.

Repetitive tasks: When faced with a large task that many people could assist with simultaneously, you've undoubtedly wished for more helping hands. Examples include moving all your possessions from one home to another, stuffing letters into envelopes for a mass mailing, and installing the same software on multiple new computers in your lab. The proverb "Many hands make light work" applies equally well to computers.

Once you dig in and start using parallelism, you will Think Parallel. You will learn to think first about the parallelism in your project and only then think about coding it.

Yale Patt, a famous computer architect, observed:

A Conventional Wisdom Problem is the belief that Thinking in Parallel is hard.

Perhaps (all) thinking is hard!

How do we get people to believe that Thinking in Parallel is natural?

(We could not agree more!)

Concurrent vs. Parallel

It is important to distinguish between the terms "concurrent" and "parallel," as they are related but subtly different. "Concurrent" means "happening during the same time span," whereas "parallel" is more specific, implying "happening at the same time (at least some of the time)." Concurrency is akin to what a single person attempts when multitasking, while parallelism resembles what multiple people can achieve together. Figure P-1 illustrates the concepts of concurrency vs. parallelism.

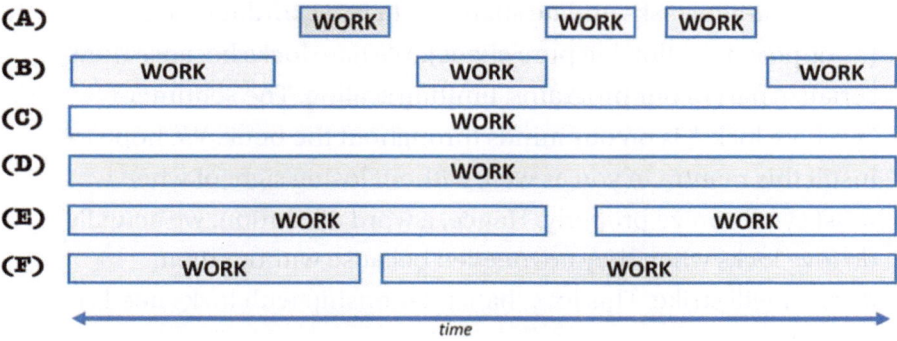

Figure P-1. *Parallel vs. concurrent: tasks A and B are concurrent relative to each other but not parallel relative to each other; all other combinations are both concurrent and parallel*

When we create effective parallel programs, our goal is to achieve more than just concurrency. Generally, speaking of concurrency implies there is no expectation of a significant amount of activity being truly parallel, meaning that two workers are not necessarily accomplishing more than one could theoretically achieve alone (see tasks A and B in Figure P-1). Since concurrent work is not completed any sooner, it does not improve the latency of a task (the delay before a task starts).

Conversely, using the term "parallel" conveys an expectation of improved latency and throughput (the amount of work done in a given time). We will explore this in greater depth when we discuss the limits of parallelism and delve into the important concepts of Amdahl's Law.

Enemies of Parallelism

Bearing in mind *the enemies of parallel programming* will help understand our advocacy for particular programming methods. Key parallel programming enemies include

Locks: In parallel programming, locks or mutual exclusion objects (mutexes) are used to provide a thread with exclusive access to a resource – blocking other threads from simultaneously accessing the same resource. Locks are the most common explicit way to ensure parallel tasks update shared data in a coordinated fashion (as opposed to allowing pure chaos). We hate locks because they serialize part of our programs, limiting scaling. The sentiment "we hate locks" is on our minds throughout the book. We hope to instill this mantra in you as well, without losing sight of when we must synchronize properly. Hence, a word of caution: we actually do love locks when they are needed because without them disaster will strike. This love/hate relationship with locks needs to be understood.

Shared mutable state: "Mutable" is another word for "can be changed." Shared mutable state happens any time we share data among multiple threads, and we allow it to change while being shared. Such sharing either reduces scaling when synchronization is needed and used correctly, or it leads to correctness issues (race conditions or deadlocks) when synchronization (e.g., a lock) is incorrectly applied. Realistically, we need shared mutable state when we write applications. Thinking about careful handling of shared mutable state may be an easier way to understand the basis of our love/hate relationship with locks. In the end, we all end up "managing" shared mutable state and the mutual exclusion (including locks) to make it work as we wish. Locks – we can't live with them, and we can't live without them.

Not "Thinking Parallel": Use of clever bandages and patches will not make up for a poorly thought-out strategy for scalable algorithms. Knowing where the parallelism is available, and how it can be exploited, should be considered before implementation.

Trying to add parallelism to an application, after it is written, is fraught with peril. Some preexisting code may shift to use parallelism relatively well, but most code will benefit from considerable rethinking of algorithms.

Forgetting that algorithms win: This may just be another way to say, "Think Parallel." The choice of algorithms has a profound effect on the scalability of applications. Our choice of algorithms determines how tasks can be divided, data structures are accessed, and results are coalesced. The optimal algorithm is really the one that serves as the basis for the optimal solution. An optimal solution is a combination of the appropriate algorithm, with the best matching parallel data structure, and the best way to schedule the computation over the data. The search for and discovery of algorithms that are better is seemingly unending for all of us as programmers. Now, as parallel programmers, we must add *scalable* to the definition of *better* for an algorithm. Achieving good scaling will require us to keep an eye on computation complexity. In particular, when comparing algorithm choices, we need to understand how time and memory requirements change with the size of the data set for any particular algorithm choice.

Terminology of Parallelism

The vocabulary of parallel programming is something we need to learn in order to converse with other parallel programmers. None of the concepts are particularly hard, but they are important to internalize. A parallel programmer, like any programmer, spends years gaining a deep intuitive feel for their craft, despite the fundamentals being simple enough to explain.

We will discuss the decomposition of work into parallel tasks, scaling terminology, correctness considerations, and the importance of locality due primarily to cache effects.

When we think about our application, how do we find the opportunities for parallelism?

At the highest level, parallelism exists either in the form of data to operate on in parallel or in the form of tasks to execute in parallel. And they are *not* mutually exclusive. In a sense, all of the important parallelism is in data parallelism. Nevertheless, we will introduce both because it can be convenient to think of both. When we discuss scaling, and Amdahl's Law, our intense bias to look for *data* parallelism will become more understandable.

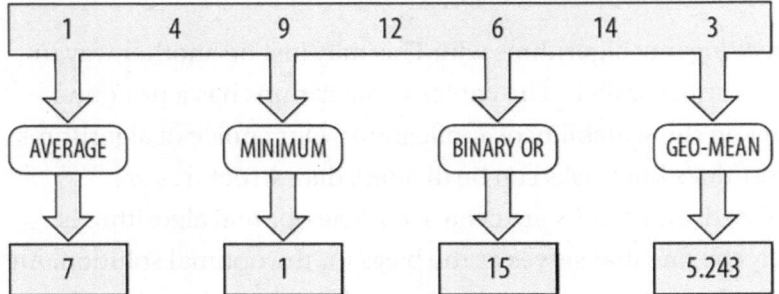

Figure P-2. *Task parallelism*

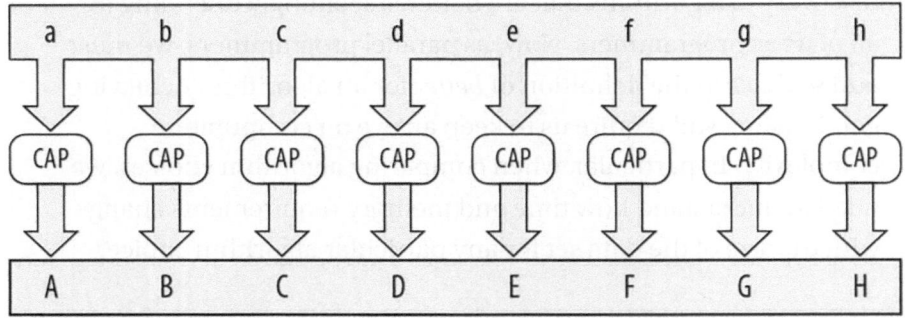

Figure P-3. *Data parallelism*

Terminology: Task Parallelism

Task parallelism refers to different, independent tasks. Figure P-2 illustrates this, showing an example of mathematical operations that can each be applied to the same data set to compute values that are independent. In this case, the average value, the minimum value, the binary OR function, and the geometric mean of the data set are computed. Finding work to do in parallel in terms of task parallelism becomes limited by the number of independent operations we can envision.

Earlier in this Preface, we have been advocating using *tasks* instead of *threads*. As we now discuss *data* vs. *task* parallelism, it may seem a bit confusing because we use the word *task* again in a different context when we compare *task parallelism* vs. *data parallelism*. For either type of parallelism, we will program for either in terms of *tasks* and not *threads*. This is the vocabulary used by parallel programmers.

Terminology: Data Parallelism

Data parallelism (Figure P-3) is easy to picture: take lots of data and apply the same transformation to each piece of the data. In Figure P-3, each letter in the data set is capitalized and becomes the corresponding uppercase letter. This simple example shows that given a data set and an operation that can be applied element by element, we can apply the same task in parallel to each element. Programmers writing code for supercomputers love this sort of problem and consider it so easy to do in parallel that it has been called *embarrassingly parallel*. A word of advice: if you have lots of data parallelism, do not be embarrassed – take advantage of it and be very happy. Consider it *happy parallelism*.

When comparing the effort to find work to do in parallel, an approach that focuses on data parallelism is limited by the amount of data we can grab to process. Approaches based on task parallelism alone are limited by the different task types we program. While both methods are valid and important, it is critical to find parallelism in the data that we process to have a truly scalable parallel program. Scalability means that our application can increase in performance as we add hardware (e.g., more processor cores) provided we have enough data. In the age of big data, it turns out that big data and parallel programming are made for each other. It seems that growth in data sizes is a reliable source of additional work. We will revisit this observation, a little later in this Preface, when we discuss Amdahl's Law.

Figure P-4. *Pipeline*

Figure P-5. *Imagine that each position is a different car in different stages of assembly; this is a pipeline in action with data flowing through it*

Terminology: Pipelining

While task parallelism is harder to find than data parallelism, a specific type of task parallelism is worth highlighting: *pipelining*. In this kind of algorithm, many independent tasks need to be applied to a stream of data. Each item is processed by each stage, as shown by the letter A in (Figure P-4). A stream of data can be processed more quickly when we use a pipeline, because different items can pass through different stages at the same time, as shown in Figure P-5. In these examples, the time to get a result may not be faster (referred to as the *latency* measured as the time from input to output) but the *throughput* is greater because it is measured in terms of completions (output) per unit of time. Pipelines enable parallelism to increase *throughput* when compared with sequential (serial) processing. A pipeline can also be more sophisticated: it can reroute data or skip steps for chosen items. TBB has specific support for simple pipelines (Chapter 2) and very complex pipelines (Chapter 4). Of course, each step in the pipeline can use data or task parallelism as well. The composability of TBB supports this seamlessly.

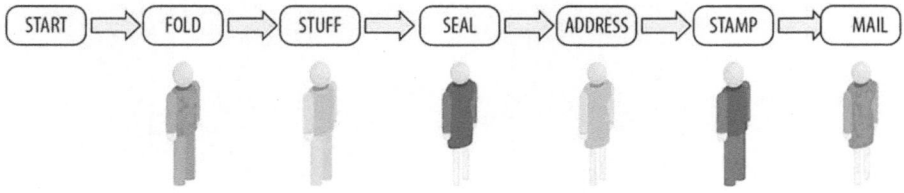

Figure P-6. *Pipelining – each person has a different job*

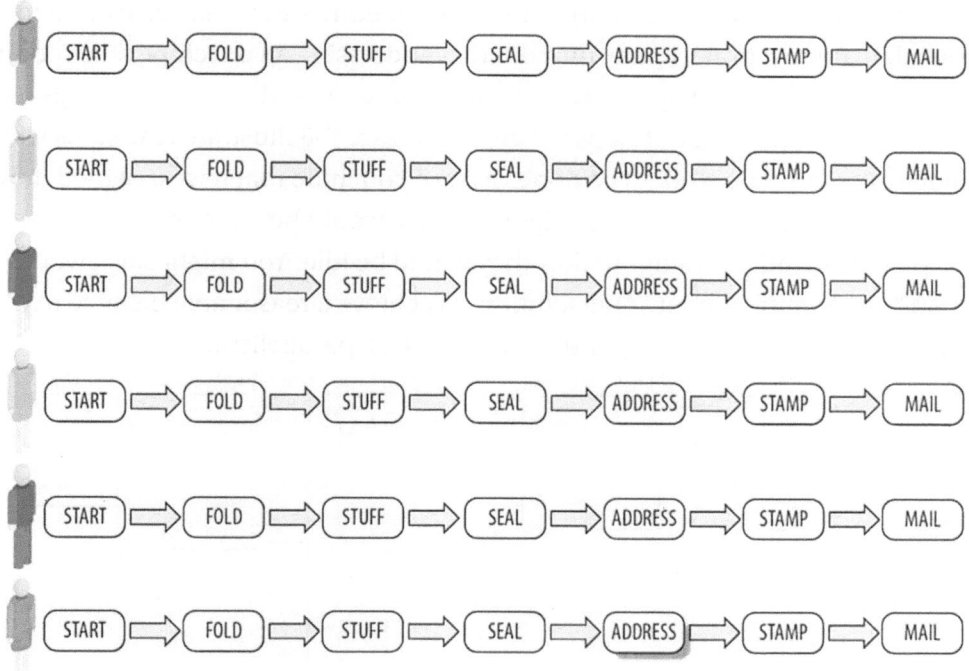

Figure P-7. *Data parallelism – each person has the same job*

Example of Exploiting Mixed Parallelism

Consider the task of folding, stuffing, sealing, addressing, stamping, and mailing letters. If we assemble a group of six people for the task of stuffing many envelopes, we can arrange each person to specialize in and perform their assigned task in a pipeline fashion (Figure P-6). This contrasts with data parallelism, where we divide up the supplies and give a batch of everything to each person (Figure P-7). Each person then does all the steps on their collection of materials.

Figure P-7 is clearly the right choice if every person must work in a different location far from each other. That is called *coarse-grained* parallelism because the interactions between the tasks are infrequent (they only come together to collect envelopes, then leave, and do their task, including mailing). The other choice shown in Figure P-6 approximates what we call *fine-grained* parallelism because of the frequent interactions (every envelope is passed along to every worker in various steps of the operation).

Neither extreme tends to fit reality, although sometimes they may be close enough to be useful. In our example, it may turn out that addressing an envelope takes enough time to keep three people busy, whereas the first two steps and the last two steps require only one person on each pair of steps to keep up. Figure P-8 illustrates the steps with the corresponding size of the work to be done. We can conclude that if we assigned only one person to each step as we see done in Figure P-6, we would be "starving" some people in this pipeline of work for things to do – they would be idle. You might say it would be hidden "underemployment." Our solution, to achieve a reasonable balance in our pipeline (Figure P-9), is really a hybrid of data and task parallelism.

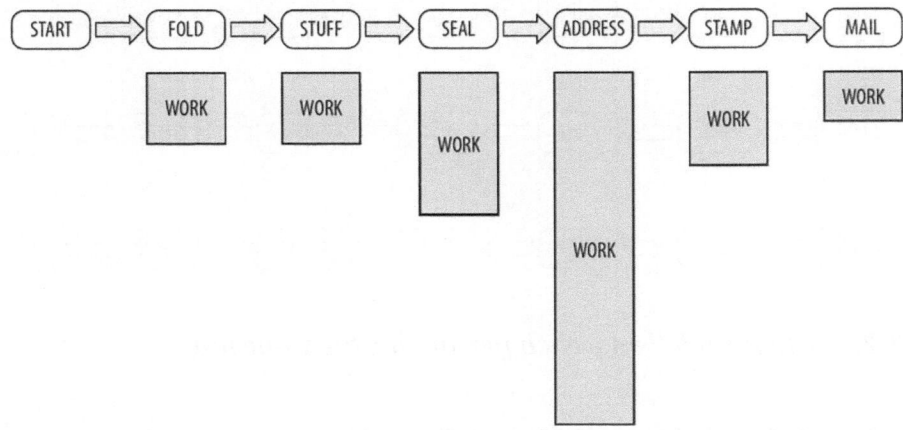

Figure P-8. *Unequal tasks are best combined or split to match people*

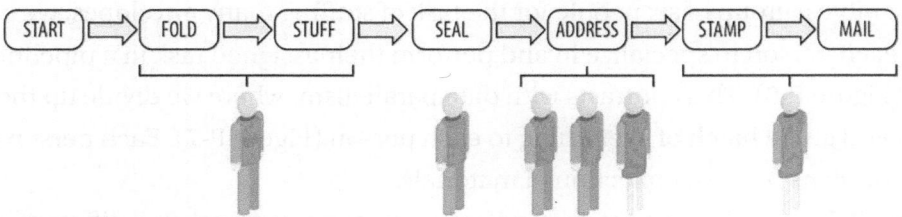

Figure P-9. *Because tasks are not equal, assign more people to addressing letters*

Achieving Parallelism

Coordinating people around the job of preparing and mailing the envelopes is easily expressed by the following two conceptual steps:

1. Assign people to tasks (and feel free to move them around to balance the workload).

2. Start with one person on each of the six tasks but be willing to split up a given task so that two or more people can work on it together.

The six tasks are folding, stuffing, sealing, addressing, stamping, and mailing. We also have six people (resources) to help with the work. That is exactly how TBB works best: we define tasks and data at a level we can explain and then split or combine data to match up with resources available to do the work.

The first step in writing a parallel program is to consider where the parallelism is. Many textbooks wrestle with task and data parallelism as though there were a clear choice. TBB allows any combination of the two that we express.

Far from decrying chaos, we love the chaos of lots of uncoordinated tasks running around getting work done without having to check in with each other (synchronization). This so-called "loosely coupled" parallel programming is great! More than locks, we hate synchronization because it makes tasks wait for other tasks. Tasks exist to work – not sit around waiting!

If we are lucky, our program will have an abundant amount of data parallelism available for us to exploit. To simplify this work, TBB requires only that we specify tasks and how to split them. For a completely data-parallel task, in TBB we will define one task to which we give all the data. That task will then be split up automatically to use the available hardware parallelism. The implicit synchronization (as opposed to synchronization we directly ask for with coding) will often eliminate the need for using locks to achieve synchronization. Referring back to our enemies list, and the fact that we hate locks, the implicit synchronization is a good thing. What do we mean by "implicit" synchronization? Usually, all we are saying is that synchronization occurred, but we did not explicitly code a synchronization. At first, this should seem like a "cheat." After all, synchronization still happened – and someone had to ask for it! In a sense, we are counting on these implicit synchronizations being more carefully planned and implemented. The more we can use the standard methods of TBB, and the less we explicitly write our own locking code, the better off we will be – in general.

By letting TBB manage the work, we hand over the responsibility for splitting up the work and synchronizing when needed. The synchronization done by the library for us, which we call implicit synchronization, in turn often eliminates the need for an explicit coding for synchronization (see Chapter 8).

We strongly suggest starting there and only venturing into explicit synchronization (Chapter 8) when absolutely necessary or beneficial. We can say, from experience, even when such things seem to be necessary, they are not. You have been warned. If you are like us, you will ignore the warning occasionally and get burned. We have. 😊

People have been exploring decomposition for decades, and some patterns have emerged. We will connect the concepts of such effective design patterns and TBB interfaces in Chapter 2 (see Figure 2-1).

Effective parallel programming is really about keeping all our tasks busy getting useful work done all the time – and hunting down and eliminating idle time is a key to our goal: scaling to achieve great speedups.

Terminology: Scaling and Speedup

The scalability of a program is a measure of how much speedup the program gets as we add more computing capabilities. Speedup is the ratio of the time it takes to run a program without parallelism vs. the time it takes to run in parallel. A speedup of 4× indicates that the parallel program runs in a quarter of the time of the serial program. An example would be a serial program that takes 100 seconds to run on a one-processor machine and 25 seconds to run on a quad-core machine.

As a goal, we would expect that our program running on two processor cores should run faster than our program running on one processor core. Likewise, running on four processor cores should be faster than running on two cores.

Any program will have a point of diminishing returns for adding parallelism. It is not uncommon for performance to even drop, instead of simply leveling off, if we force the use of too many compute resources. The granularity at which we should stop subdividing a problem can be expressed as a *grain size*. TBB uses a notion of *grain size* to help limit the splitting of data to a reasonable level to avoid this problem of dropping in performance. Grain size is generally determined automatically, by an automatic partitioner within TBB, using a combination of heuristics for an initial guess and dynamic refinements as execution progresses. However, it is possible to explicitly manipulate the grain size settings if we want to do so. We will not encourage this in this book, because we seldom will do better in performance with explicit specifications than the automatic partitioner in TBB. It tends to be somewhat machine specific, and therefore explicitly setting grain size most often reduces performance portability.

As Thinking Parallel becomes intuitive, structuring problems to scale will become second nature.

Amdahl's Law

$$S = \frac{1}{(1-P) + \dfrac{P}{N}}$$

Gustafson's Law

$$S = (1-P) + PN$$

S = maximum overall speedup
 (since for N we assume perfect speedup which means this is maximum speedup)
P = proportion that can be (perfectly) parallelized (0.0 to <1.0)
 (40% can be fully parallelized, that means 60% is serial, P=0.4)
 note: this means that $(1-P)$ = proportion that runs serially (not in parallel)
N = speedup in the region of (perfectly) parallelized code
 (for our purposes = number of processors assuming perfect (linear) speedup)
The subtle difference here is that Amdahl's Law assumes a fixed problem size.
Gustafson's Law assumes that, as we get more compute resources, we can use them
thanks to having larger problems to solve.

Figure P-10. *Amdahl's Law and Gustafson's Law – grasping "how much parallelism"*

How Much Parallelism Is There in an Application?

The topic of how much parallelism there is in an application has gotten considerable debate, and the answer is "it depends." We offer the equations for two correct views on this question in Figure P-10 presented in forms that use the same two inputs. Their meaning and difference in perspectives will become clear from our explanation that follows.

It certainly depends on the size of the problem to be solved and on the ability to find a suitable algorithm (and data structures) to take advantage of the parallelism. Before multicore processors, this debate centered on making sure we wrote efficient and worthy programs for expensive and rare parallel computers. The definition of size, the efficiency required, and the expense of the computer have all changed since the emergence of multicore processors. We need to step back and be sure we review the ground we are standing on. The world has changed.

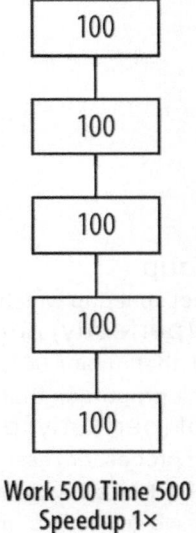

Figure P-11. *Original program without parallelism*

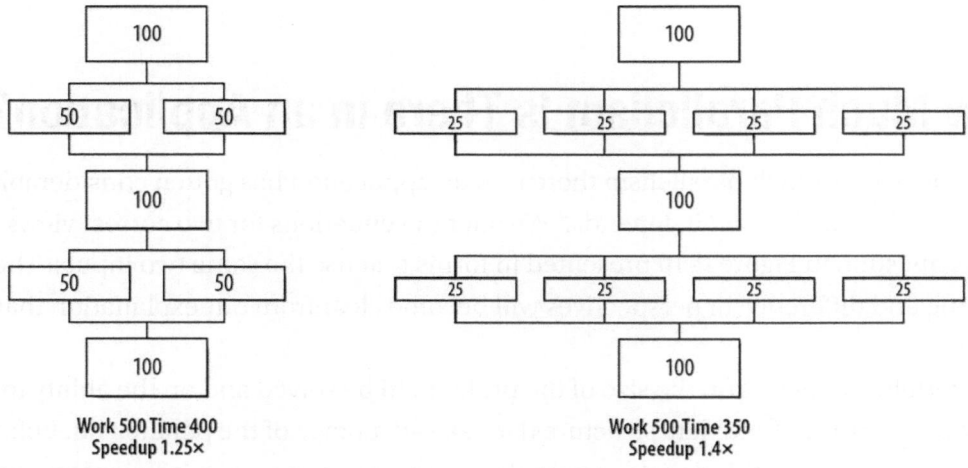

Figure P-12. *Progress on adding parallelism*

Amdahl's Law

Renowned computer architect Gene Amdahl made observations regarding the maximum improvement to a computer system that can be expected when only a portion of the system is improved. His observations in 1967 have come to be known as Amdahl's

Law. It tells us that if we speed up everything in a program by 2×, we can expect the resulting program to run 2× faster. However, if we improve the performance of only two-fifths of the program by 2×, the overall system improves only by 1.25×.

Amdahl's Law is easy to visualize. Imagine a program, with five equal parts, which runs in 500 seconds, as shown in Figure P-11. If we can speed up two of the parts by 2× and 4×, as shown in Figure P-12, the 500 seconds are reduced to only 400 (1.25× speedup) and 350 seconds (1.4× speedup), respectively. More and more, we are seeing the limitations of the portions that are not speeding up through parallelism. No matter how many processor cores are available, the serial portions create a barrier at 300 seconds that will not be broken (see Figure P-13) leaving us with only 1.7× speedup. If we are limited to parallel programming in only two-fifths of our execution time, we can never get more than a 1.7× boost in performance!

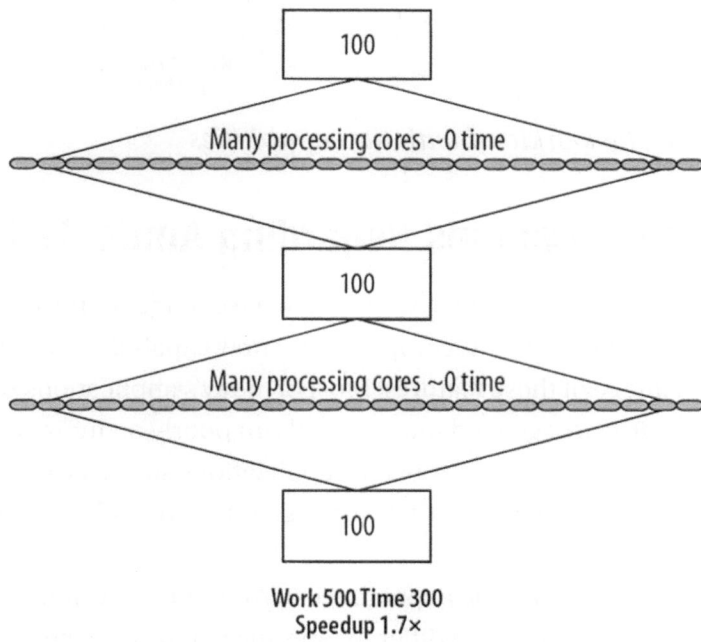

Work 500 Time 300
Speedup 1.7×

Figure P-13. *Limits according to Amdahl's Law*

Parallel programmers have long used Amdahl's Law to predict the maximum speedup that can be expected using multiple processors. This interpretation ultimately tells us that a computer program will never go faster than the sum of the parts that do not run in parallel (the serial portions), no matter how many processors we have.

Many have used Amdahl's Law to predict doom and gloom for parallel computers, but there is another way to look at things that shows much more promise.

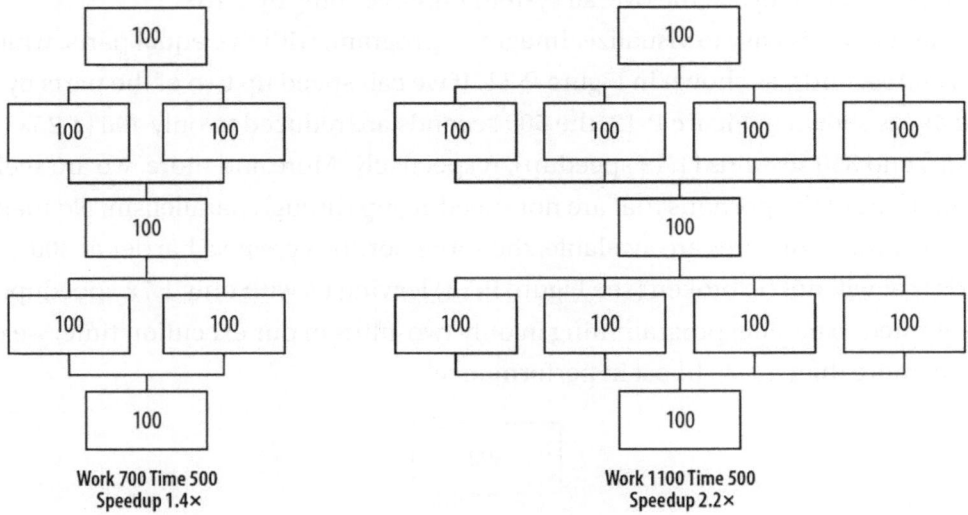

Figure P-14. *Scale the workload with the capabilities*

Gustafson's Observations Regarding Amdahl's Law

Amdahl's Law views programs as fixed, while we make changes to the computer. But experience seems to indicate that as computers get new capabilities, applications change to take advantage of these features. Most of today's applications would not run on computers from 20 years ago, and many would run poorly on more than ten years old. This observation is not limited to obvious applications such as video games and AI; it applies also to office applications, web browsers, photography, and video editing software.

More than two decades after the appearance of Amdahl's Law, John Gustafson, while at Sandia National Labs, took a different approach and suggested a reevaluation of Amdahl's Law. Gustafson noted that parallelism is more useful when we observe that workloads grow over time. This means that as computers have become more powerful, we have asked them to do more work, rather than staying focused on an unchanging workload. For many problems, as the problem size grows, the work required for the parallel part of the problem grows faster than the part that cannot be parallelized (the serial part). Hence, as the problem size grows, the serial fraction decreases, and, according to Amdahl's Law, the scalability improves. We can start with an application that looks like Figure P-11, but if the problem scales with the available parallelism, we are likely to see the advancements illustrated in Figure P-14. If the sequential parts still take the same amount of time to perform, they become less and less important as a percentage of the whole. The algorithm eventually reaches the conclusion shown in Figure P-15. Performance grows at the same rate as the number of processors, which is called linear or order of N scaling, denoted as $O(N)$.

Even in our example, the efficiency of the program is still greatly limited by the serial parts. The efficiency of using processors in our example is about 40% for large numbers of processors. On a supercomputer, this might be a terrible waste. On a system with multicore processors, one can hope that other work is running on the computer in parallel to use the processing power our application does not use. This new world has many complexities. In any case, it is still good to minimize serial code, whether we take the "glass half empty" view and favor Amdahl's Law or we lean toward the "glass half full" view and favor Gustafson's observations.

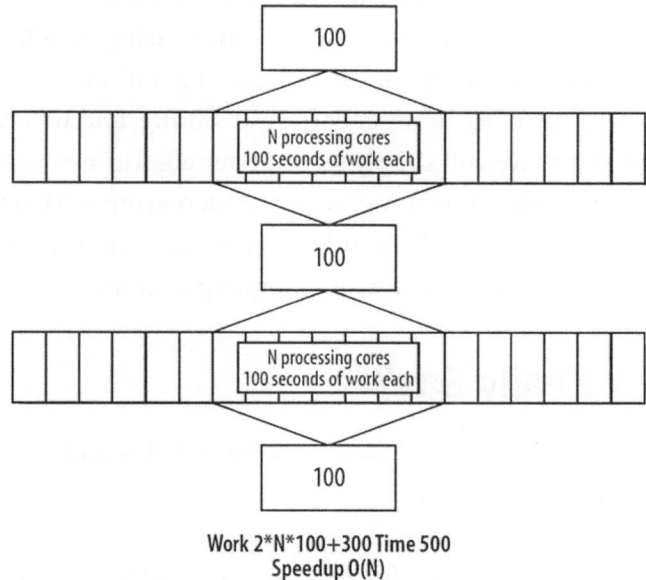

Figure P-15. *Gustafson saw a path to scaling*

Both Amdahl's Law and Gustafson's observations are correct, and they are not at odds. They highlight a different way to look at the same phenomenon. Amdahl's Law cautions us that if we simply want an existing program to run faster with the same workload, we will be severely limited by our serial code. When we envision working on a larger workload, Gustafson has pointed out we have hope. History clearly favors programs getting more complex and solving larger problems, and this is when parallel programming pays off.

The value of parallelism is easier to prove if we are looking forward than if we assume the world is not changing.

Making today's application run faster by switching to a parallel algorithm without expanding the problem is harder than making it run faster on a larger problem. The value of parallelism is easier to prove when we are not constrained to speeding up an application that already works well on today's machines.

Some have defined scaling that requires the problem size to grow as *weak scaling*. It is ironic that the term *embarrassingly parallel* is commonly applied to other types of scaling, or *strong scaling*. Because almost all true scaling happens only when the problem size scales with the parallelism available, we should just call that *scaling*. Nevertheless, it is common to apply the term *embarrassingly parallel* or *strong scaling* to scaling that occurs without growth in the problem size and refer to scaling that depends on expanding data sizes as *weak scaling*. As with embarrassing parallelism, when we have embarrassing scaling, we gladly take advantage of it and we are not embarrassed. We generally expect scaling to be the so-called *weak scaling*, and we are happy to know that any scaling is good and we will simply say that our algorithms *scale* in such cases.

The scalability of an application comes down to increasing the work done in parallel and minimizing the work done serially. Amdahl motivates us to reduce the serial portion, whereas Gustafson tells us to consider larger problems.

What Did They Really Say?

Here is what Amdahl and Gustafson articulated in their influential papers, which have sparked extensive dialogue ever since:

> ...*the effort expended on achieving high parallel processing rates is wasted unless it is accompanied by achievements in sequential processing rates of very nearly the same magnitude.*

> —Amdahl, 1967

...speedup should be measured by scaling the problem to the number of processors, not by fixing the problem size.

—Gustafson, 1988

Serial vs. Parallel Algorithms

One of the truths in programming is this: the best serial algorithm is seldom the best parallel algorithm, and the best parallel algorithm is seldom the best serial algorithm.

In practice, this means that trying to write a program that runs well on a system with one processor core, *and* also runs well on a system with a dual-core processor, is harder than just writing a good serial program (for one core) or a good parallel program (for many cores).

Supercomputer programmers know from practice that the work required grows quickly as a function of the problem size. If the work grows faster than the sequential overhead (e.g., communication, synchronization), we can fix a program that scales poorly just by increasing the problem size. It is not uncommon at all to take a program that won't scale much beyond 100 processors and scale it nicely to 300 or more processors just by doubling the size of the problem.

To be ready for the future, write parallel programs and abandon the past. That is the simplest and best advice to offer. Writing code with one foot in the world of efficient single-threaded performance and the other foot in the world of parallelism is the hardest job of all.

What Is a Thread?

If you know what a thread is, feel free to skip ahead to the section "Safety in the Presence of Concurrency." It is important to be comfortable with the concept of a thread, even though the goal of TBB is to abstract away thread management. Fundamentally, we will still be constructing a threaded program, and we will need to understand the implications of this underlying implementation.

All modern operating systems are multitasking operating systems that typically use a preemptive scheduler. Multitasking means that more than one program can be active at a time. We may take it for granted that we can have an email program and a web browser program running at the same time. Yet, not that long ago, this was not the case.

A preemptive scheduler means the operating system puts a limit on how long one program can use a processor core before it is forced to let another program use it. This is how the operating system makes it appear that our email program and our web browser are running at the same time when only one processor core is actually doing the work.

Generally, each program runs relatively independent of other programs. In particular, the memory where our program variables will reside is completely separate from the memory used by other processes. Our email program cannot directly assign a new value to a variable in the web browser program. If our email program can communicate with our web browser – for instance, to have it open a web page from a link we received in email – it does so with some form of communication that takes much more time than a memory access.

This isolation of programs from each other has value and is a mainstay of computing today. Within a program, we can allow multiple threads of execution to exist in a single program. An operating system will refer to the program as a *process* and the threads of execution as (operating system) *threads*.

All modern operating systems support the subdivision of processes into multiple threads of execution. Threads run independently, like processes, and no thread knows what other threads are running or where they are in the program unless they synchronize explicitly. The key difference between threads and processes is that the threads within a process share all the data of the process. Thus, a simple memory access can set a variable in another thread. We will refer to this as "shared mutable state" (changeable memory locations that are shared) – and we will decry the pain that sharing can cause in this book. Managing the sharing of data is a multifaceted problem that we included in our list of enemies of parallel programming. We will revisit this challenge, and solutions, repeatedly in this book.

We will note that it is common to have shared mutable state between processes. It could be memory that mapped into our memory space explicitly, or it could be data in an external store such as a database. A common example would be airline reservation systems, which can independently work with different customers to book their reservations – but ultimately, they share a database of flights and available seats. Therefore, you should know that many of the concepts we discuss for a single process can easily come up in more complex situations. Learning to Think Parallel has benefits beyond TBB! Nevertheless, TBB is almost always used within a single process with multiple threads.

Each thread has its own *instruction pointer* (a register pointing to the place in the program where it is running) and stack (a region of memory that holds subroutine return addresses and local variables for subroutines), but otherwise a thread shares its memory with all of the other threads in the same process. Even the stack memory of each thread is accessible to the other threads, though when they are programmed properly, they do not step on each other's stacks.

Threads within a process that run independently but share memory have the obvious benefit of being able to share work quickly, because each thread has access to the same memory as the other threads in the same process. The operating system can view multiple threads as multiple processes that have essentially the same permissions to regions of memory. As we mentioned, this is both a blessing and a curse – this "shared mutable state."

Programming Threads

A process usually starts with a single thread of execution and is allowed to request that more threads be started. Threads can be used to logically decompose a program into multiple tasks, such as a user interface (UI) and a main program. Threads are also useful for programming for parallelism, such as with multicore processors.

Many questions arise when we start programming with threads. How should we divide and assign tasks to keep each available processor core busy? Should we create a thread each time we have a new task, or should we create and manage a pool of threads? Should the number of threads depend on the number of cores? What should we do with a thread running out of tasks?

These are important questions for the implementation of multitasking, but that does not mean we should answer them. They detract from the objective of expressing the goals of our program. Likewise, assembly language programmers once had to worry about memory alignment, memory layout, stack pointers, and register assignments. Languages such as Fortran, C, C++, Java, and Python were created to abstract away those important details and leave them to be solved by compilers and libraries. Similarly, today we seek to abstract away thread management so that programmers can express parallelism directly.

TBB allows programmers to express parallelism at a higher level of abstraction. When used properly, TBB code is implicitly parallel.

A key notion of TBB is that we should break up the program into many more tasks than there are processors. We should specify as much parallelism as practical and let TBB runtime choose how much of that parallelism is actually exploited.

Safety in the Presence of Concurrency

When code is written in such a way that it may have problems due to the concurrency, it is said not to be thread-safe. Even with the abstraction that TBB offers, the concept of thread safety is essential. Thread-safe code is code that is written in a manner that ensures it will function as desired even when multiple threads use the same code. Common mistakes that make code not thread-safe include lack of synchronization to control access to shared data during updates (this can lead to corruption) and improper use of synchronization (can lead to deadlock, which we discuss in a few pages).

Any function that maintains a persistent state between invocations requires careful writing to ensure it is thread-safe. We need only to do this to functions that might be used concurrently. In general, functions we may use concurrently should be written to have no side effects so that concurrent use is not an issue. In cases where global side effects are truly needed, such as setting a single variable or creating a file, we must be careful to call for mutual exclusion to ensure only one thread at a time can execute the code that has the side effect.

We need to be sure to use thread-safe libraries for any code using concurrency or parallelism. All the libraries we use should be reviewed to make sure they are thread-safe. The C++ library has some functions inherited from C that are particular problems because they hold internal state between calls, specifically `asctime`, `ctime`, `gmtime`, `localtime`, `rand`, and `strtok`. We need to check the documentation when using these functions to see whether thread-safe versions are available. The C++ Standard Template Library (STL) container classes are, in general, safer than these C functions that maintain state. All STL container functions can be safely called by different threads when operating on different containers, but calling them on the same container from different threads is not always safe. The exact rules, summarized in the "Thread Safety" section of `https://en.cppreference.com/w/cpp/container`, are nontrivial. The TBB concurrent containers that we cover in Chapter 3 are designed to support concurrent access efficiently and easily. Chapter 8 explains how TBB synchronization features can be used in conjunction with thread-unsafe containers to introduce thread safety.

Mutual Exclusion and Locks

We need to think about whether concurrent accesses to the same resources will occur in our program. The resource we will most often be concerned with is data held in memory, but we also need to think about files and I/O of all kinds.

If the precise order of updates to shared data matters, then we need some form of synchronization. The best policy is to decompose our problem in such a way that synchronization is infrequent. We can achieve this by breaking up the tasks so that they can work independently, and the only synchronization that occurs is waiting for all the tasks to be completed at the end. This synchronization "when all tasks are complete" is commonly called a barrier synchronization. Barriers work when we have very coarse-grained parallelism because barriers cause all parallel work to stop (go serial) for a moment. If we do that too often, we lose scalability very quickly per Amdahl's Law.

For finer-grained parallelism, we need to use synchronization around data structures, to restrict both reading and writing by others, while we are writing. If we are updating memory based on a prior value from memory, such as incrementing a counter by ten, we would restrict reading and writing from the time that we start reading the initial value until we have finished writing the newly computed value. We illustrate a simple way to do this in Figure P-16. If we are only reading, but we read multiple related data, we would use synchronization around data structures to restrict writing while we read. These restrictions apply to other tasks and are known as *mutual exclusion*. The purpose of *mutual exclusion* is to make a set of operations appear *atomic* (indivisible).

TBB implements portable mechanisms for *mutual exclusion*. There are fundamentally two approaches: atomic (indivisible) operations for very simple and common operations (such as increment) and a general lock/unlock mechanism for longer sequences of code. These are all discussed in Chapter 8.

Thread A	Thread B	Value of X
LOCK (X)	*(wait)*	44
Read X (44)	*(wait)*	44
add 10	*(wait)*	44
Write X (54)	*(wait)*	54
UNLOCK (X)	*(wait)*	54
	LOCK (X)	54
	Read X (54)	54
	subtract 12	54
	Write X (42)	42
	UNLOCK (X)	42

Figure P-16. *Serialization that can occur when using mutual exclusion*

Consider a program with two threads that starts with X = 44. Thread A executes X = X + 10. Thread B executes X = X - 12. If we add locking (Figure P-16) so that only Thread A or Thread B can execute its statement at a time, we always end up with X = 42. If both threads try to obtain a lock at the same time, one will be excluded and will have to wait before the lock is granted. Figure P-16 shows how long Thread B might have to wait if it requested the lock at the same time as Thread A but did not get the lock because Thread A held it first.

Instead of locks, which are used in Figure P-16, we could use a small set of operations that the system guarantees to appear to be *atomic* (indivisible). We show locks here, because they are a general mechanism that allows any sequence of code to appear to be atomic. We should always keep such sequences as short as possible because they degrade scaling per Amdahl's Law. If a specific atomic operation (e.g., increment) is available, we would use that because it should be the quickest method and therefore degrade scaling the least.

Thread A	Thread B	Value of X
	Read X (44)	44
	subtract 12	44
	Write X (32)	32
Read X (32)		32
add 10		32
Write X (42)		42

Thread A	Thread B	Value of X
Read X (44)		44
add 10	Read X (44)	44
Write X (54)	subtract 12	54
	Write X (32)	32

Thread A	Thread B	Value of X
	Read X (44)	44
Read X (44)	subtract 12	44
add 10	Write X (32)	32
Write X (54)		54

RACE – A first, B second   DESIRED   RACE – B first, A second

Figure P-17. *Race conditions can lead to problems when we have no mutual exclusion. A simple fix here would be to replace each Read-operation-Write with the appropriate atomic operation (atomic increment or atomic decrement)*

As much as we hate locks, we need to concede that without them, things are even worse. Consider our example without the locks; a *race condition* exists and at least two more results are possible: X=32 or X=54 (Figure P-17). We will define this very important concept of *race condition* very soon. Additional incorrect results are now possible because each statement reads X, does a computation, and writes to X. Without locking, there is no guarantee that a thread reads the value of X before or after the other thread writes a value.

Correctness

The biggest challenge of learning to Think Parallel is understanding correctness as it relates to concurrency. Concurrency means we have multiple threads of control that may be active at one time. The operating system is free to schedule those threads in different ways. Each time the program runs, the precise order of operations will potentially be different. Our challenge as a programmer is to make sure that every legitimate way the operations in our concurrent program can be ordered will still lead to the correct result. A high-level abstraction such as TBB helps a great deal, but there are a few issues we have to grapple with on our own: potential variations in results when programs compute results in parallel and new types of programming bugs when locks are used incorrectly.

Computations done in parallel often get different results than the original sequential program. Round-off errors are the most common surprise for many programmers when a program is modified to run in parallel. We should expect numeric results, when using floating-point values, to vary when computations are changed to run in parallel because floating-point values have limited precision. For example, computing (A+B+C+D) as ((A+B)+(C+D)) enables A+B and C+D to be computed in parallel, but the final sum may be different from other evaluations such as (((A+B)+C)+D). Even the parallel results can differ from run to run, depending on the order of the operations actually taken during program execution. Such nondeterministic behavior can often be controlled by reducing runtime flexibility. We will mention such options in this book, in particular the options for deterministic reduction operations (Chapter 2). Nondeterminism can make debugging and testing much more difficult, so it is often desirable to force deterministic behavior. Depending on the circumstances, this can reduce performance because it effectively forces more synchronization.

A few types of program failures can happen only in a program using concurrency because they involve the coordination of tasks. These failures are known as *deadlocks* and *race conditions*. Determinism is also a challenge since a concurrent program has many possible paths of execution because there can be so many tasks operating independently.

Although TBB simplifies programming and reduces the likelihood of such failures, they can still occur. Multithreaded programs can be nondeterministic due to race conditions, meaning that the same program with the same input can follow different execution paths each time it is run. When this happens, failures do not consistently repeat, and debugger intrusions can easily alter the failure, making debugging especially frustrating.

Tracking down and eliminating the source of unwanted nondeterminism is not easy. Specialized tools such as Intel Advisor can help, but the first step is to understand these issues and try to avoid them.

There is also another very common problem, which is also an indication of nondeterminism, when moving from sequential code to parallel code: instability in results. Instability in results means that we get different results because of subtle changes in the order in which work is done. Some algorithms may be unstable, whereas others simply exercise the opportunity to reorder operations that are considered to have multiple correct orderings.

Next, we explain three key errors in parallel programming and solutions for each.

Deadlock

Deadlock occurs when at least two tasks wait for each other and each will not resume until the other task proceeds. This happens easily when code requires the acquisition of multiple locks. If Task A needs Lock R and Lock X, it might get Lock R and then try to get Lock X. Meanwhile, if Task B needs the same two locks but grabs Lock X first, we can easily end up with Task A wanting Lock X while holding Lock R and Task B waiting for Lock R while it holds only Lock X. The resulting impasse can be resolved only if one task releases the lock it is holding. If neither task gives up its lock, deadlock occurs and the tasks are stuck forever.

Solution for Deadlock

We recommend the use of implicit synchronization whenever possible to avoid the need for locks. In general, avoid using locks, especially multiple locks at one time. Acquiring a lock and then invoking a function or subroutine that happens to use locks is often the source of multiple lock issues. Because access to shared resources must sometimes occur, the two most common solutions are to acquire locks in a certain order (always A and then B, for instance) or to release all locks whenever any lock cannot be acquired and begin again (after a random length delay).

Race Conditions

A race condition occurs when multiple tasks read from and write to the same memory without proper synchronization. The "race" may finish correctly sometimes and therefore complete without errors, and at other times it may finish incorrectly. Figure P-17 illustrates a simple example with three different possible outcomes due to a race condition.

Race conditions are less catastrophic than deadlocks, but more pernicious because they do not necessarily produce obvious failures and yet can lead to corrupted data (an incorrect value being read or written). The result of some race conditions can be an unexpected state (and undesirable) because more than one thread may succeed in updating only part of their state (multiple data elements).

Solution for Race Conditions

Synchronization mechanisms described in Chapter 8 help us manage shared data in a disciplined manner to ensure a correct program. Avoid low-level methods based on locks because it is so easy to get things wrong. Explicit locks should be used only as a last resort. In general, we are better off using the synchronization implied by the algorithm templates and task scheduler when possible. For instance, use `parallel_reduce` (Chapter 2) instead of creating our own with shared variables. The join operation in `parallel_reduce` is guaranteed not to run until the subproblems it is joining are completed.

Instability of Results (Lack of Deterministic Results)

A parallel program will generally compute answers differently each time because the many concurrent tasks operate with slight variations between different invocations and especially on systems with differing number of processors. We explained this in our earlier discussion of correctness.

Solution for Instability of Results

TBB offers ways to ensure more deterministic behavior by reducing runtime flexibility. While this can reduce performance, the benefits of determinism are often worth it. Determinism is discussed in Chapter 2.

Abstraction

When writing a program, choosing an appropriate level of abstraction is important. Few programmers use assembly language anymore. Programming languages such as C and C++ have abstracted away the low-level details. Hardly anyone misses the old programming method.

Parallelism is no different. We can easily get caught up in writing code that is too low level. Raw thread programming requires us to manage threads, which is time-consuming and error-prone.

Programming with TBB offers an opportunity to avoid thread management. This will result in code that is easier to create, easier to maintain, and more elegant. In practice, we find that this code is also more portable and performance portable. However, it does require thinking of algorithms in terms of what work can be divided and how data can be divided.

Patterns

Experienced parallel programmers know that there are common problems for which there are known solutions. All types of programming are like this – we have concepts such as stacks, queues, and linked lists in our vocabulary as a result. Parallel programming brings forward concepts such as map, reduce, and pipeline.

We call these *patterns*, and they can be adapted to our particular needs. Learning common patterns is a perfect way to learn from those who have gone before us. TBB implements solutions for key patterns, so we can implicitly learn them simply by learning TBB. We offer a table in Chapter 2 to relate the common pattern names to the TBB algorithms (see Figure 2-1).

Locality and the Revenge of the Caches

Effective parallel programming requires that we have a sense of the importance of *locality*. The motivation for this requires that we speak briefly about the hardware, in particular memory *caches*. A "cache" is simply a hardware buffer of sorts that retains data we have recently seen or modified, closer to us so it can be accessed faster than if it was in the larger memory. The purpose of a cache is to make things faster, and therefore if our program makes better usage of caches, our application may run faster.

We say "caches" instead of "cache" because modern computer design generally consists of multiple levels of caching hardware, each level of which is a cache. For our purposes, thinking of cache as a single collection of data is generally sufficient.

We do not need to understand *caches* deeply, but a high-level understanding of them helps us understand locality, the related issues with *sharing* of *mutable state*, and the particularly insidious phenomenon known as *false sharing*.

We need to pay attention to important cache implications: locality, sharing, and false sharing. To understand these, we must understand caches and cache lines. These are fundamental to all modern computer designs.

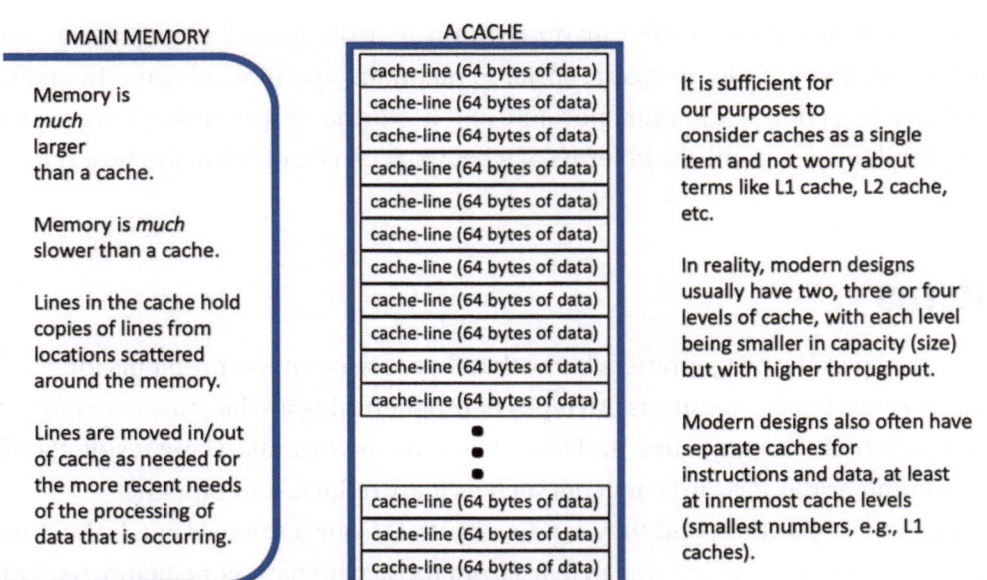

Figure P-18. *Main memory and a cache*

Hardware Motivation

We would like to ignore the details of hardware implementation as much as possible, because generally the more we cater to a particular system, the more we lose portability and performance portability. There is a notable and important exception: caches (Figure P-18).

A memory *cache* will be found in all modern computer designs. In fact, most systems will have multiple levels of caches. It was not always this way; originally, computers fetched data and instructions from memory only when needed and immediately wrote results into memory. Those were simpler times!

The speed of processors has grown to be much faster than main memory. Making all of the memory as fast as a processor would simply prove too expensive for most computers. Instead, designers make small amounts of memory, known as *caches*, which operate as fast as the processor. The main memory can remain slower and therefore more affordable. The hardware knows how to move information in and out of caches as needed, thereby adding to the number of places where data is shuffled on its journey between memory and the processor cores. Caches are critical in helping overcome the mismatch between memory speed and processor speed.

Virtually all computers use caches only for a temporary copy of data that should eventually reside in memory. Therefore, the function of a memory subsystem is to move data needed as input to caches near the requesting processor core and to move data produced by processing cores out to main memory. As data is read from memory into the caches, some data may need to be evicted from the cache to make room for the newly requested data. Cache designers work to make the data evicted be approximately the least recently used data. The hope is that data that has not been used recently is not likely to be needed in the near future. That way, caches keep in their precious space the data we are most likely to use again.

Once a processor accesses data, it is best to exhaust the program's use of it while it is still in the cache. Continued usage will hold it in the cache, while prolonged inactivity will likely lead to its eviction and future usage will need to do a more expensive (slow) access to get the data back into the cache. Furthermore, every time a new thread runs on a processor, data is likely to be discarded from the cache to make room for the data needed by the particular thread.

Locality of Reference

Consider it to be expensive to fetch data from memory the first time, but it is much cheaper to use the data for a period of time after it is fetched. This is because *caches* hold onto the information much like our own *short-term memories* allow us to remember things during a day that will be harder to recall months later.

A simple, and often cited, example of a matrix multiplication, C=AxB, with matrices A, B, and C of size nxn, is shown in Figure P-19.

```
for (i=0;i<n;i++)
  for(j=0;j<n;j++)
    for (k=0;k<n;k++)
      c[i][j] = c[i][j] + a[i][k] * b[k][j];
```

Figure P-19. *Matrix multiplication with poor locality of reference*

C and C++ store arrays in *row-major* order, which means that the contiguous array elements are in the last array dimension. This means that c[i][2] and c[i][3] are next to each other in memory, while c[2][j] and c[3][j] will be far apart (n elements apart in our example).

By switching the looping order for j and k, as shown in Figure P-20, the speedup can be dramatic because the locality of reference is greatly increased. This does not fundamentally change the mathematical result, but it improves efficiency because the memory caches are utilized more effectively. In our example, the value of n needs to be large enough that the combined size of the matrices exceeds the size of the caches. If this is not the case, the order will not matter nearly as much because either order will fit within the caches. A value of n=10,000 would make each matrix have 100 million elements. Assuming double-precision floating-point value, the three matrices together will occupy 2.4GB of memory. This will start to cause cache effects on all machines at the time of this book's publication! Almost all computers would benefit fully from the switched ordering of indices, yet almost all systems will see no effects at all when n is small enough for data to all fit in cache.

```
for (i=0;i<n;i++)
   for(k=0;k<n;k++)
      for (j=0;j<n;j++)
         c[i][j] = c[i][j] + a[i][k] * b[k][j];
```

Figure P-20. *Matrix multiplication with improved locality of reference*

Cache Lines, Alignment, Sharing, Mutual Exclusion, and False Sharing

Caches are organized in lines. And processors transfer data between the main memory and the cache at the granularity of cache lines. This causes three considerations that we will explain: data alignment, data sharing, and false sharing.

The length of a cache line is somewhat arbitrary, but 512 bits is by far the most common today – that is, 64 bytes in size, or the size of eight double-precision floating-point numbers or sixteen 32-bit integers.

Coherency/Distributed Caches

The innermost and fastest caches are located close to the computational units, specifically the processor cores. In parallel systems, this means that the innermost cache is distributed, with multiple smaller caches holding data near their respective processor cores. This distribution necessitates that all copies of data remain consistent, leading to a challenge known as cache coherency. We will not dive deeper into this; we will leave it to computer architecture courses to offer a deeper understanding of how cache coherency is maintained and the various trade-offs associated in such designs.

While we assume the mechanisms work, it's important to acknowledge that maintaining coherency incurs costs, particularly when data must be transferred back and forth between caches. Additionally, accessing the same data across multiple processors can be costly, especially if that data is subject to change.

To mitigate performance degradation from these issues, we must do two things: (1) decompose our programs to minimize real dependencies on shared data among tasks, and (2) eliminate false dependencies, commonly referred to as false sharing. The first approach is a recurring theme throughout this book and in all literature on parallel programming – it's an ongoing pursuit for developers. The second approach will be in an upcoming section dedicated to false sharing.

Alignment

It is far better for any given data item (e.g., `int`, `long`, `double`, or `short`) to fit within a single cache line. Look at Figure P-18 or Figure P-21, and consider if it were a single data item (e.g., `double`) stretching across two cache lines. If so, we would need to access (read or write) two cache lines instead of one. In general, this will take twice as much time. Aligning single data items to not span cache lines can be very important for performance. To be fair to hardware designers, some hardware has significant capabilities to lessen the penalty for data that is not aligned (often called misaligned data). Since we cannot count on such support, we strongly advise that data be aligned on its natural boundaries. Arrays will generally span cache lines unless they are very short; normally, we advise that an array is aligned to the alignment size for a single array element so that a single element never sits in two cache lines even though the array may span multiple cache lines. The same general advice holds for structures as well, although there may be some benefit to aligning small structures to fit entirely in a cache line.

A disadvantage of alignment is wasted space. Every time we align data, we are potentially skipping some memory. In general, this is simply disregarded because memory is cheap. If alignment occurs frequently, and can be avoided or rearranged to save memory, that can occasionally still be important. Therefore, we needed to mention the disadvantage of alignment. In general, alignment is critical for performance, so we should just do it. Compilers will automatically align variables, including arrays and structures, to the element sizes. We need to explicitly align when using memory allocations (e.g., `malloc`), so we recommend how to do that in Chapter 7.

The real reason we explain alignment is so we can discuss sharing and the evils of false sharing.

Sharing

Sharing copies of immutable (unchangeable) data from memory is easy because every copy is always a valid copy. Sharing immutable data does not create any special problems when doing parallel processing.

It is mutable (changeable) data that creates substantial challenges when doing parallel processing of the data. We did name *shared mutable state* as an enemy of parallelism! In general, we should minimize sharing of mutable (changeable) data between tasks. The less sharing, the less there is to debug and the less there is to go wrong. We know the reality is that sharing data allows parallel tasks to work on the same problem to achieve scaling, so we have to dive into a discussion about how to share data correctly.

Shared mutable (changeable) state creates two challenges: (1) ordering and (2) false sharing. The first is intrinsic to parallel programming and is not caused by the hardware. We previously discussed *mutual exclusion* and illustrated a key concern over correctness with Figure P-17. It is a critical topic that must be understood by every parallel programmer.

False Sharing

Because data is moved around in cache lines, it is possible for multiple, completely independent variables or memory allocations to be all or partially within the same cache line (Figure P-21). This sharing of a cache line will not cause a program to fail. However, it can greatly reduce performance. A complete explanation of the issues that arise when sharing a cache line, for mutable data being used in multiple tasks, would take many pages. A simple explanation is updating data anywhere in a cache line can create slowdowns for all accesses in the cache line from other tasks.

Regardless of the details of why false sharing slows down machines, we know that well-written parallel programs take measures to avoid false sharing. Even if one machine configuration suffers less than most, in order to be performance portable, we should always take measures to avoid false sharing.

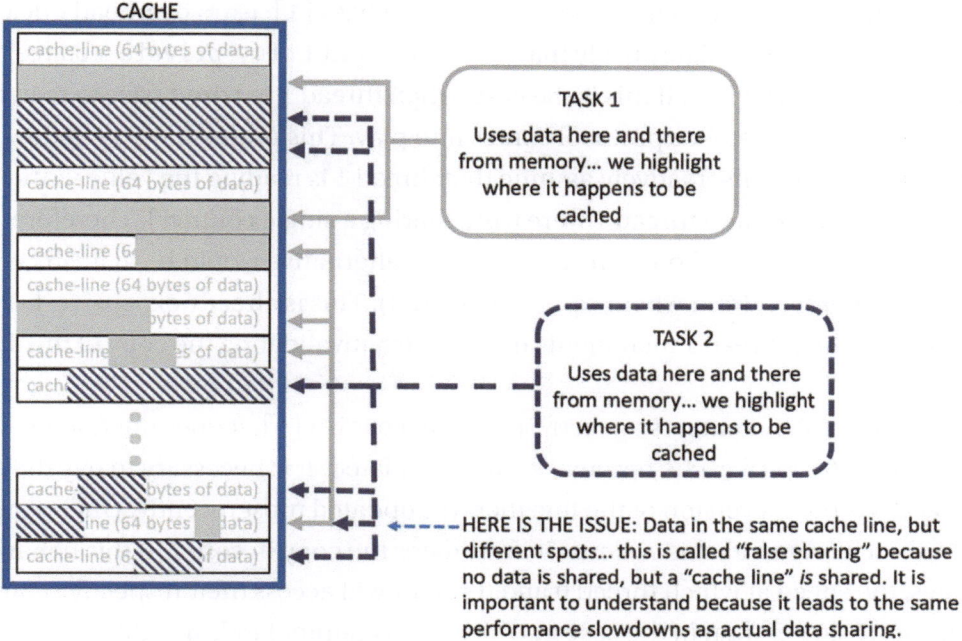

Figure P-21. *False sharing happens when data from two different tasks end up in the same cache line*

To illustrate why **false sharing** carries such a performance penalty, let us consider the extra overhead imposed on the caches and operating system when two threads access memory near each other. We will assume for the sake of this example that a cache line contains 64 bytes, at least two threads are running on processors that share the cache, and our program defines an array that threads access and update based on their thread ID:

```
int my_private_counter[MAX_THREADS];
```

Two consecutive entries in my_private_counter are likely to be in the same cache line. Therefore, our example program can experience extra overhead due specifically to the false sharing caused by having data used by separate threads land in the same cache line. Consider two threads 0 and 1 running on core 0 and core 1, respectively, and the following sequence of events:

Thread 0 increments my_private_counter[0], which translates into reading the value in the core 0 private cache, incrementing the counter, and writing the result. More precisely, core 0 reads the whole line (say 64 bytes) including this counter into the cache and then updates the counter with the new value (usually only in the cache line).

Next, if thread 1 also increments my_private_counter[1], extra overhead due to false sharing is paid. It is highly likely that positions 0 and 1 of my_private_counter fall into the same cache line. If this is the case, when thread 1 in core 1 tries to read its counter, the cache coherence protocol comes into play. This protocol works at the cache line level, and it will conservatively assume that thread 1 is reading the value written by thread 0 (as if thread 0 and thread 1 were truly sharing a single counter). Therefore, core 1 must read the cache line from core 0 (the slowest alternative would be to flush core 0 cache line to memory, from where core 1 can read it). This is already expensive, but it is even worse when thread 1 increments this counter, invalidating the copy of the cache line in core 0.

Now if thread 0 increments again my_private_counter[0], it does not find its counter in core 0's local cache because it was invalidated. It is necessary to pay the extra time to access core 1's version of the line that was updated most recently. Once again, if thread 0 then increments this counter, it invalidates the copy in core 1. If this behavior continues, the speed at which thread 0 and thread 1 will access their respective counters is significantly slower than in the case in which each counter lands in a different cache line.

This issue is called "false sharing" because actually each thread has a private (not shared) counter, but due to the cache coherence protocol working at the cache line level, and both counters "sharing" the same cache line, the two counters seem to be shared from a hardware point of view.

Now you are probably thinking that a straightforward solution would be to fix the hardware implementation of the cache coherence protocol so that it works at a word level instead of a line level. However, this hardware alternative is prohibitive, so hardware vendors ask us to solve the problem by software. Do your best to get each private counter falling in a different cache line so that it is clear to the hardware that the expensive cache coherence mechanism does not have to be dispatched.

We can see how a tremendous overhead can easily be imposed from false sharing of data. In our simple example, the right solution is to spread out the elements so they reside in different cache lines. This can be done in a number of ways, one of which would be to use the TBB cache aligned allocator (described in Chapter 7) for the data needed for a given thread instead of allocating them all together with the risk of false sharing.

Avoiding False Sharing with Alignment

To avoid false sharing (Figure P-21), we need to make sure that *distinctly different pieces of* mutable data that may be updated in parallel do not land in the same cache line. We do that with a combination of alignment and padding.

Alignment of data structures, such as arrays or structures, to a cache line boundary will prevent placement of the start of the data structure in a cache line used by something else. Usually, this means using a version of malloc that aligns to a cache line. We discuss memory allocation, including cache aligned memory allocators (e.g., tbb::cache_aligned_allocator), in Chapter 7. We can also explicitly align static and local variables with compiler directives (pragmas), but the need for that is far less common. We should note that performance slowdowns due to false sharing from memory allocation are often somewhat nondeterministic, meaning that it may affect some runs of an application and not others. This can be truly maddening because debugging a nondeterministic issue is very challenging since we cannot count on any particular run of an application to have the issue!

TBB Has Caches in Mind

TBB is designed with caches in mind and works to limit the unnecessary movement of tasks and data. When a task has to be moved to a different processor, TBB moves the task with the lowest likelihood of having data in the cache of the old processor. These considerations are built into the work (task)-stealing schedulers and therefore are part of the algorithm templates discussed in Chapter 2.

While dealing with caches has a role in many chapters, a few key chapters to note are the following:

Chapter 7 covers important considerations for memory allocators to help with caches, including alignment and padding to avoid false sharing.

Chapter 8 explains privatization and reduction.

Chapter 11 revisits data locality with an advanced discussion of options tuning for better locality.

For best performance, we need to keep data locality in mind when considering how to structure our programs. We should avoid using data regions sporadically when we can design the application to use a single set of data in focused chunks of time.

It is interesting to note that parallel quicksort is an example in which caches beat *maximum parallelism*. Parallel mergesort has more parallelism than parallel quicksort. But parallel mergesort is not an in-place sort and thus has twice the cache footprint that parallel quicksort does. Hence, quicksort usually runs faster in practice.

So we need to keep data locality in mind when considering how to structure our programs. We need to avoid using data regions sporadically when we can design the application to use a single set of data in focused chunks of time. This happens most naturally if we use data decomposition, especially at the higher levels in a program.

TBB Considers Costs of Time Slicing

Time slicing enables there to be more logical threads than physical threads. Each logical thread is serviced for a time slice – a short period of time defined by the operating system during which a thread can run before being preempted – by a physical thread. If a thread runs longer than a time slice, as most do, it relinquishes the physical thread until it gets another turn.

The most obvious cost is the time for *context switching* between logical threads. Each context switch requires that the processor save all its registers for the previous logical thread that it was executing and load its registers with information for the next logical thread it runs.

A subtler cost is cache cooling. Processors keep recently accessed data in cache memory, which is extremely fast, but also relatively insignificant compared with main memory. When the processor runs out of cache memory, it has to evict items from cache and put them back into main memory. Typically, it chooses the least recently used items in the cache. (The reality of set-associative caches is a bit more complicated, but this is not a cache primer.)

When a logical thread gets its time slice, as it references a piece of data for the first time, this data is pulled into cache, taking hundreds of cycles. If it is referenced frequently enough not to be evicted, each subsequent reference will find it in cache and take only a few cycles. Such data is called *hot* in *cache*.

Time slicing undoes this because if Thread A finishes its time slice and subsequently Thread B runs on the same physical thread, B will tend to evict data that was hot in cache for A, unless both threads need the data. When Thread A gets its next time slice, it will need to reload evicted data, at the cost of hundreds of cycles for each cache miss. Or worse yet, the next time slice for Thread A may be on a different physical thread that has a different cache altogether.

Another cost is *lock preemption*. This happens if a thread acquires a lock on a resource and its time slice runs out before it releases the lock. No matter how short a time the thread intended to hold the lock, it is now going to hold it for at least as long as it takes for its next turn at a time slice to come up. Any other threads waiting on the lock either busy-wait pointlessly or lose the rest of their time slice. The effect is called convoying because the threads end up "bumper to bumper" waiting for the preempted thread in front to resume driving.

Introduction to Vectorization (SIMD)

Parallel programming is ultimately about harnessing the parallel computational capabilities of the hardware. Throughout this book, we focus on parallelism that exploits having multiple processor cores. Such hardware parallelism is utilized by thread-level (or abstractly task-level) parallelism, which is what TBB solves for us.

There is another class of very important hardware parallelism known as vector instructions, which are instructions that can do more computation (in parallel) than a regular instruction. For instance, a regular add instruction takes two numbers, adds them, and returns a single result. An eight-way vector add would be able to handle eight pairs of inputs, add each pair, and produce eight outputs. Instead of C=A+B in a regular add instruction, we get $C_0=A_0+B_0$ and $C_1=A_1+B_1$ and $C_2=A_2+B_2$ ... and $C_7=A_7+B_7$ from a single vector add instruction. This can offer 8× in performance. These instructions do require that we have eight of the same operations to do at once, which does tend to be true of numerically intensive code.

This ability to do multiple operations in a single instruction is known as Single Instruction Multiple Data (SIMD), one of four classifications of computer architecture known by computer scientists as Flynn's taxonomy.

Vectorization is the technology that exploits SIMD parallelism, and it is a technology that relies on compilers because compilers specialize in hardware instruction selection.

We could largely ignore vector parallelism in this book and say "it's a different subject with a different set of things to study" – but we won't! A good parallel program generally uses both task parallelism (with TBB) and SIMD parallelism (with a vectorizing compiler).

We recommend learning about vectorizing capabilities of your favorite compiler and using them. #pragma SIMD is one such popular capability in compilers these days. It is also useful to understand Parallel STL options (such as oneAPI DPC++ Library (oneDPL)), including why it is generally not the best solution for effective parallel programming (Amdahl's Law favors parallelism being put at a higher level in the program than in STL calls).

While vectorization is important, using TBB offers superior speedup for most applications (if you consider choosing one or the other). This is because systems usually have more parallelism from cores than from SIMD lanes (the width of the vector instruction), plus tasks are a lot more general than the limited number of operations that are available in SIMD instructions.

ADVICE ON MULTITASKING VS. VECTORIZATION

Good advice: Multitask your code first (use TBB); vectorize second (use vectorization).

Best advice: Do both.

Doing both is generally useful when programs have computations that can benefit from vectorization. Consider a 32-core processor with AVX vector instructions. A multitasking program could hope to get a significant share of the theoretical maximum 32× in performance from using TBB. A vectorized program could hope to get a significant share of the theoretical maximum 4× in performance from using vectorization on double-precision mathematical code. However, together the theoretical maximum jump in performance is 256× – this multiplicative effect is why many developers of numerically intensive programs always do both.

Introduction to the Features of C++ (As Needed for TBB)

Since the goal of parallel programming is to have an application scale in performance on machines with more cores, C and C++ both offer an ideal combination of abstraction with a focus on efficiency. TBB makes effective use of C++ but in a manner that is approachable to C programmers.

Every field has its own terminology, and C++ is no exception. We have included a glossary at the end of this book to assist with the vocabulary of C++, parallel programming, TBB, and more. There are several terms we will review here that are fundamental to C++ programmers: lambda functions, generic programming, containers, templates, Standard Template Library (STL), overloading, ranges, and iterators.

Lambda Functions

Reading code using TBB has been easier since the inclusion of lambda functions in the C++11 standard, which allows code to be expressed inline as an anonymous function.

Support for lambda expressions was introduced in C++11. They are used to create anonymous function objects (although you can assign them to named variables) that can capture variables from the enclosing scope. The basic syntax for a C++ lambda expression is

[capture-list] (params) ->ret{body}

where

- *capture-list* is a comma-separated list of captures. We capture a variable by value by listing the variable name in the capture-list. We capture a variable by reference by prefixing it with an ampersand, for example, &v. And we can use this to capture the current object by reference. There are also defaults: [=] is used to capture all automatic variables used in the body by value and the current object by reference, [&] is used to capture all automatic variables used in the body as well as the current object by reference, and [ ] captures nothing.

- params is the list of function parameters, just like for a named function.

- ret is the return type. If ->ret is not specified, it is inferred from the return statements.

- body is the function body.

This next example shows a C++ lambda expression that captures one variable, i, by value and another, j, by reference. It also has a parameter k0 and another parameter l0 that is received by reference:

```cpp
int main(int argc, char *argv[]) {
  int i = 1, j = 10, k = 100, l = 1000;
  auto lambdaExpression = [i, &j] (int k0, int& l0) -> int {
    j = 2 * j;
    k0 = 2 * k0;
    l0 = 2 * l0;
    return i + j + k0 + l0;
  };

  printValues(i, j, k, l);
  std::cout << "First call returned " << lambdaExpression(k, l) << std::endl;
  printValues(i, j, k, l);
  std::cout << "Second call returned " << lambdaExpression(k, l) << std::endl;
  printValues(i, j, k, l);
  return 0;
}
```

Running the example will result in the following output:

```
i == 1
j == 10
k == 100
l == 1000
First call returned 2221
i == 1
j == 20
k == 100
l == 2000
Second call returned 4241
i == 1
j == 40
k == 100
l == 4000
```

We can think of a lambda expression as an instance of a function object, but the compiler creates the class definition for us. For example, the lambda expression we used in the preceding example is analogous to an instance of a class:

```
int main(int argc, char *argv[]) {
  int i = 1, j = 10, k = 100, l = 1000;
  Functor f{i,j};

  PrintValues(i, j, k, l);
  std::cout << "First call returned " << f(k, l) << std::endl;
  PrintValues(i, j, k, l);
  std::cout << "Second call returned " << f(k, l) << std::endl;
  PrintValues(i, j, k, l);
  return 0;
}
```

Wherever we use a C++ lambda expression, we can substitute it with an instance of a function object like the preceding one. In fact, the TBB library predates the C++11 standard and all of its interfaces originally required passing in instances of objects of user-defined classes. C++ lambda expressions simplify the use of TBB by eliminating the extra step of defining a class for each use of a TBB algorithm.

Generic Programming

Generic programming is where algorithms are written to generically operate on any data type. We can think of them as using parameters that are "to be specified later." C++ implements generic programming in a way that favors compile time optimization and avoids the necessity of runtime selection based on types. This has allowed modern C++ compilers to be highly tuned to minimize abstraction penalties arising from heavy use of generic programming and consequently templates and STL. A simple example of generic programming is a sort algorithm that can sort any list of items, provided we supply a way to access an item, swap two items, and compare two items. Once we have put together such an algorithm, we can instantiate it to sort a list of integers or floats or complex numbers or strings, provided that we define how the swap and the comparison are done for each data type.

A simple example of generic programming comes from considering support for complex numbers. The two elements of a complex number might be float, double, or long double types. Rather than declare three types of complex numbers and have three sets of functions to operate on the various types, with generic programming we can create the concept of a generic complex data type. When we declare an actual variable, we will use one of the following declarations, which specifies the type of the elements we want in our complex number variables:

```
complex<float> my_single_precision_complex;
complex<double> my_double_precision_complex;
complex<long double> my_quad_precision_complex;
```

These are supported in the C++ Standard Template Library (STL – definition coming up very soon) for C++ when we include the appropriate header file.

Containers

"Container" is C++ terminology for "a struct" that organizes and manages a collection of data items. A C++ container combines both object-oriented capabilities (isolates the code that can manipulate the "struct") and generic programming qualities (the container is abstract, so it can operate on different data types). We will discuss containers supplied by TBB in Chapter 3. Understanding containers is not critical for using TBB; they are primarily supported by TBB for C++ users who already understand and use containers.

Templates

Templates are patterns for creating functions or classes (such as containers) in an efficient generic programming fashion, meaning their specification is flexible with types, but the actual compiled instance is specific and therefore free of overhead from this flexibility. Creating an effective template library can be an incredibly involved task, but using one is not. TBB is a template library.

To use TBB, and other template libraries, we can really treat them as a collection of function calls. The fact that they are templates really only affects us in that we need to use a C++ compiler to compile them since templates are not part of the C language. Modern C++ compilers are tuned to minimize abstraction penalties arising from heavy use of templates.

STL

The C++ Standard Template Library (STL) is a software library for the C++ programming language, which is part of the C++ programming standard. Every C++ compiler needs to support STL.

The concept of "generic programming" runs deep in STL, which relies heavily on templates. STL algorithms, such as sort, are independent of data types (containers). STL supports more complex data types including containers and associative arrays, which can be based upon any built-in type or user-defined type provided they support some elementary operations (such as copying and assignment).

Execution Policies

The C++17 standard introduced overloads for most algorithms to accept execution policies, such as seq, par, par_unseq, and unseq. Implementations of the C++ STL that support these overloads are sometimes called Parallel STL (PSTL) libraries, even though they are just supporting parts of C++17. The C++ standard is designed for execution on a host, but standard library implementations are allowed to define additional execution polices as extensions. Some PSTL implementations have appeared that offload computations to a specific brand of accelerator when the library is linked into an application. More recently, some PSTL implementations have added support for controls to allow a program to direct the work to a particular device or to at least have the implementation selectively place the computation where it will run best. For a while, a PSTL implementation was shipped with TBB. That successful effort is now its own project called oneDPL (stands for oneAPI DPC++ Library) and is now no longer part of the TBB project. oneDPL does use TBB in its implementation to manage scheduling on the host (CPU).

Overloading

Operator overloading is an object-oriented concept that allows new data types (e.g., complex) to be used in contexts where built-in types (e.g., int) are accepted. This can be as arguments to functions or operators such as = and +. C++ templates give us a generalized overloading that can be thought of extending overloading to function names with various parameters and/or return value combinations. The goals of generic programming with templates, and object-oriented programming with overloading, are ultimately *polymorphism* – the ability to process data differently based on the type of the data but reuse the code processing. TBB does this well – so we can just enjoy it as users of the TBB template library.

Ranges and Iterators

C++ experts tell us that ranges are a powerful generalization and extension to algorithms and iterators. The C++ ranges library provides both eager range algorithms and lazy range adaptors. Adaptors can be piped together to create powerful actions that occur lazily as views are iterated over.

As users, the key concept behind an iterator or a range is much the same: a shorthand to denote a set (and some hints on how to traverse it). If we want to denote the numbers 0 to 999999, we can mathematically write this interval as [0,999999] or [0,1000000). Note the use of mathematical notation where brackets [ ] are inclusive and parentheses ( ) are non-inclusive. Using TBB syntax, we write blocked_range<size_t>(0,1000000).

We love ranges, because they match perfectly with our desire to specify "possible parallelism" instead of mandatory parallelism. Consider a "parallel for" that is planned to iterate a million times. We could immediately create a million threads to do the work in parallel, or we could create one thread with a range of [0,1000000). Such a range can be subdivided as needed to fill the available parallelism, and this is why we love ranges.

TBB supports and makes use of iterators and ranges and introduces its own concept of a TBB range that extends the C++ range concept to include the ability to divide (a recursive range). We will mention iterators, C++ ranges, and TBB ranges periodically in this book. There are plenty of examples of these starting in Chapter 2. We will show examples of how to use them, and we think those examples are easy to imitate. We will simply show which one to use where and how. Understanding the deep C++ meanings of iterators vs. ranges will not improve our ability to use TBB.
A simple explanation for now would be that iterators are less abstract than ranges, and at a minimum that leads to a lot of code using iterators which passes two parameters – something.begin() and something.end() – when all we wanted to say was "use this range – begin to end." Recursive ranges (TBB) let us take that further when we want to divide up the work (requiring we split up the range) so we can work in parallel.

Summary

We have explored how to "Think Parallel" through the lenses of decomposition, scaling, correctness, abstraction, and patterns. We have introduced locality as a critical concern in all parallel programming endeavors. Moreover, we have explained how using tasks instead of threads represents a revolutionary development in parallel programming, as supported by TBB. Additionally, we have covered the essential elements of C++ programming that extend beyond basic C knowledge to effectively utilize TBB.

With these key concepts now taking shape in your mind, you have started to "Think Parallel." You are developing an intuition about parallelism that will serve you well.

As you proceed through this book to further explore and learn parallel programming with TBB, this Preface and the Glossary will be invaluable resources.

For More Information

The C++ standard(s): `https://isocpp.org/std/the-standard`

The C++ standard(s) in useful reference online form – highly recommended: `https://cppreference.com`

"The Problem with Threads" by Edward Lee, 2006. *IEEE Computer Magazine*, May 2006, `https://tinyurl.com/ddr7thu3`, or U. C. Berkeley Technical Report: `www2.eecs.berkeley.edu/Pubs/TechRpts/2006/EECS-2006-1.pdf`

All of the code examples used in this book are available at `https://tinyurl.com/tbbBOOKexamples`

CHAPTER 1

Getting Started "Hello, oneTBB!"

In this chapter, we explore the motivations behind the oneAPI Threading Building Blocks (oneTBB) library and provide an overview of its key components, explain how to obtain the library, and present a series of straightforward examples.

Today's TBB is one of the best ways to fully exploit parallelism in standard C++. The TBB project has held this status for several decades, thanks to the project's commitment to the C++ standard, emphasis on the benefits of programming in tasks (not threads), and providing a superbly implemented task-stealing scheduler. We elaborated on those qualities in the Preface – in this chapter we are moving quickly to teaching TBB itself.

Threading Building Blocks remains unique because it rests on a few key decisions:

- Support general C++ programs with existing compilers.

- Relaxed sequential execution.

- Use recursive parallelism and generic algorithms.

- Use task stealing.

Since the TBB project was established in 2006, the landscape of C++ has evolved, and parallelism is more critical than ever. Today's TBB builds upon modern C++ standards without competing against them, ensuring seamless integration and enhanced functionality.

1

© Michael J. Voss, James R. Reinders 2025
M. J. Voss and J. R. Reinders, *Today's TBB*, https://doi.org/10.1007/979-8-8688-1270-5_1

```
1.  int main(int argc, char **argv)
2.  {
3.      auto values = std::vector<unsigned>(HOWMANY);
4.
5.      bbpHexPi bbp;
6.
7.      tbb::parallel_for(tbb::blocked_range<int>(0,values.size()),
8.          [&](tbb::blocked_range<int> r) {
9.              for (int i=r.begin(); i<r.end(); ++i) {
10.                 values[i] = bbp.EightHexPiDigits(i*8);
11.             }
12.         });
13.
14.     for (unsigned eightdigits : values)
15.         printf("%.8x", eightdigits);
16.
17.     printf("\n");
18.
19.     return 0;
20. }
```

Figure 1-1. *Filling in digits of pi (in hexadecimal) in parallel. Sample code intro/intro_pi.cpp*

Hello, oneTBB: π, Anyone?

Since we all love code, before we explain anything else, let's start by whetting our appetite with a simple example using TBB.

Figure 1-1 uses parallelism to fill in an array with the digits of pi. In order for this parallelism to scale well, we need the advanced task-stealing capabilities that come from using TBB.

In this chapter, we will stress over and over that our job as programmers is to expose parallelism to TBB. The use of tbb::parallel_for, in line 7, does exactly that by expressing work in terms of numerous tasks. A task is specified in lines 8–11 as a loop that will fill in as many elements (a range) as the TBB runtime assigns to the task from the full range of work to be done. One example cannot demonstrate all the unique aspects TBB offers, but TBB can scale much better with this example than other popular parallelism methods because TBB excels in the face of irregular parallelism. As is the case, the presence of irregular parallelism may not be obvious at first glance. While we have constructed a very simple example to illustrate this, it is important to note that irregular parallelism is quite common. The superiority of a task-stealing approach in handling irregular parallelism is a key factor in the popularity of TBB.

Our program in Figure 1-1 assumes that we have a function `EightHexPiDigits(n)` that will return the eight digits of pi (π) starting at position n in this irrational number. In this implementation, the leading "3" is at position zero (n=0), so that values $n>0$ represent the nth position right of the decimal (1st digit, 2nd digit, etc.). Since pi in hexadecimal begins with `3.243F6A8885A308D313198A2E03707344`, `EightHexPiDigits(0)` returns `0x3243F6A8` and `EightHexPiDigit(8)` returns `0x885A308D`.

Interestingly enough, it is possible to write `EightHexPiDigits(n)` so that it completes in linear time with modest memory needs. In other words, computing the nth digit of pi does not require computing all the digits before it. Note that the parallelism is irregular since some digits are computed more quickly than others.

The smallest task is filling in one vector element with eight digits from a single call to `EightHexPiDigits(n)`. When we have thousands of vector elements to fill in on a multicore system with dozens of cores, we might be tempted to allocate exactly `elements ÷ cores` tasks to each processor core. This would be a significant mistake because some elements are slower to compute. Fortunately, when we write code with TBB, the runtime has a highly efficient task-stealing scheduler that load balances with both cache reuse and scaling in mind.

The TBB runtime will automatically determine the appropriate number of threads to use, and we would normally just let it do that. However, there are several ways to assign limits (one way sets a local limit, and another sets a program-wide/global limit). Just for fun, we can test what performance looks like when we limit TBB to one thread, two threads, and so on. We did that for 1–448 threads on a system with 224 logical threads in hardware. The results are shown in Figure 1-2. This is a way to analyze the actual scaling of our program. We can see that this program scales well to the limits of the machine. We noted on the graph (Figure 1-2) limits in the hardware that naturally limit the scaling we can accomplish. It is always nice to see how TBB does well in mapping to the hardware in a way that allows us to just program to expose available parallelism without worrying about matching each machine manually. On the graph, we see that exceeding 56 threads forced use of multiple sockets, thereby reducing scaling due to Non-uniform Memory Access (NUMA) effects (we don't need to understand that now), and after 112 threads we are forced to use hyperthreads, which are not as scalable as having the whole core, and after 224 threads we've exhausted the size of the machine and therefore the limits of actual hardware parallelism. After 224 threads, the performance holds steady because the TBB runtime is able to automatically match our computation to the machine limits without degrading performance by introducing overhead that would have no benefit. This is just one example to illustrate how effective TBB is. It is very important because it means we can just count on TBB to do the best thing possible for us. The chapter's GitHub repository has the complete code for this example, including the use of the `tbb::global_control` class to set `tbb::global_control::max_allowed_parallelism` solely for the enjoyment of producing the scaling graph for Figure 1-2.

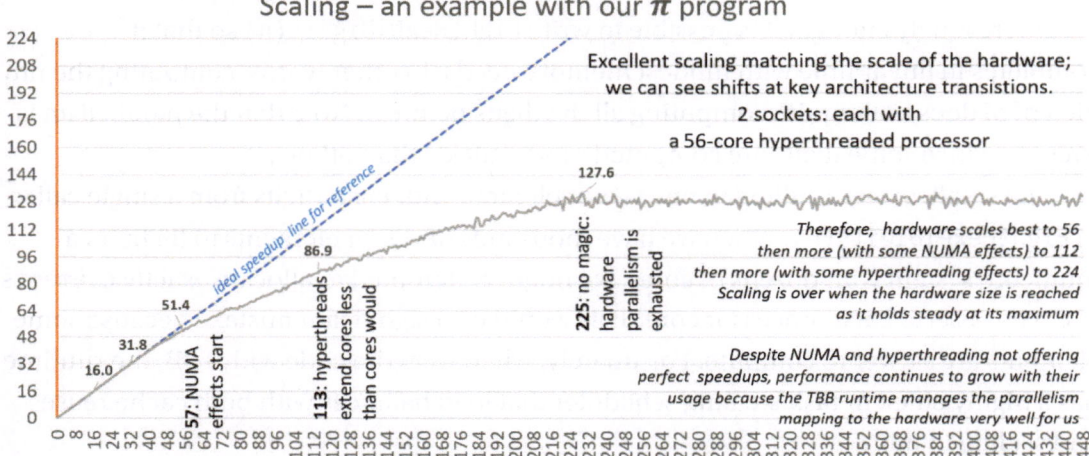

Figure 1-2. *Running on a pair of 56-core hyperthreaded processors – noting several inflection points*

That's enough to whet our appetite for now. This was just a hint of many things to come. Let's dig into the critical information we need to know about TBB in order to learn from the rest of this chapter. That will include mentioning that all the code examples (including the implementation of `EightHexPiDigits(n)`) are available in the chapter's GitHub repository.

If you are curious about the system used for Figure 1-2, it was a dual-socket system with 64G of main memory, using a pair of Intel Core i5-13500 processors. Each processor (socket) had 14 cores, each hyperthreaded (28 hardware threads each processor), and there were two processors (bringing us to 56 hardware threads). If you run this core on a variety of machines, we expect that the results will show similar curves that reflect hardware limitations when exhausting the number of physical cores or logical cores or sockets. This is excellent news for us as programmers: TBB is designed to map our algorithms to the actual hardware at runtime so we can focus on identifying potential parallelism without having to decide how much parallelism to force at runtime.

Names Over Time: TBB and oneTBB – It's Still TBB

The "Threading Building Blocks" project started with the name TBB in 2006 and then moved to the name oneAPI Threading Building Blocks (oneTBB) in late 2020. The functionality inside the library has always used the name "tbb" and continues to do so today. The technical change behind oneTBB was well motivated by the ability to embrace "modern C++." This allowed many features in oneTBB to be simplified when compared with the original TBB. This is because TBB first arrived before C++ had any support for portable parallelism, and therefore the original TBB had additional complexity to make up for this deficiency. Modern C++ (C++11 and later) includes support for portable parallelism including locking and atomic operations. When TBB was simplified to fully embrace this modern C++, it was renamed to oneTBB. It is reasonable to ask, "Why not just name it TBB v2.0?" The explanation is that TBB renaming was swept into a large push for open accelerator support, called "oneAPI," which encouraged the name oneTBB instead of TBB v2.0. It is what it is. With echoes of Billy Joel singing "It's Still Rock and Roll to Me," we'll just say, "It's Still TBB to Me."

For the purposes of the rest of this chapter, we can consider oneTBB and TBB to be equivalent terms. When writing, we will use "oneTBB" when referring to the whole implementation or the library name. Otherwise, it is simply Threading Building Blocks (TBB). As we will see, all the program interfaces are in namespace tbb:: as they always have been. What has changed with oneTBB is the shift to rely on the interfaces of modern C++ that were not available to the original TBB project in 2006.

Where Threading Building Blocks Matters

In a world where parallelism exists everywhere, it is logical to ask where TBB fits.

TBB offers an approachable programming model for parallelism that is not tailored to the limitations of an accelerator. Because of this, it can give us the full range of parallelism possible within a CPU. This matters for two reasons: first, we really do need to use the full power of our systems, and it starts with the CPU parallelism being well-used; second, it allows unfettered exploration of new techniques (not constrained by domain-specific hardware designed for a technique that was most likely first discovered using unfettered explorations).

Expanding on the most obvious "it is all about Amdahl's Law," these four main items highlight why TBB is so important:

- TBB unlocks the full potential of the foundational parallelism of CPUs in modern computers with modern C++. Note: Accelerators are critical to parallelism in modern computers, and TBB leaves their programming to other models (e.g., CUDA, SYCL, OpenCL, etc.). As we will see, optimal use of accelerators depends strongly on a well-organized parallel CPU program for obtaining the full potential of a system.,

- TBB has sophistication that allows nearly unlimited flexibility. It can implement even the most demanding new parallel algorithms while remaining simple and approachable.

- TBB is highly valuable when teaching or learning parallelism.

- TBB is a perfect instrument for parallelism for both experts and new users in this field.

Amdahl's Law Is the Heart of Why TBB Matters So Much

TBB is arguably the most important general-purpose tasking library for parallel computing. It provides a high-quality open source implementation of critical operations needed to obtain a highly scalable application. The enemy of scaling is anything that is serialized (not parallel). This observation is the essence of Amdahl's Law.

Amdahl's Law remains the most important thing to comprehend and deal with when seeking to maximize the performance of a computer system, whether it uses accelerators or not. We provided a refresher in the Preface, which precedes this chapter, to help bring it to the forefront of our thinking and to add some commentary on how to translate understanding into actions that matter for gaining performance.

In recent years, computationally intensive codes (AI, visual effects, scientific, engineering, visualization) have used accelerators. Discussion of these codes understandably focuses on maximizing the performance of core algorithms. Nevertheless, Amdahl's Law forces us to pay attention to issues that TBB is uniquely able to address better than other methods.

In this chapter, we will provide an overview of TBB and discuss strategies for structuring your application to maximize its benefits.

Two Truths – Both Tell Us to Use TBB

In the pursuit of effectively leveraging parallelism in applications, two key truths have emerged:

- Task-level programming: Application development should focus on the "task" level. This means that programmers should concentrate on identifying opportunities for parallelism, which can then be exposed to an abstraction, such as TBB. It is the responsibility of this abstraction to efficiently map these opportunities to the underlying hardware. This concept encompasses a wealth of information, and for those interested in exploring it further, we have provided a dedicated section in the Preface titled "Program Using Tasks, Not Threads."

- Avoiding custom solutions: Creating your own solution, such as a thread pool, is generally ill-advised. Not only is it more complex than it appears, but solutions like TBB already exist to handle these challenges. Moreover, as hardware continues to evolve, utilizing a common library like TBB allows for adaptation without necessitating changes to the application itself, provided that the application adheres to the abstraction offered by the library's API. This statement also carries significant implications worth considering.

The Threading Building Blocks (TBB) Library

The Threading Building Blocks (TBB) library is a C++ library that serves two key roles: (1) it fills foundational voids in support for parallelism where the C++ standard has not sufficiently expanded (and perhaps, in some cases, never should) or where new features are not fully supported by all compilers, and (2) it provides higher-level abstractions for parallelism that are beyond the scope of what the C++ language standard will likely ever include. TBB contains a number of features, as shown in Figure 1-3.

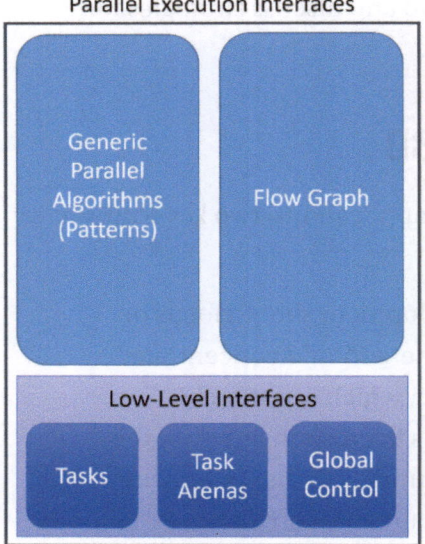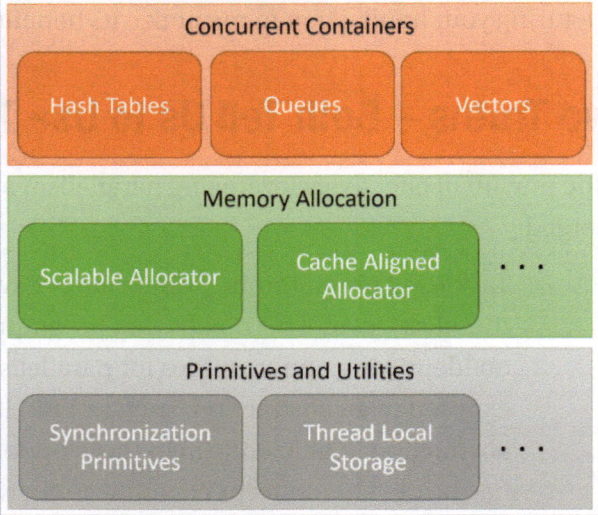

Figure 1-3. *The features of the TBB library*

These features can be categorized into two large groups: interfaces for expressing parallel computations and interfaces that are independent of the execution model.

Parallel Execution Interfaces

When we use TBB to create parallel programs, we express the parallelism in the application using one of the high-level interfaces or directly with tasks using a task group. We discuss tasks in more detail later in this chapter, but for now, we can think of a TBB task as a lightweight object that defines a small computation and its associated data. As TBB developers, we express our application using tasks, either directly or indirectly through the prepackaged TBB algorithms, and the library schedules these tasks onto the platform's hardware resources for us.

TBB provides high-level interfaces for many common parallel patterns, but there may still be cases where none of the high-level interfaces matches a problem. If that's the case, we can use other TBB features such as task groups to directly build our own algorithms.

The true power of the TBB parallel execution interfaces comes from the ability to mix them, namely, *composability*. We can create applications that have a flow graph at the top level with nodes that use nested generic parallel algorithms. In turn, they can have additional generic parallel algorithms nested within them.

One of the key properties of TBB that makes it composable is that it supports *relaxed sequential semantics*. Relaxed sequential semantics means that the parallelism we express using TBB tasks is, in fact, only a hint to the library; there is no guarantee that any of the tasks actually execute in parallel with each other. This gives the TBB library tremendous flexibility to schedule tasks as necessary to improve performance. This flexibility lets the library provide scalable performance on systems, whether they have one core, eight cores, or eighty cores. It also allows the library to adapt to the dynamic load on the platform.

Interfaces That Are Independent of the Execution Model

Unlike the parallel execution interfaces, the second large group of features in Figure 1-3 are completely independent of the execution model and TBB tasks. These features are helpful in applications that employ native threads, such as `std::jthread`, `pthreads`, or `WinThreads`, as in applications that use TBB tasks.

TBB supports concurrent containers that provide thread-friendly interfaces to common data structures like hash tables, queues, and vectors. There are also features for memory allocation, like the TBB scalable memory allocator and the cache aligned allocator. They also include lower-level features such as synchronization primitives and thread-local storage (TLS).

As developers, we can pick and choose the parts of TBB that are useful for our applications. We can, for example, use just the scalable memory allocator and nothing else. Or we can use concurrent containers and a few generic parallel algorithms. And of course, we can also choose to go all in and build an application that combines all three high-level execution interfaces and makes use of the TBB scalable memory allocator and concurrent containers, as well as the many other features in the library.

Getting the Threading Building Blocks (TBB) Library

At the time of the writing of this chapter, you can get the library from `https://github.com/uxlfoundation/oneTBB`, as part of a oneAPI toolkit, or as a stand-alone version: `https://www.intel.com/content/www/us/en/developer/tools/oneapi/onetbb.html`.

We leave it to readers to select the most appropriate route for getting TBB and to follow the directions for installing the packages that are provided at the corresponding site.

Getting a Copy of the Examples

All of the code examples used in this chapter are available at `https://tinyurl.com/tbbBOOKexamples`. The repository has a decoder published in the main directory that shows the correlation of figure numbers with the particular example (directory and filename).

Writing a First "Hello, TBB!" Example

Figure 1-4 provides a small example that uses `tbb::parallel_invoke` to evaluate two functions: one prints `Hello` and another prints `TBB!` in parallel. This example is trivial and will not benefit from parallelization, but we can use it to be sure that we have set up our environment properly to use TBB. In Figure 1-4, we include the tbb.h header to get access to the TBB functions and classes, all of which are in namespace tbb. The call to `parallel_invoke` asserts to the TBB library that the two functions passed to it are independent of each other and are safe to execute in parallel on different cores or threads and in any order. Under these constraints, the resulting output may have either `Hello` or `TBB!` appear first.

```cpp
#include <iostream>
#include <tbb/tbb.h>

int main() {
  tbb::parallel_invoke(
    []() { std::cout << " Hello " << std::endl; },
    []() { std::cout << " TBB! " << std::endl; }
  );
  return 0;
}
```

Figure 1-4. *A Hello, TBB! example. Sample code intro/intro_helloTBB.cpp*

In Figure 1-4, we use *C++ lambda expressions* to specify the functions. Lambda expressions are especially useful when using libraries like TBB to specify the user code to execute as a task. To explain C++ lambda expressions, the Preface includes a review on "lambda functions" under "Introduction to the Features of C++ (As Needed for TBB)" as our overview of this important modern C++ feature.

USING TBB.H OR NOT

A single header file, **tbb.h**, will include all the definitions for all parts of TBB. This is incredibly useful, especially as we learn TBB. Many consider it bad form to define more than is necessary, so TBB provides many individual header files for specific capabilities. Everything is defined in namespace tbb:: (which is also offered under the alias namespace oneapi::tbb::), so many just use tbb.h. Many of our examples will use tbb.h, and other examples will be selective and use only specific header files. We do this to give a flavor of both – we leave it to you to decide what works best for you in your own applications.

Today's TBB

While TBB has been critically important since 2006, much has changed in the C++ world, and that is reflected in the transition to oneTBB.

In 2006, C++ had no language support for parallel programming, and many libraries, including the Standard Template Library (STL), were not easily used in parallel programs because they were not thread-safe. The original versions of TBB had to address a lack of C++ language support.

When originally introducing TBB, we shared these thoughts: we would in fact prefer if all of the fundamental support needed for parallelism is in the C++ language itself. That would allow TBB to utilize a consistent foundation to build higher-level parallelism abstractions.

Today's C++ and TBB combine well today, just as the original TBB and C++ combined well in 2006.

Multicore processors were new in 2006 when TBB first appeared. It was a marriage made in heaven, and TBB was quickly adopted by many. TBB helped firmly establish a new standard for orchestrating parallelism on multicore systems by offering programming in terms of tasks instead of threads, being highly scalable, being composable, and tightly aligning with C++.

A subtle but critical aspect is that TBB emphasizes a model where programmers write in terms of *tasks* or high-level algorithms that generate tasks, and a runtime maps tasks onto threads. This has proven to be a critically important way to do parallel programming. The problem with a prior focus on programming threads directly is well documented in the classic paper "The Problem with Threads" by Berkeley Professor Edward A. Lee.

Figure 1-5 details key areas of modernization found in oneTBB vs. the original TBB. Years later, TBB remains highly relevant as it has evolved from the original TBB based on experience and to align with modern C++.

2006	Today
Multicore rare: Multicore processors were new and a small fraction of the processor market.	**Single core rare:** Multicore processors are the norm. In fact, the term "many core" hit the scene briefly as people debated if "multicore" would stop at 4 or 8 cores. Today, the core count on multicore processors has soared—in some cases well past where even "many core" did not imagine going.
C++ standard single thread only: C++ had no support for threading in the language or standard libraries.	**Modern C++ standard multithreaded support:** C++ has standardized support for threading – including portable atomics and locks.
Thread safety was not the norm: Most libraries were not thread-safe, and the very concept of thread-safety was not a concern for most programmers.	**Thread-safety is the norm:** Libraries either are almost always thread-safe. If not, there will be some solution for use in a multithreaded environment.
Parallel Programming niche only: Parallel programming was a niche specialty that most programmers knew little about. Parallel programming was often done at the thread level, the problems of which are well covered in previously mentioned "The Problem with Threads."	**Parallel Programming Mainstream:** Parallel programming, in many forms, is mainstream.
Clock rate rise drove acceleration: Acceleration of applications from year to year had ridden the MHz wave to a few GHz but it ended. This crisis was well announced in the seminal paper "The Free Lunch is Over: A Fundamental Turn Toward Concurrency in Software" by Herb Sutter.	**Parallelism drives acceleration:** Application acceleration today relies not only on multicore parallelism but also on domain-specific processors (GPUs, TPUs, etc.). This trend, and its importance to the future, is well covered in the seminal paper "A New Golden Age for Computer Architecture" by John L. Hennessy and David A. Patterson. Our age of 'Accelerated computing' rides on heterogeneous parallelism.
TBB had to solve the portability of threading and tasking: TBB offered tasking and threading support on top of a C++ standard that offered no such support.	**TBB focuses on portable tasking:** TBB offers tasking support on top of modern C++, which itself offers portable threading support and lambdas.

Figure 1-5. *Then (2006) and now: TBB useful more than ever*

Parallelism Support in TBB and C++ Continues to Evolve

The C++ language committee has been busy adding features for threading directly to the language and its accompanying Standard Template Library (STL). Figure 1-6 shows new and planned C++ features that address parallelism and concurrency.

ISO C++ standard	Some of the features introduced by the standard
C++11/14	Standardized memory model, `std::unique_ptr`, `std::shared_ptr`, `std::async`, `std::future`, `std::thread`, `std::atomic`, `std::mutex`, `std::lock_guard`, `std::unique_lock`, `std::conditional_variable`
C++17	Execution policies (`std::seq`, `std::par`, `std::par_unseq`, `std::unseq`), algorithm overloads that receive execution policies
C++20/23	Coroutines (`co_await`, `co_yield`, `co_return`), `std::jthread`, `std::stop_token`, `std::atomic_ref`, `std::counting_semaphore`, `std::binary_semaphore`, `std::latch`, `std::barrier`, `std::atomic_ref`
C++26 (expected)	Execution library (`sender`, `receiver`, `scheduler`), `std::simd`

Figure 1-6. *The features in the C++ standard as well as some proposed features*

C++11

As shown in Figure 1-6, the C++11 standard took a huge leap forward by introducing some low-level, basic building blocks for threading, including a standardized memory model, `std::async`, `std::future`, and `std::thread`. It also introduced atomic variables, mutual exclusion objects, and condition variables. These extensions require programmers to do a lot of coding to build up higher-level abstractions – but they do allow us to express basic parallelism directly in C++. The C++11 standard was a clear improvement when it comes to threading, but it doesn't provide us with the high-level features that make it easy to write portable, efficient parallel code. It also does not provide us with tasks or an underlying work-stealing task scheduler.

C++17

The C++17 standard introduced features that raise the level of abstraction above these low-level building blocks, making it easier for us to express parallelism without having to worry about every low-level detail. As we discuss later in this chapter, there are still some significant limitations, and so these features are not yet sufficiently expressive or performant – there's still a lot of work to do in the C++ standard.

The most pertinent of these C++17 additions are the *execution policies* that can be used with the Standard Template Library (STL) algorithms. These policies let us choose whether an algorithm can be safely parallelized, vectorized, or parallelized and vectorized or if it needs to retain its original sequenced semantics. We sometimes call an STL implementation that supports these policies a Parallel STL (PSTL). An open source implementation of PSTL is the one DPL project (see `https://tinyurl.com/uxlonedpl`). We use PSTL in our examples later in this chapter to help illustrate the power of TBB used with modern C++.

PARALLEL STL REALITIES TODAY

The C++17 standard defines Parallel STL, but that still requires support by standard library implementations. We mention the oneDPL project (see `https://tinyurl.com/uxlonedpl`) as an open source implementation of PSTL as an option used by many who work with TBB due to its great support for CPU parallelism. In earlier days of C++17, an implementation of PSTL tagged along with TBB in some distributions from Intel as a convenience for transition to the new API (but it is no longer bundled today). That implementation evolved into the oneDPL project (see `https://tinyurl.com/uxlonedpl`), and it still offers great support for CPU parallelism via TBB and is useful for those who work with TBB. Software ecosystems for accelerators often have their own solutions (as an example, oneDPL also offers a SYCL-based implementation of PSTL algorithms). Some attention may be needed if we want intelligent directing of work to the best resource rather than offloading everything to a particular vendor's accelerator when using that vendor's library. This sort of tuning is still very much a work in progress as implementations mature. We do not attempt to dive into all the nuances of these C++17 implementation issues. We just highlight to you that understanding what your particular combinations of compilers and libraries actually do for PSTL is up to you to learn elsewhere.

C++20/C++23

The C++20 and C++23 standards introduced the most basic support for coroutines to the C++ language. A coroutine is a function that can be suspended and later resumed (we introduce a similar concept available in TBB, resumable tasks, in Chapter 6). There is still no significant library support for coroutines in the C++ Standard Template Library, which remains as work in progress. `std::jthread` was added in C++20 to address concerns around `std::thread`; it automatically joins on destruction and supports cancellation (via `std::stop_token`). This standard also introduced improvements in atomics and additions of latches and barriers, very common synchronization primitives.

C++26

At the time of the writing of this chapter, the C++26 standard is on track to add the `std::simd` library for portably expressing data-parallel types and operations on those types. It also has new basic linear algebra algorithms that support standard execution policies. The new Execution library introduces senders, receivers, and schedulers, as well as a number of free functions that define a framework for managing asynchronous execution on generic execution resources.

As we can see, C++ continues to raise the bar for parallelism and concurrency support. But, even with all of these additions to grow C++ parallelism support, TBB remains a valuable capability building upon standard C++.

A More Complete Example

In this section, we write a bigger example that can benefit from parallel execution using both high-level execution interfaces shown in Figure 1-3. We do not explain all of the details of the algorithms and features, but instead we use this example to see the different layers of parallelism that can be expressed with TBB. It is simple enough to explain in a few paragraphs but complicated enough to exhibit all of the parallelism layers we can imagine. The final multilevel parallel version we create here should be viewed as a syntactic demonstration, not a how-to guide on writing an optimal TBB application. In subsequent chapters, we cover all of the features used in this section in more detail and provide guidance on how to use them to get great performance in more realistic applications.

Starting with a Serial Implementation

Let's start with the serial implementation shown in Figure 1-7. This example applies a gamma correction and a tint to each image in a vector of images, writing each result into a file. The highlighted function, `intro_gamma`, contains a for-loop that processes the elements of a vector by executing `applyGamma`, `applyTint`, and `writeImage` functions on each image. The serial implementations of each of these functions are also provided in Figure 1-7. The definitions of the image representation and some of the helper functions are contained in `intro_examples.h`. This header file is available, along with all of the source code for the example, at `https://tinyurl.com/tbbBOOKexamples`.

```cpp
#include <iostream>
#include <vector>
#include <tbb/tbb.h>
#include "intro_examples.h"

using ImagePtr = std::shared_ptr<ch01::Image>;

ImagePtr applyGamma(ImagePtr image_ptr, double gamma);
ImagePtr applyTint(ImagePtr image_ptr, const double *tints);
void writeImage(ImagePtr image_ptr);

void myfuncG(const std::vector<ImagePtr>& image_vector) {
  const double tint_array[] = {0.75, 0, 0};
  for (ImagePtr img : image_vector) {
    img = applyGamma(img, 1.4);
    img = applyTint(img, tint_array);
    writeImage(img);
  }
}

ImagePtr applyGamma(ImagePtr image_ptr, double gamma) {
  auto output_image_ptr =
    std::make_shared<ch01::Image>(image_ptr->name() + "_gamma",
      ch01::IMAGE_WIDTH, ch01::IMAGE_HEIGHT);
  auto in_rows = image_ptr->rows();
  auto out_rows = output_image_ptr->rows();
  const int height = in_rows.size();
  const int width = in_rows[1] - in_rows[0];

  for ( int i = 0; i < height; ++i ) {
    for ( int j = 0; j < width; ++j ) {
      const ch01::Image::Pixel& p = in_rows[i][j];
      double v = 0.3*p.bgra[2] + 0.59*p.bgra[1] + 0.11*p.bgra[0];
      double res = pow(v, gamma);
      if(res > ch01::MAX_BGR_VALUE) res = ch01::MAX_BGR_VALUE;
      out_rows[i][j] = ch01::Image::Pixel(res, res, res);
    }
  }
  return output_image_ptr;
}
```

Figure 1-7. *A serial implementation of an example that applies a gamma correction and a tint to a vector of images. Sample code intro/intro_gamma.cpp*

```cpp
ImagePtr applyTint(ImagePtr image_ptr, const double *tints) {
  auto output_image_ptr =
    std::make_shared<ch01::Image>(image_ptr->name() + "_tinted",
      ch01::IMAGE_WIDTH, ch01::IMAGE_HEIGHT);
  auto in_rows = image_ptr->rows();
  auto out_rows = output_image_ptr->rows();
  int height = in_rows.size();

  const int width = in_rows[1] - in_rows[0];

  for ( int i = 0; i < height; ++i ) {
    for ( int j = 0; j < width; ++j ) {
      const ch01::Image::Pixel& p = in_rows[i][j];
      std::uint8_t b = (double)p.bgra[0] +
                          (ch01::MAX_BGR_VALUE-p.bgra[0])*tints[0];
      std::uint8_t g = (double)p.bgra[1] +
                          (ch01::MAX_BGR_VALUE-p.bgra[1])*tints[1];
      std::uint8_t r = (double)p.bgra[2] +
                          (ch01::MAX_BGR_VALUE-p.bgra[2])*tints[2];
      out_rows[i][j] =
        ch01::Image::Pixel(
          (b > ch01::MAX_BGR_VALUE) ? ch01::MAX_BGR_VALUE : b,
          (g > ch01::MAX_BGR_VALUE) ? ch01::MAX_BGR_VALUE : g,
          (r > ch01::MAX_BGR_VALUE) ? ch01::MAX_BGR_VALUE : r
        );
    }
  }
  return output_image_ptr;
}

void writeImage(ImagePtr image_ptr) {
  image_ptr->write( (image_ptr->name() + ".bmp").c_str());
}

int main(int argc, char* argv[]) {
  std::vector<ImagePtr> image_vector;

  for ( int i = 2000; i < 20000000; i *= 10 )
    image_vector.push_back(ch01::makeFractalImage(i));

  tbb::tick_count t0 = tbb::tick_count::now();
  myfuncG(image_vector);
  std::cout << "Time : " << (tbb::tick_count::now()-t0).seconds()
            << " seconds" << std::endl;
  return 0;
}
```

Figure 1-7. (*continued*)

Both the applyGamma function and the applyTint function traverse across the rows of the image in an outer for-loop and the elements of each row in an inner for-loop. New pixel values are computed and assigned to the output image. The applyGamma function applies a gamma correction. The applyTint function applies a blue tint to the image. The functions receive and return std::shared_ptr objects to simplify memory management; readers that are unfamiliar with std::shared_ptr can refer to the sidebar discussion "A Note on Smart Pointers." Figure 1-8 shows example outputs for an image fed through the example code.

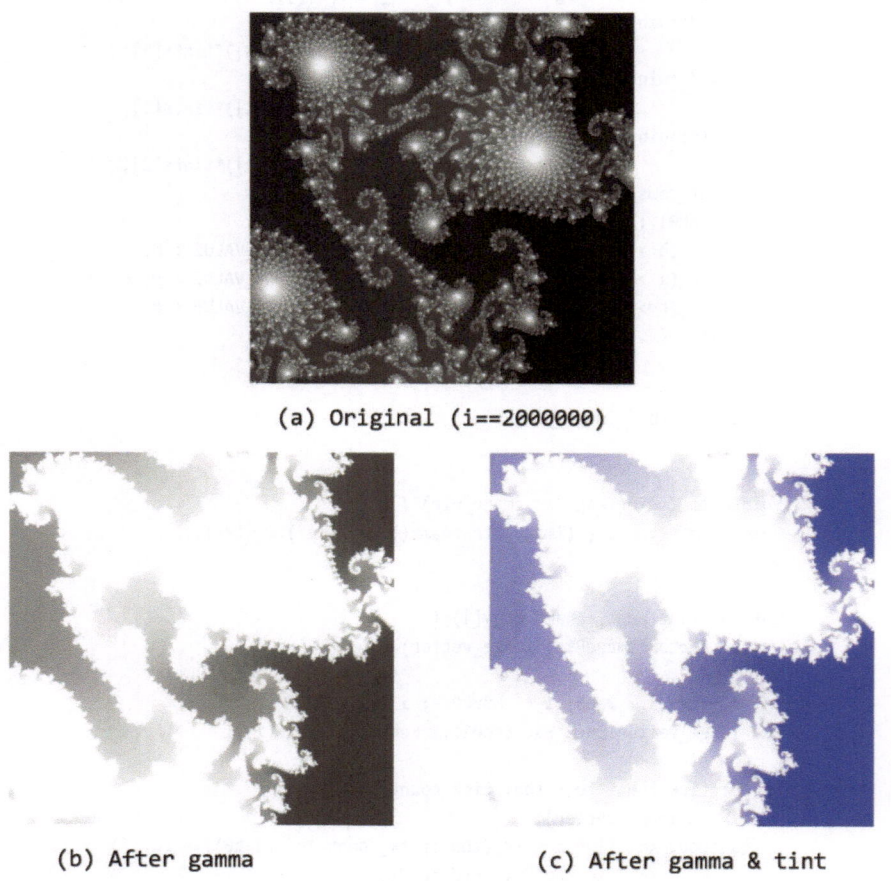

(a) Original (i==2000000)

(b) After gamma   (c) After gamma & tint

Figure 1-8. *Outputs for Figure 1-7 example: (a) the original generated image, (b) the image after it has been gamma corrected, and (c) the image after it has been gamma corrected and tinted*

A NOTE ON SMART POINTERS

One of the most challenging parts of programming in C/C++ can be dynamic memory management. When we use new/delete or malloc/free, we have to be sure that we match them up correctly to avoid memory leaks and double frees. Smart pointers, including `unique_ptr`, `shared_ptr`, and `weak_ptr,` were introduced in C++11 to provide automatic, exception-safe memory management. For example, if we allocate an object by using `make_shared`, we receive a smart pointer to the object. As we assign this shared pointer to other shared pointers, the C++ library takes care of reference counting for us. When there are no outstanding references to our object through any smart pointers, then the object is automatically freed. In most of the examples in this chapter, including in Figure 1-7, we use smart pointers instead of raw pointers. Using smart pointers, we don't have to worry about finding all of the points where we need to insert a free or delete – we can just rely on the smart pointers to do the right thing.

Adding a Message-Driven Layer Using a Flow Graph

Using a top-down approach, we can replace the outer loop in Figure 1-7 with a TBB flow graph that streams images through a set of filters, as shown in Figure 1-9. We admit that this is the most contrived of our choices in this particular example. We could have easily used an outer parallel loop in this case; or we could have merged the gamma and tint loop nests together. But for demonstration purposes, we choose to express this as a graph of separate nodes to show how TBB can be used to express message-driven parallelism. In Chapter 4, we will learn more about the TBB flow graph interfaces and discover more natural applications for this high-level, message-driven execution interface.

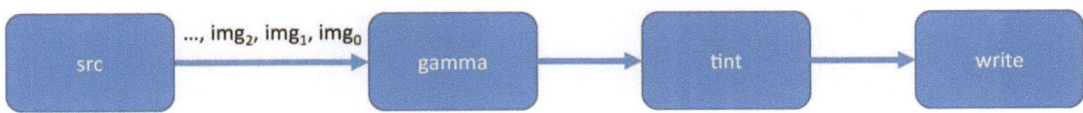

Figure 1-9. *A data flow graph that has four nodes: (1) a node that gets or generates images, (2) a node that applies the gamma correction, (3) a node that applies the tint, and (4) a node that writes out the resulting image*

By using the data flow graph in Figure 1-9, we can overlap the execution of different stages of the pipeline as they are applied to different images. For example, when the first image, img_0, completes in the gamma node, the result is passed to the `tint` node, while a new image img_1 enters the gamma node. Likewise, when this next step is done, img_0, which has now passed through both the gamma and `tint` nodes, is sent to the `write` node. Meanwhile, img_1 is sent to the `tint` node, and a new image, img_2, begins processing in the gamma node. At each step, the execution of the filters is independent of each other, and so these computations can be spread across different cores or threads. Figure 1-10 shows the loop now expressed as a TBB flow graph.

```cpp
void myfuncFG(const std::vector<ImagePtr>& image_vector) {
  const double tint_array[] = {0.75, 0, 0};

  tbb::flow::graph g;
  int i = 0;
  tbb::flow::input_node<ImagePtr> src( g, [&]( tbb::flow_control &fc ) -> ImagePtr
  {
      if ( i < image_vector.size() )
      {
          return image_vector[i++];
      }
      else
      {
          fc.stop();
          return nullptr;
      }
  });

  tbb::flow::function_node<ImagePtr, ImagePtr> gamma(g,
    tbb::flow::unlimited,
    [] (ImagePtr img) -> ImagePtr {
      return applyGamma(img, 1.4);
    }
  );

  tbb::flow::function_node<ImagePtr, ImagePtr> tint(g,
    tbb::flow::unlimited,
    [tint_array] (ImagePtr img) -> ImagePtr {
      return applyTint(img, tint_array);
    }
  );

  tbb::flow::function_node<ImagePtr> write(g,
    tbb::flow::unlimited,
    [] (ImagePtr img) {
      writeImage(img);
    }
  );

  tbb::flow::make_edge(src, gamma);
  tbb::flow::make_edge(gamma, tint);
  tbb::flow::make_edge(tint, write);
  src.activate();
  g.wait_for_all();
}
```

Figure 1-10. *Using a TBB flow graph in place of the outer for-loop. Sample code intro/intro_flowgraph.cpp*

As we will see in Chapter 4, several steps are needed to build and execute a TBB flow graph. First, a graph object, g, is constructed. Next, we construct the nodes that represent the computations in our data flow graph. The node that streams the images to the rest of the graph is an input_node named src. The computations are performed by the function_node objects named gamma, tint, and write. We can think of an input_node as a node that has no input and continues to send data until it runs out of data to send. We can think of a function_node as a wrapper around a function that receives an input and generates an output.

After the nodes are created, we connect them using edges. Edges represent the dependencies or communication channels between nodes. Since, in our example in Figure 1-10, we want the src node to send the initial images to the gamma node, we make an edge from the src node to the gamma node. We then make an edge from the gamma node to the tint node. And likewise, we make an edge from the tint node to the write node. Once we complete the construction of the graph's structure, we call src.activate() to start the input_node and g.wait_for_all() to wait until the graph completes.

When the application in Figure 1-10 executes, each image generated by the src node passes through the pipeline of nodes as described previously. When an image is sent to the gamma node, the TBB library creates and schedules a task to apply the gamma node's body to the image. When that processing is done, the output is fed to the tint node. Likewise, TBB will create and schedule a task to execute the tint node's body on that output of the gamma node. Finally, when that processing is done, the output of the tint node is sent to the write node. Again, a task is created and scheduled to execute the body of the node, in this case writing the image to a file. Each time an execution of the src node finishes and returns true, a new task is spawned to execute the src node's body again. Only after the src node stops generating new images and all of the images it has already generated have completed processing in the write node will the wait_for_all call return.

Adding a Fork-Join Layer Using a `parallel_for`

Now, let's turn our attention to the implementation of the applyGamma and applyTint functions. In Figure 1-11, we replace the outer i-loops in the serial implementations with calls to tbb::parallel_for. We use a parallel_for generic parallel algorithm to execute across different rows in parallel. A parallel_for creates tasks that can be spread across multiple processor cores on a platform.

```
ImagePtr applyGamma(ImagePtr image_ptr, double gamma) {
  auto output_image_ptr =
    std::make_shared<ch01::Image>(image_ptr->name() + "_gamma",
      ch01::IMAGE_WIDTH, ch01::IMAGE_HEIGHT);
  auto in_rows = image_ptr->rows();
  auto out_rows = output_image_ptr->rows();
  const int height = in_rows.size();
  const int width = in_rows[1] - in_rows[0];

  tbb::parallel_for( 0, height,
    [&in_rows, &out_rows, width, gamma](int i) {
      for ( int j = 0; j < width; ++j ) {
        const ch01::Image::Pixel& p = in_rows[i][j];
        double v = 0.3*p.bgra[2] + 0.59*p.bgra[1] + 0.11*p.bgra[0];
        double res = pow(v, gamma);
        if(res > ch01::MAX_BGR_VALUE) res = ch01::MAX_BGR_VALUE;
        out_rows[i][j] = ch01::Image::Pixel(res, res, res);
    } }
  );
  return output_image_ptr;
}

ImagePtr applyTint(ImagePtr image_ptr, const double *tints) {
  auto output_image_ptr =
    std::make_shared<ch01::Image>(image_ptr->name() + "_tinted",
      ch01::IMAGE_WIDTH, ch01::IMAGE_HEIGHT);
  auto in_rows = image_ptr->rows();
  auto out_rows = output_image_ptr->rows();
  const int height = in_rows.size();
  const int width = in_rows[1] - in_rows[0];

  tbb::parallel_for( 0, height,
    [&in_rows, &out_rows, width, tints](int i) {
      for ( int j = 0; j < width; ++j ) {
        const ch01::Image::Pixel& p = in_rows[i][j];
        std::uint8_t b = (double)p.bgra[0] +
                         (ch01::MAX_BGR_VALUE-p.bgra[0])*tints[0];
        std::uint8_t g = (double)p.bgra[1] +
                         (ch01::MAX_BGR_VALUE-p.bgra[1])*tints[1];
        std::uint8_t r = (double)p.bgra[2] +
                         (ch01::MAX_BGR_VALUE-p.bgra[2])*tints[2];
        out_rows[i][j] =
          ch01::Image::Pixel(
            (b > ch01::MAX_BGR_VALUE) ? ch01::MAX_BGR_VALUE : b,
            (g > ch01::MAX_BGR_VALUE) ? ch01::MAX_BGR_VALUE : g,
            (r > ch01::MAX_BGR_VALUE) ? ch01::MAX_BGR_VALUE : r
          );
    } }
  );
  return output_image_ptr;
}
```

Figure 1-11. *Adding* parallel_for *to apply the gamma correction and tint across rows in parallel. Sample code intro/intro_parallel_for.cpp*

Adding Vectorization Using Standard C++17 Execution Policies

We can further optimize our two computational kernels by replacing the inner j-loops with calls to the STL function transform. The transform algorithm applies a function to each element in an input range, storing the results into an output range. The arguments to transform are (1) the execution policy, (2 and 3) the input range of elements, (4) the beginning of the output range, and (5) the lambda expression that is applied to each element in the input range and whose result is stored to the output elements.

In Figure 1-12, we use the C++17 std::unseq execution policy to tell the compiler to use the SIMD version of the transform function.

```cpp
#include <algorithm>
#include <execution>
#include <iostream>
#include <vector>
#include <tbb/tbb.h>
#include "intro_examples.h"

using ImagePtr = std::shared_ptr<ch01::Image>;
void writeImage(ImagePtr image_ptr);

ImagePtr applyGamma(ImagePtr image_ptr, double gamma) {
  auto output_image_ptr =
    std::make_shared<ch01::Image>(image_ptr->name() + "_gamma",
      ch01::IMAGE_WIDTH, ch01::IMAGE_HEIGHT);
  auto in_rows = image_ptr->rows();
  auto out_rows = output_image_ptr->rows();
  const int height = in_rows.size();
  const int width = in_rows[1] - in_rows[0];

  tbb::parallel_for( 0, height,
    [&in_rows, &out_rows, width, gamma](int i) {
      auto in_row = in_rows[i];
      auto out_row = out_rows[i];
      std::transform(std::execution::unseq, in_row, in_row+width,
        out_row, [gamma](const ch01::Image::Pixel& p) {
          double v = 0.3*p.bgra[2] + 0.59*p.bgra[1] + 0.11*p.bgra[0];
          double res = pow(v, gamma);
          if(res > ch01::MAX_BGR_VALUE) res = ch01::MAX_BGR_VALUE;
          return ch01::Image::Pixel(res, res, res);
      });
    }
  );
  return output_image_ptr;
}

ImagePtr applyTint(ImagePtr image_ptr, const double *tints) {
  auto output_image_ptr =
    std::make_shared<ch01::Image>(image_ptr->name() + "_tinted",
      ch01::IMAGE_WIDTH, ch01::IMAGE_HEIGHT);
  auto in_rows = image_ptr->rows();
  auto out_rows = output_image_ptr->rows();
  const int height = in_rows.size();
  const int width = in_rows[1] - in_rows[0];

  tbb::parallel_for( 0, height,
    [&in_rows, &out_rows, width, tints](int i) {
      auto in_row = in_rows[i];
      auto out_row = out_rows[i];
      std::transform(std::execution::unseq, in_row, in_row+width,
        out_row, [tints](const ch01::Image::Pixel& p) {
          std::uint8_t b = (double)p.bgra[0] +
                           (ch01::MAX_BGR_VALUE-p.bgra[0])*tints[0];
          std::uint8_t g = (double)p.bgra[1] +
                           (ch01::MAX_BGR_VALUE-p.bgra[1])*tints[1];
          std::uint8_t r = (double)p.bgra[2] +
                           (ch01::MAX_BGR_VALUE-p.bgra[2])*tints[2];
          return ch01::Image::Pixel(
            (b > ch01::MAX_BGR_VALUE) ? ch01::MAX_BGR_VALUE : b,
            (g > ch01::MAX_BGR_VALUE) ? ch01::MAX_BGR_VALUE : g,
            (r > ch01::MAX_BGR_VALUE) ? ch01::MAX_BGR_VALUE : r
          );
      });
    }
  );
  return output_image_ptr;
}
```

Figure 1-12. *Using* `std::transform` *to add SIMD parallelism to the inner loops. Sample code intro/intro_parallel_for_transform.cpp*

In Figure 1-12, each `Image::Pixel` object contains an array with four single-byte elements representing the blue, green, red, and alpha values for that pixel. By using the unseq execution policy, a vectorized loop is used to apply the function across the row of elements. This level of parallelization takes advantage of the vector units in the CPU core that the code executes on but does not spread the computation across different cores.

Note   Passing an execution policy to an STL algorithm does not guarantee parallel execution. It is legal for the library to choose a more restrictive execution policy than the one requested. Therefore, it is important to check the impact of using an execution policy – especially one that depends on compiler implementations!

While the examples we created in Figures 1-7 through 1-12 are a bit contrived, they demonstrate the breadth and power of the TBB library's parallel execution interfaces.

Summary

In this chapter, we showed why a library such as TBB remains very relevant today as when it was first introduced. We then briefly looked at the major features in the library, including the parallel execution interfaces and the other features that are independent of the execution interfaces. We shared how to verify that our TBB development environment is correctly set up by writing, compiling, and executing very simple examples. We concluded the chapter by building a more complete example that uses three levels of parallelism, demonstrating the composability of TBB with itself and standard C++ parallelism.

We are now ready to walk through the key support for parallel programming in the upcoming chapters.

CHAPTER 2

Algorithms

Writing an effective parallel program depends heavily on how we implement our algorithms. A number of key tasking patterns have proven effective in practice, and TBB algorithms offer highly effective paths to success by guiding us down these proven paths.

TBB provides eight *parallel algorithms to support key tasking patterns*. Relying on only eight algorithms might seem surprising if you are familiar with the C++ Standard Template Library (STL) and its over 100 algorithms or with Parallel STL (PSTL) libraries that contain more than 80 different parallel algorithms. TBB offers eight algorithms because these are the parallel algorithms that are both general and essential – they are implementations of what are commonly referred to as *parallel patterns*. By focusing on this necessary and sufficient set of patterns, the TBB library is able to provide a set of highly tuned generic algorithms that can be used to implement a wide range of additional algorithms across a wide range of application domains.

CHOOSING EIGHT AS KEY

We think of the eight TBB algorithms as seven key algorithm building blocks plus one useful algorithm: *sort*. The inclusion of *sort* as a TBB algorithm has always been useful but different. The TBB list of algorithms was informed by the MIT research that created task stealing, a project known as Cilk, which found difficulties for programmers in practice when originally restricted to only `cilk_spawn` and `cilk_sync` as building blocks. Cilk later added a cilk_for, which still proved less than ideal for users. A decade ago, Microsoft directly supported a subset of the TBB algorithms hoping `fewer` than all eight would be sufficient. User feedback strongly favored the eight that TBB supports. It is notable that TBB added flow graph support and task group support based on community feedback to round out support for parallel patterns (those are covered in Chapters 4 and 5). While eight algorithms may not be provably perfect, the eight that remain in TBB today have proven effective over time at meeting the needs of a very broad user base.

© Michael J. Voss, James R. Reinders 2025
M. J. Voss and J. R. Reinders, *Today's TBB*, https://doi.org/10.1007/979-8-8688-1270-5_2

TBB algorithms are generic, general functions that express commonly used parallel execution patterns found in a wide range of application domains. They typically do not solve specific domain or mathematical problems, such as finding an element in a collection or performing a matrix multiplication, but instead can be used to efficiently express solutions for specific problems. In fact, many of the domain-specific and performance libraries in the oneAPI ecosystem, including the oneAPI Data Parallel Library (an implementation of the C++ Parallel STL), express their wide range of algorithms on top of these eight TBB algorithms.

Figure 2-1 shows the set of functions provided by TBB alongside a brief description of each one and the primary software design patterns they are used to implement. Do not worry if you are not familiar with the design patterns in the third column; we will briefly describe those later in this section. Figure 2-1 is roughly ordered by the scalability of the algorithms; the earlier an algorithm appears in the table, the fewer constraints it has on the ordering of its tasks.

Parallel Algorithm	Brief Description	Primary Design Pattern	Discussed in section (where to learn about it!)
Making independent tasks out of a known set			
parallel_for	Performs parallel iteration of a range of values.	map	Independent Tasking Patterns (starts p. 36)
parallel_invoke	Evaluates several functions in parallel.	Primarily serves to implement the fork-join pattern. When combined with nesting it can be used to implement divide-and-conquer, branch-and-bound, and other tree-based patterns.	Independent Tasking Patterns (starts p. 36)
Making independent tasks out of an expanding set			
parallel_for_each	A parallel implementation of std::for_each, with the option to dynamically add more values to the range.	work-pile	Independent Tasking Patterns (starts p. 36)
Making a task graph for associative operations			
parallel_reduce	Computes a reduction over a range of values.	reduction	Tasking Patterns That Compute a Single Value (starts p. 54)
parallel_deterministic_reduce	Computes a reduction over a range of values with a deterministic associativity.	reduction with reproducible results	Tasking Patterns That Compute a Single Value (starts p. 54)
parallel_scan	Computes a parallel prefix over a range of values	scan/prefix	Tasking Patterns That Compute a Single Value (starts p. 54)
Making a task graph that implements a pipelined execution of functions			
parallel_pipeline	Performs a pipelined execution of filters.	pipeline	Pipeline Patterns (starts p. 68)
Sorting			
parallel_sort	Performs a parallel quicksort.	**N/A** While sort is a very common specific algorithm, it is not considered a fundamental parallel pattern.	parallel_sort (starts p. 79)

Figure 2-1. *The generic algorithms in the Threading Building Blocks library are roughly ordered from the least to the most constrained in the dependencies between tasks*

In this chapter, we provide more detail about all eight TBB algorithms as listed in Figure 2-1. The first seven algorithms, in Figure 2-1, serve as building blocks on which we build our own algorithms to meet our particular needs. While `parallel_sort` can be useful, it is a bit of an outlier since it solves a specific problem, sorting. When TBB was first introduced, sorting was identified by users as a key algorithm and has been maintained ever since.

A Few Comments on Mapping Parallel Patterns to TBB

Software design patterns, such as those listed in Figure 2-1 and again in Figure 2-2, have a long history in programming. The value of object-oriented programming was described by the Gang of Four (Gamma, Helm, Johnson, and Vlissides) and their landmark work *Design Patterns: Elements of Reusable Object-Oriented Software* (Addison-Wesley). Many credit that book with bringing more order to the world of object-oriented programming. Their book gathered the collective wisdom of the community and boiled it down into simple named "patterns," so people could talk about them.

Design Pattern	Description
nesting	The execution of a pattern inside of another pattern. All of TBB supports nesting.
fork-join	Splits control flow into two or more parallel paths and then rejoins them into a single path. All TBB algorithms are internally fork-join patterns. We can think locally and incrementally about TBB algorithms because the parallelism created by each algorithm begins during the call and rejoins before the call completes. Beyond this characteristic of all TBB algorithms, the `parallel_invoke` algorithm, task_group (described in Chapter 6), and flow graph (described in Chapter 4) are APIs that let us easily express fork-join patterns in our own applications.
map	Divides work into uniform independent tasks. This is the best pattern to use because it requires the least ordering and synchronization. The TBB `parallel_for` can be used to implement map.
work-pile	Divides work into uniform independent tasks and new work items can be added dynamically as other items are being processed. The TBB `parallel_for_each` can be used to implement work-pile.
divide-and-conquer	Divides work recursively into increasingly smaller units of work. This pattern typically involves three steps at each layer: (1) dividing into subproblems, (2) solving each subproblem and (3) combing the subproblems' solutions. The subproblems are recursively solved in the same way until reaching a base case. The `parallel_invoke` algorithm and task_group are the TBB features typically used to implement divide-and-conquer patterns.
branch-and-bound	Divides work recursively into increasingly smaller units of work but may prune or cancel unnecessary items to reduce the need for an exhaustive execution of all subproblems. Often used for searches. The `parallel_invoke` algorithm and task_group combined with cancellation are the TBB features typically used to implement branch-and-bound patterns.
reduction	Divides work into independent tasks that compute partial results that are then reduced (combined) into a single result. A specialized example of divide-and-conquer. TBB provides two algorithms to solve reductions: `parallel_reduce` and `parallel_deterministic_reduce`.
scan / prefix	Divides work into independent tasks that compute partial results that are then combined, but intermediate results are also computed for each individual work item. A parallel implementation of y[i]=y[i-1] op f(i). The TBB `parallel_scan` implements a scan / prefix.
pipeline	Passes items through a fixed, linear chain of producer-consumer operations. The TBB `parallel_pipeline` is used to implement pipelines.
event-based coordination	A pattern that expresses producer-consumer and data flow patterns. The flow graph (described in Chapter 4) is used for event-based coordination.

Figure 2-2. *A glossary of the important design patterns associated with parallel programming and their relationship to TBB algorithms*

Patterns for Parallel Programming by Mattson, Sanders, and Massingill (Addison-Wesley) similarly collects wisdom from the parallel programming community. Experts use common tricks and have their own language to discuss techniques. With parallel patterns in mind, programmers can quickly come up to speed in parallel programming, just as object-oriented programmers have done with the famous Gang-of-Four book.

Patterns for Parallel Programming is longer than this book and very dense reading, but with some help from author Tim Mattson, we can summarize how the patterns relate to TBB.

Mattson et al. propose that programmers need to work through four design spaces to develop a parallel program. We describe them next.

Finding Concurrency

For this design space, we work within our problem domain to identify available concurrency and expose it for use in the algorithm design. TBB simplifies this effort by encouraging us to find as many tasks as we can without having to worry about how to map them to hardware threads. We also provide information on how to best make the tasks split in half when the task is considered large enough. Using this information, TBB then automatically divides large tasks repeatedly to help spread work evenly among processor cores. An abundance of tasks leads to scalability for our algorithms.

Algorithm Structures

This design space embodies our high-level strategy for organizing a parallel algorithm. We need to figure out how we want to organize our workflow. Figure 2-2 lists important patterns that we can consult to guide our selection toward a pattern that best suits our needs. These "patterns that work" are the focus of *Structured Parallel Programming* by McCool, Robison, and Reinders (Elsevier), a useful text for anyone interested in diving into the world of patterns more. Doing so is *not* needed to be an effective user of TBB.

Supporting Structures

This step involves the details for turning algorithm strategy into actual code. We consider how the parallel program will be organized and the techniques used to manage shared (especially mutable) data. These considerations are critical and have an impact that reaches across the entire parallel programming process. TBB is well designed to encourage the right level of abstraction, so this design space is satisfied by using TBB well (something we hope we teach in this book).

Implementation Mechanisms

This design space includes thread management and synchronization. TBB manages all the thread management, leaving us free to worry only about tasks at a higher level of design. When using TBB, most programmers code to avoid explicit synchronization coding and debugging. The TBB algorithms described in this chapter and the flow graph API are used to minimize explicit synchronization.

Using a pattern language can guide the creation of better parallel programming environments and help us make the best use of TBB to write parallel software. When discussing mapping parallel patterns to TBB algorithms, we are motivated by finding a scalable algorithm that matches the pattern. A scalable algorithm effectively uses additional cores and hardware resources as they become available. Historically, scaling has been divided into two types: *strong scaling* and *weak scaling.*

An algorithm shows strong scaling if it takes less time to solve a problem of a fixed size as additional cores are added. For example, an algorithm that shows strong scaling may complete the processing of a given data set two times faster than the sequential algorithm when two cores are available but complete the processing of that same data set 100 times faster when 100 cores are available.

An algorithm shows weak scaling if it takes the same amount of time to solve a problem with a fixed data set size *per processor* as more processors are added. For example, an algorithm that shows weak scaling may be able to process two times the data than its sequential version in a fixed period using two processors and 100 times the data than its sequential version in that same fixed period when using 100 processors.

Neither *strong scaling* nor *weak scaling* is inherently better than the other; it all depends on the use case. If you have a fixed sized problem and want to solve it faster, you need strong scaling. If you have a problem and want to increase the amount of data processed to get a more accurate (or somehow better) result, then you need weak scaling.

Independent Tasking Patterns

In order to achieve the most effective parallel program, we must always consider how to keep computations as independent as possible. Therefore, we start by discussing algorithms for fully independent tasks. We are wise to try to map our programming problem onto these algorithms if at all possible. As we progress further in the chapter, we will introduce algorithms to help with dependencies in manners that still seek to maximize independence since that is what is needed to maximize the effectiveness of parallel programming.

Independent tasks require no messy synchronization and so are a task scheduler's dream – they offer complete freedom. In this section, we cover three different algorithms that generate independent tasks. We use `parallel_invoke` to submit a set of functions to be executed as parallel tasks. We use `parallel_for` to create tasks out of loop iterations – but the range must be recursively splitable; that is, it is efficient to break the range repeatedly into two parts. And finally, with `parallel_for_each`, we spawn tasks from loops that traverse containers or that traverse from a beginning to an ending iterator. To increase scalability, `parallel_for_each` also lets us add new tasks as we execute the known tasks. The unifying feature of these patterns is that, once created, the tasks generated by these algorithms are not ordered with respect to each other; they can be executed in any order and by any of TBB's worker threads.

In Figures 2-1 and 2-2, we noted that these algorithms can be used to implement design patterns. The primary differences between `parallel_invoke`, `parallel_for`, and `parallel_for_each` are how developers describe the independent tasks, and this difference has huge implications on scalability and the types of workloads that can be mapped.

`parallel_invoke`: Independent Tasks from Function Calls

The TBB function `parallel_invoke` is the simplest of TBB algorithms to understand; it schedules calls to user-provided functions as parallel tasks and then blocks the calling thread until those tasks are complete. Pass in four functions, execute four parallel tasks, and then wait until they are done. This is a quintessential example of the fork-join pattern.

parallel_invoke is a function template that executes two or more user-provided functions in parallel as shown in Figure 2-3.

```
// Defined in header <tbb/parallel_invoke.h>
namespace tbb {
    template<typename... Functions>
    void parallel_invoke(Functions&&... fs);
} // namespace tbb
```

Figure 2-3. *The* parallel_invoke *algorithm as described in [algorithms. parallel_invoke]*

As an example, if we have two vectors, v1 and v2, we can sort these two vectors by calling a serialQuicksort on each vector consecutively:

```
serialQuicksort(v1.begin(), v1.end());
serialQuicksort(v2.begin(), v2.end());
```

When we execute them one after the other, the total time to execute these calls is equal to the time it takes to execute the first serialQuicksort plus the time it takes to execute the second serialQuicksort.

WHAT DOES [ALGORITHMS.PARALLEL_INVOKE] MEAN IN THE CAPTION FOR FIGURE 2-3?

As mentioned in the Preface, we will use a notation [X.Y] (e.g., [algorithms.parallel_invoke]) to refer to the specification (https://tinyurl.com/tbbspec) page where the relevant online specification lives. The title X (e.g., algorithms) will be under either oneTBB Interfaces or oneTBB Auxiliary Interfaces, and that will take you to the page where the link for Y (e.g., parallel_invoke) exists.

We can use the oneTBB parallel_invoke algorithm to execute these two calls in parallel as shown in Figure 2-4.

```cpp
#include <vector>
#include <tbb/tbb.h>

struct DataItem { int id; double value; };
using QSVector = std::vector<DataItem>;

template<typename Iterator> void serialQuicksort(Iterator b, Iterator e);

void example(QSVector& v1, QSVector& v2) {
  tbb::parallel_invoke(
    [&]() { serialQuicksort(v1.begin(), v1.end()); },
    [&]() { serialQuicksort(v2.begin(), v2.end()); }
  );
}
```

Figure 2-4. *Using* `parallel_invoke` *to execute two* `serialQuicksort` *calls in parallel. Sample code algorithms/parallel_invoke_two_quicksorts.cpp*

The call to the oneTBB `parallel_invoke` in Figure 2-4 creates two tasks that can be executed in parallel by different worker threads, overlapping the executions of these functions in time. If the two invocations of `serialQuicksort` each execute for roughly the same amount of time and if the CPUs on the system are not busy doing other things, this parallel implementation can be completed in roughly half the time it takes to invoke the functions consecutively on a single thread.

This simple use of `parallel_invoke` to execute two sorts in parallel, however, demonstrates neither strong nor weak scaling. The example can only create two independent sorts and, therefore, only uses two processors. If we have 100 processors available, 98 of them will be idle because we have not given them anything to do. So no strong scaling. And increasing the problem size does not help. Whether we execute two very small sorts or two very large sorts, we still can, at most, improve performance by a factor of two. So, if this were your application, there would be no reason to be excited when you get a new computer with more cores.

`parallel_for`: Independent Tasks from a Known Set of Loop Iterations

The `parallel_for` algorithm is a function template that executes the iterations of a for-loop as independent tasks. There are quite a few function signatures available for `parallel_for` as shown in Figure 2-5. What all the signatures have in common is that the TBB library can efficiently generate tasks by recursively subdividing the range.

```
namespace tbb {

//! Parallel iteration over a range of integers, with no step
template<typename Index, typename Func>
void parallel_for(Index first, Index last, const Func& f,
                  partitioner, task_group_context& context);
template<typename Index, typename Func>
void parallel_for(Index first, Index last, const Func& f);
/* … plus 2 other similar signatures not shown here … */

//! Parallel iteration over a range of integers, with step
template<typename Index, typename Func>
void parallel_for(Index first, Index last, Index step, const Func& f,
                  partitioner, task_group_context& context);
/* … plus 3 other similar signatures not shown here … */

//! Parallel iteration over TBB range
template<typename Range, typename Body>
void parallel_for(const Range& range, const Body& body,
                  partitioner, task_group_context& context);
/* … plus 3 other similar signatures not shown here … */

} // namespace tbb
```

Figure 2-5. *The function signatures for* `parallel_for` *as described in [algorithms. parallel_for]*

The `parallel_for` algorithm is the most widely used feature of TBB because many parallel applications are expressed as a series of parallel loops or as nested parallel loops. The `parallel_for` algorithm creates independent tasks from loop iterations, so if there are many iterations, there are many potential tasks. `parallel_for` is therefore typically more scalable than `parallel_invoke` when expressing a single layer of fork-join parallelism.

For example, we know there will be exactly N iterations in the following loop and there are no data dependencies across the iterations:

```
for (int i = 0; i < N; ++i) {
    a[i] = f(a[i]);
}
```

We can use a `parallel_for` to make this loop parallel using the highlighted signature from Figure 2-5:

```
tbb::parallel_for(0, N, [&](int i) {
    a[i] = f(a[i]));
});
```

It is important to understand that by using a `parallel_for`, we are asserting that it is safe to execute the iterations of the loop in any order and in parallel with each other. The TBB library does nothing to check that executing the iterations of a `parallel_for` in parallel (or in fact any of the tasks created by the generic algorithms in parallel) will generate the same results as a serial execution of the algorithm – it is our job as developers to be sure that this is the case when we choose to use a parallel algorithm. Ultimately, we need to ensure when we use a parallel algorithm that any potential changes in read and write access patterns do not change the validity of the results. We also need to ensure that we are using only thread-safe libraries and functions from within our parallel code.

For example, the following loop is *not* safe to execute as a `parallel_for` since each iteration depends on the result of the previous iteration. Changing the order of execution of this loop will alter the final values stored in the elements of array a:

```
for (int i = 0; i < N; ++i) {
    a[i] = a[i-1] + 1;
}
```

Imagine if the array a={1,0,0,0,...,0}. After executing this loop sequentially, it will hold {1,2,3,4,...,N}. But if the loop executes out of order, the results will be different. A mental exercise, when looking for loops that are safe to execute in parallel, is to ask yourself whether the results will be the same if the loop iterations are executed all at once or in random order or in reverse order. In this case, if a={1,0,0,0,...,0} and the iterations of the loop are executed in reverse order, a will hold {1,2,1,1,...,1} when the loop is complete. Obviously, execution order matters for this loop!

Figure 2-6 shows a nonoptimized serial implementation of a matrix multiplication loop nest that computes c = ab for NxK and KxM matrices. ***Before going any further, we must warn that most developers should never write their own matrix multiplication code!*** We use this kernel here for demonstration purposes – if you ever need to use matrix multiply in a real application and do not consider yourself to be an optimization guru, you will almost certainly be better served by using a highly optimized implementation from a math library that implements the Basic Linear Algebra

Subprograms (BLAS) like the Math Kernel Library (MKL), BLIS, or ATLAS. But, with that caveat in mind, matrix multiplication is a good example here because it is a small kernel and performs a basic operation that we are all familiar with. It also contains interesting memory access patterns that we will revisit in Chapter 11. With these disclaimers covered, let us continue with Figure 2-6.

```cpp
template<typename InMat1, typename InMat2, typename OutMat>
void simpleSerialMatrixProduct(int M, int N, int K, const InMat1& a,
                               const InMat2& b, OutMat& c) {
  for (int i0 = 0; i0 < M; ++i0) {
    for (int i1 = 0; i1 < N; ++i1) {
      auto& c0 = c[i0*N+i1];
      for (int i2 = 0; i2 < K; ++i2) {
        c0 += a[i0*K+i2] * b[i2*N + i1];
      }
    }
  };
}
```

Figure 2-6. *A simple serial matrix product implementation. Sample code algorithms/parallel_for_unoptimized_mxm.cpp*

We can quickly implement a parallel version of the matrix multiplication in Figure 2-6 by using `parallel_for` as shown in Figure 2-7. In this implementation, we make the outer i0 loop parallel. An iteration of the outer i0 loop executes the enclosed i1 and i2 loops. It is often better to make outer loops parallel whenever possible, to keep overheads low.

```cpp
template<typename InMat1, typename InMat2, typename OutMat>
void simpleParallelMatrixProduct(int M, int N, int K, const InMat1& a,
                                 const InMat2& b, OutMat& c) {
  tbb::parallel_for( 0, M, [&](int i0) {
    for (int i1 = 0; i1 < N; ++i1) {
      double& c0 = c[i0*N+i1];
      for (int i2 = 0; i2 < K; ++i2) {
        c0 += a[i0*K+i2] * b[i2*N + i1];
      }
    }
  });
}
```

Figure 2-7. *A simple parallel matrix product implementation that uses a single parallel_for. Sample code algorithms/parallel_for_unoptimized_mxm.cpp*

The code in Figure 2-7 quickly gets us a basic parallel version of matrix multiply. While this is a correct parallel implementation, it will leave a lot of performance on the table because of the way it traverses the arrays. Later, we will talk about the advanced features unlocked by the other function signatures for `parallel_for` that are used to tune performance.

`parallel_for_each` for Creating Independent Tasks from an Expanding Set

With both `parallel_invoke` and `parallel_for`, the parallel tasks can be identified very efficiently. For `parallel_invoke`, the tasks are the arguments. For `parallel_for`, the tasks can be generated by recursively dividing the range, using multiple threads. The `parallel_for_each` algorithm lets us express what is called a *work-pile* in Figure 2-2. A work-pile is used when we create independent tasks but cannot efficiently enumerate them all at the start.

A simple example would be if we want to make a parallel version of a while-loop:

```
while (auto i = get_image()) {
    f(i);
}
```

This loop keeps reading in images until there are no more images to read. After each image is read, it is processed by the function f. We cannot use a `parallel_for` because we do not know how many images there will be and so cannot provide a range.

A more subtle case is when we have a container that does not provide random-access iterators:

```
std::list<image_type> my_images = get_image_list();
for (auto &i : my_list) {
    f(i);
}
```

Because a `std::list` does not support random access to its elements, we can obtain the delimiters of the range `my_images.begin()` and `my_images.end()`, but we cannot get to elements in between these points without sequentially traversing the list. The TBB library therefore cannot quickly create chunks of iterations to hand out to multiple threads as tasks since it cannot point to the beginning and ending points of these chunks without traversing the container.

To manage loops like these, the TBB library provides `parallel_for_each`. A TBB `parallel_for_each` applies a Body to work items until there are no more items to process. Some work items can be provided up front when the loop begins, and others can be added by Body executions as they are processing other items.

The `parallel_for_each` function signatures have two variants, as shown in Figure 2-8, one that accepts a first and a last iterator and another that accepts a C++ range.

```cpp
namespace tbb {

//! Parallel iteration over a range,
//   with optional addition of more work.
template<typename InputIterator, typename Body>
void parallel_for_each(InputIterator first, InputIterator last,
                       Body body);
template<typename InputIterator, typename Body>
void parallel_for_each(InputIterator first, InputIterator last,
                       Body body, task_group_context& context);
template<typename Container, typename Body>
void parallel_for_each(Container& c, Body body);
template<typename Container, typename Body>
void parallel_for_each(Container& c, Body body,
                       task_group_context& context);
template<typename Container, typename Body>
void parallel_for_each(const Container& c, Body body);
template<typename Container, typename Body>
void parallel_for_each(const Container& c, Body body,
                       task_group_context& context);

} // namespace tbb
```

Figure 2-8. *The function signatures for* `parallel_for_each` *as described in [algorithms.parallel_for_each]*

As a simple example, let us start with a `std::list` of `std::pair<int, bool>` elements, each of which contains a random integer `value` and `false`. For each element, we will calculate if the `int` value is a prime number; if so, we store `true` to the `bool` value. We will assume that we are given functions that populate the container and determine if a number is prime. A serial implementation is shown in Figure 2-9.

```cpp
#include <list>
#include <utility>
#include <tbb/tbb.h>

using PrimesValue = std::pair<int, bool>;
using PrimesList = std::list<PrimesValue>;
bool isPrime(int n);

//
// Simple serial implementation that checks each element in the list
// and assigns true if it is a prime number
//
void serialPrimesList(PrimesList& values) {
  for (PrimesList::reference v : values) {
    if (isPrime(v.first))
      v.second = true;
  }
}
```

Figure 2-9. *A serial implementation of the primes example using a* std::list. *Sample code algorithms/parallel_for_each_primes.cpp*

```cpp
void parallelPrimesList(PrimesList& values) {
  tbb::parallel_for_each(values,
    [](PrimesList::reference v) {
      if (isPrime(v.first))
        v.second = true;
    }
  );
}
```

Figure 2-10. *A parallel implementation of the primes example using a TBB parallel_for_each to process the* std::list. *Sample code algorithms/parallel_ for_each_primes.cpp*

We can create a parallel implementation of this loop using a TBB `parallel_for_each` as shown in Figure 2-10.

The TBB `parallel_for_each` algorithm will safely traverse the container sequentially while creating tasks to apply the body to each element. Because the container must be traversed sequentially, a `parallel_for_each` may not be as scalable as a `parallel_for`, but as long as the body is relatively large (e.g., runtime is a microsecond or more), the traversal overhead will be negligible compared with the parallel executions of the body on the elements.

In addition to handling containers that do not provide random access, the parallel_ for_each also allows us to add additional work items from within the body executions. If bodies are executing in parallel and they add new items, these items can be spawned in parallel too, avoiding the sequential task spawning limitations of parallel_for_each.

Figure 2-11 provides a serial implementation that calculates whether values are prime numbers, but the values are now stored in a tree instead of a list.

```
void serialPrimesTree(PrimesTreeElement::Ptr e) {
  if (e) {
    if (isPrime(e->v.first))
      e->v.second = true;
    if (e->left) serialPrimesTree(e->left);
    if (e->right) serialPrimesTree(e->right);
  }
}
```

Figure 2-11. *A serial implementation of the primes example using a binary tree of elements. Sample code algorithms/parallel_for_each_primes.cpp*

We create a parallel implementation of this tree version using a parallel_for_each, as shown in Figure 2-12. To highlight the different ways to provide work items in this implementation, we use a container that holds a single tree of values. The parallel_ for_each starts with only a single work item, but two items are added in each body execution, one to process the left subtree and the other to process the right subtree. We use the tbb::feeder<T>::add method to add new work items to the iteration space. The class tbb::feeder<T> is defined by the TBB library, and an instance of this class is passed as the second argument to the body.

The number of available work items increases exponentially as the bodies traverse down the levels of the tree. In Figure 2-12, we add new items through the feeder even before we check if the current element is a prime number, so that the other tasks are spawned as quickly as possible.

```
void parallelPrimesTree(PrimesTreeElement::Ptr root) {
  PrimesTreeElement::Ptr tree_array[] = {root};
  tbb::parallel_for_each(tree_array,
    [](PrimesTreeElement::Ptr e,
       tbb::feeder<PrimesTreeElement::Ptr>& f) {
      if (e) {
        if (e->left) f.add(e->left);
        if (e->right) f.add(e->right);
        if (isPrime(e->v.first))
          e->v.second = true;
      }
    }
  );
}
```

Figure 2-12. *A parallel implementation of the primes example using a binary tree of elements, a* parallel_for_each, *and a feeder to add new elements to the workpile. Sample code algorithms/parallel_for_each_primes.cpp*

We should note that the two uses we considered of parallel_for_each have the potential to scale for different reasons. The first implementation, without the feeder in Figure 2-10, can show good performance if each body execution has enough work to do to mitigate the overheads of traversing the list sequentially. In the second implementation, with the feeder in Figure 2-12, we start with only a single work item, but the number of available work items grows quickly as the bodies execute and add new items.

An even more complicated example, which we will revisit a few times in this book, is forward substitution. Forward substitution is a simple method to solve a set of equations Ax = b, where A is an nxn lower triangular matrix. The same caveat that was raised about our matrix multiplication example in Figure 2-6 holds here; there are highly tuned libraries for parallel solvers. Unless you are an expert in this domain, you should rely on those instead and not write your own. But as with matrix multiplication, this is a good example for demonstrating parallelism.

Viewed as matrices, the set of equations looks like

$$\begin{bmatrix} a_{11} & 0 & \cdots & 0 \\ a_{21} & a_{22} & \cdots & 0 \\ \vdots & \vdots & \ddots & \vdots \\ a_{n1} & a_{n2} & \cdots & a_{nn} \end{bmatrix} \begin{bmatrix} x_1 \\ x_2 \\ \vdots \\ x_n \end{bmatrix} = \begin{bmatrix} b_1 \\ b_2 \\ \vdots \\ b_n \end{bmatrix}$$

and can be solved a row at a time:

$$x_1 = b_1 / a_{11}$$

$$x_2 = (b_2 - a_{21}x_1) / a_{22}$$

$$x_3 = (b_3 - a_{31}x_1 - a_{32}x_2) / a_{33}$$

...

$$x_m = (b_n - a_{n1}x_1 - a_{n2}x_2 - \ldots - a_{nn-1}x_{n-1}) / a_{nn}$$

The serial code for a direct implementation of this algorithm is shown in Figure 2-13. In the serial code, b is destructively updated to store the sums for each row.

```cpp
void serialFwdSub(std::vector<double>& x,
                  const std::vector<double>& a,
                  std::vector<double>& b) {
  const int N = x.size();
  for (int i = 0; i < N; ++i) {
    for (int j = 0; j < i; ++j) {
      b[i] -= a[j + i*N] * x[j];
    }
    x[i] = b[i] / a[i + i*N];
  }
}
```

Figure 2-13. *The serial code for a direct implementation of forward substitution. This implementation is written to make the algorithm clear – not for best performance. Sample code algorithms/parallel_for_each_fwd_substition.cpp*

Figure 2-14(a) shows the dependencies between the iterations of the body of the i,j loop nest in Figure 2-13. Each iteration of the inner j loop (shown by the rows in the figure) performs a reduction into b[i] and depends on all elements of x that were written in earlier iterations of the i loop. We could use a parallel_reduce to parallelize the inner j loop, but there may not be enough work in the early iterations of the i loop to make this profitable. The dotted line in Figure 2-14(a) shows that there is another way to find parallelism in this loop nest by looking diagonally across the iteration space. We can exploit this parallelism by using a parallel_for_each to add iterations only as their dependencies are satisfied, like how we added new tree elements as we discovered them in Figure 2-12.

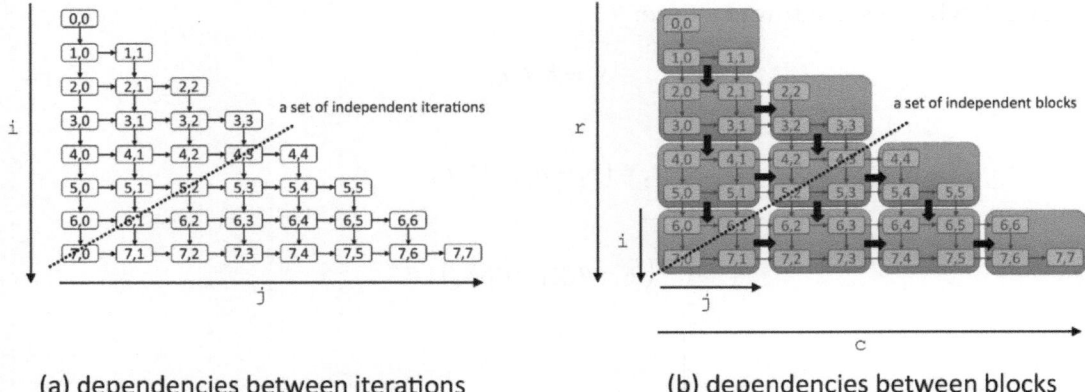

(a) dependencies between iterations   (b) dependencies between blocks

Figure 2-14. *The dependencies in forward substitution for a small 8 × 8 matrix. In (a), the dependencies between iterations are shown. In (b), the iterations are grouped into blocks to reduce scheduling overheads. In both (a) and (b), each block must wait for its neighbor above and its neighbor to its left to complete before it can safely execute*

If we express the parallelism for each iteration separately, we will create tasks that are too small to overcome scheduling overheads since each task will only be a few floating-point operations. Instead, we can modify the loop nest to create blocks of iterations, as shown in Figure 2-14(b). The dependence pattern stays the same, but we will be able to schedule these larger blocks of iterations as tasks. A blocked version of the serial code is shown in Figure 2-15.

```cpp
const int block_size = 512;

void serialFwdSub(std::vector<double>& x,
                  const std::vector<double>& a,
                  std::vector<double>& b) {
  const int N = x.size();
  for (int i = 0; i < N; ++i) {
    for (int j = 0; j < i; ++j) {
      b[i] -= a[j + i*N] * x[j];
    }
    x[i] = b[i] / a[i + i*N];
  }
}

static inline void
computeBlock(int N, int r, int c,
             std::vector<double>& x,
             const std::vector<double>& a,
             std::vector<double>& b);

void serialFwdSubTiled(std::vector<double>& x,
                       const std::vector<double>& a,
                       std::vector<double>& b) {
  const int N = x.size();
  const int num_blocks = N / block_size;

  for ( int r = 0; r < num_blocks; ++r ) {
    for ( int c = 0; c <= r; ++c ) {
      computeBlock(N, r, c, x, a, b);
    }
  }
}
```

Figure 2-15. *A blocked version of the serial implementation of forward substitution. Sample code algorithms/parallel_for_each_fwd_substition.cpp*

A parallel implementation that uses `parallel_for_each` is shown in Figure 2-16. Here, we use the interface to `parallel_for_each` that allows us to specify a beginning and an ending iterator, instead of an entire container.

Unlike with the prime number tree example in Figure 2-12, we do not want to simply send every neighboring block to the feeder. Instead, we initialize an array of counters, `ref_count`, to hold the number of blocks that must complete before each block is allowed to start executing. Atomic variables will be discussed more in Chapter 8. For our purposes here, we can view these as variables that we can modify safely in parallel; in particular, the decrements are done in a thread-safe way. We initialize the counters so that the top-left element has no dependencies, the first column and the blocks along the diagonal have a single dependency, and all others have two dependencies. These counts match the number of predecessors for each block as shown in Figure 2-14.

```cpp
void parallelFwdSub(std::vector<double>& x,
                    const std::vector<double>& a,
                    std::vector<double>& b) {
  const int N = x.size();
  const int num_blocks = N / block_size;

  // create reference counts
  std::vector<std::atomic<char>> ref_count(num_blocks*num_blocks);
  ref_count[0] = 0;
  for (int r = 1; r < num_blocks; ++r) {
    ref_count[r*num_blocks] = 1;
    for (int c = 1; c < r; ++c) {
      ref_count[r*num_blocks + c] = 2;
    }
    ref_count[r*num_blocks + r] = 1;
  }

  using BlockIndex = std::pair<size_t, size_t>;
  BlockIndex top_left(0,0);

  tbb::parallel_for_each( &top_left, &top_left+1,
    [&](const BlockIndex& bi, tbb::feeder<BlockIndex>& f) {
      auto [r, c] = bi;
      computeBlock(N, r, c, x, a, b);
      // add successor to right if ready
      if (c + 1 <= r && --ref_count[r*num_blocks + c + 1] == 0) {
        f.add(BlockIndex(r, c + 1));
      }
      // add successor below if ready
      if (r + 1 < (size_t)num_blocks &&
          --ref_count[(r+1)*num_blocks + c] == 0) {
        f.add(BlockIndex(r+1, c));
      }
    }
  );
}
```

Figure 2-16. *An implementation of forward substitution using parallel_for_each. Sample code* `algorithms/parallel_for_each_fwd_substition.cpp`

In the call to `parallel_for_each` in Figure 2-16, we initially provide only the top-left block, [`&top_left`, `&top_left+1`). The `&top_left+1` points to one past the `top_left` variable, acting as an end iterator. But in each body execution, the `if`-statements at the bottom decrement the atomic counters of the blocks that are dependent on the block that was just processed. If a counter reaches zero, that block has its dependencies satisfied, and it is passed to the feeder.

Like the previous prime number examples, this example demonstrates the hallmark of applications that use `parallel_for_each`: the parallelism is constrained by the need to sequentially access a container or by the need to dynamically find and feed work items to the algorithm.

Recursive, Tree-Based Tasking Patterns

Earlier, we used `parallel_invoke` to spawn a set of completely independent tasks. But we were left a bit disappointed when we realized that spawning two independent calls to quicksort, as done in Figure 2-4, could only get us a factor of 2 improvement even if we have 100 cores. This is because the downside to using `parallel_invoke` is that the scaling of a single call to this algorithm is limited because each function, which becomes an independent task, is provided as an explicit argument. To keep 100 cores busy, we would need to list 100 functions – which is not very practical. In contrast, a single call to `parallel_for` or `parallel_for_each` might generate many tasks.

Luckily for `parallel_invoke` and for us, TBB is very efficient at handling nested parallelism, and so calls to `parallel_invoke` can be nested inside of other calls to `parallel_invoke`. In fact, efficient nesting is a hallmark of TBB in general, and any TBB algorithm can be efficiently nested inside of other TBB algorithms. By combining the fork-join pattern with nesting, we can use `parallel_invoke`, which previously may have seemed very limited, to implement design patterns that are highly scalable such as divide-and-conquer and branch-and-bound. Take that, `parallel_for` and `parallel_for_each`!

Quicksort itself is a divide-and-conquer algorithm, as shown in Figure 2-17(a). Quicksort works by recursively shuffling an array around pivot values, placing the values that are less than or equal to the pivot value in the left partition of the array and the values that are greater than the pivot value in the right partition of the array. When the recursion reaches the base case, arrays of size one, the whole array has been sorted. We should note that recursive calls at the bottom of Figure 2-17(b) are exactly like the calls we made parallel in Figure 2-4; they are just part of a larger recursive algorithm.

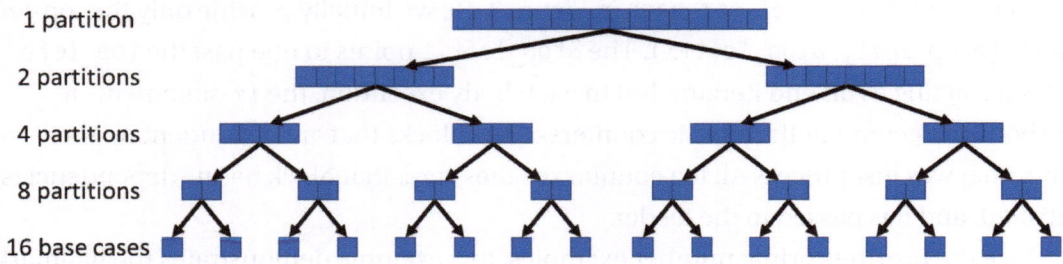

(a) A divide-and-conquer quicksort partitions the iterations space into recursively smaller pieces.

```cpp
void serialQuicksort(Iterator b, Iterator e) {
  if (b >= e) return;

  // do shuffle
  double pivot_value = b->value;
  Iterator i = b, j = e-1;
  while (i != j) {
    while (i != j && pivot_value < j->value) --j;
    while (i != j && i->value <= pivot_value) ++i;
    std::iter_swap(i, j);
  }
  std::iter_swap(b, i);

  // recursive call
  serialQuicksort(b, i);
  serialQuicksort(i+1, e);
}
```

(b) A serial implementation of a recursive quicksort.

Figure 2-17. *A serial implementation of quicksort. Sample code algorithms/ parallel_invoke_two_quicksorts.cpp*

Figure 2-18 shows a parallel implementation of quicksort that replaces the two recursive calls to serialQuicksort with a parallel_invoke that creates tasks that make recursive calls. These two tasks are parallel tasks. However, and this is important, each call to parallel_invoke is a fork-join pattern, so we have introduced some synchronization points here. A call to parallel_invoke generates independent tasks, but the function call does not return until those tasks are completed. Luckily, this behavior is just what we need to express divide-and-conquer algorithms like quicksort. Certainly, we would not want our parallel quicksort to return before all of the sorting work is done. Similarly, we would not want any function that is sorting one of the partitions shown in Figure 2-17(a) to return until all its children partitions are sorted.

In addition to the use of `parallel_invoke` in Figure 2-18, we also introduce a cutoff value. In the original serial quicksort, we recursively partition all the way down to arrays of a single element. Spawning and scheduling a TBB task is not free, and so we do not want to create extremely small tasks. To limit overheads in our parallel implementation, we recursively call `parallel_invoke` only until we dip below 100 elements and then directly call `serialQuicksort` instead. We will discuss appropriate task sizes later in Chapter 11.

```cpp
template<typename Iterator>
void parallelQuickSort(Iterator b, Iterator e) {
  const int cutoff = 100;

  if (e - b < cutoff) {
    serialQuicksort(b, e);
  } else {
    // do shuffle
    double pivot_value = b->value;
    Iterator i = b, j = e - 1;
    while (i != j) {
      while (i != j && pivot_value < j->value) --j;
      while (i != j && i->value <= pivot_value) ++i;
      std::iter_swap(i, j);
    }
    std::iter_swap(b, i);

    // recursive call
    tbb::parallel_invoke(
      [=]() { parallelQuickSort(b, i); },
      [=]() { parallelQuickSort(i + 1, e); }
    );
  }
}
```

Figure 2-18. *A parallel implementation of quicksort using `parallel_invoke`. Sample code algorithms/parallel_invoke_recursive_quicksort.cpp*

You may also notice that the parallel implementation of quicksort has a big limitation – the shuffle is done completely serially. At the top level, this means we have an O(n) operation that is done on a single thread before any of the parallel work can begin. This can limit the speedup.

Tasking Patterns That Compute a Single Value

As we saw in Figure 2-2, a common parallel pattern found in applications is a reduction, commonly known as the "reduce pattern" or "map-reduce" because it tends to be used with a map pattern. A reduction computes a single value from a collection of values. Example applications include calculating a sum, a minimum value, or a maximum value. Another less common, but still important, pattern found in applications is a scan (sometimes called a prefix). A scan is like a reduction, but it also calculates an intermediate result for each element in the collection (the prefixes).

Both reductions and scans compute a single final value (and in the case of scans, intermediate values) from a collection of values. To break up the computation into parallel tasks, the TBB algorithms that implement reductions and scans rely on *associativity*. If an operation is associative, it will produce the same mathematical result regardless of how the elements are grouped together. For example, when using integers or real numbers, a + b + c can be computed as (a + b) + c or a + (b + c); mathematically, the grouping does not matter!

Intuitively, this means we can break an associative operation into independent groups that become tasks, like breaking r = a + b + c + d into three tasks: t1 = a + b, t2 = c + d and then a third task. The third task must wait for the first two tasks to finish and then combines the partial results, r = t1 + t2. If we have more than four elements, we have more options on how elements are grouped and how many intermediate values we store and then combine. We cannot execute all the tasks independently; we need to make sure that tasks that combine intermediate results only occur after the intermediate results are available. But even so, we can create independent tasks that we can execute in parallel.

Associativity and Floating-Point Arithmetic

Before we go further, we need to mention a complication that arises when depending on associativity on computer systems. It is not always practical to represent real numbers on computers with exact precision. Instead, floating-point types such as float, double, and long double are used as an approximation. The consequence of these approximations is that mathematical properties that apply to operations on real numbers do not apply to floating-point types. For example, while addition is associative and commutative on real numbers, it is neither of these for floating-point numbers.

For example, if we compute the sum of N real values, each of which is equal to 1.0, we expect the result to be N:

```
float r = 0.0;
for (uint64_t i = 0; i < N; ++i) {
  r += 1.0;
}
std: :cout << "in-order sum == " << r << std :: endl;
```

But there is a limited number of significant digits in the float representation, and so not all integer values can be represented exactly as floating-point values. So, for example, if we run this loop with N == 10e6 (10 million), we will get an output of 10000000. But if we execute this loop with N == 20e6 (20 million), we get an output of 16777216. The variable r simply cannot represent 16777217 since the standard float representation has a 24-bit mantissa (for significant digits) and 16777217 requires 25 bits. When we add 1.0 to 16777216, the result rounds down to 16777216, and each subsequent addition of 1.0 also rounds down to 16777216. To be fair, at each step, the result of 16777216 is a good approximation of 16777217. It is the accumulation of these rounding errors that makes the final result so bad.

If we break this sum into two loops and combine partial results, we get the right answer in both cases (remember we could successfully sum up to 10 million):

```
float tmp1 = 0.0, tmp2 = 0.0;
for (uint64_t i = 0; i < N/2; ++i)
  tmp1 += 1.0;
for (uint64_t i = N/2; i < N; ++i)
  tmp2 += 1.0;
float r = tmp1 + tmp2;
std :: cout << "associative sum == " << r << std :: endl;
```

Why? Because r can represent larger numbers, just not always exactly. The values in tmp1 and tmp2 are of similar magnitude, and therefore the addition impacts the available significant digits in the representation, and we get a result that is a good approximation of 20 million. This example is an extreme case of how associativity can change the results of a computation using floating-point numbers.

The takeaway of this discussion is parallel_reduce and parallel_scan depend on associativity to compute and combine partial results in parallel. So, when using floating-point numbers, we may get different results when compared with a serial implementation. And in fact, depending on the number of participating threads, the implementation of these algorithms may choose to create a different number of partial results from run to run.

Before we panic and conclude that we should never use these algorithms, we should keep in mind that implementations that use floating-point numbers generally result in an approximation. Even the serial implementation results in an approximation. Getting different results on the same input does not necessarily mean that one of the results is wrong. It just means that the rounding errors accumulated differently for two different runs. It is up to us as developers to decide whether these differences matter for our application.

Okay, now let us get back to the algorithms themselves.

parallel_reduce

parallel_reduce is a function template in TBB that depends on associativity to execute a reduction using parallel tasks.

```
namespace tbb {

//! Lambda-friendly signatures
template<typename Range, typename Value,
         typename Func, typename Reduction>
Value parallel_reduce(const Range& range, const Value& identity,
                      const Func& real_body, const Reduction& reduction,
                      partitioner, task_group_context& context);
template<typename Range, typename Value,
Value parallel_reduce(const Range& range, const Value& identity,
                      const Func& real_body, const Reduction& reduction);
/* … plus 2 other similar signatures not shown here … */

//! Class-friendly signatures
template<typename Range, typename Body>
void parallel_reduce(const Range& range, Body& body,
                     partitioner, task_group_context& context);
template<typename Range, typename Body>
void parallel_reduce(const Range& range, Body& body);
/* … plus 2 other similar signatures not shown here … */

} // namespace tbb
```

Figure 2-19. *The* `parallel_reduce` *algorithm as described in the [algorithms. parallel_reduce] section of the oneTBB specification. Specification as described in [algorithms.parallel_reduce]*

A TBB `parallel_reduce` (see Figure 2-19) requires a Range (`range`) and Body (`real_body`), just like `parallel_for`. But we also need to provide an Identity Value (`identity`) and a Reduction Body (`reduction`).

To create parallelism for a `parallel_reduce`, the TBB library divides the `range` into chunks and creates tasks that apply `real_body` to each chunk. In Chapter 11, we discuss how to use partitioners to control the size of the chunks that are created, but for now, we can assume that TBB creates chunks of an appropriate size to minimize overheads and balance load. Each task that executes `real_body` starts with a value `init` that is initialized with `identity` and then computes and returns a partial result for its chunk. The TBB library combines these partial results by calling the `reduction` function to create a single result for the whole loop.

The identity argument is a value that leaves other values unchanged when combined with it using the operation that is being parallelized. For example, the additive identity is "0" (since x + 0 = x) and the multiplicative identity is "1" (since x * 1 = x). So, if we are parallelizing a sum, we would provide "0," but if we were parallelizing a multiplication, we would provide "1." The reduction function takes two partial results and combines them.

Figure 2-20 illustrates how real_body and reduction functions may be applied to compute the maximum value from an array of 16 elements if the Range is broken into four chunks. In this example, the associative operation applied by real_body to the elements of the array is max() and the identity element is $-\infty$, since max(x,-∞)=x. In C++, we can use std::max as the operation and std::numeric_limits<int>::min() as an approximation of $-\infty$.

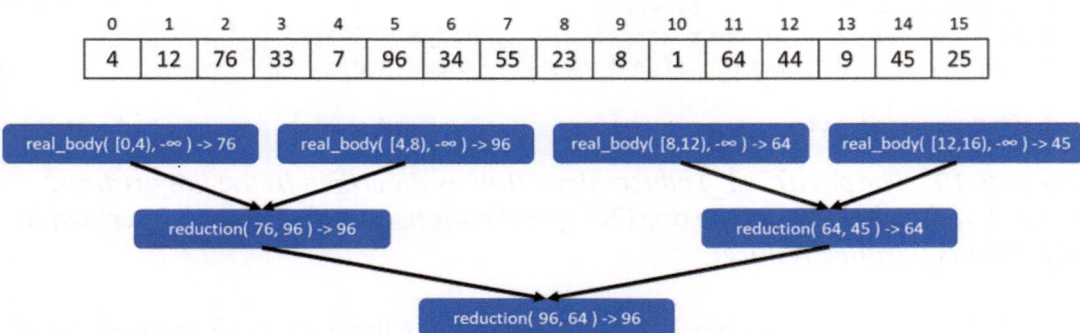

Figure 2-20. *How the* real_body *and* reduction *functions are called to compute a maximum value*

```cpp
#include <limits>
#include <tbb/tbb.h>

int simpleParallelMax(const std::vector<int>& v) {
  int max_value = tbb::parallel_reduce(
    /* the range = */ tbb::blocked_range<int>(0, v.size()),
    /* identity = */ std::numeric_limits<int>::min(),
    /* func = */
    [&](const tbb::blocked_range<int>& r, int init) -> int {
      for (int i = r.begin(); i != r.end(); ++i) {
        init = std::max(init, v[i]);
      }
      return init;
    },
    /* reduction = */
    [](int x, int y) -> int {
      return std::max(x,y);
    }
  );
  return max_value;
}
```

Figure 2-21. *Using* `parallel_reduce` *to compute a maximum value. Sample code algorithms/parallel_reduce_max.cpp*

We can express our simple maximum value loop using a `parallel_reduce` as shown in Figure 2-21.

You may notice in Figure 2-21 that we use a `blocked_range` object for the Range, instead of just providing the beginning and ending of the range as we did with `parallel_for`. The `parallel_for` algorithm provides a simplified syntax that is not available with `parallel_reduce`. For `parallel_reduce`, we pass a Range object directly, but luckily, we can use one of the predefined ranges provided by the TBB library, which include `blocked_range`, `blocked_range2d`, and `blocked_range3d` among others. These other range objects will be described in more detail in Chapter 11.

A `blocked_range`, used in Figure 2-21, represents a 1D iteration space. To construct one, we provide the beginning and the ending value. In the Body, we use its `begin()` and `end()` functions to get the beginning and ending values of the chunk of values that this body execution has been assigned and then iterate over that subrange. In Figure 2-7, each individual value in the Range is sent to the `parallel_for` Body, and so there is no need for an i-loop to iterate over a range. In Figure 2-21, the Body receives a `blocked_range` object that represents a chunk of iterations, and therefore we still have an i-loop that iterates over the entire chunk assigned to it. We can opt in to using this Range-based syntax for a `parallel_for` too if we want to reduce overheads. We will revisit that in Chapter 11.

Now let us look at a slightly more complicated example. Figure 2-22 shows an approach to calculate π by numerical integration. The height of each rectangle is calculated using the Pythagorean Theorem. The area of one quadrant of a unit circle is computed in the loop and multiplied by 4 to get the total area of the circle, which is equal to π.

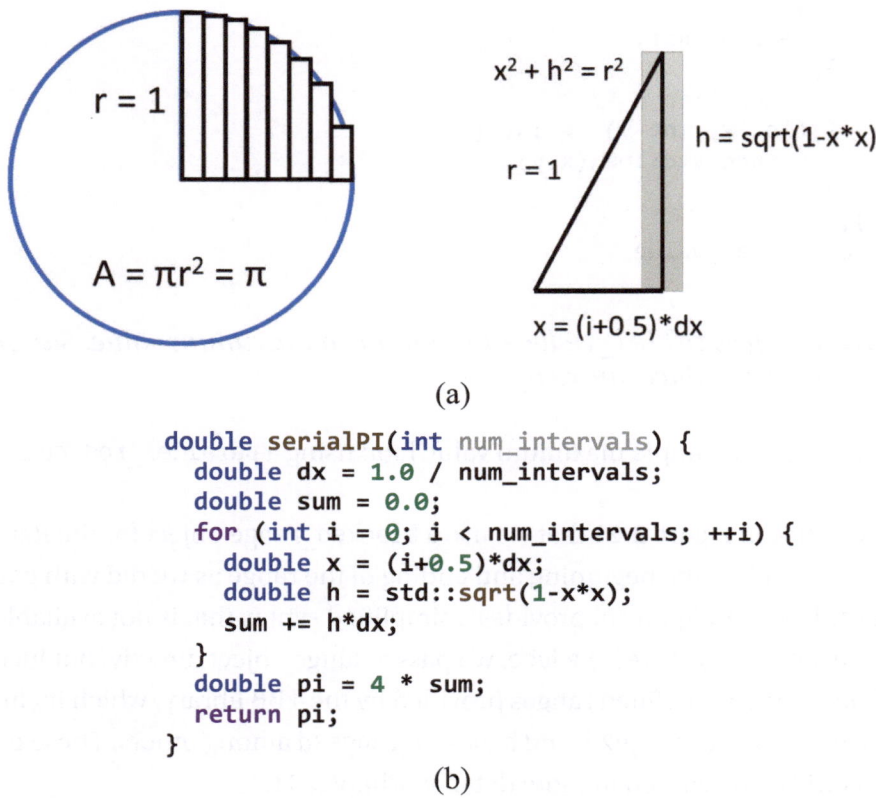

(a)

```
double serialPI(int num_intervals) {
    double dx = 1.0 / num_intervals;
    double sum = 0.0;
    for (int i = 0; i < num_intervals; ++i) {
        double x = (i+0.5)*dx;
        double h = std::sqrt(1-x*x);
        sum += h*dx;
    }
    double pi = 4 * sum;
    return pi;
}
```

(b)

Figure 2-22. *A serial π calculation using the rectangular integral method. Sample code* `algorithms/parallel_reduce_pi.cpp`

The code in Figure 2-22(b) computes the sum of the areas of all the rectangles, a reduction operation. To use TBB `parallel_reduce`, we need to identify the range, `real_body`, `identity`, and `reduction`. For this example, the range is `[0, num_intervals)`, and the `real_body` will be like the `i`-loop in Figure 2-22(b). The `identity` value is `0.0` since we are performing a sum. And the reduction body, which needs to combine partial results, will return the sum of two values. The parallel implementation using a TBB parallel_reduce is shown in Figure 2-23.

```cpp
#include <cmath>
#include <tbb/tbb.h>
//
// Estimating pi using numerical integration
// with a TBB parallel_reduce
//
double parallelPI(int num_intervals) {
  double dx = 1.0 / num_intervals;
  double sum = tbb::parallel_reduce(
    /* range = */ tbb::blocked_range<int>(0, num_intervals),
    /* identity = */0.0,
    /* func */
    [=](const tbb::blocked_range<int>& r, double init) -> double {
      for (int i = r.begin(); i != r.end(); ++i) {
        double x = (i + 0.5)*dx;
        double h = std::sqrt(1 - x*x);
        init += h*dx;
      }
      return init;
    },
    /* reduction */
    [](double x, double y) -> double {
      return x + y;
    }
  );
  double pi = 4 * sum;
  return pi;
}
```

Figure 2-23. *Implementation of pi using tbb::parallel_reduce. Sample code algorithms/parallel_reduce_pi.cpp*

As with parallel_for, there are advanced features and options that can be used with parallel_reduce to tune performance and manage rounding errors (see "Associativity and Floating-Point Arithmetic").

parallel_deterministic_reduce

parallel_deterministic_reduce is a function template in TBB that depends on associativity to execute a reduction using parallel tasks as with parallel_reduce while ensuring we will get the same results for each execution on the same input data when executed on the same machine. This may result in a slight loss of performance, but in practice, it is negligible. This function is used instead of `parallel_reduce` only when there is a specific desire for deterministic results. Often, this is used for testing. It is certainly very useful when debugging a program!

Restricting the Scheduler for Determinism

As we mentioned earlier, the implementation of floating-point numbers is an approximation. This means that parallelism can lead to different results when we depend on properties like associativity or commutativity. The various results are not necessarily wrong, but they are just different. TBB provides a `parallel_deterministic_reduce` algorithm if we want to ensure that we get the same results for each execution on the same input data when executed on the same machine.

`parallel_deterministic_reduce` only accepts `simple_partitioner` or `static_partitioner`, since the number of subranges is deterministic for both of these partitioner types. The different types of partitioners are further explored in Chapter 11. The `parallel_deterministic_reduce` also always executes the same set of split and join operations on a given machine no matter how many threads dynamically participate in execution and how tasks are mapped to threads – the `parallel_reduce` algorithm may not. The result is that `parallel_deterministic_reduce` will always return the same result when run on the same machine – but sacrifices some flexibility to do so.

While `parallel_deterministic_reduce` will have some additional overhead because it must perform all the splits and joins, this overhead is typically small. The bigger limitation is that we cannot use any of the partitioners that automatically find a chunk size for us like `auto_partitioner` and `affinity_partitioner`.

parallel_scan: A Reduction with Intermediate Values

A less common, but still important, pattern found in applications is a scan (sometimes called a prefix). A scan is similar to a reduction, but not only does it compute a single value from a collection of values, but it also calculates an intermediate result for each element in the Range (*the prefixes*). An example is a running sum of the values x0, x1, ... xN. The results include each value in the running sum, y0, y1, ... yN, and the final sum yN.

The values in the series can first appear to be hopelessly not independent enough for any parallelism:

```
y0 = x0
y1 = x0+ x1
...
yN = x0+ x1 + ... + xN
```

A serial loop that computes a running sum from a vector v would look something like Figure 2-24.

```cpp
int serialImpl(const std::vector<int> &v, std::vector<int> &rsum) {
  int N = v.size();
  rsum[0] = v[0];
  for (int i = 1; i < N; ++i) {
    rsum[i] = rsum[i-1] + v[i];
  }
  int final_sum = rsum[N-1];
  return final_sum;
}
```

Figure 2-24. *A serial loop that computes a running sum from a vector v. Sample code algorithms/ serial_running_sum.cpp*

On the surface, a scan looks like a serial algorithm. Each prefix depends on the results computed in all of the previous iterations. While it might seem surprising, there are however efficient parallel implementations of this seemingly serial algorithm. The TBB parallel_scan algorithm implements an efficient parallel scan. Its interface requires that we provide a range, an identity value, a scan body, and a combine body as shown in Figure 2-25.

```cpp
template<typename Range, typename Value,
         typename Scan, typename Combine>
Value parallel_scan(const Range& range, const Value& identity,
                    const Scan& scan, const Combine& combine);
```

Figure 2-25. *The parallel_scan algorithm as described in the [algorithms. parallel_scan] section of the oneTBB specification. Specification as described in [algorithms.parallel_scan]*

The range, identity value, and combine body are analogous to the range, identity value, and reduction body of `parallel_reduce`. And, as with the other loop algorithms, the range is divided by the TBB library into chunks, and TBB tasks are created to apply the body (scan) to these chunks. A complete description of the `parallel_scan` interfaces is provided in [algorithms.parallel_scan].

What is different about `parallel_scan` is that the scan body may be executed more than once on the same chunk of iterations – first in a *pre-scan* mode and then later in a *final-scan* mode.

In *final-scan* mode, the body is passed an accurate prefix result for the iteration that immediately precedes its subrange. Using this value the body computes and stores the prefixes for each iteration in its subrange and returns the accurate prefix for the last element in its subrange.

However, when the scan body is executed in *pre-scan* mode, it receives a starting prefix value that is not the final value for the element that precedes its given range. Just like with `parallel_reduce`, a `parallel_scan` depends on associativity. In pre-scan mode, the starting prefix value may represent a subrange that precedes it, but not the complete range that precedes it. Using this value, it returns a (not yet final) prefix for the last element in its subrange. The returned value represents a partial result for the starting prefix combined with its subrange. By using these *pre-scan* and *final-scan* modes, it is possible to exploit useful parallelism in a scan algorithm.

How does this work?

Let's look at the running sum example again and think about computing it in three chunks A, B, and C. In a sequential implementation we compute all of the prefixes for A, then B, and then C (three steps done in order). We can do better with a parallel scan as shown in Figure 2-26.

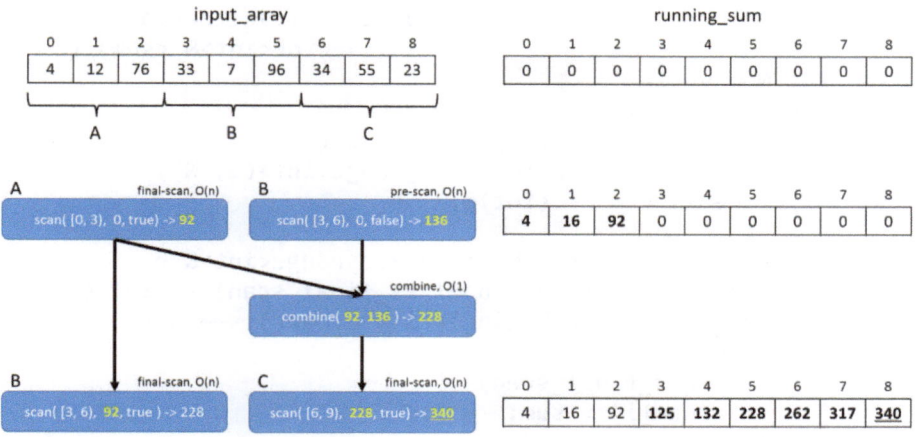

Figure 2-26. *Performing a scan in parallel to compute a sum*

First, we compute the scan of A in final-scan mode since it is the first set of values and so its prefix values will be accurate if it is passed an initial value of identity. At the same time that we start A, we start B in pre-scan mode. Once these two scans are done, we can now calculate accurate starting prefixes for both B and C. To B we provide the final result from A (92) and to C we provide the final scan result of A combined with the pre-scan result of B (92+136 = 228).

The combine operation takes constant time, so it is much less expensive than the scan operations. Unlike the sequential implementation that takes three large steps that are applied one after the other, the parallel implementation executes final scan of A and pre-scan of B in parallel, then performs a constant-time combine step, and then finally computes final scan of B and C in parallel. If we have at least two cores and N is sufficiently large, a parallel prefix sum that uses three chunks can therefore be computed in about two-thirds of the time of the sequential implementation. And parallel_prefix can of course execute with more than three chunks to take advantage of more cores.

Figure 2-27 shows an implementation of the simple partial sum example using a TBB parallel_scan. The range is the interval [1, N), the identity value is 0, and the combine function returns the sum of its two arguments. The scan body returns the partial sum for all of the values in its subrange, added to the initial sum it receives. However, only when its is_final_scan argument is true does it assign the prefix results to the running_sum array.

```
int simpleParallelRunningSum(const std::vector<int>& v,
                             std::vector<int>& rsum) {
  int N = v.size();
  rsum[0] = v[0];
  int final_sum = tbb::parallel_scan(
    /* range = */ tbb::blocked_range<int>(1, N),
    /* identity = */ (int)0,
    /* scan body */
    [&v, &rsum](const tbb::blocked_range<int>& r,
                int sum, bool is_final_scan) -> int {
      for (int i = r.begin(); i < r.end(); ++i) {
        sum += v[i];
        if (is_final_scan)
          rsum[i] = sum;
      }
      return sum;
    },
    /* combine body */
    [](int x, int y) {
      return x + y;
    }
  );
  return final_sum;
}
```

Figure 2-27. *Implementation of a running sum using parallel_scan. Sample code algorithms/parallel_scan_running_sum.cpp*

A Slightly More Complicated Scan Example: Line of Sight

Figure 2-28 shows a serial implementation of a line-of-sight problem similar to the one described in *Vector Models for Data-Parallel Computing* (Guy E. Blelloch, The MIT Press). Given the altitude of a viewing point and the altitudes of points at fixed intervals from the viewing point, the line-of-sight code determines which points are visible from the viewing point. As shown in Figure 2-28(a), a point is not visible if any point between it and the viewing point, altitude[0], has a larger angle Θ. The serial implementation performs a scan to compute the maximum Θ value for all points between a given point and the viewing point. If the given point's Θ value is larger than this maximum angle, then it is a visible point; otherwise, it is not visible.

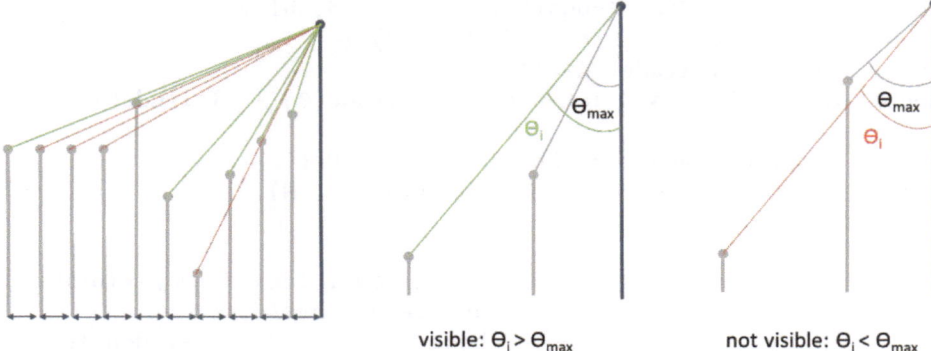

visible: $\Theta_i > \Theta_{max}$ not visible: $\Theta_i < \Theta_{max}$

(a) Calculating points that are visible from a viewing point.

```cpp
void serialLineOfSight(const std::vector<double>& altitude,
                       std::vector<bool>& is_visible, double dx) {
  const int N = altitude.size();

  double max_angle = std::atan2(dx, altitude[0] - altitude[1]);
  double my_angle = 0.0;

  for (int i = 2; i < N; ++i ) {
    my_angle = std::atan2(i * dx, altitude[0] - altitude[i]);
    if (my_angle >= max_angle) {
      max_angle = my_angle;
    } else {
      is_visible[i] = false;
    }
  }
}
```

(b) The serial implementation.

Figure 2-28. *A line-of-sight example. Sample code algorithms/parallel_scan_line_of_sight.cpp*

Figure 2-29 shows a parallel implementation of the line-of-sight example that uses a TBB parallel_scan. When the algorithm completes, the is_visible array will contain the visibility of each point (true or false). It is important to note that this code needs to compute the maximum angle at each point in order to determine the point's visibility, but the final output is the visibility of each point, not the maximum angle at each point. Because the max_angle is needed but is not a final result, it is computed in both pre-scan and final-scan modes, but only the is_visible values are stored for each point during final-scan executions.

```
    void parallelLineOfSight(const std::vector<double>& altitude,
  std::vector<bool>& is_visible, double dx) {
    const int N = altitude.size();
    double max_angle = std::atan2(dx, altitude[0] - altitude[1]);

    double final_max_angle = tbb::parallel_scan(
      /*  range = */ tbb::blocked_range<int>(1, N),
      /* identity */ 0.0,
      /* scan body */
      [&altitude, &is_visible, dx](const tbb::blocked_range<int>& r,
                                   double max_angle,
                                   bool is_final_scan) -> double {
        for (int i = r.begin(); i != r.end(); ++i) {
          double my_angle = atan2(i*dx, altitude[0] - altitude[i]);
          if (my_angle >= max_angle)
            max_angle = my_angle;
          if (is_final_scan && my_angle < max_angle)
            is_visible[i] = false;
        }
        return max_angle;
      },
      [](double a, double b) -> double {
        return std::max(a,b);
      }
    );
  }
```

Figure 2-29. *An implementation of the line-of-sight problem using* parallel_
scan. *Sample code algorithms/parallel_scan_line_of_sight.cpp*

Pipeline Patterns

A pipeline is a linear sequence of *filters* that transform *items* as they pass through them. Pipelines are often used to process data that stream into an application such as video or audio frames or financial data. In Chapter 4, we will discuss the flow graph interfaces that let us build more complex graphs that include fan-in-to and fan-out-from filters. In this section, we discuss parallel_pipeline, which only addresses linear sequences of filters.

Figure 2-30 shows a small example loop that reads in arrays of characters, transforms the characters by changing all the lowercase characters to uppercase and all the uppercase characters to lowercase, and then writes the results in order to an output file.

```
#include <algorithm>
#include <cctype>
#include <fstream>
#include <iostream>
#include <memory>
#include <string>
#include <tbb/tbb.h>

using CaseStringPtr = std::shared_ptr<std::string>;
CaseStringPtr getCaseString(std::ofstream& f);
void writeCaseString(std::ofstream& f, CaseStringPtr s);

void serialChangeCase(std::ofstream& caseBeforeFile,
                      std::ofstream& caseAfterFile) {
  while (CaseStringPtr s_ptr = getCaseString(caseBeforeFile)) {
    std::transform(s_ptr->begin(), s_ptr->end(), s_ptr->begin(),
      [](char c) -> char {
        if (std::islower(c))
          return std::toupper(c);
        else if (std::isupper(c))
          return std::tolower(c);
        else
          return c;
      }
    );
    writeCaseString(caseAfterFile, s_ptr);
  }
}
```

Figure 2-30. *A serial case change example. Sample code algorithms/parallel_
pipeline_case.cpp*

The operations have to be done in order on each buffer, but we can overlap the
execution of different filters applied to different buffers. Figure 2-31(a) shows this
example drawn as a pipeline, where the "write buffer" operates on $buffer_i$, while in
parallel the "process" filter operates on $buffer_{i+1}$ and the "get buffer" filter reads in
$buffer_{i+2}$.

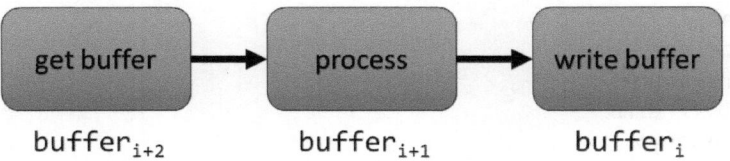

buffer$_{i+2}$ buffer$_{i+1}$ buffer$_i$

(a) Three buffers processed in parallel by different filters.

buffer #

get buffer	0	1	2	3	4	5		
process		0	1	2	3	4	5	
write buffer			0	1	2	3	4	5

time

(b) The steady-state behavior if all filters can work on one item at a time.

buffer #

get buffer	0	1	2	3	4	5							
process		0	0	1	1	2	2	3	3	4	4	5	5
write buffer				0		1		2		3		4		5

time

(c) The steady-state behavior if process takes 2x the time of the other filters.

Figure 2-31. *The case change example using a pipeline*

As illustrated in Figure 2-31(b), in the steady state, each filter is busy, and their executions are overlapped. However, as shown in Figure 2-31(c), unbalanced filters decrease speedup. The performance of a pipeline of serial filters is limited by the slowest serial stage.

The TBB library supports both serial and parallel filters. A parallel filter can be applied in parallel to different items to increase the throughput of the filter. Figure 2-32(a) shows the "case change" example drawn with the middle/process filter executing in parallel on two items. Figure 2-32(b) illustrates that if the middle filter takes twice as long as the other filters to complete on any given item, then assigning two threads to this filter will allow it to match the throughput of the other filters.

Figure 2-33 shows the types and functions associated with the TBB `parallel_pipeline`.

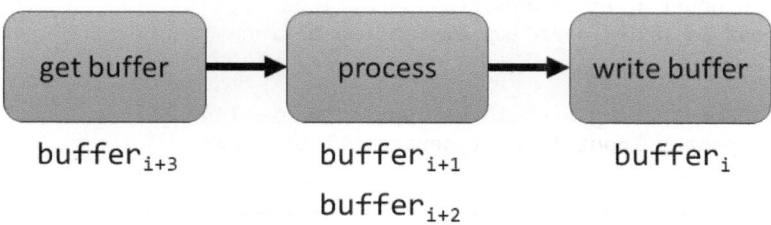

(a) A parallel filter can process multiple items in parallel.

	buffer #								
get buffer	0	1	2	3	4	5			
process		0	0	2	2	4	4		
			1	1	3	3	5	5	
write buffer			0	1	2	3	4	5	

time →

(b) More threads can be provided to a parallel filter to increase throughput.

Figure 2-32. *The case change example using a pipeline with a parallel filter. By using two copies of the parallel filter, the pipeline maximizes throughput*

```
namespace tbb {
  enum class filter_mode {
    parallel = /* implementation defined */,
    serial_in_order = /* implementation defined */,
    serial_out_of_order = /* implementation defined */
  };

  //! Class representing a chain of type-safe pipeline filters
  template<typename Input Type, typename OutputType>
  class filter;
```

```
  //! Create a filter to participate in parallel_pipeline
  template<typename Body> filter<filter_input<Body>, filter_output<Body>>
  make_filter( filter_mode mode, const Body& body );
```

```
  //! Composition of filters left and right.
  template<typename T, typename V, typename U> filter<T, U>
  operator&( const filter<T,V>& left, const filter<V,U>& right );
```

```
  //! Parallel pipeline over chain of filters with user-supplied context.
  inline void
  parallel_pipeline(size_t max_number_of_live_tokens,
                    const filter<void, void>& filter_chain,
                    task_group_context& context);
```

```
  //! Parallel pipeline over chain of filters.
  inline void
  parallel_pipeline(size_t max_number_of_live_tokens,
                    const filter<void, void>& filter_chain);
```

```
  //! Parallel pipeline over sequence of filters.
  template<typename F1, typename F2, typename ... FiltersContext> void
  parallel_pipeline(size_t max_number_of_live_tokens,
                    const F1& filter1,
                    const F2& filter2,
                    FiltersContext&& ... filters);
} // namespace tbb
```

Figure 2-33. *The* parallel_pipeline *algorithm as described in the [algorithms. parallel_pipeline] section of the oneTBB specification. Specification as described in [algorithms.parallel_pipeline]*

The first argument of the highlighted parallel_pipeline function in Figure 2-33 is max_number_of_live_tokens. This argument is used to set the maximum number of items that will be allowed to flow through the pipeline at any given time. This value is necessary to constrain resource consumption. For example, consider the simple three-filter pipeline. What if the middle filter is a serial filter and it takes 1,000 times longer than the filter that gets new buffers? The first filter might allocate 1,000 buffers only to queue them up before the second filter – wasting a lot of memory.

The second argument to parallel_pipeline is filter_chain, a series of filters created by concatenating filters that are created using the make_filter function by calling the operator& function. These two functions are also highlighted in Figure 2-33.

The make_filter template function receives two arguments: a filter_mode and a Body. The input and output types of created filters are set from the input and output types of the Body. The filter_mode argument is serial_in_order, serial_out_of_ order, or parallel. Figure 2-34 shows the implementation of the case change example using a TBB parallel_pipeline.

```
  void parallelChangeCase(std::ofstream& caseBeforeFile,
                          std::ofstream& caseAfterFile) {
    int num_tokens = tbb::info::default_concurrency();
    tbb::parallel_pipeline(
      /* tokens */ num_tokens,
      /* the get filter */
      tbb::make_filter<void, CaseStringPtr>(
        /* filter node */ tbb::filter_mode::serial_in_order,
        /* filter body */
        [&](tbb::flow_control& fc) -> CaseStringPtr {
          CaseStringPtr s_ptr = getCaseString(caseBeforeFile);
          if (!s_ptr)
            fc.stop();
          return s_ptr;
        }) & // concatenation operation
      /* make the change case filter */
      tbb::make_filter<CaseStringPtr, CaseStringPtr>(
        /* filter node */ tbb::filter_mode::parallel,
        /* filter body */
        [](CaseStringPtr s_ptr) -> CaseStringPtr {
          std::transform(s_ptr->begin(), s_ptr->end(), s_ptr->begin(),
            [](char c) -> char {
              if (std::islower(c))
                return std::toupper(c);
              else if (std::isupper(c))
                return std::tolower(c);
              else
                return c;
            });
          return s_ptr;
        }) & // concatenation operation
      /* make the write filter */
      tbb::make_filter<CaseStringPtr, void>(
        /* filter node */ tbb::filter_mode::serial_in_order,
        /* filter body */
        [&](CaseStringPtr s_ptr) -> void {
          writeCaseString(caseAfterFile, s_ptr);
        })
    );
  }
```

Figure 2-34.   *The case change example implemented using a TBB parallel_ pipeline, two serial_in_order filters, and a parallel filter in the middle. Sample code algorithms/parallel_pipeline_case.cpp*

We can note that the first filter receives a special argument of type `tbb::flow_control`. We use this argument to signal when the first filter in a pipeline is no longer going to generate new items. For example, in the first filter in Figure 2-34, we call `fc.stop()` when the pointer returned by `getCaseString()` is `null`.

In this implementation, the first and last filters are created using the `serial_in_order` mode. This specifies that both filters should run on only one item at a time and that the last filter should execute the items in the same order that the first filter generated them in. A `serial_out_of_order` filter is allowed to execute the items in any order. The middle filter is passed `parallel` as its mode, allowing it to execute on different items in parallel.

A more complicated example of a pipeline is shown in Figure 2-35. A while-loop reads in frame numbers, and then for each frame it reads a left and a right image and adds a red coloring to the left image and a blue coloring to the right image. It then merges the resulting two images into a single red–cyan 3D stereoscopic image.

(a) Two images combined into a red–cyan 3D stereoscopic image. Elena Adams took the original photograph.

```cpp
class PNGImage {
public:
  uint64_t frameNumber = -1;
  unsigned int width = 0, height = 0;
  std::shared_ptr<std::vector<unsigned char>> buffer;
  static const int numChannels = 4;
  static const int redOffset = 0;
  static const int greenOffset = 1;
  static const int blueOffset = 2;

  PNGImage() {}
  PNGImage(uint64_t frame_number, const std::string& file_name);
  PNGImage(const PNGImage& p);
  virtual ~PNGImage() {}
  void write() const;
};

int getNextFrameNumber();
PNGImage getLeftImage(uint64_t frameNumber);
PNGImage getRightImage(uint64_t frameNumber);
void increasePNGChannel(PNGImage& image, int channel_offset, int increase);
void mergePNGImages(PNGImage& right, const PNGImage& left);

void serial3DStereo() {
  while (uint64_t frameNumber = getNextFrameNumber()) {
    auto left = getLeftImage(frameNumber);
    auto right = getRightImage(frameNumber);
    increasePNGChannel(left, PNGImage::redOffset, 10);
    increasePNGChannel(right, PNGImage::blueOffset, 10);
    mergePNGImages(right, left);
    right.write();
  }
}
```

(b) A serial implementation that applies the 3D effect.

Figure 2-35. *A serial example that applies the 3D stereoscopic effect. Sample code* *algorithms/3Dstereo_serial_no_pipeline.cpp*

Like the simple case change sample, we again have a series of inputs that pass through a set of filters. We identify the crucial functions and convert them to pipeline filters: getNextFrameNumber, getLeftImage, getRightImage, increasePNGChannel (to left image), increasePNGChannel (to right image), mergePNGImages, and right.write(). Figure 2-36 shows the example drawn as a pipeline. The increasePNGChannel filter is applied twice, first on the left image and then on the right image.

Figure 2-36. *The 3D stereoscopic sample application as a pipeline*

The parallel implementation using a TBB parallel_pipeline is shown in Figure 2-37.

```cpp
      void parallel3DStereo() {
        using Image = PNGImage;
        using ImagePair = std::pair<PNGImage, PNGImage>;
        tbb::parallel_pipeline(
          /* tokens */ 8,
          /* make the left image filter */
          tbb::make_filter<void, Image>(
            /* filter type */ tbb::filter_mode::serial_in_order,
            [&](tbb::flow_control& fc) -> Image {
              if (uint64_t frame_number = getNextFrameNumber()) {
                return getLeftImage(frame_number);
              } else {
                fc.stop();
                return Image{};
              }
            }) &
          tbb::make_filter<Image, ImagePair>(
            /* filter type */ tbb::filter_mode::serial_in_order,
            [&](Image left) -> ImagePair {
              return ImagePair(left, getRightImage(left.frameNumber));
            }) &
          tbb::make_filter<ImagePair, ImagePair>(
            /* filter type */ tbb::filter_mode::parallel,
            [&](ImagePair p) -> ImagePair {
              increasePNGChannel(p.first, Image::redOffset, 10);
              return p;
            }) &
          tbb::make_filter<ImagePair, ImagePair>(
            /* filter type */ tbb::filter_mode::parallel,
            [&](ImagePair p) -> ImagePair {
              increasePNGChannel(p.second, Image::blueOffset, 10);
              return p;
            }) &
          tbb::make_filter<ImagePair, Image>(
            /* filter type */ tbb::filter_mode::parallel,
            [&](ImagePair p) -> Image {
              mergePNGImages(p.second, p.first);
              return p.second;
            }) &
          tbb::make_filter<Image, void>(
            /* filter type */ tbb::filter_mode::parallel,
            [&](Image img) {
              img.write();
            })
        );
      }
```

Figure 2-37. *The 3D stereoscopic sample using* parallel_pipeline. *Sample code* algorithms/3Dstereo_parallel_pipeline.cpp

The TBB `parallel_pipeline` function imposes a linearization of the pipeline filters. The filters are applied one after the other as the input from the first stage flows through the pipeline. This is an unneeded constraint imposed on this sample due to the limitations of `parallel_pipeline`. The left image processing and right image processing are independent until the `mergeImageBuffers` filter, but because of the interface of `parallel_pipeline`, the filters must be linearized. Even so, only the filters that read in the images are serial filters, and therefore this implementation can still be scalable if the execution time is dominated by the later, parallel stages.

In Chapter 4, we introduce the TBB flow graph, which will allow us to more directly express applications that benefit from nonlinearized execution of filters.

parallel_sort

In the preceding sections, we discussed seven of the eight TBB algorithms in terms of key patterns they help us implement. The last algorithm, sort, is undeniably useful but in a different sense because it is really just an algorithm and not a building block.

`parallel_sort` sorts a sequence or a container, possibly in parallel. The sort is *neither* stable *nor* deterministic – the relative ordering of elements with equal keys is *not* preserved and *not* guaranteed to repeat if the same sequence is sorted again. The requirements on the iterator and sequence are the same as for `std::sort`.

There are three invocation types for `parallel_sort`:

1. A call `parallel_sort(begin,end,comp)` sorts the sequence
   [begin, end) using the argument `comp` to determine relative
   orderings. If `comp(x,y)` returns true, then x appears before y in the
   sorted sequence.

2. A call `parallel_sort(begin, end)` is equivalent to `parallel_sort`
   `(begin,end,std::less<T>)`.

3. A call `parallel_sort(c[,comp])` is equivalent to `parallel_`
   `sort(std::begin(c),std::end(c)[,comp])`.

Figure 2-38 provides a simple example of using `parallel_sort`.

```
#include <cstdio>
#include <tbb/tbb.h>
#include <array>

#define PV(X) printf(" %02d", X);
#define PN(Y) printf( "\nHello, Sorted " #Y ":\t");
#define P(N) PN(N); std::for_each(N.begin(),N.end(),[](int x) { PV(x); });
#define V(Z) myvect.push_back(Z);

int main( int argc, char *argv[] ) {
  int myvalues[]                  = {  3,  9,  4,  5,  1,  7,  6,  8, 10,  2 };
  std::array<int, 10> myarray     = { 19, 13, 14, 11, 15, 20, 17, 16, 12, 18 };
  std::array<int, 10> disarray    = { 23, 29, 27, 25, 30, 21, 26, 24, 28, 22 };
  tbb::concurrent_vector<int> myvect;
  V(40); V(31); V(37); V(33); V(34); V(32); V(34); V(35); V(38); V(36);

  tbb::parallel_sort( myvalues,myvalues+10 );
  tbb::parallel_sort( myarray.begin(), myarray.end() );
  tbb::parallel_sort( disarray );
  tbb::parallel_sort( myvect );

  PN(myvalues); for(int i=0;i<10;i++) PV(myvalues[i]);
  P(myarray);
  P(disarray);
  P(myvect);
  printf("\n\n");
  return 0;
}

This output is deterministic!

Hello, Sorted myvalues:  01 02 03 04 05 06 07 08 09 10

Hello, Sorted myarray:   11 12 13 14 15 16 17 18 19 20

Hello, Sorted disarray:  21 22 23 24 25 26 27 28 29 30

Hello, Sorted myvect:    31 32 33 34 34 35 36 37 38 40
```

Figure 2-38. *`parallel_sort` example. Sample code algorithms/parallel_sort.cpp*

The Other Algorithms, Patterns, and Features

In this chapter, we discussed all the TBB algorithms, but we have not yet covered all of the parallel patterns introduced in Figure 2-2.

The event-based coordination parallel pattern is covered well by TBB's flow graph API. The flow graph is such a large topic that we reserve Chapter 4 to introduce it and Chapter 5 to put it to good use.

The TBB `task_group` is a very general and widely applicable way to create and manage tasks more directly. Many of the parallel patterns in Figure 2-2 can be expressed in one way or another using a `task_group`. We will dive into `task_group` in Chapter 6.

Summary

This chapter offered an overview of the generic parallel algorithms provided by the TBB library and described how parallel patterns can be implemented using them. These prepackaged algorithms provide well-tested and tuned implementations that can be applied incrementally to an application to improve performance.

The code shown in this chapter provides small examples that show how these algorithms can be used. In later chapters, we discuss how to get the most out of TBB by combining these algorithms in composable ways and tuning applications using the library features available for optimizing locality, minimizing overheads, and adding priorities.

In the next chapter (Chapter 3), because data independence is an important consideration in addition to task independence, we consider concurrent containers. Then, we finish covering parallel patterns by discussing flow graph and task groups in Chapters 4–6.

CHAPTER 3

Data Structures for Concurrency

Data sharing between concurrent tasks can lead to significant correctness and performance challenges if not managed properly. TBB provides well-tested, open source solutions that have established themselves as reliable tools over the years. TBB containers can be used independently or alongside other TBB components.

It's important to note that concurrent containers are not necessary when performing parallel read operations. Special support is only needed when parallel code modifies a container. For occasional modifications – where no new keys are introduced – the standard C++ library is typically sufficient. However, developers must familiarize themselves with the thread safety guidelines outlined in the C++ reference (`https://en.cppreference.com/w/cpp/container`).

In scenarios where collections grow dynamically, such as adding new elements, using parallel-aware containers like those described in this chapter becomes essential. Performance enhancement is the primary reason for adopting TBB containers in these cases.

C++ Standard Template Library (STL) containers have limited concurrency support, as they do not safely support concurrent updates that alter the container's structure. Concurrent modifications without proper synchronization can easily lead to container corruption. While STL containers can be protected by wrapping them in a mutex to ensure safe concurrent access, this approach restricts execution to a single thread at a time, limiting parallel speedup as described by Amdahl's Law. In contrast, TBB's highly concurrent containers provide a superior solution for managing key data structures in concurrent environments.

This chapter introduces the highly concurrent containers available in the TBB project, following a brief overview of fundamental data structures.

© Michael J. Voss, James R. Reinders 2025
M. J. Voss and J. R. Reinders, *Today's TBB*, https://doi.org/10.1007/979-8-8688-1270-5_3

CHOOSE ALGORITHMS WISELY: CONCURRENT CONTAINERS ARE NOT A CURE-ALL

Parallel data access is best when it stems from a clear parallelism strategy, a key part of which is the proper choice of algorithms. Controlled access, such as that offered by concurrent containers, comes at a cost and may not always possible. TBB offers concurrent containers when such support can work well in practice (queues, hash tables, and vectors).

TBB does not attempt to support concurrency for containers such as "lists" and "trees," where fine-grained sharing will not scale well – the better opportunity for parallelism lies in revising algorithms and/or data structure choices.

Concurrent containers offer a thread-safe version for containers where concurrent support can work well in parallel programs. They offer a higher-performance alternative to using a serial container with a coarse-grained lock around it. Internally, TBB containers utilize fine-grained locking or lockless implementations.

Key Data Structures: Basics

If you are familiar with hash tables, maps, sets, queues, and vectors, then you may want to skip this section and resume reading in the "Concurrent Containers" section. To help review the fundamentals, we provide a quick introduction to key data structures before we jump into talking about how TBB supports these for parallel programming.

Vectors

A vector is a dynamic, sequenced container that stores elements without using fixed indexing. Unlike an array, which maintains a fixed size and stores a collection of elements of the same type in an indexed manner, a vector can automatically adjust its size as elements are added or removed. This flexibility allows vectors to grow in capacity, accommodating varying amounts of data, whereas arrays remain static once initialized, limiting their adaptability.

Associative Containers, Ordered and Unordered

Associative containers can be thought of as collections, often referred to as "sets" in simpler terms. However, in technical language, we use specific terms like maps, sets, and hash tables to describe different types of collections.

In C++, associative containers are class templates designed to implement associative arrays. Each container relies on a key for organizing its elements. In map and set containers, each key is unique, while multimap and multiset containers allow for multiple instances of the same key. For set and multiset containers, we can only check for the existence of keys, such as "Glass of Juice," "Loaf of Bread," or "Puppy in the Window." In contrast, map and multimap containers store key–value pairs, enabling queries for values like Info["Glass of Juice"].cost, Info["Loaf of Bread"].cost, and Info["Puppy in the Window"].cost.

These containers are versatile templates that can hold various data types, including integers, floating-point numbers, or custom classes. Additionally, they offer both unordered and ordered versions. Each type of container has specific constraints on its elements.

Our associative containers come in three varieties:

1. Ordered vs. unordered

2. Map vs. set: Is there a *key and value*? Or just a *key*?

3. Multiple values: Can two items with the same *keys* be inserted in the same collection?

Ordered vs. Unordered

An unordered associative container does not order its elements. With ordered associative containers, elements are stored in a predefined order (e.g., ascending values).

Operations on an unordered collection may be faster, especially on large data, since operations are O(1) average time instead of O(log n). Therefore, we should only choose to use the ordered versions if our algorithm requires the ability to traverse (*iterate* in C++ jargon) all members in a specific order.

With an unordered container, the only guarantee when we iterate over all members is that we will visit each member of the container once and only once. The order in which members are encountered with an unordered container is not guaranteed and may vary run to run, machine to machine, and so on.

Map vs. Set

What we call a "map" is really just a "set" with a value attached. Maps are occasionally referred to as a dictionary. Imagine a basket of fruits (Apple, Orange, Banana, Pear, Lemon). A *set* containing fruits could tell us if we had a particular type of fruit in the basket. A simple *yes* or *no*. We can add a fruit type into the basket or remove it. A *map* adds to this a value, often a data structure itself with information. With a *map* of a fruit type in a collection (fruit basket), we could choose to keep a count, a price, and other information. Instead of a simple *yes* or *no* question, we can ask about Info[Apple].cost or Info[Banana].ripeness. If the value is a structure with multiple fields, then we can query multiple things such as cost, ripeness, and color.

Multiple Values

Inserting something into a map/set using the same *key* as an item already in the map is not allowed (ensuring uniqueness) in the regular "map" or "set" containers but is allowed in the "multimap" and "multiset" versions. In the "multiple" versions, duplicates are allowed, but we lose the ability to look up something like Info[Apple].cost because the key Apple is no longer unique in a map/set. In such cases, we would need to iterate over all the elements with the key Apple to examine each recorded cost.

Hashing and Comparing

The unordered versions of everything we have mentioned (associative arrays, map/set, single/multiple) are commonly implemented using *hash* functions. To understand what a *hash* function is, it is best to understand its motivation. Consider an associative array LibraryCardNumber[Name of Patron]. The array LibraryCardNumber returns the library card number for a patron given the name (specified as a string of characters) that is supplied as the index. One way to implement this associative array would be with a linked list of elements. Unfortunately, looking up an element would require searching the list one by one for a match. That might require traversing the entire list, which is highly inefficient in a parallel program because of contention over access to the share list structure. Even without parallelism, when inserting an item, verification that there is no other entry with the same *key* requires searching the entire list. If the list has thousands or millions of patrons, this can require excessive amounts of time. More exotic data structures, such as trees, can correct some but not all of these issues.

Imagine, instead, a vast array in which to place data. This array is accessed by a traditional array[integer] method. This is very fast. In this case, all we need is a magical *hash* function that takes the index for the associative array (*Name of Patron*) and turns it into the integer we need.

Concurrent Containers

TBB provides highly concurrent container classes that are useful for all C++ threaded applications; the TBB concurrent container classes can be used with any method of threading, including TBB of course!

The C++ STL was not initially designed with concurrency in mind. Therefore, attempts to modify STL containers concurrently may result in corrupted containers for operations that change structure (some operations are safe). Of course, STL containers can be wrapped in a coarse-grained mutex to make them safe for concurrent access by letting only one thread operate on the container at a time. However, that approach eliminates concurrency and thereby restricts parallel speedup if done in performance-critical code. This is a crucial point: conversion of containers to TBB concurrent containers should be motivated by need. Data structures that are used in parallel should be designed for concurrency to enable scaling for our applications. Data structures that are not accessed in parallel need not change. However, we would strongly advise writing new code with the assumption it may be used concurrently at some point in the future.

The concurrent containers in TBB provide functionality similar to containers provided by the STL, but do so in a thread-safe way. For example, the tbb::concurrent_vector is similar to the std::vector class but lets us safely grow the vector in parallel. As mentioned early on, we do *not* need a concurrent container if we *only* read from it in parallel; it is only when we have parallel code that modifies a container that we need special support.

TBB offers several container classes, meant to replace corresponding STL containers in a compatible manner, which permit multiple threads to simultaneously invoke certain methods on the same container.

Important   Use concurrent containers if (and probably only if) the speedup from the additional concurrency that they enable outweighs their slower sequential performance.

It is worth noting that TBB concurrent containers do come at a small cost. They typically have slightly higher overheads than regular STL containers, and therefore operations on them may take slightly longer than on the STL containers. When the possibility of concurrent access exists, concurrent containers should be used. However, if concurrent access is not possible, the use of STL containers is advised. We should use concurrent containers when the speedup from the additional concurrency that they enable outweighs their slower sequential performance.

The interfaces for the containers remain the same as in STL, except where a change is required in order to support concurrency. Let's jump ahead for a moment and make this a suitable time to consider a classic example of why some interfaces are not thread-safe – *and this is a critical point to understand!* The classic example (see Figure 3-1) is the need for a new *pop-if-not-empty* capability (called try_pop) for queues in place of relying on a code sequence using STL *test-for-empty* followed by a *pop* if the test returned not empty. A danger in such STL code is that another thread might be running, empty the container (after the original thread's test, but before pop), and therefore create a race condition where the *pop* may result in undefined behavior. That means the STL code is not thread-safe. We could throw a lock around the whole sequence to prevent modification of the queue between our test and our pop, but such locks are known to destroy performance when used in parallel parts of an application. Understanding this simple example (Figure 3-1) will help illuminate what is required to support parallelism well.

std:: code, *not* thread-safe	tbb:: code, thread-safe

```cpp
#include <iostream>
#include <queue>
#include <tbb/parallel_invoke.h>

int main() {
  int sum0(0), sum1(0);

  std::priority_queue<int> myPQ;

  for(int i=0; i<10001; i+=1) {
    myPQ.push(i);
  }

  tbb::parallel_invoke(
    [&]() {
      while( !myPQ.empty() ) {
        sum0 += myPQ.top();
        myPQ.pop();
      }
    },
    [&]() {
      while( !myPQ.empty() ) {
        sum1 += myPQ.top();
        myPQ.pop();
      }
    });

  // if correct (which it is not) this
  // would always print "total: 50005000"
  std::cout << "total: "
            << sum0+sum1 << '\n';
  return 0;
}
// Sample outputs:
// total: 128379594
// total: 124432912
// total: 107697942
// total: 50005000
// total: 115224669
// total: 146790135
// total: 130683763
// total: 126960607
```

```cpp
#include <iostream>
#include <tbb/concurrent_priority_queue.h>
#include <tbb/parallel_invoke.h>
#include <tbb/parallel_for.h>

int main() {
  int sum0(0), sum1(0);

  tbb::concurrent_priority_queue<int> myPQ;

  tbb::parallel_for(0,10001,1,
      [&](size_t i){ myPQ.push(i); } );

  tbb::parallel_invoke(
    [&]() {
      int item = 0;
      while( myPQ.try_pop(item) )
        sum0 += item;
    },
    [&]() {
      int item = 0;
      while( myPQ.try_pop(item) )
        sum1 += item;
    });

  // thanks to being correct, this
  // always prints "total: 50005000"
  std::cout << "total: "
            << sum0+sum1 << '\n';
  return 0;
}


// Always outputs:
// total: 50005000
```

Figure 3-1. *Motivation for* try_pop *instead of* top *and* pop *shown in a side-by-side comparison of STL and TBB priority queue code. Using the STL priority queue in parallel is unsafe and therefore results in unpredictable results. Sample code* containers/pop_danger.cpp *and* pop_danger_fixed.cpp

Like STL, TBB containers are templated with respect to an allocator argument. Each container uses that allocator to allocate memory for user-visible items. The default allocator for TBB is the scalable memory allocator supplied with TBB (discussed in Chapter 7). Regardless of the allocator specified, the implementation of the container may also use a different allocator for strictly internal structures.

TBB offers the following concurrent containers:

- Associative containers (ordered and unordered versions): Map, multimap, set, and multiset

- Hash map (this is an unordered associative container class – a concept predating C++11 STL)

- Queues: Regular, bounded, and priority

- Vector

WHY DO TBB CONTAINERS' ALLOCATOR ARGUMENTS DEFAULT TO TBB?

Allocator arguments are supported with all TBB containers, and they default to the TBB scalable memory allocators (see Chapter 7).

The containers default to using a mix of `tbb::cache_aligned_allocator` and `tbb:tbb_allocator`. We document the defaults in this chapter, but the oneTBB specification and the TBB header files are the definitive resources for learning the defaults. There is no requirement to link in the TBB scalable allocator library (see Chapter 7), as TBB dynamically loads the scalable allocator if it can find it. The containers will silently fall back to using `malloc` when the library is not present. Of course, this fallback will not help us with performance.

Class name *and C++11 connection notes*	Concurrent traversal and insertion.	Keys have a value associated with them.	Support concurrent erasure	Built-in locking (requires us to release).	No visible locking (lock-free interface).	Identical items allowed to be inserted.	`[]` and `at` accessors	Elements ordered (with some added overhead).
`concurrent_hash_map` *Predates C++11.*	✓	✓	✓	✓	✗	✗	✗	✗
`concurrent_map` *Closely resembles the C++11* `map`.	✓	✓	✗	✗	✓	✗	✓	✓
`concurrent_multimap` *Closely resembles the C++11* `multimap`.	✓	✓	✗	✗	✓	✓	✗	✓
`concurrent_set` *Closely resembles the C++11* `set`.	✓	✗	✗	✗	✓	✗	✗	✓
`concurrent_multiset` *Closely resembles the C++11* `multiset`.	✓	✗	✗	✗	✓	✓	✗	✓
`concurrent_unordered_map` *Closely resembles the C++11* `unordered map`.	✓	✓	✗	✗	✓	✗	✓	✗
`concurrent_unordered_multimap` *Closely resembles the C++11* `unordered multimap`.	✓	✓	✗	✗	✓	✓	✗	✗
`concurrent_unordered_set` *Closely resembles the C++11* `unordered set`.	✓	✗	✗	✗	✓	✗	✗	✗
`concurrent_unordered_multiset` *Closely resembles the C++11* `unordered multiset`.	✓	✗	✗	✗	✓	✓	✗	✗

Figure 3-2. *Comparison of concurrent ordered and unordered associative containers*

Concurrent Unordered Associative Containers

Unordered associative containers are a group of class templates that implement hash table variants. Figure 3-2 lists these containers and their key differentiating features. Concurrent unordered associative containers can be used to store arbitrary elements, such as integers or custom classes, because they are templates. TBB offers implementations of associative containers that can perform well concurrently. Figure 3-2 is a handy reference to compare the nine TBB implementations for associative containers.

Starting with C++11, a hash table implementation was added to the STL, and the name unordered_map was chosen for the class to prevent confusion and collisions with pre-standard implementations. It could be said that the name unordered_map is more descriptive as it hints at the interface to the class and the unordered nature of its elements. Along with unordered_map, C++11 also added unordered_set, unordered_multimap, and unordered_multiset.

Avoid STL Interfaces That Are Unsafe with Concurrency

TBB offers safe concurrency, but we must avoid the unsafe STL interfaces that TBB labels as such.

The original TBB hash table support, called tbb::concurrent_hash_map, predates C++11. It remains quite valuable and did not need to change to match the standard. TBB now includes support for the eight variants (see Figure 3-2) of map and set to mirror the C++11 additions, with the interfaces augmented or adjusted only as needed to support concurrent access. Avoiding a few parallel-unfriendly interfaces is part of the "nudging us" to effective parallel programming. Two noteworthy adjustments for better parallel scaling are as follows:

1. Erase methods (other than for concurrent_hash_map) are not thread-safe. The erase methods for C++ standard functions are prefixed with unsafe_ to indicate that they are not concurrency safe because concurrent erasure is only supported for concurrent_hash_map. This does not apply to concurrent_hash_map because it *does* support concurrent erasure.

2. Bucket methods are not thread-safe. They are prefixed with unsafe_ as a reminder that they are not concurrency safe with respect to insertion. They are supported for compatibility with STL but should be avoided if possible. If used, they should be protected from being used concurrently with insertions occurring. These interfaces do not apply to concurrent_hash_map because the TBB designers avoided such functions.

Unsafe Really Means Unsafe

Using methods labeled "unsafe" is a really bad idea and hopefully only done in debug code on a temporary basis with an understanding of their evils.

Erase methods are unsafe to do in a parallel program, and a lock around the erase itself will not solve the problem. If we do need to make erasures, it is our responsibility to ensure no part of our application is holding onto a view into the container that could be affected by an erase happening. It is best to avoid algorithms that utilize erasures, but if we must, then we will need to ensure concurrent views are managed properly.

Iterating methods are unsafe in a parallel program because such traversals are not atomic. This means that if items are being added concurrently to a traversal, the traversal will not necessarily see a view that ever existed (see sidebar).

SEEING A LIST OF ELEMENTS THAT NEVER EXISTED

Consider a set that contains A-C-E when we start traversing (iterating over). After visiting A and moving to C, imagine that a concurrent task adds B so that the set contains A-B-C-E and then a concurrent task adds D so that the set contains A-B-C-D-E. Our original traversal may continue from C to D and then E. In such an example, we would have visited A-C-D-E as our view of the contents of the set. Oddly, there was never a point in time when the set actually was just A-C-D-E as we saw it. The set had actually been A-C-E, then A-B-C-E, and finally A-B-C-D-E. If we are going to do traversals concurrent with list changes, then we need to be sure that such views are okay. As long as the contents of a set/map are independent, it is relatively easy for this to be okay. However, if the members of a set/map have interdependencies, this can be a real mess.

Resist the impulse to ignore such effects of concurrency. Use traversals with appropriate caution.

Iterating Through These Structures Is Asking for Trouble

We will sneak in some concurrency-unsafe code at the end of Figure 3-4 when we iterate through the hash table to dump it out. If insertions or deletions were made while we walked the table, this could be problematic. We could just say, "It is debug code – we do not care!" But experience has taught us that it is all too easy for code like this to creep into non-debug code. Beware!

The TBB designers left the iterators available for concurrent_hash_map for debug purposes, but they purposefully did not tempt us with iterators as return values from other members.

Unfortunately, STL tempts us in ways we should learn to resist. The concurrent_ unordered_* containers are different from concurrent_hash_map – the API follows the C++ standard for associative containers (keep in mind, the original TBB concurrent_ hash_map predates any standardization by C++ for unordered containers). The operations to add or find data return an iterator, so this tempts us to iterate with it. In a parallel program, we risk this being simultaneous with other operations on the map/set.

If we give into temptation, protecting data integrity is completely left to us as programmers; the API of the container does not help. One could say that the C++ standard containers offer additional flexibility but lack the built-in protection that concurrent_hash_map offers. The STL interfaces are easy enough to use concurrently, if we avoid the temptation to use the iterators returned from an add or find operation for anything other than referencing the item we looked up. If we give into the temptation (we should not!), then we have a lot of thinking to do about concurrent updates in our application (for a little motivation, see the prior explanation: "Seeing a List of Elements That Never Existed"). Of course, if there are no updates happening – only lookups – then there are no parallel programming issues with using the iterators.

HASH MAP

A hash map (also commonly called a hash table) is a data structure that maps keys to values using a hash function. A hash function computes an index from a key, and the index is used to access the "bucket" in which value(s) associated with the key are stored.

Choosing a good hash function is especially important! A perfect hash function would assign each key to a unique bucket so there will be no *collisions* for different keys. In practice, however, hash functions are not perfect and will occasionally generate the same index for more than one key. These collisions require some form of accommodation by the hash table implementation, and this will introduce overhead – hash functions should be designed to minimize collisions by hashing inputs into a nearly even distribution across the buckets.

The advantage of a hash map comes from the ability to, in the average case, provide O(1) time for searches and insertions. The advantage of a TBB hash map is support for concurrent usage both for correctness and performance. This assumes that a good hash function is being used – one that does not cause many collisions for the keys that are used. The theoretical worst case of O(n) remains whenever an imperfect hash function exists or if the hash table is not well-dimensioned.

Often hash maps are, in actual usage, more efficient than other table lookup data structures including search trees. This makes hash maps the data structure of choice for many purposes including associative arrays, database indexing, caches, and sets.

concurrent_hash_map

TBB supplies concurrent_hash_map, which maps keys to values in a way that permits multiple threads to concurrently access values via find, insert, and erase methods. As we will discuss later, tbb::concurrent_hash_map was designed for parallelism, and therefore its interfaces are thread-safe unlike the STL map/set interfaces we will cover later in this chapter.

The keys are unordered. There is at most one element in a concurrent_hash_map for each key. The key may have other elements in flight but not in the map. Type HashCompare specifies how keys are hashed *and* how they are compared for equality. As is generally expected for hash tables, if two keys are equal, then they must hash to the same hash code. This is why HashCompare ties the concept of comparison and hashing into a single object instead of treating them separately. Another consequence of this is that we must not change the hash code of a key while the hash table is nonempty.

A concurrent_hash_map acts as a container of elements of type std::pair<const Key,T>. Typically, when accessing a container element, we are interested in either updating it or reading it. The template class concurrent_hash_map supports these two purposes, respectively, with the classes accessor and const_accessor that function as smart pointers. An accessor represents update (write) access. As long as it points to an element, all other attempts to look up that key in the table are blocked until the accessor is done. A const_accessor is similar, except that it represents read-only access. Multiple accessors can point to the same element at the same time. This feature can greatly improve concurrency in situations where elements are frequently read and infrequently updated.

We share a simple example of code using the concurrent_hash_map container in Figures 3-3 and 3-4 with example output in Figure 3-5. We can improve the performance of this example by reducing the lifetime of the element access. The methods find and insert take an accessor or const_accessor as an argument. The choice tells concurrent_hash_map whether we are asking for update or read-only access. Once the method returns, the access lasts until the accessor or const_accessor is destroyed. Because having access to an element can block other threads, try to shorten the lifetime of the accessor or const_accessor. To do so, declare it in the innermost block possible. To release access even sooner than the end of the block, use method release. Figure 3-6 shows a rework of the loop body from Figure 3-3 that uses release instead of depending upon destruction to end thread lifetime. The method remove(key) can also operate concurrently. It implicitly requests write access. Therefore, before removing the key, it waits on any other extant accesses on key.

BUILT-IN LOCKING VS. NO VISIBLE LOCKING

The containers concurrent_hash_map and concurrent_unordered_* have some differences concerning the locking of accessed elements. Therefore, they may behave very differently under contention. The accessors of concurrent_hash_map are essentially locks: accessor is an exclusive lock, and const_accessor is a shared lock. Lock-based synchronization is built into the usage model for the container, protecting not only container integrity but to some degree data integrity as well. The code in Figure 3-3 uses an accessor when performing an insert into the table.

```cpp
#include <tbb/concurrent_hash_map.h>
#include <tbb/blocked_range.h>
#include <tbb/parallel_for.h>
#include <string>

// Structure that defines hashing and comparison operations for user's type.
struct MyHashCompare {
  static size_t hash( const std::string& x ) {
    size_t h = 0;
    for( const char* s = x.c_str(); *s; ++s )
      h = (h*17)^*s;
    return h;
  }
  //! True if strings are equal
  static bool equal( const std::string& x, const std::string& y ) {
    return x==y;
  }
};

// A concurrent hash table that maps strings to ints.
typedef tbb::concurrent_hash_map<std::string,int,MyHashCompare> StringTable;

// Function object for counting occurrences of strings.
struct Tally {
  StringTable& table;
  Tally( StringTable& table_ ) : table(table_) {}
  void operator()( const tbb::blocked_range<std::string*> range ) const {
    for( std::string* p=range.begin(); p!=range.end(); ++p ) {
      StringTable::accessor a;
      table.insert( a, *p );
      a->second += 1;
    }
  }
};
```

Figure 3-3. *Hash table example, part 1 of 2. Sample code containers/concurrent_hash_maps.cpp*

```
const size_t N = 10;

std::string Data[N] = { "Hello", "World", "TBB", "Hello",
      "So Long", "Thanks for all the fish", "So Long",
      "Three", "Three", "Three" };

int main() {
  // Construct empty table.
  StringTable table;

  // Put occurrences into the table
  tbb::parallel_for( tbb::blocked_range<std::string*>( Data, Data+N, 1000 ),
        Tally(table) );

  // Display the occurrences using a simple walk
  // (note: concurrent_hash_map does not offer const_iterator)
  // see a problem with this code???
  // read "Iterating through these structures is asking for trouble"
  // coming up in a few pages
  for( StringTable::iterator i=table.begin();
       i!=table.end();
       ++i )
    printf("%s %d\n",i->first.c_str(),i->second);

  return 0;
}
```

Figure 3-4. *Hash table example, part 2 of 2. Sample code containers/concurrent_hash_maps.cpp*

```
                    Three 3
                    So Long 2
                    Hello 2
                    TBB 1
                    World 1
                    Thanks for all the fish 1
```

Figure 3-5. *Output of the example program in Figures 3-3 and 3-4*

```
      for( std::string* p=range.begin(); p!=range.end(); ++p ) {
        StringTable::accessor a;
        table.insert( a, *p );
        a->second += 1;
        a.release();
      }
```

Figure 3-6. *Revision to Figure 3-3 to reduce accessor lifetime hoping to improve scaling. Sample code containers/concurrent_hash_maps.cpp*

PERFORMANCE TIPS FOR HASH MAPS

- Always specify an initial size for the hash table. The default of one will scale horribly! Good sizes definitely start in the hundreds. If a smaller size seems correct, then using a lock on a small table will have an advantage in speed due to cache locality.

- Check your hash function – and be sure that there is good pseudo-randomness in the low-order bits of the hash value. In particular, you should not use pointers as keys because generally a pointer will have a set number of zero bits in the low-order bits due to object alignment. If this is the case, it is strongly recommended that the pointer be divided by the size of the type it points to, thereby shifting out the always zero bits in favor of bits that vary. Multiplication by a prime number, and shifting out some low-order bits, is a strategy to consider. As with any form of hash table, keys that are equal must have the same hash code, and the ideal hash function distributes keys uniformly across the hash code space. Tuning for an optimal hash function is definitely application specific, but using the default supplied by TBB tends to work well.

- Do not use accessors if they can be avoided and limit their lifetime as much as possible when accessors are needed (see example of this in Figure 3-6). They are effectively fine-grained locks, inhibit other threads while they exist, and therefore potentially limit scaling.

- Use the TBB memory allocator (see Chapter 7). Use scalable_allocator as the template argument for the container if you want to enforce its usage and not allow a fallback to malloc. This also provides a good sanity check during development when testing performance.

Concurrent Support for **map** and **set**

Standard C++ STL defines set, map, multiset, multimap, unordered_set, unordered_ map, unordered_multiset, and unordered_multimap. Each of these containers differs only by the constraints that are placed on their elements. TBB offers concurrent support for each of these interfaces. Figure 3-2 shows that the STL names are prepended with concurrent_ for the eight interfaces compatible with STL for map and set.

Please be sure to heed the warnings that iterating through the elements is unsafe to do concurrently. The fact that it is unsafe is why the original TBB supported only the unordered versions of these interfaces. The ordered versions were added later based on customer requests and were accompanied with cautions from the TBB development team about the dangers of concurrent traversal (iterating).

Figure 3-7 shows quick examples of concurrent_map and concurrent_unordered_ map, followed by a debug dump of the contents that uses the unsafe traversal (but it is just for debug!). Note how the ordered map is alphabetized (not in Greek order), which scrambles the numbers we assigned as values when inserting in order of the Greek alphabet. Also note that the order of traversal of the unordered map does not match the order in which they we inserted – order really does not matter for the unordered map.

```cpp
#include <iostream>
#include <vector>
#include <tbb/concurrent_map.h>
#include <tbb/concurrent_unordered_map.h>

using namespace std;

int main()
{
  vector<string> names {"alpha", "beta", "gamma", "delta", "epsilon",
                        "zeta", "eta", "theta", "iota", "kappa",
                        "lambda", "mu", "nu", "xi", "omicron",
                        "pi", "rho", "sigma", "tau", "upsilon",
                        "phi", "chi", "psi", "omega"};

  tbb::concurrent_map<string,int> greekOrdered;
  tbb::concurrent_unordered_map<string,int> greekToMe;

  for(int i=0; i<names.size(); i++) {
    greekOrdered[names[i]] = i;
    greekToMe[names[i]] = i;
  }

  for(auto i=greekOrdered.begin(); i!=greekOrdered.end(); i++) {
    cout << i->first << "(" << i->second << ")  ";
  }
  cout << "\n\n";
  for(auto i=greekToMe.begin(); i!=greekToMe.end(); i++) {
    cout << i->first << "(" << i->second << ")  ";
  }
  cout << "\n";

  return 0;
}
```

Output:

```
alpha(0)  beta(1)  chi(21)  delta(3)  epsilon(4)  eta(6)  gamma(2)  iota(8)
kappa(9) lambda(10) mu(11) nu(12) omega(23) omicron(14) phi(20) pi(15)
psi(22)  rho(16)  sigma(17)  tau(18)  theta(7)  upsilon(19)  xi(13)  zeta(5)

rho(16)  omega(23)  omicron(14)  tau(18)  pi(15)  delta(3)  mu(11)  eta(6)
kappa(9)  alpha(0)  nu(12)  xi(13)  epsilon(4)  theta(7)  beta(1)  psi(22)
sigma(17)  lambda(10)  gamma(2)  phi(20)  iota(8)  upsilon(19)  zeta(5)
chi(21)
```

Figure 3-7. *Quick example of using concurrent_map and concurrent_unordered_map. Sample code containers/concurrent_maps.cpp*

Concurrent Queues: Regular, Bounded, and Priority

Queues are useful data structures where items are added or removed with operations known as push (add) and pop (remove). The unbounded queue interfaces provide a try_pop that tells us if the queue was empty and no value was popped from the queue. This steers us away from writing our own logic to avoid a blocking pop by testing empty – an operation that is not thread-safe (see Figure 3-1). Sharing a queue between multiple threads can be an effective way to pass work items from thread to thread – a queue holding "work" to do could have work items added to request future processing and removed by tasks that want to do the processing.

Normally, a queue operates in a first-in-first-out (FIFO) fashion. If we start with an empty queue, do a push(10) and then a push(25); then the first pop operation will return 10, and the second pop will return a 25. This is much different from the behavior of a stack, which would usually be last-in-first-out. But we are not talking about stacks here!

We show a simple example in Figure 3-8 that clearly shows that the pop operations return the values in the same order as the push operations added them to the queue.

```cpp
#include <tbb/concurrent_queue.h>
#include <tbb/concurrent_priority_queue.h>
#include <iostream>

int myarray[10] = { 16, 64, 32, 512, 1, 2, 512, 8, 4, 128 };

void pval(int test, int val) {
  if (test) {
    std::cout << " " << val;
  } else {
    std::cout << " ***";
  }
}

void simpleQ() {
  tbb::concurrent_queue<int> queue;
  int val = 0;

  for( int i=0; i<10; ++i )
    queue.push(myarray[i]);

  std::cout << "Simple  Q   pops are";

  for( int i=0; i<10; ++i )
    pval( queue.try_pop(val), val );

  std::cout << std::endl;
}
```

Output:

```
Simple  Q   pops are 16 64 32 512 1 2 512 8 4 128
```

Figure 3-8. *Example of using the simple (FIFO) queue. Sample code containers/*
concurrent_queues.cpp

There are two twists offered for queues: *bounding* and *priorities*. Bounding enforces
a limit on the size of a queue. This means that a push might not be possible if the queue
is full. To manage this, the bounded queue interfaces offer us ways to have a push wait
until it can add to the queue or have a "try to push" operation that does the push if it
can or lets us know the queue was full. A queue is by default unbounded! If we want
a bounded queue, we need to use concurrent_bounded_queue and call method set_
capacity to set the size for the queue. We show in Figure 3-9 a simple usage of bounded

queue in which only the first six items pushed made it into the queue. We could add a test on try_push and do something. In this case, we have the program print *** when the pop operation finds that the queue was empty.

```
void boundedQ() {
  tbb::concurrent_bounded_queue<int> queue;
  int val = 0;

  queue.set_capacity(6);

  for( int i=0; i<10; ++i )
    queue.try_push(myarray[i]);

  std::cout << "Bounded Q   pops are";

  for( int i=0; i<10; ++i )
    pval( queue.try_pop(val), val );

  std::cout << std::endl;
}
```

Output:

```
Simple  Q   pops are 16 64 32 512 1 2 512 8 4 128
Bounded Q   pops are 16 64 32 512 1 2 *** *** *** ***
```

Figure 3-9. *This routine expands our program to show bounded queue usage. Sample code containers/concurrent_queues.cpp*

A priority adds a second twist to first-in-first-out policy by effectively sorting items in the queue. The default priority, if we do not specify one in our code, is std::less<T>. This means that a pop operation will return the highest-valued item in the queue.

Figure 3-10 shows two examples of priority usage, one defaulting to std::less<int> while the other specifying std::greater<int> explicitly.

```cpp
void prioQ() {
  tbb::concurrent_priority_queue<int> queue;
  int val = 0;

  for( int i=0; i<10; ++i )
    queue.push(myarray[i]);

  std::cout << "Prio    Q   pops are";

  for( int i=0; i<10; ++i )
    pval( queue.try_pop(val), val );

  std::cout << std::endl;
}

void prioQgt() {
  tbb::concurrent_priority_queue<int,std::greater<int>> queue;
  int val = 0;

  for( int i=0; i<10; ++i )
    queue.push(myarray[i]);

  std::cout << "Prio    Qgt pops are";

  for( int i=0; i<10; ++i )
    pval( queue.try_pop(val), val );

  std::cout << std::endl;
}
```

Output:

```
Simple  Q    pops are 16 64 32 512 1 2 512 8 4 128
Bounded Q    pops are 16 64 32 512 1 2 *** *** *** ***
Prio    Q    pops are 512 512 128 64 32 16 8 4 2 1
Prio    Qgt pops are 1 2 4 8 16 32 64 128 512 512
```

Figure 3-10. *These routines expand our program to show priority queueing. Sample code containers/concurrent_queues.cpp*

As our examples in the prior three figures show, to implement these three variations on queues, TBB offers three container classes: concurrent_queue, concurrent_bounded_queue, and concurrent_priority_queue. All concurrent queues permit multiple threads to concurrently push and pop items. The interfaces are similar to STL std::queue or std::priority_queue except where it must differ to make concurrent modification of a queue safe.

The fundamental methods on a queue are push and try_pop. The push method works as it would with a std::queue. It is important to note that there is no support for front or back methods because they would not be safe in a concurrent environment since these methods return a reference to an item in the queue. In a parallel program, the front or back of a queue could be changed by another thread in parallel making the use of front or back meaningless.

Similarly, pop and testing for empty are not supported for unbounded queues – instead, the method try_pop is defined to pop an item if it is available and return a true status; otherwise, it returns no item and a status of false. The test-for-empty and pop methods are combined into a single method to encourage thread-safe coding. For bounded queues, there is a non-blocking try_push method in addition to the potentially blocking push method. These help us avoid the size methods to inquire about the size of the queue. Generally, the size methods should be avoided, especially if they are holdovers from a sequential program. Since the size of a queue can change concurrently in a parallel program, the size method needs careful thought if it is used. For one thing, TBB can return a negative value for size methods when the queue is empty and there are pending pop methods. The empty method is true when size is zero or less.

Bounding Size

For concurrent_queue and concurrent_priority_queue, capacity is unbounded, subject to memory limitations on the target machine. The concurrent_bounded_queue offers controls over bounds – a key feature being that a push method will block until the queue has room. A bounded queue is useful in slowing a supplier to match the rate of consumption instead of allowing a queue to grow unconstrained.

concurrent_bounded_queue is the only concurrent_queue_* container that offers a pop method. The pop method will block until an item becomes available. A push method can be blocking only with a concurrent_bounded_queue so this container type also offers a non-blocking method called try_push.

Using bounding to rate match, to avoid overflowing memory or overcommitting cores, also exists in flow graphs (see Chapter 4) through the use of a limiter_node.

Priority Ordering

A priority queue maintains an ordering in the queue based on the priorities of individual queued items. As we mentioned earlier, a normal queue has a first-in-first-out policy, whereas a priority queue sorts its items. We can provide our own compare function to change the ordering from the default of `std::less<T>`. For instance, using `std::greater<T>` causes the smallest element to be the next to be retrieved for a pop method. We did exactly that in our example code in Figure 3-10.

Staying Thread-Safe: Try to Forget About Top, Size, Empty, Front, and Back

It is important to note that there is no `top` method, and we probably should avoid using `size` and `empty` methods. Concurrent usage means that the values from all three can change due to push/pop methods in other threads. Also, the `clear` and `swap` methods, while supported, are not thread-safe. TBB forces us to rewrite code using `top` when converting a `std::priority_queue` usage to `tbb::concurrent_priority_queue` because the element that would be returned could be invalidated by a concurrent pop. Because the return values are not endangered by concurrency, TBB does support `std::priority_queue` methods of `size`, `empty`, and `swap`. However, we recommend carefully reviewing the wisdom of using either function in a concurrent application, since a reliance on either is likely to be a hint that the code needs rewriting for concurrency.

Iterators

For debugging purposes alone, all three concurrent queues provide limited iterator support (`iterator` and `const_iterator` types). This support is intended solely to allow us to inspect a queue during debugging. Both `iterator` and `const_iterator` types follow the usual STL conventions for forward iterators. The iteration order is from least recently pushed to most recently pushed. Modifying a queue invalidates any iterators that reference it. The iterators are relatively slow. They should be used only for debugging. An example of usage is shown in Figure 3-11.

```cpp
#include <tbb/concurrent_queue.h>
#include <iostream>

int main() {
  tbb::concurrent_queue<int> queue;
  for( int i=0; i<10; ++i )
    queue.push(i);
  for( tbb::concurrent_queue<int>::const_iterator
       i(queue.unsafe_begin());
       i!=queue.unsafe_end();
       ++i )
    std::cout << *i << " ";
  std::cout << std::endl;
  return 0;
}
```

Output:
0 1 2 3 4 5 6 7 8 9

Figure 3-11. *Sample debugging code for iterating through a concurrent queue – note the* unsafe_ *prefix on* begin *and* end *to emphasize the debug-only non-thread-safe nature of these methods. Sample code containers/debugging_queue.cpp*

Why to Use This Concurrent Queue: The A-B-A Problem

We mentioned at the outset of this chapter that there is significant value in having containers that have been written by parallelism experts for us to "just use." None of us should want to reinvent good scalable implementations for each application. As motivation, we diverge to mention the A-B-A problem – a classic computer science example of parallelism gone wrong! At first glance, a concurrent queue might seem easy enough to simply write our own. It is not. Using the concurrent_queue from TBB, or any other well-researched and well-implemented concurrent queue, is a good idea. Humbling as the experience can be, we would not be the first to learn it is not as easy as we could naively believe. The update idiom (compare_exchange_strong) from Chapter 8 is inappropriate if the A-B-A problem (see sidebar) thwarts our intent. This is a frequent problem when trying to design a non-blocking algorithm for linked data structures, including a concurrent queue. The TBB designers have a solution to the

A-B-A problem already packaged in the solutions for concurrent queues. We can just rely upon it. Of course, it is open source code so you can hunt around in the code to see the solution if you are feeling curious. If you do look in the source code, you'll see that arena management (Chapter 11) has to deal with the A-B-A problem as well. Of course, you can just use TBB without needing to know any of this. We just wanted to emphasize that working out concurrent data structures is not as easy as it might appear – hence the love we have for using the concurrent data structures supported by TBB.

THE A-B-A PROBLEM

Understanding the A-B-A problem is a key way to train ourselves to think through the implications of concurrency when designing our own algorithms. While TBB avoids the A-B-A problems while implementing concurrent queues and other TBB structures, it is a reminder that we need to "Think Parallel."

The A-B-A problem occurs when a thread checks a location to be sure the value is A and proceeds with an update only if the value was A. The question arises whether it is a problem if other tasks change the same location in a way that the first task does not detect:

1. A task reads a value A from globalx.

2. Other tasks change globalx from A to B and then back to A.

3. The task in step 1 does its compare_and_swap, reading A and thus not detecting the intervening change to B.

If the task erroneously proceeds under an assumption that the location has not changed since the task first read it, the task may proceed to corrupt the object or otherwise get the wrong result.

Consider an example with linked lists. Assume a linked list W(1)→X(9)→Y(7)→Z(4), where the letters are the node locations and the numbers are the values in the nodes. Assume that some task traverses the list to find a node X to dequeue. The task fetches the next pointer, X.next (which is Y), with the intent to put it in W.next. However, before the swap is done, the task is suspended for some time.

During the suspension, other tasks are busy. They dequeue X and then happen to reuse that same memory and queue a new version of node X as well as dequeuing Y and adding Q at some point in time. Now, the list is W(1)→X(2)→Q(3)→Z(4).

Once the original task finally wakes up, it finds that W.next still points to X, so it swaps out W.next to become Y, thereby making a complete mess out of the linked list.

Atomic operations are the way to go if they embody enough protection for our algorithm. If the A-B-A problem can ruin our day, we need to find a more complex solution. tbb::concurrent_queue has the necessary additional complexity to get this right!

When to NOT Use Queues: Think Algorithms

Queues are widely used in parallel programs to buffer consumers from producers. Before using an explicit queue, we need to consider using parallel_for_each or parallel_pipeline instead (see Chapter 2). These options are often more efficient than queues for the following reasons:

Queues are inherently bottlenecks because they must maintain an order.

A thread that is popping a value will stall if the queue is empty until a value is pushed.

A queue is a passive data structure. If a thread pushes a value, it could take time until it pops the value, and in the meantime the value (and whatever it references) becomes *cold* in cache. Or worse yet, another thread pops the value, and the value (and whatever it references) must be moved to the other processor core.

In contrast, parallel_for_each and parallel_pipeline avoid these bottlenecks. Because their threading is implicit, they optimize use of worker threads so that they do other work until a value shows up. They also try to keep items *hot* in cache. For example, when another work item is added to a parallel_for_each, it is kept local to the thread that added it unless another idle thread can steal it before the *hot* thread processes it. This way, items are more often processed by the *hot* thread, thereby reducing delays in fetching data.

Concurrent Vector

TBB offers a class called concurrent_vector. A concurrent_vector<T> is a dynamically growable array of T. It is safe to grow a concurrent_vector even while other threads are also operating on elements of it or even growing it themselves. For safe concurrent growing, concurrent_vector has three methods that support common uses of dynamic arrays: push_back, grow_by, and grow_to_at_least.

Figure 3-12 shows a simple usage of concurrent_vector, and Figure 3-13 shows, in the dump of the vector contents, the effects of parallel threads having added concurrently. The outputs from the same program would prove identical if sorted into numerical order.

When to Use **tbb::concurrent_vector** Instead of **std::vector**

The key value of concurrent_vector<T> is its ability to grow a vector concurrently and its ability to guarantee that elements do not move around in memory.

concurrent_vector does have more overhead than std::vector. So we should only use concurrent_vector when we need the ability to dynamically resize it while other accesses are (or might be) in flight or require that an element never move.

```cpp
#include <iostream>
#include <tbb/concurrent_vector.h>
#include <tbb/parallel_for.h>

void oneway() {
// Create a vector containing integers
    tbb::concurrent_vector<int> v = {3, 14, 15, 92};

    // Add more integers to vector SERIALLY
    for( int i = 100; i < 1000; ++i ) {
        v.push_back(i*100+11);
        v.push_back(i*100+22);
        v.push_back(i*100+33);
        v.push_back(i*100+44);
    }

    // Iterate and print values of vector (debug use only)
    for(int n : v) {
      std::cout << n << std::endl;
    }
}

void allways() {
// Create a vector containing integers
    tbb::concurrent_vector<int> v = {3, 14, 15, 92};

    // Add more integers to vector IN PARALLEL
    tbb::parallel_for( 100, 999, [&](int i){
        v.push_back(i*100+11);
        v.push_back(i*100+22);
        v.push_back(i*100+33);
        v.push_back(i*100+44);
      });

    // Iterate and print values of vector (debug use only)
    for(int n : v) {
      std::cout << n << std::endl;
    }
}
```

Figure 3-12. *Concurrent vector small example. Sample code containers/
concurrent_vectors.cpp*

```
3                           3
14                          14
15                          15
92                          92
10011                       10011
.  .  .                     .  .  .
84911                       72611
84922                       91211
84933                       87111
84944                       72622
85011                       91222
85022                       87122
85033                       72633
85044                       91233
.  .  .                     .  .  .
99933                       99833
99944                       99844
```

Figure 3-13. *The left side is output generated while using for (not parallel), and the right side shows output when using parallel_for (concurrent pushing into the vector)*

Elements Never Move

A concurrent_vector never moves an element as it grows. This can be an advantage over the STL std::vector even for single-threaded code. The container allocates a series of contiguous arrays. The first reservation, growth, or assignment operation determines the size of the first array. Using a small number of elements as initial size incurs fragmentation across cache lines that may increase element access time. shrink_to_ fit() merges several smaller arrays into a single contiguous array, which may improve access time.

Concurrent Growth of concurrent_vectors

While concurrent growing is fundamentally incompatible with ideal exception safety, concurrent_vector does offer a practical level of exception safety. The element type must have a destructor that never throws an exception, and if the constructor can throw an exception, then the destructor must be nonvirtual and work correctly on zero-filled memory.

The push_back(x) method safely appends x to the vector. The grow_by(n) method safely appends n consecutive elements initialized with T(). Both methods return an iterator pointing to the first appended element. Each element is initialized with T(). The following routine safely appends a C string to a shared vector:

```
void Append( tbb::concurrent_vector<char>& vector,
        const char* string ) {
  size_t n = strlen(string)+1;
  std::copy( string, string+n, vector.grow_by(n) );
}
```

grow_to_at_least(n) grows a vector to at least size n if it is not already at least that large. Concurrent calls to the growth methods do not necessarily return in the order that elements are appended to the vector.

size() returns the number of elements in the vector, which may include elements that are still undergoing concurrent construction by methods push_back, grow_by, or grow_to_at_least. The previous example uses std::copy and iterators, not strcpy and pointers, because elements in a concurrent_vector might not be at consecutive addresses. It is safe to use the iterators while the concurrent_vector is being grown, as long as the iterators never go past the current value of end(). However, the iterator may reference an element undergoing concurrent construction. Therefore, we are required to synchronize construction and access.

Operations on concurrent_vector are concurrency safe with respect to growing, not for clearing or destroying a vector. Never invoke clear() if there are other operations in flight on the concurrent_vector.

Summary

In this chapter, we discussed three key data structures (hash/map/set, queues, and vectors) that have support in TBB. This support from TBB offers thread safety (okay to run concurrently) as well as an implementation that scales well. We offered advice on things to avoid, because they tend to cause trouble in parallel programs – including using the iterators returned by map/set for anything other than the one item that was looked up. We reviewed the A-B-A problem both as a motivation for using TBB instead of writing our own concurrent_queue and as an excellent example of the thinking we need to do when parallel programs share data.

As with other chapters, the code shown in figures is all downloadable.

Despite all the wonderful support for parallel use of containers, we cannot emphasize enough the concept that thinking through algorithms to minimize synchronization of any kind is critical to effective parallel programming. If you can avoid sharing data structures, by using `parallel_for_each`, `parallel_pipeline`, `parallel_reduce`, and so on, as we mentioned in the section "When to NOT Use Queues: Think Algorithms!", you may find your programs scale better. We mention this in multiple ways throughout this book, because thinking this through is important for the most effective parallel programming.

CHAPTER 4

Flow Graphs: The Basics

The flow graph interfaces [flow_graph] let us express programs as graphs of interconnected computations that model the event-based coordination parallel pattern described in Figure 2-2 of Chapter 2. In many cases, these applications stream data through a set of filters or stages. We call these *data flow graphs*. Graphs can also express happens-before relationships between operations without explicitly passing data, allowing us to express dependency structures that cannot be easily expressed with a parallel loop or pipeline. Some linear algebra computations, such as Cholesky decomposition, have efficient parallel implementations that avoid heavyweight synchronization points by tracking dependencies on smaller operations instead. We call graphs that express these happens-before relationships *dependency graphs*.

A flow graph is inherently asynchronous. Messages are passed to nodes using non-blocking functions, and TBB tasks are created eagerly in response to the arrival of these messages. Available TBB worker threads participate in executing those tasks. The most common use cases create a complete graph structure before sending any messages into the graph. However, we can also dynamically change the graph structure as it is running (see Chapter 5 for more details).

Why Use Graphs to Express Parallelism?

Graphs are a convenient way to express applications. When sketching the relationships between computations on a whiteboard, we often naturally use graphs to capture those relationships. If we then express our application as a graph of computations, we are just translating those relationships in the design to C++ code. With these relationships now explicit in the code, the graph exposes information that can be effectively used at runtime to schedule computations in parallel. Take the code in Figure 4-1(a) as an example.

117

© Michael J. Voss, James R. Reinders 2025
M. J. Voss and J. R. Reinders, *Today's TBB*, https://doi.org/10.1007/979-8-8688-1270-5_4

```
while (auto img = getImage())
{
    auto x = f1(img);
    auto y = f2(x);
    auto z = f3(x);
    f4(y,z);
}
```

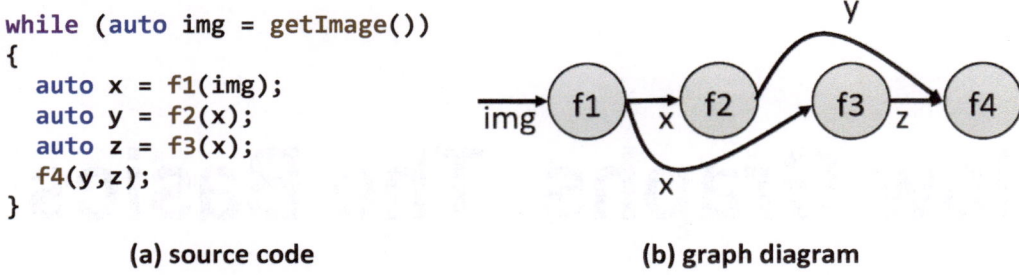

(a) source code   **(b) graph diagram**

Figure 4-1. *A serial sequence of computations expressed as a graph*

In each iteration of the while-loop in Figure 4-1(a), an image is read and then passed through a series of filters: f1, f2, f3, and f4. We can draw the flow of data between these filters as shown in Figure 4-1(b). In this figure, the variables that are used to pass the data returned from each function are replaced by edges from the node that generates the value to the subsequent node(s) that consume the values. For example, the value returned by f1 is stored into variable x in Figure 4-1(a) and this variable is passed to f2 and f3. In Figure 4-1(b), variable x is replaced by two edges: one flowing from f1 to f2 and another from f1 to f3. Figure 4-1(b) does not yet represent a TBB flow graph. As we will see soon, if we want to pair together inputs in a TBB flow graph, such as y and z as an input to f4, we need to use join nodes to combine them.

For now, let's assume that the graph in Figure 4-1(b) captures all the data that is shared between these functions. If so, we (and in turn a library like TBB) can infer a lot about what is legal to execute in parallel as shown in Figure 4-2. The edges mandate a partial ordering of the nodes.

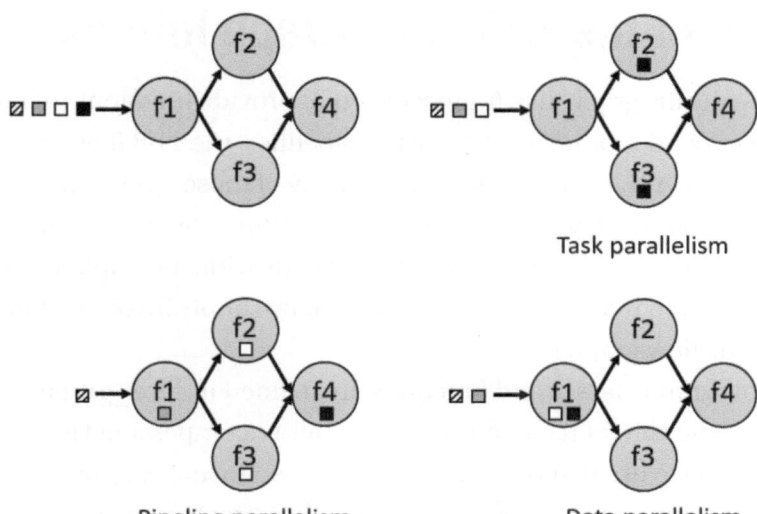

Task parallelism

Pipeline parallelism

Data parallelism

Figure 4-2. *The kinds of parallelism that can be inferred from the graph in Figure 4-1. Boxes with the same fill pattern are related to the same input message and not necessarily a common shared object. For example, the solid black boxes in the Task parallelism graph represent copies of the x value generated by applying f1 to the first* img *that entered the graph in Figure 4-1*

If we stream four images through the graph in Figure 4-1(b), there are several types of parallelism that can be exposed by the TBB library as shown in Figure 4-2. There are no edges between nodes f2 and f3, so they can be executed in parallel. Executing two different functions in parallel on the same data is an example of *task parallelism*. If the functions do not update shared global states, then we can also overlap the processing of different images in the graph, exploiting *pipeline parallelism*. Finally, if the functions are *thread-safe*, that is, it is safe to execute each function in parallel with itself on different data, we can overlap the processing of two different images in the same node to exploit *data parallelism*.

When we use the TBB flow graph interface, we provide the library with the information it needs to take advantage of these different kinds of parallelism so it can map our computation to the platform hardware in the most effective way.

The Basics of the TBB Flow Graph Interface

Unlike domain-specific graph-like frameworks that provide functions to build AI models, neural networks, or image processing pipelines, the TBB flow graph is a general-purpose and generic API. It can be used to build any of those applications, but it does not provide the domain-specific functions and algorithms themselves. It lets us build a graph of connected computations, but we need to provide the implementations of those computations. In many cases, we can do that by simply invoking domain-specific functions from the flow graph nodes.

The TBB flow graph classes and functions are defined in `flow_graph.h` and are contained within the `tbb::flow` namespace. The all-encompassing `tbb.h` also includes `flow_graph.h`, so if we use that header, we do not need to include anything else.

To use a flow graph, we create a *graph* object, then create *nodes* to perform operations, and make *edges* to express the message channels or dependencies between these nodes. The flow graph API is asynchronous and eager and allows the addition and removal of edges while the graph is executing. For simplicity, however, we will describe in most detail the simplest case in this section, where we fully define the graph before we start executing any work in it. In that scenario, there are five steps in using a graph: (1) create the graph object, (2) create the nodes, (3) add edges between the nodes' input and output ports, (4) send messages into the graph directly or by activating `input_node` objects, and (5) wait for the graph to complete so that we can use the generated results.

Figure 4-3 shows a small example that performs these five steps. In this section, we will discuss each of these steps in more detail. We should note that in our first examples in this chapter, we use `std::cout` to display output, and this means that our nodes are in fact not side-effect-free. Eventually, we will see this can result in jumbled output as we introduce more parallelism. However, in Figure 4-3, the sharing of the `std::cout` object across nodes is harmless since only a single message flows through the graph and so there is no overlap in node executions.

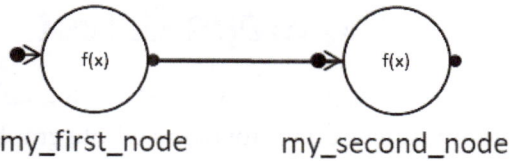

my_first_node   my_second_node

Diagram of a simple two-node graph

```cpp
void graphTwoNodes() {
  // step 1: construct the graph
  tbb::flow::graph g;

  // step 2: make the nodes
  tbb::flow::function_node<int, std::string> my_first_node{g,
    tbb::flow::unlimited,
    []( const int& in ) {
      std::cout << "first node received: " << in << std::endl;
      return std::to_string(in);
    }
  };

  tbb::flow::function_node<std::string> my_second_node{g,
    tbb::flow::unlimited,
    []( const std::string& in ) {
      std::cout << "second node received: " << in << std::endl;
    }
  };

  // step 3: add edges
  tbb::flow::make_edge(my_first_node, my_second_node);

  //
  my_first_node.try_put(10);

  // step 5: wait for graph to complete
  g.wait_for_all();
}
```

Figure 4-3. *A simple two-node flow graph. In this example, the nodes receive inputs as const references, even when they are fundamental types, such as* int. *In real code, flow graph messages are rarely fundamental types. If we were using* int *messages in non-sample code, we would receive them by value instead; both options are legal. But, for larger messages, it is almost always better to avoid copying, and so we highlight that expected pattern by using const references here. Sample code graph/graph_two_nodes.cpp*

Step 1: Create the Graph Object

The first step to create a flow graph is to construct a graph object. In the flow graph interface, a graph object is used for invoking whole graph operations such as waiting for all tasks related to the graph's execution to complete, resetting the state of all nodes in the graph, and canceling the execution of all nodes in the graph. When building a graph, each node belongs to exactly one graph, and edges are made between nodes in the same graph. Making edges between nodes in different graphs results in undefined behavior. The graph object must be created before any nodes are added to it, and it must also outlive all tasks executing on behalf of the graph, as well as all nodes associated with it. Graph objects cannot be copied, since the copy constructor and assignment operator are deleted. Figure 4-4 shows the key public functions in the graph class.

```
namespace tbb {
namespace flow {

  class graph : no_copy {
  public:

    //! Constructs a graph with isolated task_group_context (see Chapter 9)
    graph();

    //! Constructs a graph with use_this_context as context
    explicit graph(task_group_context& use_this_context);

    //! Destroys the graph.
    ~graph();

    //! Wait until graph is idle and the number of
    //! release_wait calls equals
    //! to the number of reserve_wait calls.
    void wait_for_all();

    // thread-unsafe state reset.
    void reset(reset_flags f = rf_reset_protocol);

    //! cancels execution of the associated task_group_context
    void cancel();

    //! return status of graph execution
    bool is_cancelled();
    bool exception_thrown();

  }; // class graph

} }
```

Figure 4-4. *The key member functions in class graph as described in [flow_graph.graph]*

Step 2: Construct Nodes

The TBB flow graph API defines a rich set of node types (Figure 4-5) that we break into four groups: functional node types, join node types, buffering node types, and control flow node types. The symbols used in Figure 4-5 are used throughout this book to make clear which node type is being used in diagrams.

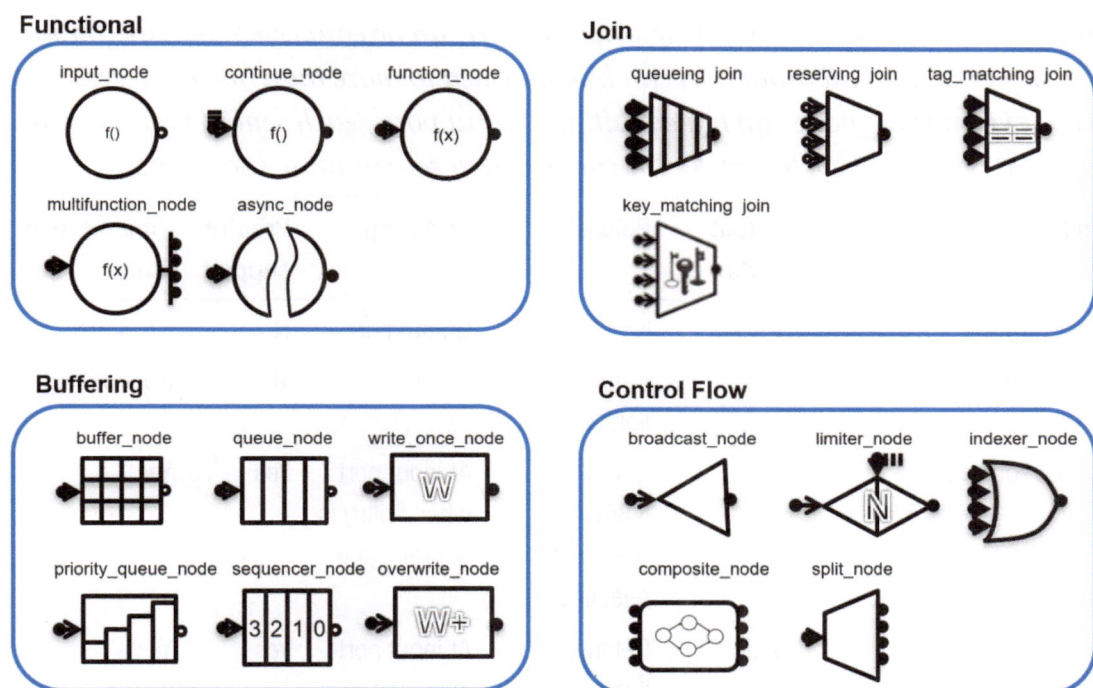

Figure 4-5. *The types of nodes in the flow graph API*

Functional Nodes

Functional nodes are the heart of the flow graph API. These nodes execute user-defined code. All the functional node constructors take at least the graph object as an argument and a user-provided function object. The functional nodes differ in what incoming messages they respond to (if any at all), the signature expected of the user's function object (body), and how the output(s) of the user-provided computation are propagated to other nodes.

Table 4-1 describes the properties of each of the node types, including how many input and output ports it supports, its policy for handling arriving messages, if it buffers its input or output messages, whether it supports node-level priorities, and if the concurrency of the node can be limited. Node-level priorities, policies, and concurrency limits are explored further when we discuss more advanced topics in Chapter 5.

Table 4-1. *The functional node types in the flow graph API. Ports act as connection points for edges. A single output port can be connected to more than one successor, and an input port can be connected to more than one predecessor. A* multifunction_node *can have multiple output ports, each sending messages of different types, and each port can be connected to zero or more successors*

Node	Input ports	Output ports	Policies	Buffering	Priority support	Concurrency limit
input_node	0	1	N/A	Output port	No	No, serial
continue_node	1	1	Default, lightweight	None	Yes	No, unlimited
function_node	1	1	Default, lightweight, queueing, rejecting	At input port when Policy is not rejecting	Yes	Yes
multifunction_ node	1	0...N	Default, lightweight, queueing, rejecting	At input port when Policy is not rejecting	Yes	Yes
async_node	1	1	Default, lightweight, queueing, rejecting	At input port when Policy is not rejecting	Yes	Yes

We use the body arguments in functional nodes to provide the code we want to apply to messages. Table 4-2 describes the required signatures of these body objects as well as the named requirement used in the oneTBB specification for this signature.

Table 4-2. *The signatures required of the user-provided bodies*

Node	Named requirement	Body signature
input_node	***InputNodeBody***	Output operator()(flow_control& fc)
continue_node	***ContinueNodeBody***	Output operator()(const continue_msg& v)
function_node	***FunctionNodeBody***	Output operator()(const Input& v)
multifunction_node	***MultifunctionNodeBody***	void operator()(const Input& v, OutputPortsType& p)
async_node	***AsyncNodeBody***	void operator()(const Input& v, GatewayType& gateway)

In Figure 4-3, we defined my_first_node to receive an int value, print the value, and then convert it to a std::string, returning the converted value. In the Figure 4-3 example, we provide all the template arguments when constructing the object, but TBB includes deduction guides to support better class template argument deduction (CTAD). You can read more about CTAD and deduction guides at https://en.cppreference. com/w/cpp/language/class_template_argument_deduction. In many cases when using C++17 or later, the template arguments for flow graph classes can be deduced and do not need to be explicitly provided. For example, my_first_node can also be constructed without providing the template arguments or return type directly, as shown in Figure 4-6.

```
tbb::flow::function_node my_first_node{g,
  tbb::flow::unlimited,
  []( const int& in ) {
    std::cout << "first node received: " << in << std::endl;
    return std::to_string(in);
  }
};
```

Figure 4-6. *my_first_node constructed without providing arguments or return type directly. Sample code graph/graph_two_nodes_deduced.cpp*

Important member functions of function_node are shown in Figure 4-7. These include constructors and a function try_put. We can directly pass messages to any node in a flow graph by calling its try_put function, but typically messages are passed implicitly across edges. Usually, the only time we call try_put explicitly is to submit messages to the nodes that serve as primary inputs to the graph. For example, in Figure 4-3, we called try_put on my_first_node but not on my_second_node, which receives its inputs through the output edge from my_first_node.

```cpp
namespace tbb {
namespace flow {

  template < typename Input,
             typename Output = continue_msg,
             typename Policy = /*implementation-defined*/ >
  class function_node : public graph_node,
                        public receiver<Input>,
                        public sender<Output> {
  public:
    //! Constructor
    template<typename Body>
    function_node( graph& g, size_t concurrency, Body body,
                   Policy /*unspecified*/ = Policy(),
                   node_priority_t priority = no_priority );

    template<typename Body>
    function_node( graph& g, size_t concurrency, Body body,
                   node_priority_t priority = no_priority );

    ~function_node();

    //! Copy constructor
    function_node( const function_node& src );

    //! Explicitly pass a message to the node
    bool try_put( const Input& v );
  };

}
}
```

Figure 4-7. *The key member functions of class* function_node *as described in [flow_graph.function_node]*

A `function_node` generates a single output value from a single input value, but there are several other kinds of functional nodes available for flow graphs as shown in Table 4-2.

Join Nodes

A `join_node` combines inputs from multiple input ports to create an output `std::tuple`. The key members of `join_node` are shown in Figure 4-8. A `join_node` can have one of four join policies: `queueing`, `reserving`, `key_matching`, and `tag_matching` as described in Table 4-3.

```cpp
namespace tbb {
namespace flow {
  using tag_value = /*implementation-defined*/;

  // JoinNodePolicies:
  struct reserving;
  struct queueing;
  template<typename K,
           class KHash=tbb_hash_compare<K> > struct key_matching;
  using tag_matching = key_matching<tag_value>;

  template<typename OutputTuple,
           class JoinPolicy = /*implementation-defined*/>
  class join_node {
  public:
    using input_ports_type = /*implementation-defined*/;

    explicit join_node( graph& g );
    join_node( const join_node& src );

    input_ports_type& input_ports();

    bool try_get( OutputTuple& v );

    template<typename OutputTuple, typename K,
             class KHash=tbb_hash_compare<K> >
    class join_node< OutputTuple, key_matching<K, KHash> > {
    public:
      using input_ports_type = /*implementation-defined*/;

      explicit join_node( graph& g );
      join_node( const join_node& src );

      template<typename ... TagBodies>
      join_node( graph& g, TagBodies ... );

      input_ports_type& input_ports();

      bool try_get( OutputTuple& v );
    };
} }
```

Figure 4-8. *The key types and functions for join nodes as described in [flow_graph.join_node]*

Table 4-3. *The join policies available for* join_node *as described in [flow_graph. join_node_policies]*

Join policy	Buffering	Description
queueing	FIFO queue at each input port	Stores incoming messages in per-port queues, joining the messages into a tuple using a first-in-first-out approach.
key_matching	Hash table across input ports	Stores the incoming messages in per-port maps and joins messages based on matching keys.
tag_matching	Hash table across input ports	Stores the incoming messages in per-port maps and joins messages based on matching tag_value tags (an unsigned integral). A specialization of key_matching.
reserving	Does not buffer messages but records (possible) availability of inputs	Stores the known state of availability of messages for each input port. When all ports are marked as possibly available, it tries to reserve a message for each port. If unsuccessful, it unmarks that port and releases all previously acquired reservations. If successful, it broadcasts a tuple containing these messages to all successors. If at least one successor accepts the tuple, the reservations are consumed; otherwise, they are released.

The join_node that follows, j, has three input ports and one output port. Input port 0 will accept messages of type int. Input port 1 will accept messages of type std::string. Input port 2 will accept messages of type double. There will be a single output port that combines the incoming messages and then broadcasts messages of type std::tuple<int, std::string, double>:

```
tbb::flow::join_node<std::tuple<int, std::string, double>,
                     tbb::flow::queueing> j(g);
```

For the queueing, key_matching, and tag_matching policies, the join_node buffers incoming messages as they arrive at each of its input ports. These policies never reject an incoming message.

As a special case, a reserving join_node does not buffer the incoming messages at all. Instead, it tracks the state of the preceding buffers – when it detects that there are messages available for each of its input ports, it tries to reserve an item for each input port. A reservation prevents any other node from consuming the item while the reservation is held. Only if the join_node can successfully acquire a reservation on an element for each input port does it then consume these messages; otherwise, it releases all the reservations and leaves the messages in the preceding buffers. If a reserving join_node fails to reserve all the inputs, it tries again later when it detects a change in state of one or more of the predecessors. The reserving policy is used to limit message production as described more in "Controlling Repetition with Tokens" in Chapter 5.

Figures 4-9 and 4-10 show an example of a graph that contains a join_node that creates a tuple from a double and std::string.

```cpp
#include <iostream>
#include <tbb/tbb.h>

void graphJoin() {
  // step 1: construct the graph
  tbb::flow::graph g;

  // step 2: make the nodes
  tbb::flow::function_node my_node{g,
    tbb::flow::unlimited,
    []( const int& in ) {
      std::cout << "received: " << in << std::endl;
      return std::to_string(in);
    }
  };

  tbb::flow::function_node my_other_node{g,
    tbb::flow::unlimited,
    [](const int& in) {
      std::cout << "other received: " << in << std::endl;
      return double(in);
    }
  };

  tbb::flow::join_node<std::tuple<std::string, double>>
  my_join_node{g};

  tbb::flow::function_node my_final_node{g,
    tbb::flow::unlimited,
    [](const std::tuple<std::string, double>& in) {
      std::cout << "final: " << std::get<0>(in)
                << " and " << std::get<1>(in) << std::endl;
      return 0;
    }
  };

  // step 3: add the edges
  make_edge(my_node, tbb::flow::input_port<0>(my_join_node));
  make_edge(my_other_node, tbb::flow::input_port<1>(my_join_node));
  make_edge(my_join_node, my_final_node);

  // step 4: send messages
  my_node.try_put(1);
  my_other_node.try_put(2);
  // step 5: wait for the graph to complete
  g.wait_for_all();
}
```

Figure 4-9. *An implementation of the graph depicted in Figure 4-10. Note that we rely on CTAD to deduce input and output types for the functional nodes. Sample code graph/graph_with_join.cpp*

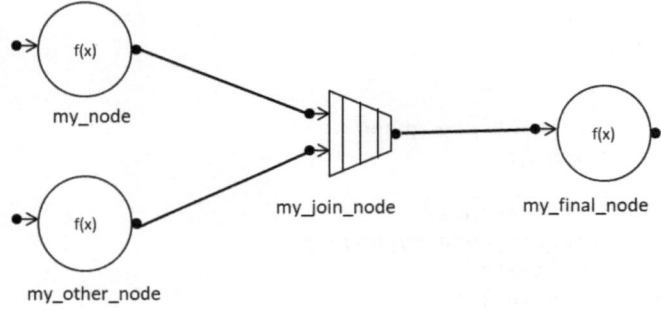

Figure 4-10. *A four-node graph with a join_node*

Buffering Nodes

Buffering nodes are used in limited but important circumstances. In Chapter 5, we discuss more advanced topics, including how to limit resource usage, manage tasking overheads, control repetition, dynamically change the structure of a graph, and more. Buffering nodes play critical roles in these topics, and we defer discussion of these important nodes to that chapter.

Control Flow Nodes

The last category of nodes are control flow nodes. A broadcast_node simply forwards an incoming message to all its successors. This kind of node is useful in situations where we want to create a single entry-point into a graph or section of a graph. A limiter_node is used to control the number of messages that can pass through a point in the graph and is typically used to limit memory use. An indexer_node is used to join disjoint paths through the graph, forwarding a single message at a time to the node's successors, tagged with the port number on which that message arrived. A split_node breaks an incoming tuple into its constituent elements, forwarding each element through a different output port. Finally, a composite_node is used to encapsulate a subgraph as a single node so it can be more easily integrated into larger graphs.

As with buffering nodes, control flow nodes are often used for the important patterns and optimizations that are further described in Chapter 5.

Step 3: Add Edges

As we have already seen in Figures 4-3 and 4-9, after we construct a graph object and nodes, we use `make_edge` calls to set up the message channels or dependencies:

```
make_edge(predecessor_node, successor_node);
```

If a node has more than one input port or output port, `make_edge` must be invoked on a specific port and not the node itself. This can be done by using the `input_port` and `output_port` function templates:

```
make_edge(tbb::flow::output_port<0>(predecessor_node),
          tbb::flow::input_port<1>(successor_node));
```

In Figure 4-3, we made an edge between `my_first_node` and `my_second_node` in our simple two-node graph. Figure 4-9 shows a slightly more complicated flow graph that has four nodes.

The first two nodes in Figure 4-9 generate results that are joined together into a tuple by a queueing `join_node`, `my_join_node`. When the edges are made to the input ports of the `join_node`, we need to specify the port number:

```
make_edge(my_node, tbb::flow::input_port<0>(my_join_node));
make_edge(my_other_node, tbb::flow::input_port<1>(my_join_node));
```

The output of the `join_node`, a `std::tuple<std::string, double>`, is sent to `my_final_node`. We do not need to specify a port number when there is only a single port:

```
make_edge(my_join_node, my_final_node);
```

Step 4: Send Messages to the Graph

The fourth step in creating and using a TBB flow graph is to start the graph execution by sending messages to the graph. There are two main ways that messages enter a graph, either (1) through an explicit `try_put` to a node or (2) as the output of an `input_node`. In both Figures 4-3 and 4-9, we call `try_put` on nodes to start messages flowing into the graph.

For example, in Figure 4-9, we send a message to my_node by directly calling try_put on it:

```
my_node.try_put(1);
```

This causes the TBB library to spawn a task to execute the body of my_node on the int message 1, resulting in output such as "received: 1". It is legal to call try_put on any input port of any node, including internal nodes, but it is most common to only call try_put on the root nodes of a graph.

The second way to send a message into a graph is to use an input_node. An input_node is constructed by default in an inactive state, that is, it won't immediately start sending messages. This prevents it from sending messages before the graph is completely constructed, which is the most common usage scenario. To get messages flowing after a graph is completely constructed, we need to call the activate() function on all the input_node objects.

Figure 4-11 demonstrates how an input_node can be used as a replacement for a serial loop to feed messages to a graph. In Figure 4-11(a), a loop repeatedly calls try_put on a node my_node, sending messages to it. In Figure 4-11(b), an input_node is used for the same purpose.

As described in Table 4-2, the input_node body must meet the named requirement **InputNodeBody**. An input_node applies the body to generate the next item. When a new element cannot be generated, the body calls fc.stop() to indicate the input is now done. When fc.stop() is called, any valid value of Output can be returned and it will be immediately discarded. After fc.stop() is called, the body will not be invoked again unless the graph or node is reset. In Figure 4-11(b), the input_node body maintains internal state (count) that tracks the number of messages it has sent and calls fc.stop() when it reaches a predefined limit.

```cpp
void tryPutLoop() {
  const int limit = 3;
  tbb::flow::graph g;
  tbb::flow::function_node my_node{g, tbb::flow::unlimited,
    [](const int& i) {
      std::printf("my_node: %d\n", i);
      return 0;
    }
  };
  for (int count = 0; count < limit; ++count) {
    my_node.try_put(count);
  }
  g.wait_for_all();
}
```

(a) Using calls to try_put inside of a loop.

```cpp
void inputNodeLoop() {
  tbb::flow::graph g;

  tbb::flow::input_node my_input{g,
    [](tbb::flow_control& fc) {
      const int limit = 3;
      static int count = 0;
      if (count >= limit)
        fc.stop();
      return count++;
    }
  };
  tbb::flow::function_node my_node{g,
    tbb::flow::unlimited,
    [](const int& i) {
      std::printf("my_node: %d\n", i);
      return 0;
    }
  };

  tbb::flow::make_edge(my_input, my_node);

  my_input.activate();

  g.wait_for_all();
}
```

(b) Using an input_node to submit the messages.

Figure 4-11. *(a) A loop is used to send the int values 0, 1, and 2 to a node my_node, and (b) an input_node sends the int values 0, 1, and 2 to the node my_node. Sample code graph/graph_loops.cpp*

The main advantage of using an input_node, instead of a loop, is that it responds to other nodes in the graph. In Chapter 5, we discuss tips on how an input_node can be used in conjunction with a reserving join_node or a limiter_node to control how many messages are allowed to enter regions of a graph. If we use a simple loop, we can inadvertently flood our graph with inputs, forcing nodes to buffer many messages if they cannot keep up.

In all the examples in this chapter, we fully define the graph structure before sending any messages into it. A TBB flow graph uses an eager execution model, and there is no finalization step where a graph representation is transformed into an executable form. A TBB flow graph is always executable and ready to receive messages. However, if we start sending messages to a graph before we have constructed all the nodes and connected all the edges in the way we intend, we will start executing the graph as it is currently expressed. This property of TBB flow graph is powerful since it can be used to dynamically grow and change a graph but can also be problematic because it can lead to unexpected results if not done carefully. Later in Chapter 5, we discuss how to dynamically grow a graph safely.

Step 5: Wait for the Graph to Complete Executing

Once we have sent messages into a graph either using try_put or an input_node, we can wait for the execution of the graph to complete by calling wait_for_all() on the graph object. We can see these calls in Figures 4-3, 4-9, and 4-11. Destroying nodes or the graph without first calling wait_for_all leads to undefined behavior.

If we build and execute the graph in Figure 4-3, we see an output like

```
first node received: 10
second node received: 10
```

If we build and execute the graph in Figure 4-9, we see an output like

```
other received: received: 21
final: 1 and 2
```

The output from Figure 4-9 looks a little jumbled, and it is. The first two function nodes execute in parallel, and both are streaming to std::cout. In our output, we see a combination of the two outputs jumbled together because we broke the assumption we made earlier in this chapter when we discussed graph-based parallelism – our nodes are not side-effect-free! These two nodes execute in parallel, and both affect the state of the global `std::cout` object. In this example, that's okay since this output is printed just to show the progress of the messages through the graph. But it is an important point to remember.

The final `function_node` in Figure 4-9 only executes when both values from the preceding function nodes are joined together by the `join_node` and are passed to it. This final node therefore executes by itself, and so it streams the expected final output to `std::cout`: "final: 1 and 2".

A More Complicated Example of a Data Flow Graph

In Chapter 2, we introduced an example that applied a red–cyan 3D stereoscopic effect to pairs of left and right images. In Chapter 2, we parallelized this example with a TBB `parallel_pipeline`, but in doing so admitted that we left some parallelism on the table by linearizing the pipeline stages. An example output is shown in Figure 2-35. Now let's use a flow graph.

Let's step through the construction of a TBB flow graph that implements our stereoscopic 3D sample. The structure of the flow graph we will create is shown in Figure 4-12. This diagram looks different from Figure 2-36, because now the nodes represent TBB flow graph node objects and the edges represent TBB flow graph edges.

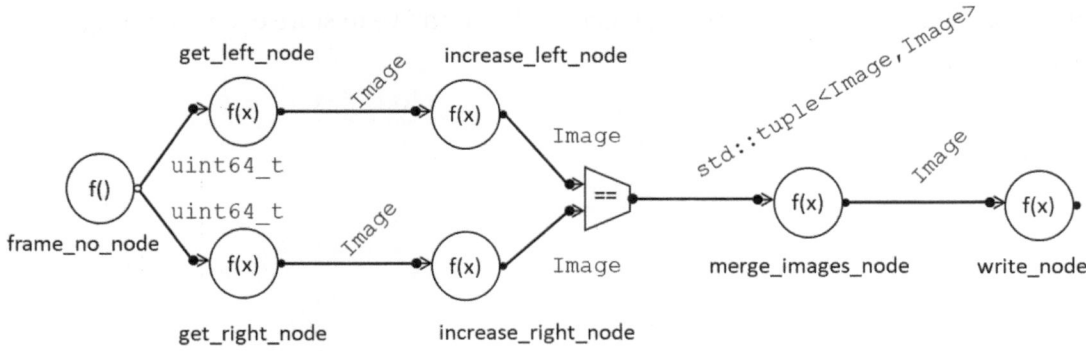

Figure 4-12. *A graph that represents the calls in Figure 2-36. Sample code graph/ graph_stereoscopic_3d.cpp*

Figure 4-13 shows the stereoscopic 3D example implemented using the TBB flow graph interfaces. The five basic steps are outlined in boxes. First, we create a graph object. Next, we create the eight nodes, including an `input_node`, several `function_node` instances, and a join_node. The details of node creation are shown in Figure 4-14. We then connect the nodes using calls to make_edge. After making the edges, we activate the input_node. Finally, we wait for the graph to be completed.

As we noted earlier, the getLeftImage and getRightImage functions execute independently, but serially since they read images sequentially from a file or camera. In the code in Figure 4-13, we communicate this constraint to the runtime library by setting the concurrency constraint for these nodes to flow::serial.

In contrast, the increase_left_node and the increase_right_node objects are constructed with a concurrency constraint of flow::unlimited. The runtime library will immediately spawn a task to execute the body of these nodes whenever an incoming message arrives.

In Figure 4-12, we see that the merge_images_node function needs both a right and a left image. In the original serial code, we were ensured that the images would be from the same frame, because the while-loop only operated on one frame at a time. In our flow graph version, however, multiple frames may be pipelined through the flow graph and therefore may be in progress at the same time. To provide our merge_images_node with a pair of matching left and right images, we create the join_images_node with a tag_matching policy. The call to the constructor includes two lambda expressions that are used to obtain the tag values from the incoming messages on the two input ports. The merge_images_node accepts a tuple and generates a single merged image.

The last node created in Figure 4-14 is write_node. It is a flow::unlimited function_node that receives Image objects and calls write to store each incoming buffer to an output file.

```
// step 1: create graph object
tbb::flow::graph g;
```

```
// step 2: create nodes
// see Figure 4-14
```

```
// step 3: add edges
tbb::flow::make_edge(frame_no_node, get_left_node);
tbb::flow::make_edge(frame_no_node, get_right_node);
tbb::flow::make_edge(get_left_node, increase_left_node);
tbb::flow::make_edge(get_right_node, increase_right_node);
tbb::flow::make_edge(increase_left_node,
                     tbb::flow::input_port<0>(join_images_node));
tbb::flow::make_edge(increase_right_node,
                     tbb::flow::input_port<1>(join_images_node));
tbb::flow::make_edge(join_images_node, merge_images_node);
tbb::flow::make_edge(merge_images_node, write_node);
```

```
// step 4: send messages in to the graph
frame_no_node.activate();
```

```
// step 5: wait for graph to complete
g.wait_for_all();
```

Figure 4-13. *The stereoscopic 3D example as a TBB flow graph. The five steps for using a flow graph are highlighted. Sample code* graph/graph_ stereoscopic_3d.cpp

```cpp
// step 2: create nodes
tbb::flow::input_node<uint64_t> frame_no_node{g,
  []( tbb::flow_control &fc ) -> uint64_t {
    uint64_t frame_number = getNextFrameNumber();
    if (frame_number)
      return frame_number;
    else {
      fc.stop();
      return frame_number;
} } };
tbb::flow::function_node<uint64_t, Image> get_left_node{g,
  /* concurrency */ tbb::flow::serial,
  [] (uint64_t frame_number) -> Image {
    return getLeftImage(frame_number);
} };
tbb::flow::function_node<uint64_t, Image> get_right_node{g,
  /* concurrency */ tbb::flow::serial,
  [] (uint64_t frame_number) -> Image {
    return getRightImage(frame_number);
} };
tbb::flow::function_node<Image, Image> increase_left_node{g,
  /* concurrency */ tbb::flow::unlimited,
  [] (Image left) -> Image {
      increasePNGChannel(left, Image::redOffset, 10);
      return left;
} };
tbb::flow::function_node<Image, Image> increase_right_node{g,
  /* concurrency */ tbb::flow::unlimited,
  [] (Image right) -> Image {
      increasePNGChannel(right, Image::blueOffset, 10);
      return right;
} };
tbb::flow::join_node<std::tuple<Image, Image>, tbb::flow::tag_matching >
  join_images_node(g, [] (Image left) { return left.frameNumber; },
                      [] (Image right) { return right.frameNumber; } );
tbb::flow::function_node<std::tuple<Image, Image>, Image> merge_images_node{g,
  /* concurrency */ tbb::flow::unlimited,
  [] (std::tuple<Image, Image> t) -> Image {
    auto& l = std::get<0>(t);
    auto& r = std::get<1>(t);
    mergePNGImages(r, l);
    return r;
} };
tbb::flow::function_node<Image> write_node{g,
  /* concurrency */ tbb::flow::unlimited,
  [] (Image img) {
    img.write();
} };
```

Figure 4-14. *The "create nodes" step for the stereoscopic 3D example (see Figure 4-13). Sample code graph/graph_stereoscopic_3d.cpp*

Implementing a Dependency Graph

The steps for using a dependency graph are the same as for a data flow graph; we create a graph object, make nodes, add edges, and feed messages into the graph. The main differences are that the functional nodes are continue_node objects, the graph must be acyclic, and we must wait for the graph to execute to completion each time we feed a message into the graph. The advantage of a dependency graph is that the overhead is low because we are passing messages that increment and decrement counters, instead of joining messages into std::tuple objects. continue_node objects are used in dependency graphs because they simply count the number of received messages. It is legal to use a continue_node in a data flow graph, but useful applications for it are rare.

In this section, the graph is constructed completely before it is started. In Chapter 5, an example is described that uses write_once nodes to allow concurrent construction and execution of a dependency graph.

Now, let us build an example dependency graph. For our example, we implement the same forward substitution example that we implemented in Chapter 2 using a TBB parallel_for_each. You can refer to the detailed description of the serial and parallel_for_each-based example in that chapter.

Using a dependency graph, we can simply express the dependencies directly and allow the TBB library to discover and exploit the available parallelism in the graph. We do not have to maintain counts or track completions explicitly like in the parallel_for_each version in Chapter 2, and we do not introduce unneeded synchronization points.

Figure 4-15 shows a dependency graph version of this example. We use a std::vector to hold a set of shared pointers to continue_node objects, each node representing a block of iterations. To create the graph, we follow the common pattern: (1) create a graph object, (2) create nodes, (3) add edges, (4) feed a message into the graph, and (5) wait for the graph to complete. However, we now create the graph structure using a loop nest as shown in Figure 4-15. The function createNode creates a new continue_node object for each block, and the function addEdges connects the node to the neighbors that must wait for its completion.

```
using Node = tbb::flow::continue_node<tbb::flow::continue_msg>;
using NodePtr = std::shared_ptr<Node>;

void graphFwdSub(std::vector<double>& x,
                 const std::vector<double>& a,
                 std::vector<double>& b) {
  const int N = x.size();
  const int block_size = 1024;
  const int num_blocks = N / block_size;

  std::vector<NodePtr> nodes(num_blocks*num_blocks);
  tbb::flow::graph g;
  for (int r = num_blocks - 1; r >= 0; --r) {
    for (int c = r; c >= 0; --c) {
      nodes[r*num_blocks + c] = createNode(g, r, c, block_size, x, a, b);
      addEdges(nodes, r, c, block_size, num_blocks);
    }
  }
  nodes[0]->try_put(tbb::flow::continue_msg{});
  g.wait_for_all();
}
```

Figure 4-15. *A dependency graph implementation of the forward substitution example. The five steps for using a flow graph are highlighted. Sample code is graph/graph_fwd_substitution.cpp*

In Figure 4-16, we show the implementation of the **createNode.** In Figure 4-17, we show the implementation of the **addEdges** function.

```cpp
NodePtr createNode(tbb::flow::graph& g,
                   int r, int c, int block_size,
                   std::vector<double>& x,
                   const std::vector<double>& a,
                   std::vector<double>& b) {
  const int N = x.size();
  return std::make_shared<Node>(g,
    [r, c, block_size, N, &x, &a, &b] (const tbb::flow::continue_msg& msg) {
      int i_start = r*block_size, i_end = i_start + block_size;
      int j_start = c*block_size, j_max = j_start + block_size - 1;
      for (int i = i_start; i < i_end; ++i) {
        int j_end = (i <= j_max) ? i : j_max + 1;
        for (int j = j_start; j < j_end; ++j) {
          b[i] -= a[j + i*N] * x[j];
        }
        if (j_end == i) {
          x[i] = b[i] / a[i + i*N];
        }
      }
      return msg;
    }
  );
}
```

Figure 4-16. *The implementation of* `createNode`. *Sample code graph/graph_fwd_substitution.cpp*

The `continue_node` objects created in `createNode` use a lambda expression that encapsulates the inner two loops from the blocked version of forward substitution shown in Chapter 2. Since no data is passed across the edges in a dependency graph, the data each node needs is accessed via shared memory using the pointers that are captured by the lambda expression. In Figure 4-16, the node captures by value the integers r, c, N, and `block_size` as well as references to the vectors x, a, and b.

In Figure 4-17, the function `addEdges` uses `make_edge` calls to connect each node to its right and lower neighbors, since they must wait for the new node to complete before they can execute. When the loop nest in Figure 4-15 is finished, a dependency graph similar to the one found in Chapter 2 has been constructed.

```
void addEdges(std::vector<NodePtr>& nodes,
              int r, int c, int block_size, int num_blocks) {
  NodePtr np = nodes[r*num_blocks + c];
  if (c + 1 < num_blocks && r != c)
    tbb::flow::make_edge(*np, *nodes[r*num_blocks + c + 1]);
  if (r + 1 < num_blocks)
    tbb::flow::make_edge(*np, *nodes[(r + 1)*num_blocks + c]);
}
```

Figure 4-17. *The implementation of addEdges. Sample code graph/graph_fwd_substitution.cpp*

As shown in Figure 4-15, once the complete graph is constructed, we start it by sending a single continue_msg to the upper-left node. Any continue_node that has no predecessors will execute whenever it receives a message. Sending a message to the top-left node starts the dependency graph. Again, we use g.wait_for_all() to wait until the graph is finished executing.

Summary

In this chapter, we reviewed flow graphs as a fundamental tool for implementing parallel patterns in applications, building upon the algorithms introduced in Chapter 2. Flow graphs allow us to represent programs as interconnected graphs of computations, effectively modeling the event-based coordination parallel pattern. This enables the expression of data flow through filters or stages, as well as the representation of dependencies between operations without the need for explicit data transfer.

We saw how flow graphs are inherently asynchronous, utilizing non-blocking message passing to trigger TBB tasks, which can then be executed by available worker threads. While the common approach is to construct a complete graph before initiating message passing, the graph's structure can also be modified dynamically during execution. We look at dynamic modification in Chapter 5.

We saw the advantages of using graphs to express parallelism, noting that they provide a natural and clear way to depict relationships between computations. This clarity allows TBB to efficiently schedule tasks in parallel, leveraging various types of parallelism such as task, pipeline, and data parallelism.

We included examples showing the steps involved in using a flow graph, including creating the graph object, constructing various types of nodes (functional, join, buffering, and control flow), and managing message flow between nodes. By illustrating these concepts with examples and diagrams, this chapter provided a foundational understanding of flow graphs, setting the stage for more advanced applications in concurrent programming.

In Chapter 5, we describe advanced aspects of using flow graphs in more detail, including how to limit resource usage, manage tasking overheads, use node priorities, dynamically change the structure of a graph, interoperate with accelerators, and more.

CHAPTER 5

Flow Graphs: Expressing Applications

As we learned in the prior chapter, the flow graph API is remarkably versatile, allowing us to construct graphs that incorporate loops, utilize nodes such as `multifunction_node` to generate multiple messages for each incoming message, and introduce parallelism in various ways. This level of flexibility enables us to represent the same application in numerous forms, ranging from highly efficient to less efficient implementations. While each approach can produce correct results, they may differ significantly in terms of complexity and overhead. Therefore, in this chapter, we explore strategies that help us develop flow graph applications that optimize execution efficiency.

Choose the Best Message Type

Messages may be buffered at various points in the graph, for example, in input or output ports (see Table 4-1). When messages are buffered, they are copied into the buffer (they are not moved, because there may be other receivers besides the buffer). The cost in time and memory used for copying a message depends on its type. When possible, we should pass around small objects or pointers, so that these copy-related costs will be low.

We therefore need to carefully select our message types. If we need to pass large objects, it's best to pass these via pointer (or more safely using a smart pointer such as `shared_ptr`) instead of by value. When passing pointers though, we need to be aware of potential concurrent accesses enabled by the parallelism in the graph and protect those accesses as needed. It might also be possible to break a large object into the read-only parts and read–write parts, accessing the read-only parts via pointer and passing the read–write parts by value. Splitting the read-only and read–write data will allow each concurrent access to have its own protected copy of read–write parts and share the read -only parts to minimize memory footprint.

Limiting Resource Usage When Streaming Messages

When streaming messages into a flow graph, it may be necessary to constrain resource usage so that we do not generate an unlimited number of tasks or buffer an unlimited number of messages within the graph. Table 5-1 shows the differences between the approaches we will further explore in this section. First in Figure 5-1, we look at using concurrency limits on functional nodes to constrain generation of messages by an input_node. In Figure 5-2, we show how limiter_node can control the number of messages that reach a subgraph. And finally, in Figure 5-4, we show that tokens can constrain parallelism while also acting like a cache that limits the total number of message allocations.

Table 5-1. *Approaches to control task and memory growth described in this section*

Approach	Description
Concurrency limits (Figure 5-1)	Per-node concurrency limits constrain an input node's generation of new messages.
Limiter node (Figure 5-2)	A limiter_node constrains the number of messages that pass through a point in the graph. The final node in the subgraph sends a message to the limiter_node when new messages may enter.
Token passing (Figure 5-4)	A reserving join_node constrains the number of messages that pass through a point in the graph. Pre-allocated tokens stored in a buffer_node limit message generation and can also serve as a form of cache.

Control Task and Memory Growth with Per-Node Concurrency Limits

The `function_node`, `multifunction_node`, and `async_node` constructors take a `concurrency_limit` argument that limits the number of tasks that can concurrently execute to process messages for that specific node. We can set this value to 1 or to `flow::serial` to protect a node that contains thread-unsafe code or set the value to `flow::unlimited` so that a task is spawned as each message arrives, maximizing the potential parallelism generated by the node.

Setting the `concurrency_limit` to values between 1 and `flow::unlimited`, such as a constant 4 or perhaps the result of a call to `std::thread::hardware_concurrency()`, caps the number of tasks, allowing some parallelism but not unlimited parallelism. We can use this to limit task and memory growth. If there is no reason to limit parallelism, using `flow::unlimited` should be preferred since it allows for the most potential parallelism and incurs the least bookkeeping overhead.

Using the `concurrency_limit` is not the whole story though. By default, a `function_node`, `multifunction_node`, or `async_node` has an unbounded queue at its input port. In this default mode when the concurrency limit is exceeded, a task cannot be spawned immediately and instead the incoming message is stored in this queue, and when a task eventually finishes, another message is retrieved in FIFO order from this queue and a new task is spawned. This means that if messages arrive at a faster rate than the node is processing messages, this queue can grow in an unbounded way. If buffering is only needed to deal with the bursty arrival of messages until the node catches up, there's no problem. But if the arrival rate continually exceeds the processing rate, we might run out of memory!

In Figure 5-1, we construct a `function_node limited_to_3_node` with a `rejecting` policy and a concurrency limit of 3. Using a `rejecting` policy turns off the implicit buffering in the node. At most there will be four messages in this graph at a time. There can be at most three messages being processed in parallel by the `function_node limited_to_3_node` and one being generated or buffered by the `input_node source`.

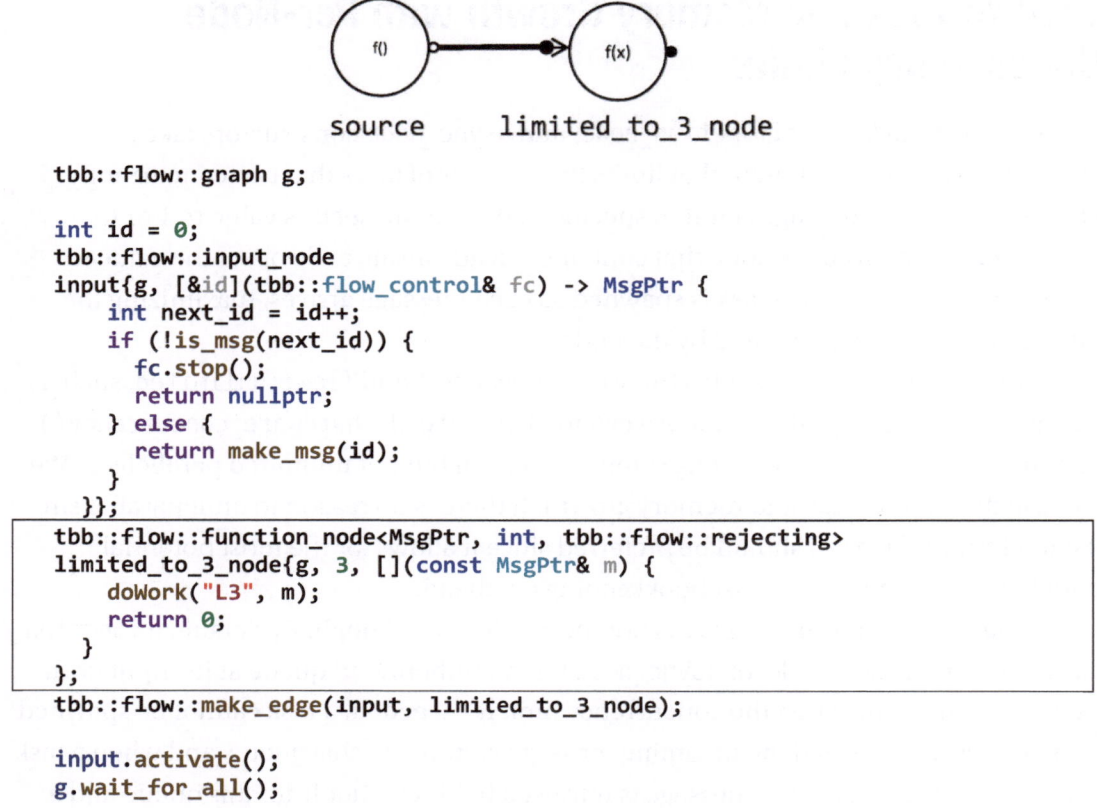

```
tbb::flow::graph g;

int id = 0;
tbb::flow::input_node
input{g, [&id](tbb::flow_control& fc) -> MsgPtr {
    int next_id = id++;
    if (!is_msg(next_id)) {
      fc.stop();
      return nullptr;
    } else {
      return make_msg(id);
    }
}};
tbb::flow::function_node<MsgPtr, int, tbb::flow::rejecting>
limited_to_3_node{g, 3, [](const MsgPtr& m) {
    doWork("L3", m);
    return 0;
  }
};
tbb::flow::make_edge(input, limited_to_3_node);

input.activate();
g.wait_for_all();
```

Figure 5-1. *Using an* input_node *connected to a node with limited concurrency to limit task creation and memory use. Sample code graph/graph_limiting_ messages.cpp*

If this graph were to generate a total of 12 messages, at most four messages and three work tasks would be alive at a time. Node concurrency limits, however, only affect a single node, and while they can be used to create back pressure on a preceding node, they are not sufficient for limiting whole-graph concurrency or to limit concurrency within a subgraph.

Controlling Task and Memory Growth with `limiter_node`

To limit whole-graph concurrency or to limit concurrency within a subgraph, one approach is to use a limiter_node [flow_graph.limiter_node]. A limiter_node counts and limits the number of messages that flow through it. It has a constructor that takes a threshold argument and has a decrementer function that returns a reference to the embedded receiver that is used to decrement the count. In Figure 5-3, we implement the graph that is shown in Figure 5-2. We construct a limiter_node with a threshold of 3 and connect the output of last node in the subgraph to its decrementer. Once the threshold is reached, new messages will only be allowed to pass through via the limiter when a message is received from that last node.

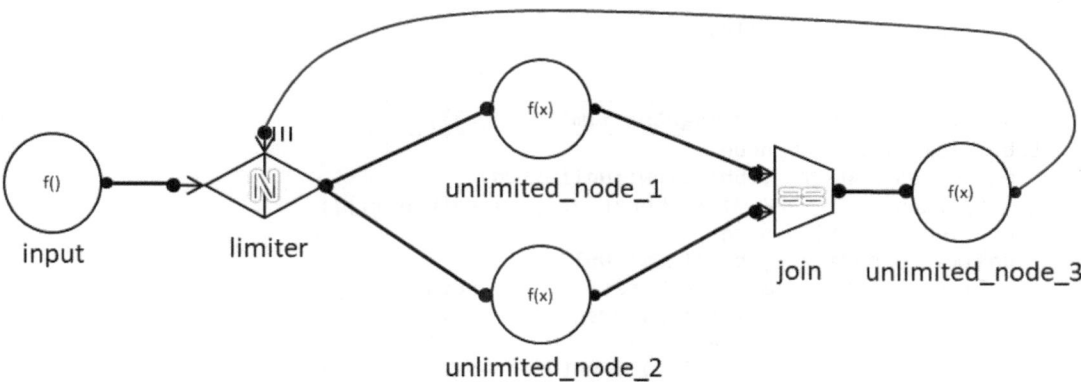

Figure 5-2. *Diagram of a graph using a* limiter_node. *The* input_node *is constrained by the limit in the limiter, but messages that pass through are sent to both nodes that succeed it.*

Just like in the previous example, the number of messages in flight is limited, but now when 12 messages are generated by the input, at most four messages and *six tasks* are alive concurrently. The key difference between this approach and the one in Figure 5-1 is that we can place an entire subgraph after the limiter_node. This has two main consequences. First, we can limit the resources used by an entire subgraph via this single point in the graph. But second, there is not a simple one-to-one correspondence between the messages that pass through the limiter_node and the number of tasks generated by the graph. For example, while the limiter allows only three messages to pass through, there can be up to six concurrent tasks executing. Each of the three messages can create two concurrently executing tasks, one from unlimited_node_1 and one from unlimited_node_2.

```
tbb::flow::graph g;

int id = 0;
tbb::flow::input_node
input{g, [&id](tbb::flow_control& fc) -> MsgPtr {
    int next_id = id++;
    if (!is_msg(next_id)) {
      fc.stop();
      return nullptr;
    } else {
      return make_msg(id);
    }
  }};
tbb::flow::limiter_node<MsgPtr> limiter{g, 3};
tbb::flow::function_node
  unlimited_node_1{g,tbb::flow::unlimited,
    [] (const MsgPtr& m) {doWork("U1", m);return m;}};
tbb::flow::function_node
  unlimited_node_2{g,tbb::flow::unlimited,
    [] (const MsgPtr& m) {doWork("U2", m);return m;}};
tbb::flow::join_node<std::tuple<MsgPtr, MsgPtr>,
  tbb::flow::key_matching<int>>
  join{ g, [](const MsgPtr& p) { return p->get_id(); },
           [](const MsgPtr& p) { return p->get_id(); }};
tbb::flow::function_node
unlimited_node_3{g, tbb::flow::unlimited,
[] (const std::tuple<MsgPtr, MsgPtr>& m) {
    doWork("U3", std::get<0>(m));return tbb::flow::continue_msg{};}};

tbb::flow::make_edge(input, limiter);
tbb::flow::make_edge(limiter, unlimited_node_1);
tbb::flow::make_edge(limiter, unlimited_node_2);
tbb::flow::make_edge(unlimited_node_1, tbb::flow::input_port<0>(join));
tbb::flow::make_edge(unlimited_node_2, tbb::flow::input_port<1>(join));
tbb::flow::make_edge(join, unlimited_node_3);
tbb::flow::make_edge(unlimited_node_3, limiter.decrementer());

input.activate();
g.wait_for_all();
```

Figure 5-3. *Using a* `limiter_node` *to limit task creation and memory use. The code in boxes shows the creation of the* `limiter_node` *and the edges that are connected to it. Sample code graph/graph_limiting_messages.cpp.*

Controlling Repetition with Tokens

Another approach to managing growth for a whole graph or subgraph is to use a token-passing scheme as shown in Figure 5-4. Now, tokens take the place of per-node concurrency limits or `limiter_node` thresholds. As described earlier in Table 4-3, a `join_node` that is constructed with a `reserving` policy does not buffer incoming messages, but only consumes messages once it can reserve a message in each incoming port. In Figure 5-4, this behavior is used to limit the number of messages generated by the `input` by only consuming a message from the `source` if it can be paired with a token from the `token_buffer`.

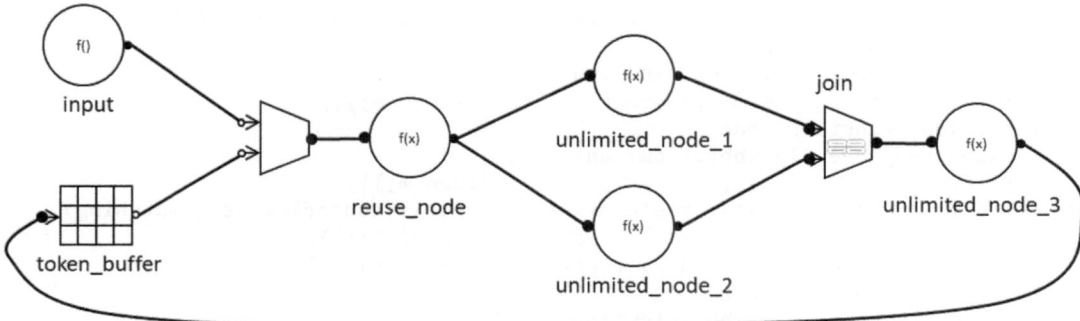

Figure 5-4. *Using a reserving* `join_node` *and tokens to limit task creation and memory use. Sample code graph/graph_limiting_messages.cpp*

A token can be any type, such as a primitive type, an empty object, a pre-allocated buffer, etc. We can therefore use the `token_buffer` to act like a cache of unused items, where large, costly-to-allocate objects are stored to be reused as they are matched with incoming messages. In Figure 5-5, the `token_buffer` stores three messages that are pre-allocated and explicitly put into the graph in a for-loop. Like with our `limiter_node` example, this graph may execute as many as six tasks concurrently but over the whole lifetime of the application only allocates three messages since these objects are reused and are accessed by pointer.

```cpp
using token_t = MsgPtr;
tbb::flow::graph g;
int id = 0;
tbb::flow::input_node
input{g, [&id](tbb::flow_control& fc) {
    int next_id = id++;
    if (!is_msg(next_id)) {fc.stop();return -1;} else {return next_id;}
  }};
tbb::flow::buffer_node<MsgPtr> token_buffer{g};
tbb::flow::join_node<std::tuple<int, token_t>,
                     tbb::flow::reserving> token_join{g};
tbb::flow::function_node<std::tuple<int, token_t>,
  MsgPtr, tbb::flow::lightweight>
    reuse_node{g, tbb::flow::unlimited,
      [] (const  std::tuple<int, token_t>& m) -> MsgPtr {
        return recycle_token_as_msg(std::get<1>(m), std::get<0>(m));}};
tbb::flow::function_node
  unlimited_node_1{g, tbb::flow::unlimited,
    [] (const MsgPtr& m) {doWork("U1", m);return m;}};
tbb::flow::function_node
  unlimited_node_2{g,tbb::flow::unlimited,
    [] (const MsgPtr& m) {doWork("U2", m);return m;}};
tbb::flow::join_node<std::tuple<MsgPtr, MsgPtr>, tbb::flow::tag_matching>
  join{ g, [](const MsgPtr& p) { return p->get_id(); },
           [](const MsgPtr& p) { return p->get_id(); }};
tbb::flow::function_node
  unlimited_node_3{g, tbb::flow::unlimited,
    [] (const std::tuple<MsgPtr, MsgPtr>& t) {
      auto m = std::get<0>(t);doWork("U3", m);return m;}};
tbb::flow::make_edge(input, tbb::flow::input_port<0>(token_join));
tbb::flow::make_edge(token_buffer, tbb::flow::input_port<1>(token_join));
tbb::flow::make_edge(token_join, reuse_node);
tbb::flow::make_edge(reuse_node, unlimited_node_1);
tbb::flow::make_edge(reuse_node, unlimited_node_2);
tbb::flow::make_edge(unlimited_node_1, tbb::flow::input_port<0>(join));
tbb::flow::make_edge(unlimited_node_2, tbb::flow::input_port<1>(join));
tbb::flow::make_edge(join, unlimited_node_3);
tbb::flow::make_edge(unlimited_node_3, token_buffer);

for (int i = 0; i < 3; ++i)
  token_buffer.try_put(make_msg(-1));
input.activate();
g.wait_for_all();
```

Figure 5-5. *Using tokens to limit task creation and memory use. This implementation uses the* `token_buffer` *as a cache for unused large messages. The boxed code shows the creation of the token buffer, the reserving* `join_node`, *and the edges that are connected to them. Sample code graph/graph_limiting_ messages.cpp*

Managing Tasking Overheads

Typically, the functional nodes execute their user-provided bodies by spawning a TBB task. Task creation and scheduling is not free, and therefore we need to be thoughtful about the amount of work in a task. If a node does too little work, the costs associated with packaging and running it as a task may exceed any benefits we gain from possible concurrent execution with other tasks. The cost for scheduling varies from system to system, and so we cannot give a hard-and-fast rule for how much work is enough to amortize the cost of task scheduling. But a general rule of thumb is that tasks should be larger than 1 microsecond.

But what if the natural expression of an application results in nodes that are too small? There are two common ways to address the issue: (1) manually combine nodes, even if it makes the code a bit harder for a human reader to understand, or (2) use a tbb::flow::lightweight policy to hint to the TBB library that the body should be executed immediately by the calling thread when a message arrives instead of packaged as a separately scheduled task. The use of a tbb::flow::lightweight policy acts as a hint to the TBB scheduler, so TBB may still choose to create a task. In addition, the function call operator() of a node body must be noexcept for lightweight policies to have effect.

Figure 5-6 shows an example that, in function small_nodes, implements a three-node graph with an add, a multiply, a and cube node. Each node does very little work. Function small_nodes_combined shows the same example with the nodes combined into a single node. While the intent of the code might be a bit obfuscated, it will now have significantly lower overhead. In function small_nodes_lightweight, the multiply and cube nodes are constructed with a lightweight policy. This graph allows some parallelism since each try_put to the add node starts a new task. But no additional tasks will be created and scheduled, since the multiply and cube nodes will be directly executed from within the tasks created for their preceding add.

Which approach is best will vary according to the use case. When combining nodes, the compiler has an additional advantage since it can now see across the combined code and may be better able to optimize. When using a lightweight policy, the code retains the same readability while reducing overheads.

We should note that the lightweight policy can be combined with concurrency limits as well as other policies. For example, we can create a node that has a concurrency limit of 3 and that rejects messages when that limit is reached, as shown below:

```
function_node< int, int, rejecting_lightweight >
my_node( g, 3, [](const int &v) noexcept { f(v); } );
```

We should also note that the use of lightweight is just a hint. TBB can choose to schedule a task to execute the body.

Because small nodes are, by definition, small, their impact is often overshadowed by the parallelism exposed by larger nodes unless they are executed very frequently. So, while techniques shown in Figure 5-6 can be useful, they are typically not necessary unless the application time becomes significantly impacted by repeatedly executed small nodes.

```cpp
void small_nodes() {
  tbb::flow::graph g;
  tbb::flow::function_node add( g, tbb::flow::unlimited,
                    [](const int &v) { return v+1; } );
  tbb::flow::function_node multiply( g, tbb::flow::unlimited,
                        [](const int &v) { return v*2; } );
  tbb::flow::function_node cube( g, tbb::flow::unlimited,
                    [](const int &v) { return v*v*v; } );
  tbb::flow::make_edge(add, multiply);
  tbb::flow::make_edge(multiply, cube);
  for(int i = 1; i <= N; ++i)
    add.try_put(i);
  g.wait_for_all();
}

void small_nodes_combined() {
  tbb::flow::graph g;
  tbb::flow::function_node< int, int >
    combined_node( g, tbb::flow::unlimited,
      [](const int &v) {auto v2 = (v+1)*2;return v2*v2*v2;});
  for(int i = 1; i <= N; ++i)
    combined_node.try_put(i);
  g.wait_for_all();
}

void small_nodes_lightweight() {
  tbb::flow::graph g;
  tbb::flow::function_node< int, int >
    add( g, tbb::flow::unlimited,[](const int &v) { return v+1; } );
  tbb::flow::function_node< int, int, tbb::flow::lightweight >
    multiply( g, tbb::flow::unlimited,
              [](const int &v) noexcept { return v*2; } );
  tbb::flow::function_node< int, int, tbb::flow::lightweight >
    cube( g, tbb::flow::unlimited,
              [](const int &v) noexcept { return v*v*v; } );
  tbb::flow::make_edge(add, multiply);
  tbb::flow::make_edge(multiply, cube);
  for(int i = 1; i <= N; ++i)
    add.try_put(i);
  g.wait_for_all();
}
```

Figure 5-6. *Combining nodes or using a lightweight policy to reduce task scheduling overheads. Sample code graph/graph_small_nodes.cpp*

Use Nested Parallelism Instead of Many Messages

As discussed in Chapter 2, TBB provides several algorithms that are optimized for common parallel patterns. While we can express graphs that include loops and use nodes like multifunction_node to output many messages from each invocation, we should be on the lookout for cases where we take advantage of nested parallelism. One simple example is shown in Figure 5-7.

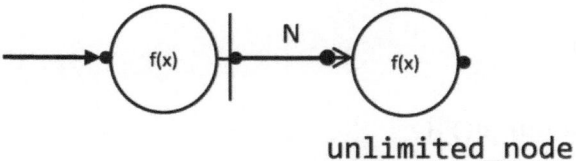

unlimited_node

Figure 5-7. *A multifunction_node that sends many messages for each message it receives. This pattern may be better expressed as a nested parallel_for loop*

In Figure 5-7, for each message that the multifunction_node receives, it generates many output messages that flow into a subsequent function_node with unlimited concurrency. This graph will act a lot like a parallel loop, with the multifunction_node acting as the control loop and the function_node as the body. But this is a very inefficient way to implement a parallel loop! While there might be valid uses of this pattern, it is likely more efficient to use a highly optimized parallel loop algorithm instead. This entire graph might collapse into a single node that contains a nested parallel_for. Of course, whether this replacement is possible or desirable depends on the application.

Node Priorities Can Improve Scheduling

Typically, we should not try to control the choices made by the TBB scheduler. However, there are cases where some nodes in a flow graph clearly have higher priority than others. The most common case is when a node interacts with an asynchronous agent, such as an accelerator or GPU. A delay in executing a node that submits work to an accelerator can cause the accelerator to be underutilized.

Figure 5-8 shows an example of a flow graph where one of the nodes is more important than the others – it exclaims, "Me first!" But when we execute this graph, using only two threads, the TBB library needs to select which nodes to execute and tries to be fair between the three nodes.

```
tbb::flow::graph g;

tbb::flow::broadcast_node<int> b{g};

tbb::flow::function_node
  n1{g, tbb::flow::unlimited,
  [](const int& t) { std::printf("Hi from n1\n"); return 0; }};

tbb::flow::function_node
  n2{g, tbb::flow::unlimited,
  [](const int& t) { std::printf("Hi from n2\n"); return 0; }};

tbb::flow::function_node
  n3{g, tbb::flow::unlimited,
    [](const int& t) { std::printf("n3: Me first!\n"); return 0; }};

tbb::flow::make_edge(b, n1);
tbb::flow::make_edge(b, n2);
tbb::flow::make_edge(b, n3);

for (int i = 0; i < 5; ++i) b.try_put(10);
g.wait_for_all();
```

Figure 5-8. *A flow graph with one node that is more time-consuming than the others. Sample code graph/graph_node_priorities.cpp*

An example run of Figure 5-8 using only two threads showed the output in the following order:

```
Hi from n1
Hi from n2
n3: Me first!
Hi from n1
Hi from n2
n3: Me first!
Hi from n1
Hi from n2
n3: Me first!
n3: Me first!
Hi from n1
Hi from n2
Hi from n2
Hi from n1
n3: Me first!
```

However, if we really want node n3 to be given priority over the other two nodes, we can rewrite and add a node priority [flow_graph.node_priorities] as shown in Figure 5-9.

```
tbb::flow::function_node
  n3{g, tbb::flow::unlimited,
    [](const int& t) { std::printf("n3: Me first!\n"); return 0; },
    tbb::flow::node_priority_t(1)};
```

Figure 5-9. *Using a node priority to bias execution towards n3. Sample code graph/graph_node_priorities.cpp*

A TBB node priority is an unsigned integer value, where higher values mean higher priorities. Any node not given an explicit priority has a default priority of 0. If we change n3 as shown in Figure 5-9 and again execute using only two threads, the TBB library shows a preference for n3:

```
n3: Me first!
n3: Me first!
n3: Me first!
n3: Me first!
n3: Me first!
Hi from n2
Hi from n1
Hi from n1
Hi from n2
Hi from n1
Hi from n2
Hi from n1
Hi from n2
Hi from n1
Hi from n2
```

You Can Overlap Graph Construction with Execution

The TBB flow graph API uses an eager execution model. Whenever a functional node receives a message, and as long as its concurrency limits and policies allow, it will immediately spawn a task to execute its body on the incoming message. Due to this eager design, it is common practice to fully define a whole graph before activating its input_node objects or before sending explicit messages to it. However, that is not strictly required. We can overlap execution of a graph with its construction, but we need to be mindful how messages will flow in a partially defined graph if we do so.

To demonstrate this, we will build a dependency graph like the one shown in Figure 5-10, but overlap building the graph with executing it. In this graph, write_once_node objects [flow_graph.write_once_node] are used to buffer messages so that they are not lost as the graph is built. A write_once_node buffers a single value and broadcasts it to all its successors, including successors that are added after its value is written. Figure 5-10 uses write_once_node objects like futures.

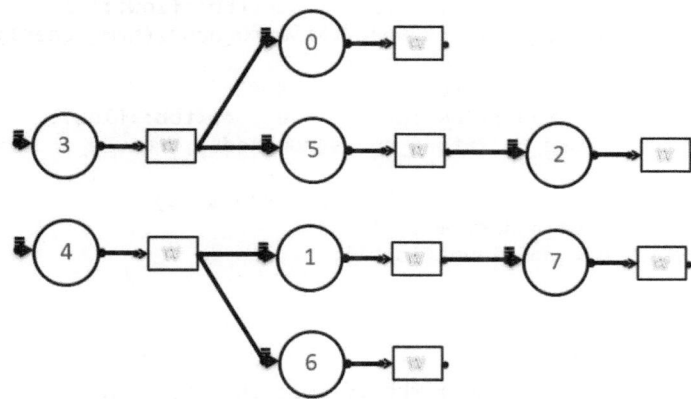

Figure 5-10. *A dependency graph that can be safely built while executing some of the nodes since it uses* write_once_node *objects to act like futures*

Figure 5-11 shows the code that builds and executes this dependency graph. The for-loop in the main function iterates through the configuration vector. This vector stores the node dependencies shown in Figure 5-10. As each element is processed, the continue_node that corresponds to the id is created. As shown in the boxed part of the code, if there is a predecessor for the new node, an edge is made from that predecessor's "future" write_once_node to the new node's input. If the node has no predecessor, try_put is called to start the node.

When executed, this sample will show that the partial ordering of the nodes shown in Figure 5-10 is respected, even though the nodes are created in order from id 0 to id 7 and nodes without predecessors are immediately started as they are encountered. When run, we saw the nodes execute in the order 3, 0, 4, 1, 5, 2, 6, 7.

Although we show a dependency graph in this section, the same idea applies to data flow graphs. We can build graphs dynamically but need to be careful to buffer messages that may arrive at a point in the graph before the (eventual) receiving node has been constructed and an edge established.

```cpp
struct config_t { int id; int predecessor; };
std::vector<config_t> configuration =
  {{0,3}, {1,4}, {2,5}, {3,-1}, {4,-1}, {5,3}, {6,4}, {7,1}};
int num_nodes = configuration.size();

int main() {
  tbb::flow::graph g;

  // create a vector of pointers to work nodes
  using work_node_t = tbb::flow::continue_node<tbb::flow::continue_msg>;
  std::vector<std::unique_ptr<work_node_t>> work_nodes(num_nodes);

  // create fully populated vector of "promises"
  using future_node_t = tbb::flow::write_once_node<tbb::flow::continue_msg>;
  std::vector<future_node_t> future_nodes(num_nodes, future_node_t{g});

  // build graph (starting nodes with no predecessors)
  for(int i = 0; i < num_nodes; ++i) {
    const config_t& c = configuration[i];

    // create the work node for that element
    work_nodes[c.id].reset(
        new work_node_t{g,
                        [c](const tbb::flow::continue_msg& m) {
                          std::printf("Executing %d\n", c.id);
                          return m;
                        }});
    // connect the new node to its future
    tbb::flow::make_edge(*work_nodes[c.id], future_nodes[c.id]);

    // start the node or link it to predecessor's promise
    if (c.predecessor != -1) {
      std::printf("new %d with %d -> %d\n", c.id, c.predecessor, c.id);
      tbb::flow::make_edge(future_nodes[c.predecessor], *work_nodes[c.id]);
    } else {
      std::printf("starting %d from main\n", c.id);
      work_nodes[c.id]->try_put(tbb::flow::continue_msg{});
    }
    std::printf("**** wait a bit in main\n");
    std::this_thread::sleep_for(std::chrono::milliseconds(1000));
    std::printf("**** done waiting in main\n");
  }
  g.wait_for_all();
  return 0;
}
```

Figure 5-11. *Overlapping graph construction with execution. Sample code graph/*
graph_execute_with_building.cpp

Reestablish Order After Parallelism as Needed

Because a flow graph is less structured than a simple `tbb::parallel_pipeline`, we may sometimes need to establish an ordering of messages at points in the graph. There are three common approaches for establishing order in a data flow graph: use a key-matching `join_node`, use a `sequencer_node`, or use a `multifunction_node`.

For example, in Chapter 4, the parallelism in our stereoscopic 3D flow graph allowed the left and right images to arrive out of order at the `mergeImageBuffersNode`. In that example, we ensured that the correct two images were paired together as inputs to the `mergeImageBuffersNode` by using a tag-matching `join_node`. The different join node policies are described in Table 4-3.

Another way to establish order is to use a `sequencer_node`. A `sequencer_node` is a buffer that outputs messages in sequence order, using a user-provided body object to obtain the sequence number from the incoming message.

In Figure 5-12, we can see a three-node graph, with nodes `first_node`, `sequencer`, and `last_node`. We use a `sequencer_node` to reestablish the input order of the messages before the final serial output node `last_node`. Because `function_node first_node` is unlimited, its tasks can finish out of order and send their output as they complete. The `sequencer_node` reestablishes the input order by using the sequence number assigned when each message was originally constructed.

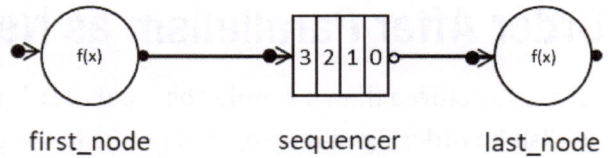

```
void orderWithSequencer() {
  const int N = 10;
  tbb::flow::graph g;
  tbb::flow::function_node
  first_node{g, tbb::flow::unlimited,
  [] (const MessagePtr& m) {
    m->my_string += " with sequencer";
    return m;
  }};
  tbb::flow::sequencer_node
  sequencer(g, [] (const MessagePtr& m) {
    return m->my_seq_no;
  });
  tbb::flow::function_node<MessagePtr, int, tbb::flow::rejecting>
  last_node{g, tbb::flow::serial, [] (MessagePtr m) {
      std::cout << m->my_string << std::endl;
      return 0;
  }};
  tbb::flow::make_edge(first_node, sequencer);
  tbb::flow::make_edge(sequencer, last_node);

  for (int i = 0; i < N; ++i)
    first_node.try_put(std::make_shared<Message>(i));
  g.wait_for_all();
}
```

Figure 5-12. *A* `sequencer_node` *is used to ensure that the messages print in the order dictated by their* `my_seq_no` *member variables. Sample code graph/graph_reestablish_order.cpp.*

If we execute a similar example without a sequencer node and N=10, the output is scrambled as the messages pass each other on their way to `last_node`:

```
9 no sequencer
8 no sequencer
7 no sequencer
0 no sequencer
1 no sequencer
2 no sequencer
6 no sequencer
5 no sequencer
4 no sequencer
3 no sequencer
```

When we execute the code shown in Figure 5-12, we see the following output:

```
0 with sequencer
1 with sequencer
2 with sequencer
3 with sequencer
4 with sequencer
5 with sequencer
6 with sequencer
7 with sequencer
8 with sequencer
9 with sequencer
```

As we can see, a `sequencer_node` can reestablish the order of the messages, but it does require us to assign the sequence number and provide a body to the `sequencer_node` that can obtain that number from an incoming message.

A final approach to establishing order is to use a serial `multifunction_node`. A `multifunction_node` can output zero or more messages on any of its output ports for a given input message. Since it is not forced to output a message for each incoming message, it can buffer incoming messages and hold them until some user-defined ordering constraint is met.

For example, Figure 5-13 shows how we can implement a `sequencer_node` using a `multifunction_node` by buffering incoming messages until the next message in sequencer order has arrived. This example assumes that at most N messages are sent to a node `sequencer` and that the sequence numbers start at 0 and are continuous up to N-1. Vector v is created with N elements initialized as empty `shared_ptr` objects. When a message arrives at `sequencer`, it is assigned to the corresponding element of v. Then starting at the last sent sequence number, each element of v that has a valid message is sent, and the sequence number is incremented. For some incoming messages, no output message will be sent; for others, one or more messages may be sent.

```
using MessagePtr = std::shared_ptr<Message>;
using MFNSequencer =
  tbb::flow::multifunction_node<MessagePtr, std::tuple<MessagePtr>>;
using MFNPorts = typename MFNSequencer::output_ports_type;

int seq_i = 0;
std::vector<MessagePtr> v{(const unsigned)N, MessagePtr{}};

MFNSequencer sequencer{g, tbb::flow::serial,
[N, &seq_i, &v](MessagePtr m, MFNPorts& p) {
  v[m->my_seq_no] = m;
  while (seq_i < N && v[seq_i].use_count()) {
    std::get<0>(p).try_put(v[seq_i++]);
  }
}};
```

Figure 5-13. *Using a multifunction_node to buffer and reestablish order. Sample code graph/graph_reestablish_order.cpp*

While Figure 5-13 shows how a multifunction_node can be used to reorder messages by sequence order, in general, any user-defined ordering or bundling of messages can be used.

If we need to combine messages related to the same input, but the order in which we process these combined messages doesn't matter, a key- or tag-matching join_node is a good choice. If we need to reestablish the order in which messages entered (or passed through) the graph, we can use a sequencer_node. Finally, if we need something more complicated, we can create our own logic using a multifunction_node.

Group Nodes for Easy Reuse

Encapsulating a group of nodes is convenient if there is a common pattern that needs to be created many times or if there is too much detail in one large flat graph.

To do so, we can use a tbb::flow::composite_node. A composite_node is used to encapsulate a collection of other nodes so they can be used like a first-class graph node. Its interface follows:

```cpp
template<typename... InputTypes, typename... OutputTypes>
class composite_node <std::tuple<InputTypes...>, std::tuple<OutputTypes...>> :
public graph_node {
  public:
    typedef std::tuple< receiver<InputTypes>&...> input_ports_type;
    typedef std::tuple< sender<OutputTypes>&...> output_ports_type;

    composite_node ( graph &g );
    virtual ~composite_node();

    void set_external_ports(input_ports_type&& input_ports_tuple,
                            output_ports_type&& output_ports_tuple);
    input_ports_type& input_ports();
    output_ports_type& output_ports();
};
```

Unlike the other node types that we have discussed in this chapter, we need to create a new class that inherits from `tbb::flow::composite_node` [flow_graph.composite_node] to make use of its functionality. For example, let's consider the flow graph in Figure 5-14(a). This graph combines two inputs from `source1` and `source2` and uses a token-passing scheme to limit memory consumption.

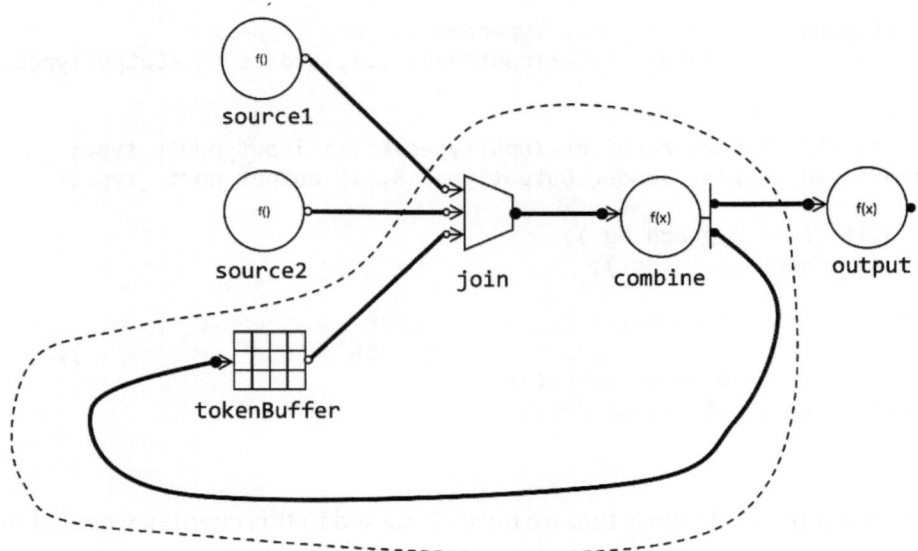

(a) a graph that includes a pattern that might be reusable elsewhere.

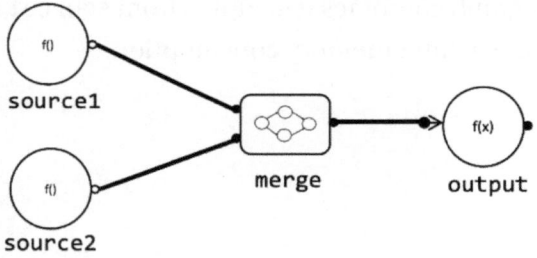

(b) the graph refactored to use a composite_node.

Figure 5-14. *Encapsulating a reusable pattern as a* composite_node

If this token-passing pattern is commonly used in our application, or by members of our development team, it might make sense to encapsulate it into its own node type, as shown in Figure 5-14(b). It also cleans up the high-level view of our application by hiding the details. Figure 5-15 shows what a flow graph implementation looks like if we have a node that implements the dashed part of Figure 5-14(a), replacing it with a single merge node.

```cpp
void usingMergeNode() {
  tbb::flow::graph g;

  tbb::flow::input_node<BigObjectPtr> source1{g,
  [&] (tbb::flow_control& fc) {
    static int in1_count = 0;
    BigObjectPtr p;
    if (in1_count < A_LARGE_NUMBER)
      p = std::make_shared<BigObject>(in1_count++);
    else
      fc.stop();
    return p;
  }};

  tbb::flow::input_node<BigObjectPtr> source2{g,
  [&] (tbb::flow_control& fc) {
    static int in2_count = 0;
    BigObjectPtr p;
    if (in2_count < A_LARGE_NUMBER)
      p = std::make_shared<BigObject>(in2_count++);
    else
      fc.stop();
    return p; }};

  MergeNode merge{g};

  tbb::flow::function_node<BigObjectPtr> output{g,
    tbb::flow::serial,
    [] (BigObjectPtr b) {
      std::cout << "Received id == " << b->getId()
                << " in final node" << std::endl;
  }};

  tbb::flow::make_edge(source1, tbb::flow::input_port<0>(merge));
  tbb::flow::make_edge(source2, tbb::flow::input_port<1>(merge));
  tbb::flow::make_edge(merge, output);

  reset_counters();
  source1.activate();
  source2.activate();
  g.wait_for_all();
}
```

Figure 5-15. *Creating a flow graph that uses a class* MergeNode *that inherits from* tbb::flow::composite_node. *Sample code graph/graph_composite_node.cpp*

In Figure 5-15, we use the merge node object like any other flow graph node, making edges to its input and output ports. Figure 5-16 shows how we use tbb::flow::composite_node to implement our MergeNode class. In Figure 5-16, MergeNode inherits from CompositeType, which is an alias for

```
tbb::flow::composite_node<std::tuple<BigObjectPtr, BigObjectPtr>,
                          std::tuple<BigObjectPtr>>;
```

The two template arguments indicate that a MergeNode will have two input ports, which both receive BigObjectPtr messages, and a single output port that sends BigObjectPtr messages.

The class MergeNode has a member variable for each node it encapsulates: a tokenBuffer, a join, and a combine node. And these member variables are initialized in the member initializer list of the MergeNode constructor. In the constructor body, calls to tbb::flow::make_edge set up all the internal edges.

A call to set_external_ports is used to assign the ports from the member nodes to the external ports of the MergeNode. In this case, the first two input ports of join become the inputs of the MergeNode and the output of combine becomes the output of the MergeNode. Finally, because the node is implementing a token-passing scheme, the tokenBuffer is filled with tokens.

While creating a new type that inherits from tbb::flow::composite_node may appear daunting at first, using this interface can lead to more readable and reusable code, especially as your flow graphs become larger and more complicated.

```cpp
using BigObjectPtr = std::shared_ptr<BigObject>;
using CompositeType =
  tbb::flow::composite_node<std::tuple<BigObjectPtr, BigObjectPtr>,
                            std::tuple<BigObjectPtr>>;
class MergeNode : public CompositeType {
  using token_t = int;
  tbb::flow::buffer_node<token_t> tokenBuffer;
  tbb::flow::join_node<std::tuple<BigObjectPtr, BigObjectPtr, token_t>,
                       tbb::flow::reserving> join;
  using MFNode =
    tbb::flow::multifunction_node<std::tuple<BigObjectPtr,
      BigObjectPtr, token_t>,std::tuple<BigObjectPtr, token_t>>;
  MFNode combine;

public:
  MergeNode(tbb::flow::graph& g) :
```
```cpp
    // make the nodes
    CompositeType{g},
    tokenBuffer{g},
    join{g},
    combine{g, tbb::flow::unlimited,
      [] (const MFNode::input_type& in, MFNode::output_ports_type& p) {
        BigObjectPtr b0 = std::get<0>(in);
        BigObjectPtr b1 = std::get<1>(in);
        token_t t = std::get<2>(in);
        spinWaitForAtLeast(0.0001);
        b0->mergeIds(b0->getId(), b1->getId());
        std::get<0>(p).try_put(b0);
        std::get<1>(p).try_put(t);
      }}
```
```cpp
  {
    // make the edges
    tbb::flow::make_edge(tokenBuffer, tbb::flow::input_port<2>(join));
    tbb::flow::make_edge(join, combine);
    tbb::flow::make_edge(tbb::flow::output_port<1>(combine), tokenBuffer);
```
```cpp
    // set the input and output ports
    CompositeType::set_external_ports(
      CompositeType::input_ports_type(
        tbb::flow::input_port<0>(join),
        tbb::flow::input_port<1>(join)
      ),
      CompositeType::output_ports_type(
        tbb::flow::output_port<0>(combine)
      ));
```
```cpp
    // populate the token buffer
    for (token_t i = 0; i < 3; ++i)
      tokenBuffer.try_put(i);
  }};
```

Figure 5-16. *Implementing* MergeNode. *Sample code graph/graph_composite_node.cpp*

Use Asynchrony Instead of Blocking a Worker Thread

The flow graph API is itself asynchronous. Any call to `try_put` (except if made to a node with a lightweight policy) returns immediately after injecting a message into the graph. The thread does not block, waiting for the message to be processed by the graph. If we want to block a thread until the graph completes its work, we must call `wait_for_all` on the graph object.

The interactions with a flow graph are primarily asynchronous. Even so, there are times when we need to introduce even more asynchrony, and that is where `async_node` [flow_graph.async_node] enters the picture. We can demonstrate this with the example in Figure 5-17. The goal of this example is to send a message from an `input_node`, `in_node`, through processing in an `asynchronous node`, `offload_node`, and display the result in the `out_node`. However, instead of processing the message directly inside of the user-provided body of the `offload_node`, the body offloads the work via SYCL queue to a device managed by the SYCL Runtime (a GPU, an FPGA, or even a set of CPUs). As soon as the device is done, another dependent SYCL task is used to send the results back to the flow graph via a gateway object. No TBB worker thread is blocked or actively waits for the value to be returned through the gateway.

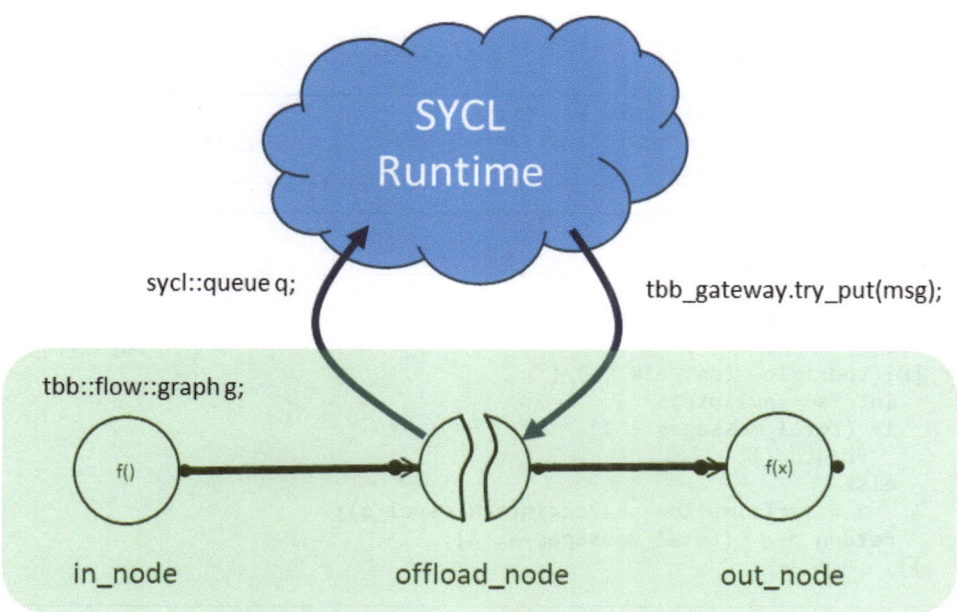

Figure 5-17. *A simple example that offloads a fill operation to a SYCL queue*

In this section, we use SYCL for demonstration purposes only. An async_node works to hide any asynchrony, whether it is offloaded to SYCL, CUDA, OpenCL, or even a native CPU thread pool.

Figure 5-18 shows the implementation of a graph that represents Figure 5-17. In Figure 5-18, both a tbb::flow::graph and a sycl::queue are constructed. The flow graph manages the work assigned to TBB worker threads. The SYCL queue manages the work offloaded to the device. The async_node manages the interface between the TBB flow graph nodes and the SYCL queue. This is a book about TBB; there is a book titled *Data Parallel C++* that is an excellent resource if you want to learn more about SYCL. For this discussion, we just need to know that SYCL queues are used to offload work to accelerators and that we can create dependent tasks in SYCL that run after work is done.

```cpp
const int N = 1000;
int total_messages = 3;
```

```cpp
using msg_t = std::pair<int, int *>;
using offload_node_t = tbb::flow::async_node<msg_t, msg_t>;
using gateway_t = offload_node_t::gateway_type;
```

```cpp
sycl::queue sycl_q;
tbb::flow::graph g;
```

```cpp
tbb::flow::input_node<msg_t>
in_node{g,
    [&](tbb::flow_control& fc) {
      int *a = nullptr;
      if (total_messages < 1)
        fc.stop();
      else
        a = sycl::malloc_shared<int>(N, sycl_q);
      return msg_t{total_messages--, a};
    }};
```

```cpp
offload_node_t offload_node{ /* See Figure 5-19 */ };
```

```cpp
tbb::flow::function_node<msg_t>
out_node{g, tbb::flow::serial,
    [=](const msg_t& msg) {
      int id = msg.first;
      int* a = msg.second;
      if (a == nullptr
          || std::any_of(a, a+N, [id](int i) { return i != id; })) {
        std::cout << "ERROR: unexpected msg in out_node\n";
      } else {
        std::cout << "Received well-formed msg for id " << id << "\n";
      }
    }};
```

```cpp
tbb::flow::make_edge(in_node, offload_node);
tbb::flow::make_edge(offload_node, out_node);
in_node.activate();
g.wait_for_all();
```

Figure 5-18. *A flow graph that includes an* async_node *to implement our simple SYCL offloading example. Sample code graph/graph_async_sycl.cpp*

Figure 5-19 shows the details of how the offload_node is constructed. First, like other functional node types, its constructor receives both a graph object and a concurrency limit. But its body, as shown in Figure 5-19, receives not only the incoming message but also a reference to a gateway [req.gateway_type].

```
offload_node_t
offload_node{g, tbb::flow::unlimited,
            [&sycl_q](const msg_t& msg, gateway_t& tbb_gateway) {

    // tell the graph we are doing something asynchronously
    tbb_gateway.reserve_wait();

    // submit the async work
    int id = msg.first;
    int* a = msg.second;
    auto sycl_event = sycl_q.fill(a, id, N);

    // tell the graph the work is done
    sycl_q.submit([&](sycl::handler& sycl_h) {
      sycl_h.depends_on(sycl_event); // wait for sycl_event
      sycl_h.host_task([&tbb_gateway, msg]() {
        // send the result
        tbb_gateway.try_put(msg);
        // tell the graph to no longer wait for this agent
        tbb_gateway.release_wait();
      });
    });
}};
```

Figure 5-19. *The details of the user-provided body of the* offload_node. *Sample code graph/graph_async_sycl.cpp*

An async_node gateway type gateway_t represents a way to interact with both the flow graph and the async_node object and provides three member functions:

```
bool gateway_t::try_put(const Output &v);
void gateway_t::reserve_wait();
void gateway_t::release_wait();
```

In Figure 5-19, a call to tbb_gateway.reserve_wait() notifies the graph that asynchronous work is being initiated. If the number of reserve_wait calls exceeds the number of release_wait calls, even if there are no TBB tasks actively working in the graph, the graph's work is not considered to be complete. So, for example, the call to g.wait_for_all() in the last line of Figure 5-18 will continue to block, awaiting the graph's completion.

The work offloaded through the SYCL queue in Figure 5-19 is trivial; it is the call to sycl_q.fill(a, id, N), which simply sets all the elements of a to be equal to id. Again, we are not going to describe how SYCL works in this book, so you will just have to trust us. The call to fill submits the work to the device. However, the tbb_gateway needs to be used to send back the result to the TBB world and notify the flow graph that the asynchronous work is complete. This is accomplished in Figure 5-19 by adding a SYCL host_task that depends on the completion of the fill operation. A SYCL host_task is run, by the SYCL Runtime, on the host and can contain any valid C++ code. In Figure 5-19 the body of the host_task calls try_put followed by release_wait on the gateway.

It should be noted that while there is a lot of code in Figure 5-19, the actual execution of the fill operation, as well as the dependent host task body, is done asynchronously; no TBB worker is blocked waiting for them to complete. Instead, the async_node body offloads the execution of those tasks to the SYCL Runtime via the SYCL queue, and work only resumes on a TBB worker thread in response to a task spawned by the call to tbb_gateway.try_put when executed by the SYCL host task. We should also note that the tbb_gateway is passed by reference, and this reference is valid for the duration of the async_node's lifetime, so it should not be used after the node is destroyed.

In this example, we used SYCL but, as mentioned earlier, there's nothing special about the relationship between TBB and SYCL in this context. We could have equally well used CUDA or HIP.

We May Optimize `reserve_wait` calls

A call to graph::wait_for_all() will not exit while the number of calls to reserve_wait() is greater than the number of calls to release_wait(). However, there is no requirement to call reserve_wait() for each input message received by an async_node. We need to call reserve_wait() to prevent graph::wait_for_all() from returning prematurely, but we may be able to (carefully) optimize the number of times we call reserve_wait() and release_wait() if we choose to.

Summary

The flow graph API offers a flexible and powerful interface for constructing dependency and data flow graphs. In this chapter, we examined various approaches to utilizing the flow graph high-level execution interface to enhance application performance. Since the flow graph interfaces are built on TBB tasks, they inherit valuable composability and optimization features. We hope the tips provided in this chapter will help you maximize the potential of this robust set of APIs for flow graphs.

CHAPTER 6

Tasks and Task Group

One of the things that we like the most about TBB is its "multiresolution" nature. In the context of parallel programming models, multiresolution means that we can choose among different levels of abstraction to code our algorithm, such as using high-level algorithms or using low-level threading or tasking APIs. In TBB, we have flow graphs to coordinate functions (see Chapter 4), and we have high-level templates, such as `parallel_for` or `pipeline` (see Chapter 2), that are ready to use when our algorithms fit into these particular patterns. But what if our algorithm is not that simple? Or what if the available high-level abstraction is not squeezing out the last drop of performance of our parallel hardware? Should we just give up and remain prisoners of the high-level features of the programing model? Of course not! There should be a capability to get closer to the hardware, a way to build our own templates from the ground up, and a way to thoroughly optimize our implementation using low-level and more tunable characteristics of the programming model. In TBB, this capability exists. In this chapter, we focus on one of the most powerful low-level features of TBB, the `task_group` programming interface. As we have said throughout the book, tasks are at the heart of TBB, and tasks are the building blocks used to construct the high-level templates such as `parallel_for` and `pipeline`. But there is nothing that prevents us from venturing into these deeper waters and starting to code our algorithms directly with `task_group`, from building our own high-level templates for future use on top of tasks, or, as we describe in the next chapters, from fully optimizing our implementation by fine-tuning the way in which tasks are executed. In essence, this is what you will learn by reading this chapter and the ones that follow. Enjoy the deep dive!

© Michael J. Voss, James R. Reinders 2025
M. J. Voss and J. R. Reinders, *Today's TBB*, https://doi.org/10.1007/979-8-8688-1270-5_6

A Running Example: The Fibonacci Sequence

Task-based TBB implementations are particularly appropriate for algorithms in which a problem can be recursively divided into smaller subproblems following a tree-like decomposition. There are plenty of problems like these. The divide-and-conquer and branch-and-bound parallel patterns (Chapter 2) are examples of classes of such algorithms. If the problem is big enough, it usually scales well on a parallel architecture because it is easy to break it into enough tasks to fully utilize the hardware and avoid load imbalance.

What is big enough in task size and big enough in the number of tasks? That depends a bit on the application, but we should remember the rule of thumb that a task should be greater than 1 microsecond in execution time if we want it to amortize overheads. And if we want the TBB scheduler to have flexibility in utilizing the hardware and balancing load, then we need to create enough tasks to provide that flexibility – so at least a multiple of the number of hardware threads.

For the purpose of this chapter, we have chosen one of the simplest problems that can be implemented following a tree-like approach. The problem is known as the Fibonacci sequence, and it consists in computing the integer sequence that starts with zero and one, and afterward, every number in the sequence is the sum of the two preceding ones:

0, 1, 1, 2, 3, 5, 8, 13, 21, 34, 55, 89, 144, ...

Mathematically, the nth number in the sequence, Fn, can be computed recursively as

$$F_n = F_{n-1} + F_{n-2}$$

with initial values F0=0 and F1=1. There are several algorithms that compute Fn, but in the interest of illustrating how TBB tasks work, we chose the one presented in Figure 6-1, although it is not the most efficient one.

```cpp
long fib(long n) {
  if(n<2)
    return n;
  else
    return fib(n-1)+fib(n-2);
}
```

Figure 6-1. *Recursive implementation of the computation of* Fn. *Sample code tasks/parallel_invoke_fib.cpp*

Fibonacci number computation is a classic computer science example for showing recursion, but it is also a classic example in which a simple algorithm is inefficient. A more efficient method would be to compute

$$F_n = \begin{bmatrix} 1 & 1 \\ 1 & 0 \end{bmatrix}^{n-1}$$

and take the upper-left element. The exponentiation over the matrix can be done quickly via repeated squaring. But we'll go ahead in this section and use the classic recursion example for teaching purposes.

The code presented in Figure 6-1 clearly resembles the recursive equation to compute Fn = Fn-1 + Fn-2. While it may be easy to understand, we clarify it further in Figure 6-2 where we depict the recursive calling tree when calling fib(4).

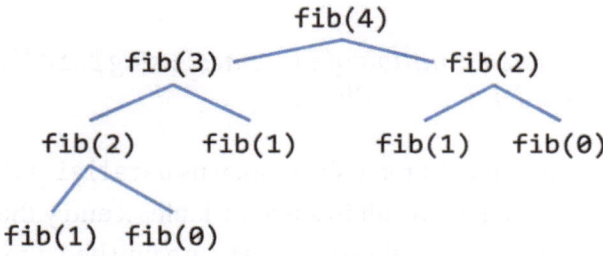

Figure 6-2. *Recursive calling tree for fib(4)*

The if (n<2) line at the beginning of the serial code of Figure 6-1 caters for what is called the *base case* that is always needed in recursive codes to avoid infinite recursion, which is nice because we don't want to nuke the stack, do we?

We will parallelize this first sequential implementation using different task-based approaches, from simpler to more elaborated and optimized versions. The lessons we learn with these examples can be mimicked in other tree-like or recursive algorithms, and the optimizations we show can also be put to work to make the most out of our parallel architecture in similar situations.

The High-Level Approach: `parallel_invoke`

In Chapter 2, we already presented a high-level class that suits our needs when it comes to spawning parallel tasks: `parallel_invoke`. Relying on this class, we can produce a first parallel implementation of the Fibonacci algorithm that we present in Figure 6-3.

```cpp
long parallel_fib(long n) {
  if(n<2) {
    return n;
  }
  else {
    long x, y;
    tbb::parallel_invoke([&]{x=parallel_fib(n-1);},
                         [&]{y=parallel_fib(n-2);});
    return x+y;
  }
}
```

Figure 6-3. *Parallel implementation of Fibonacci using* `parallel_invoke`*. Sample code tasks/parallel_invoke_fib.cpp*

The `parallel_invoke` function recursively spawns `parallel_fib(n-1)` and `parallel_fib(n-2)` returning the result in stack variables x and y that are captured by reference in the two lambdas. When these two tasks are finished, the caller task simply returns the sum of x+y. The recursive nature of the implementation keeps invoking parallel tasks until the base case is reached when n<2. This means that TBB will create tasks even for computing `parallel_fib(1)` and `parallel_fib(0)`, which just return 1 and 0, respectively. As we have said throughout the book, we want to expose enough parallelism to the architecture creating a sufficiently large number of tasks, but at the same time tasks must also have a minimum degree of granularity (>1 microsecond) so that task creation overhead pays off. This trade-off is usually implemented in this kind of algorithm using a "cutoff" parameter as we show in Figure 6-4.

```cpp
long parallel_fib_cutoff(log n) {
  if(n<cutoff) {
    return fib(n);
  }
  else {
    long x, y;
    tbb::parallel_invoke([&]{x=parallel_fib_cutoff(n-1);},
                         [&]{y=parallel_fib_cutoff(n-2);});
    return x+y;
  }
}
```

Figure 6-4. *Cutoff version of the* `parallel_invoke` *implementation. Sample code tasks/parallel_invoke_fib.cpp*

The idea is to modify the base case so that we stop creating more tasks when n is not large enough (n<cutoff) and instead call the serial algorithm. Computing a suitable cutoff value requires some experimentation, so it is advisable to write our code so that cutoff can be an input parameter to ease the search of a suitable one. For example, in our test bed, fib(30) only takes around 1 millisecond, and this is a fine-grained-enough task to discourage further splitting. This cutoff results in large-sized tasks, but still generates enough tasks to keep our hardware busy for our test case of fib(40). So, based on our experimentation, it makes sense to set cutoff=30, which results in calling the serial version of the code for tasks that receive n=29 and n=28, as we can see in Figure 6-5.

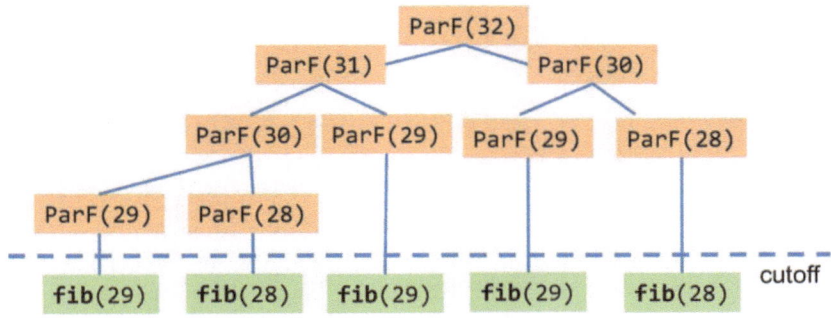

Figure 6-5. *Calling tree after invoking* `parallel_fib(32)` – `ParF(32)` *in the figure for the sake of saving space –* `fib()` *is the base case serially implemented*

If after looking at Figure 6-5 you think that it is silly to compute fib(29) in three different tasks and fib(28) in two additional ones, you are right – it is silly! As a disclaimer, we already said that this is not the optimal implementation but a commonly used recursive example that serves our educational interests. A clear optimization would be to implement recursion in a manner such that already computed Fibonacci numbers are not recomputed again, thus achieving the optimal $O(n)$ complexity, but this is not our goal today. You may also be thinking, after looking at Figure 6-4, why in the world we are once again revisiting the parallel_invoke that was already covered way back in Chapter 2. But not to worry, it's just a way to introduce a small example that can start our journey into directly using tasks with task_group.

The Lower-Level Approach: **task_group**

Figure 6-6 shows the member functions of the class task_group. task_group is the way to create and manage tasks in oneTBB. If you are familiar with the old very low-level tasking API, tbb::task, from earlier versions of TBB, you can find a comparison and migration examples in Chapter 12.

```
namespace tbb {

    class task_group {
    public:
        task_group();
        task_group(task_group_context& context);

        ~task_group();

        template<typename Func>
        void run(Func&& f);

        template<typename Func>
        task_handle defer(Func&& f);

        void run(task_handle&& h);

        template<typename Func>
        task_group_status run_and_wait(const Func& f);

        task_group_status run_and_wait(task_handle&& h);

        task_group_status wait();
        void cancel();
    };

    bool is_current_task_group_canceling();

} // namespace tbb
```

Figure 6-6. *The class definition for* task_group *as described in [scheduler.task_ group]. The Func type must meet the Function Objects requirements described in the [function.objects] section of the ISO C++ standard*

A re-implementation of the Fibonacci code that relies on task_group is presented in Figure 6-7. At first glance, this is just a more verbose way of implementing the code of Figure 6-4, where we used parallel_invoke. However, we would like to underscore that, unlike the parallel_invoke alternative, we now have a handle to a group of tasks, g, and as we will discuss later, this enables some additional possibilities, such as task cancellation. Also, by explicitly calling the member functions g.run() and g.wait(), we spawn the new tasks and wait for them to finish their computation at two different program points; separation between run() and wait() would allow for the caller thread to do some computation between spawning some tasks and waiting for them in the blocking call wait().

```
long parallel_fib(long n) {
  if(n<cutoff) {
    return fib(n);
  }
  else {
    long x, y;
    tbb::task_group g;
    g.run([&]{x=parallel_fib(n-1);}); // spawn a task
    g.run([&]{y=parallel_fib(n-2);}); // spawn another task
    g.wait();                         // wait for both tasks to complete
    return x+y;
  }
}
```

Figure 6-7. *Parallel Fibonacci based on* task_group. *Sample code tasks/task_group_fib.cpp*

In addition, task_group also offers other interesting member functions that can come handy in some situations:

void run_and_wait(const Func& f) is equivalent to {run(f); wait();} but guarantees that f runs on the current thread. By choosing this combined function, we allow the implementation to bypass the TBB scheduler. If we first call run(f), we basically spawn a task that gets enqueued in the worker thread-local queue. When calling wait(), we call the scheduler that dequeues the just enqueued task if nobody else has stolen it in the meantime. The purpose of run_and_wait is twofold: first, we can avoid the overhead of enqueueing-scheduling-dequeuing steps, and second, we avoid the potential stealing that can happen while the task is in the queue.

void cancel() cancels all tasks in this task_group. Maybe the computation was triggered from a user interface (UI) that also includes a "cancel" button. If the user now presses this button, there is a way to stop the computation. In Chapter 9, we further elaborate on cancellation and exception handling.

Until all the tasks in the task_group are complete or are canceled, task_group_status wait() blocks. It returns the final status of the task_group. Return values can be complete (all tasks in the group have finished) or canceled (task_group received a cancellation request).

In our parallel implementation of Figure 6-7, each call to parallel_fib creates a new task_group so it is possible to cancel one branch without affecting the others, as we will see in Chapter 9.

When we use a single `task_group`, we need to be careful to avoid submitting all of the tasks sequentially from a single task or thread. Consider, for example, that we might be tempted to write code like Figure 6-8.

```
#include <tbb/tbb.h>

void f();

void serializedCallsToRun(tbb::task_group& g,
                          int depth) {
  int n = 1<<depth;
  for (int i = 1; i < n; ++i) {
    g.run([]() { f(); });
  }
}

void serialCalls(int depth) {
  tbb::task_group g;
  serializedCallsToRun(g, depth);
  g.wait();
}
```

Figure 6-8. *Serialized calls to* `task_group::run` *that create a bottleneck by spawning all tasks from a single thread. Sample code* `tasks/task_group_poor_scaling.cpp`

As we see in Figure 6-8, n tasks will be spawned one after the other and by the same thread. The other worker threads will be forced to steal every task created by the one executing `g.run()`. This will certainly kill the performance, especially if `f()` is a fine-grained task and the number of worker threads is high. The recommended alternative is the one used in Figure 6-7 where a recursive deployment of tasks is exercised. In that approach, the worker threads steal at the beginning of the computation, and ideally, in log2(p) steps, where p is the number of threads, all p threads are working in their own tasks that in turn enqueue more tasks in their local queues. For example, for p=4, the first thread, A, spawns two tasks and starts working in one, while Thread B steals the other. Now, Threads A and B spawn two tasks each (four in total) and start working in two of them, but the other two are stolen by Threads C and D. From then on, all four threads are working and enqueueing more tasks in their local queues and stealing again only when they run out of local tasks. When working from local queues, synchronization overheads are lower, and cache locality tends to be higher. The benefits of this type of distribution of tasks are described in detail in Chapter 10, including in Figure 10-11.

We can change the code in Figure 6-8 to recursively spawn tasks as a tree as shown in Figure 6-9. On our test system, the tree-based creation of tasks in Figure 6-9 was able to execute the same number of tasks as the serial case in 30% of the time, even though there are the same total number of calls to f() in both Figures 6-8 and 6-9.

```cpp
#include <tbb/tbb.h>

void f();

void treeCallsToRun(tbb::task_group& g, int depth) {
  if (depth>1) {
    g.run([&g, depth]() {
      treeCallsToRun(g, depth-1);
    });
    g.run([&, depth]() {
      treeCallsToRun(g, depth-1);
    });
  }
  f();
}

void treeCalls(int depth) {
  tbb::task_group g;
  treeCallsToRun(g, depth);
  g.wait();
}
```

Figure 6-9. *A recursive algorithm that uses* task_group *to spawn tasks recursively from within possibly different worker threads. Sample code* tasks/task_group_ poor_scaling.cpp

The **task_group** Functions Are Thread-Safe

The code in Figure 6-9 works because the member functions in task_group are thread-safe. Therefore, different threads can safely call run and wait on the same task_group object in parallel. Even so, accessing the same task_group from different threads (or tasks) must be done carefully if calls to run and wait might overlap. The function wait returns when there are no more tasks executing in the task_group. If one thread is calling run at roughly the same time another thread is calling wait, there may be a race to determine if the run happens before or after the call to wait. If run happens before wait, then wait will not return until after that task is complete. If wait happens first, and the count of tasks is zero when wait is called, it will return without waiting for the task that has not yet been run.

In Figure 6-9, there is no dangerous race. Tasks are added recursively from within other tasks, and so the count of tasks executing in the task_group g can never be zero when a call to g.run is made from one of these tasks.

Deferred Tasks

Earlier we noted that one advantage of task_group is that it lets us separate the running of a task (task_group::run) from the point in the code where we wait for the tasks to complete (task_group::wait). Deferred tasks provide yet another point of code separation. A deferred task is represented by a tbb::task_handle and is created by calling (task_group::defer). Using tbb::task_handle we have a separate point to define the task without immediately spawning it. In Figure 6-6, we can see that the functions in task_group that spawn tasks, task_group::run and task_group::run_and_wait, have overloads that receive a tbb::task_handle in place of the function object.

A tbb::task_handle is more than just a pointer to the user body – it is also a handle to the structure that TBB will use for scheduling and executing the task.

Figure 6-10 expands on the Fibonacci example from Figure 6-7 but uses deferred tasks. In this example, it does not seem necessary to create a separate function to define the tasks, but in cases where there is complicated logic for creating the task, it is often convenient to encapsulate that logic in a separate function. task_group::defer and tbb::task_handle allow us to define our tasks in one part of our code and run them later in another part.

```
tbb::task_handle make_task(tbb::task_group& g, long& r, long n);

long parallel_fib(long n) {
  if(n<cutoff) {
    return fib(n);
  }
  else {
    long x, y;
    tbb::task_group g;
    tbb::task_handle h1 = make_task(g, x, n-1);
    tbb::task_handle h2 = make_task(g, y, n-2);
    g.run(std::move(h1));
    g.run(std::move(h2));
    g.wait();                    // wait for both tasks to complete
    return x+y;
  }
}

tbb::task_handle make_task(tbb::task_group& g, long& r, long n) {
  return g.defer([&r,n]{r=parallel_fib(n);});
}
```

Figure 6-10. *Parallel Fibonacci based on* `task_group` *that spawns all tasks recursively and uses deferred tasks to separate the definition of the tasks from the running of the tasks. Sample code* `tasks/task_group_fib_defer.cpp`

If you are familiar with some of the optimizations exposed by the lowest-level tasking API in older versions of TBB, deferred tasks can be used as a migration strategy for existing code that uses continuation passing, task recycling and scheduler bypass. See Chapter 12 for more information on migration of those techniques.

Tasks with Dependencies

In general, the flow graph is now the high-level way to express dependencies in TBB. Even so, we can implement manual reference counting if needed and then use `tbb::task_group` to run tasks once they are ready. In Chapter 2, we already explored how explicit reference counting can be used with `tbb::parallel_for_each` to add more work as it is ready to run. In Chapter 2, we implemented a forward substitution example using `tbb::parallel_for_each` and referencing counting. We can do the same for tasks run using `tbb::task_group` as shown in Figures 6-11 and 6-12.

```
const int block_size = 512;
using BlockIndex = std::pair<size_t, size_t>;

void parallelFwdSubTaskGroup(std::vector<double>& x,
                             const std::vector<double>& a,
                             std::vector<double>& b) {
  const int N = x.size();
  const int num_blocks = N / block_size;

  // create reference counts
  std::vector<std::atomic<char>> ref_count(num_blocks*num_blocks);
  ref_count[0] = 0;
  for (int r = 1; r < num_blocks; ++r) {
    ref_count[r*num_blocks] = 1;
    for (int c = 1; c < r; ++c) {
      ref_count[r*num_blocks + c] = 2;
    }
    ref_count[r*num_blocks + r] = 1;
  }

  BlockIndex top_left(0,0);

  tbb::task_group tg;
  tg.run([&]() {
    fwdSubTGBody(tg, N, num_blocks, top_left, x, a, b, ref_count);
  });
  tg.wait();
}
```

Figure 6-11. *Forward substitution based on* task_group *that uses reference counting to track dependencies before running tasks. Sample code* tasks/task_group_with_dependencies.cpp. *The forward substitution problem was discussed in detail in Chapter 2, with a diagram of the dependencies shown in Figure 2-14*

```
void fwdSubTGBody(tbb::task_group& tg,
                  int N, int num_blocks,
                  const std::pair<size_t, size_t> bi,
                  std::vector<double>& x,
                  const std::vector<double>& a,
                  std::vector<double>& b,
                  std::vector<std::atomic<char>>& ref_count) {
  auto [r, c] = bi;
  computeBlock(N, r, c, x, a, b);
  // add successor to right if ready
  if (c + 1 <= r && --ref_count[r*num_blocks + c + 1] == 0) {
    tg.run([&, N, num_blocks, r, c]() {
      fwdSubTGBody(tg, N, num_blocks,
                   BlockIndex(r, c+1), x, a, b, ref_count);
    });
  }
  // add successor below if ready
  if (r + 1 < (size_t)num_blocks
      && --ref_count[(r+1)*num_blocks + c] == 0) {
    tg.run([&, N, num_blocks, r, c]() {
      fwdSubTGBody(tg, N, num_blocks,
                   BlockIndex(r+1, c), x, a, b, ref_count);
    });
  }
}
```

Figure 6-12. *The body of the tasks used for the forward substitution sample based on* task_group. *Sample code **tasks/task_group_with_dependencies.cpp**. The forward substitution problem was discussed in detail in Chapter 2, with the code for* computeBlock *provided in Figure 2-15*

In Figure 6-11, std::atomic variables are used to track the readiness of a task to run. In the example, as described in more detail in Chapter 2, a task is ready to run when the block to its left and above are complete. Figure 6-12 shows the implementation of the fwdSubTGBody function that tracks these dependencies and runs tasks to process each block as their dependencies are satisfied.

MORE TASK GRAPH CONTROLS?

In the older versions of TBB, there was specific support in the lowest-level tasking API for reference counting, and this could be used to create low-level task graphs. The older tasking API also could be used to implement low-level optimizations. At the time of publication for this book, this support is not (yet?) available in the current version of TBB. Some in the TBB community have expressed interest in having an API that reintroduces a more direct approach for creating and managing task dependencies, and there is ongoing work in that direction – stay tuned to discussions in the oneTBB community to find out more as this develops. In the meantime, Chapter 12 provides guidance on how to migrate many of these older low-level task-based implementations and optimizations.

Suspending and Resuming Tasks

In general, TBB tasks are executed non-preemptively. The TBB scheduler does not stop a task that is currently executing on a worker thread and starts executing another task in its place. This means that if our task is blocked waiting for something to happen, for example, an I/O operation to finish or an offload to an accelerator to complete, the task occupies one of the TBB worker threads while it is waiting.

TBB is designed for computational parallelism, and so non-preemptive execution makes sense in most cases – but not always.

In those cases where it does not make sense, developers can use TBB's *resumable* task support to pause a task and then resume it later, freeing up the worker thread. This is a form of cooperative threading, where different user functions may suspend and later resume tasks when the results they need to continue are ready. The two primary functions in the API are tbb::task::suspend and tbb::task::resume:

```
using tbb::task::suspend_point = /* implementation-defined */;
template < typename Func > void tbb::task::suspend( Func );
void tbb::task::resume( tbb::task::suspend_point );
```

The tbb::task::suspend function is called from within a task. The task can be created by a generic algorithm, flow graph, or task_group. tbb::task::suspend captures the current context, invokes the user-provided function with a tbb::task::suspend_point as an argument, and then suspends the current task execution. For example, tbb::task::suspend might be called from within the body of a parallel_for:

```
tbb::parallel_for(0, N, [&](int) {
  tbb::task::suspend(
    [&] (tbb::task::suspend_point tag) {
      async_activity.submit(tag);
    });
  // once resumed will start executing here:
  next_thing_to_do_after_resumed();
});
```

The user-provided function is executed to completion, but the program flow does not return from the call to suspend until tbb::task::resume(tag) has been called. This frees up the thread that was executing the suspended task to execute other TBB tasks.

The suspended task can be resumed by the same thread or any other thread by calling tbb::task::resume(tag) with the matching tag:

```
tbb::task::resume(tag);
```

When resumed, the task is scheduled to pick up execution again where the call to suspend would have returned. We should be aware that when the task is resumed after the suspension point, there is no guarantee that the same thread that called suspend will continue after the suspension point. The TBB implementation does guarantee that the same thread will execute the code in the case of top-level TBB calls (such as tbb::parallel_for and tbb::flow::graph::wait_for_all and tbb::task_arena::execute calls made from the main thread). But for nested cases, there is no such guarantee.

In Chapter 5, we used tbb::flow::async_node in a flow graph to prevent a worker thread from blocking while waiting for work on an accelerator to complete. Figure 6-13 shows a modified version of that example using resumable tasks.

```cpp
#include <iostream>
#include <utility>
#include <sycl/sycl.hpp>
#include <tbb/tbb.h>

int main() {
  const int N = 1000;
  int num_iterations = 3;

  try {
    sycl::queue sycl_q;

    tbb::parallel_for(0, num_iterations,
      [&](int id) {
        int *a = sycl::malloc_shared<int>(N, sycl_q);
        tbb::task::suspend([=,&sycl_q](tbb::task::suspend_point tag) {
          auto sycl_event = sycl_q.fill(a, id, N);
          sycl_q.submit([=](sycl::handler& sycl_h) {
            sycl_h.depends_on(sycl_event); // run after sycl_event is done
            sycl_h.host_task([tag]() {
              tbb::task::resume(tag);
            });
          });
        });
        if (std::any_of(a, a+N, [id](int i) { return i != id; })) {
          std::printf("ERROR: unexpected fill result\n");
        } else {
          std::printf("Well-formed fill for id %d\n", id);
        }
      }
    );
  } catch (const sycl::exception&) {
    std::cout << "No CPU SYCL device on this platform\n";
  }
  return 0;
}
```

Figure 6-13. *`tbb::task::suspend` is used to prevent a task created by a parallel_for from blocking while work is offloaded to a device using SYCL. A SYCL host task (which is run by the SYCL Runtime) resumes the task when the work is done by calling `tbb::task::resume`. Sample code **tasks/resumable_tasks.cpp***

In Figure 6-13, each iteration of a `parallel_for` allocates an array and offloads that array to a SYCL device using a SYCL queue, on which it is filled with values. Just like in Chapter 5, this example still does not do any useful work and is for demonstration purposes only. And again, as in Chapter 5, we are not going to explain the SYCL code itself. If you want to learn more about SYCL, we recommend the book titled *Data Parallel C++* that James Reinders helped author.

The function passed to `tbb::task::suspend` in Figure 6-13 submits a kernel to do the fill operation and then attaches another SYCL task that depends on its completion. This dependent task calls `resume` to restart the `parallel_for` task when the work on the device is complete.

Summary

In this chapter, we introduced `task_group` as the primary way to execute tasks outside of high-level TBB algorithms. We showed that it can be used in recursive algorithms to generate task trees and with reference counting to create task graphs. We noted that developers that are familiar with the older TBB low-level tasking API can find additional information on how to migrate to `task_group` in Chapter 12.

We also touched on resumable tasks, a feature for cooperative threading that can free up worker threads that are waiting on asynchronous work. Resumable tasks work with tasks that are generated by any of the high-level TBB algorithms, a `task_group`, or a flow graph. We saw a similar feature that is specific for the flow graph, `async_node`, in Chapter 5.

CHAPTER 7

Memory Allocation

This chapter discusses a *critical* part of any parallel program: scalable memory allocation, which includes the use of new as well as explicit calls to malloc, calloc, and so on. Scalable memory allocation can be used regardless of whether we use any other part of Threading Building Blocks (TBB). In addition to interfaces to use directly, TBB offers "proxy" libraries to automatically replace C/C++ functions for dynamic memory allocation, which is an easy, effective, and popular way to get a performance boost without any code changes. This is important and works regardless of how advanced you are in your usage of C++, specifically whether you use the modern and encouraged smart pointers (std::unique_ptr, std::shared_ptr, or std::weak_ptr) or the now discouraged raw pointers. The performance benefits of using a scalable memory allocator are significant because they directly address issues that would otherwise limit scaling and risk false sharing. TBB was among the first widely used scalable memory allocators, in no small part because it came free with TBB to help highlight the importance of including memory allocation considerations in any parallel program. It remains extremely popular today and is one of the best scalable memory allocators available.

Modern C++ programming (which favors smart pointers), combined with parallel thinking, encourages us to use TBB scalable memory allocators explicitly with std::allocate_shared or implicitly with std::make_shared.

Modern C++ Memory Allocation

While performance is especially interesting for parallel programming, *correctness* is a critical topic for *all* applications. Memory allocation/deallocation issues are a significant source of bugs in applications, and this has led to many additions to the C++ standard and a shift in what is considered modern C++ programming!

© Michael J. Voss, James R. Reinders 2025
M. J. Voss and J. R. Reinders, *Today's TBB*, https://doi.org/10.1007/979-8-8688-1270-5_7

Modern C++ programming *encourages* the use of managed memory allocation with the introduction of smart pointers in C++11 (make_shared, allocate_shared, etc.) and *discourages* extensive use of malloc or new. We have used std::make_shared in examples since the very first chapter of this book. The addition of std::aligned_alloc in C++17 provides for cache alignment to avoid false sharing but does not address scalable memory allocation. Many additional capabilities are in the works for future C++ revisions but without explicit support for scalability.

TBB continues to offer this critical piece for parallel programmers: *scalable memory allocation*. TBB does this in a fashion that fits perfectly with all versions of C++ and C standards. The heart and soul of the support in TBB can be described as *memory pooling by threads*. This pooling avoids performance degradations caused by unnecessary shifting of data between caches. TBB also offers scalable memory allocation combined with cache alignment, which offers the scalable attribute above what one can expect from simply using std::aligned_alloc. Cache alignment is not a default behavior because indiscriminate usage can greatly expand memory usage.

As we discuss in this chapter, the use of scalable memory allocation can be critical to performance. std::make_shared does not provide for the specification of an allocator, but there is a corresponding std::allocate_shared, which does allow the specification of an allocator.

This chapter focuses on scalable memory allocators, which should be used in whatever manner of C++ memory allocation is chosen for an application. Modern C++ programming, with parallel thinking, would encourage us to use std::allocate_shared explicitly with TBB scalable memory allocators or use std::make_shared implicitly with TBB by overriding the default new to use the TBB scalable memory allocator. Note std::make_shared is not affected by the new operator for a particular class because it actually allocates a larger block of memory to manage both the contents for a class and its extra space for bookkeeping (specifically, the atomic that is added to make it a smart pointer). That is why overriding the default new (to use the TBB allocator) will be sufficient to affect std::make_shared.

Manner of Use	Summary	Figure listing interfaces
C/C++ proxy	Most popular usage. Automatic replacements of standard memory allocation methods. No code changes required.	Figure 7-4 has a list of functions replaced by the proxy library.
C functions	C standard functions (e.g., malloc).	List of functions in Figure 7-10.
C++ classes	C++ standard interfaces (std:allocator).	List of classes in Figure 7-12.
Performance optimization tweaks	Ways to tweak performance (across any manner of usage) to meet particular needs, including use of large pages. Useful when optimizing for the ultimate in performance.	Functional interfaces and an environment variable listed in Figure 7-14.

Figure 7-1. *Ways to use the TBB scalable memory allocator*

Scalable Memory Allocation: What

This chapter is organized to discuss the scalable memory capabilities of TBB in four categories as listed in Figure 7-1. Features from all four categories can be freely mixed; we break them into categories only as a way to explain all the functionality. The C/C++ proxy library is by far the most popular way to use the scalable memory allocator.

The scalable memory allocator is cleanly separated from the rest of TBB so that our choice of memory allocator for concurrent usage is independent of our choice of parallel algorithm and container templates.

Scalable Memory Allocation: Why

While most of this book shows us how to improve the performance of our application by doing work in parallel, memory allocations and deallocations that are not thread-aware can undo our hard work! There are two primary issues at play in making careful memory allocation critical in a parallel program: contention for the allocator and cache effects.

When ordinary, nonthreaded allocators are used, memory allocation can become a serious bottleneck in a multithreaded program because each thread competes for a global lock for each allocation and deallocation of memory from a single global heap. Programs that run this way are not scalable. In fact, because of this contention, programs that make intensive use of memory allocation may actually slow down as the number of processor cores increases! Scalable memory allocators solve this by using more sophisticated data structures to largely avoid contention.

The other issue, caching effects, happens because the use of memory has an underlying mechanism in hardware for the caching of data. Data usage in a program will, therefore, have an implication on where data needs to be cached. If we allocate memory for Thread B and the allocator gives us memory that was recently freed by Thread A, it is highly likely that we are inadvertently causing data to be copied from cache to cache, which may reduce the performance of our application needlessly. Additionally, if memory allocations for separate threads are placed too closely together, they can share a cache line. We can describe sharing as *true sharing* (sharing the same object) or *false sharing* (no objects are shared, but objects happen to fall in the same cache line). Either type of sharing can have particularly dramatic negative consequences on performance, but *false sharing* is of particular interest because it can be avoided since no sharing was intended. We can avoid false sharing by using class `cache_aligned_allocator<T>` to always allocate beginning on a cache line and maintaining per-thread heaps, which are rebalanced from time to time if needed. This organization also helps with the prior contention issue.

The benefits of using a scalable memory allocator can easily be a 20–30% performance, and we have even heard of 4× program performance in extreme cases by simply relinking with a scalable memory allocator.

Avoiding False Sharing with Padding

Padding is needed if the internals of a data structure cause issues due to false sharing. In Chapter 8, we will use a histogram example. The buckets of the histogram and the locks for the buckets are both possible data structures that are packed tightly enough in memory to have more than one task updating data in a single cache line.

The idea of padding, in a data structure, is to space out elements enough that we do not share adjacent elements that would be updated via multiple tasks.

Regarding false sharing, the first measure we have to take is to rely on the `tbb::cache_aligned_allocator` or `std::aligned_alloc`, instead of `std::allocator` or `malloc`, when declaring the shared histogram (see Figure 8-20) as shown in Figure 7-2.

```
std::vector<atom_bin, tbb::cache_aligned_allocator<atom_bin>>
    hist_p(num_bins);
```

Figure 7-2. *Simple histogram vector of atomics. Sample code synchronization/ histogram_07_3rd_safe_parallel_cache_aligned.cpp*

However, this is just aligning the beginning of the histogram vector and ensuring that hist_p[0] will land at the beginning of a cache line. This means that hist_p[0], hist_p[1], ... , hist_p[15] are stored in the same cache line, which translates into false sharing when a thread increments hist_p[0] and another thread increments hist_p[15]. To solve this issue, we need to assure that each position of the histogram, each bin, is occupying a full cache line, which can be achieved using a padding strategy shown in Figure 7-3.

```
struct atom_bin {
  alignas(128) std::atomic<int> count;
};
std::vector<atom_bin, tbb::cache_aligned_allocator<atom_bin>>
  hist_p(num_bins);

std::for_each(image.begin(), image.end(),
              [&](uint8_t i){hist[i]++;});
```

Figure 7-3. *Getting rid of false sharing using padding in the histogram vector of atomics. Sample code synchronization/histogram_07_3rd_safe_parallel_cache_aligned.cpp*

As we can see in Figure 7-3, the array of bins, hist_p, is now a vector of structs, each one containing the atomic variable, with an alignment of 128 to ensure a false sharing safe implementation for caches lines on Intel processors (as of today).

Our false-sharing-free data structure does occupy 16 times more space than the original one. It is yet another example of the space–time trade-off that frequently arises in computer programming: now we occupy more memory, but the code is faster. Other examples are smaller code vs. loop unrolling, calling functions vs. function inlining, or processing of compressed data vs. uncompressed data.

This warrants that each bin of hist_p is occupying a full cache line, thanks to the alignas() method. Just one more thing! We love to write portable code, right? What if in a different or future architecture cache line size is different. No problem, the C++17 standard has the solution we are looking for:

```
struct atom_bin {
  alignas(std::hardware_destructive_interference_size)
    std::atomic<int> count;
};
std::vector<atom_bin, tbb::cache_aligned_allocator<atom_bin>>
  hist_p(num_bins);
```

Great, assuming that we have fixed the *false sharing* problem, what about the true sharing one?

Two different threads will eventually increment the same bin, which will be ping-pong from one cache to other. We need a better idea to solve this one! We show how to deal with this in Chapter 8 when we discuss *privatization and reduction*.

Scalable Memory Allocation Alternatives

These days, TBB is not the only option for scalable memory allocations. While we are very fond of it, we will introduce the most popular options in this section. When using TBB for parallel programming, it is essential that we use a scalable memory allocator whether it is the one supplied by TBB or another. Programs written using TBB can utilize any memory allocator solution.

TBB was the first popular parallel programming method to promote scalable memory allocation alongside the other parallel programming techniques because the creators of TBB understood the importance of including memory allocation considerations in any parallel program. The TBB memory allocator remains extremely popular today and is definitely still one of the best scalable memory allocators available.

The TBB scalable memory allocator can be used regardless of whether we use any other part of Threading Building Blocks (TBB). Likewise, TBB can operate with any scalable memory allocator.

The most popular alternatives to the TBB scalable memory allocator are jemalloc, tcmalloc, and llalloc. Like the scalable memory allocator in TBB, there are alternatives to malloc that emphasize fragmentation avoidance while offering scalable concurrency support. (Fragmentation in memory allocation is the inefficient use of memory, caused when free memory becomes a collection of small non-contiguous blocks, leading to difficulty in fulfilling allocation requests.) All three are available open source with liberal licensing (BSD or Apache).

There are some people who will tell you that they have compared tbbmalloc for their application with others and have found it to be superior for their application. This is quite common. However, there are some people who choose jemalloc or tcmalloc or llalloc even when using the rest of TBB extensively. This works too. The choice is yours to make.

jemalloc is the FreeBSD libc allocator. More recently, additional developer support features such as heap profiling and extensive monitoring/tuning hooks have been added. jemalloc is used by Facebook.

tcmalloc is part of Google's gperftools, which includes tcmalloc and some performance analysis tools. tcmalloc is used by Google.

llalloc from Lockless Inc. is available freely as an open source lockless memory allocator or can be purchased for use with closed source software.

The behavior of individual applications, and in particular patterns of memory allocations and releases, makes it impossible to pick a single fits-all winner from these options. We are confident that any choice of TBBmalloc, jemalloc, tcmalloc, and llalloc will be far superior to a default malloc function or new operator if they are of the non-scalable variety (this is becoming less and less an issue as time goes by – many mallocs are now optimized for threaded code, whereas none were when TBB first appeared).

Compilation Considerations

When compiling with programs with the Intel compilers or gcc, it is best to pass in the following flags:

- -fno-builtin-malloc (on Windows: /Qfno-builtin-malloc)

- -fno-builtin-calloc (on Windows: /Qfno-builtin-calloc)

- -fno-builtin-realloc (on Windows: /Qfno-builtin-realloc)

- -fno-builtin-free (on Windows: /Qfno-builtin-free)

This is because a compiler may make some optimizations assuming it is using its own built-in functions. These assumptions may not be true when using other memory allocators. Failure to use these flags may not cause a problem, but it is not a bad idea to be safe. It might be wise to check the compiler documentation of your favorite compiler.

Most Popular Usage (C/C++ Proxy Library): How

Using the proxy libraries, we can globally replace new/delete and malloc, calloc, realloc, free, and other routines with a dynamic memory interface replacement technique. This automatic way to replace malloc and other C/C++ functions for dynamic memory allocation is by far the most popular way to use the TBB scalable memory allocator capabilities. It is also very effective.

We can replace `malloc`, `calloc`, `realloc`, `free`, etc. (see Figure 7-4 for a complete list) and new/delete by using the `tbbmalloc_proxy` library. Using this method is easy and sufficient for most programs. The details of the mechanism used on each operating system vary a bit, but the net effect is the same everywhere. The library names are shown in Figure 7-5.

	Linux	macOS	Windows
Replaceable global C++ operators `new` and `delete`	YES	YES	YES
Standard C library functions: `malloc, calloc, realloc, free`	YES	YES	YES
Standard C library functions (added in C11): `aligned_alloc`	YES		
Standard POSIX function: `posix_memalign`	YES	YES	
Depending on the platform, other functions are also replaced (a list, current as of publication, follows below – any additions/changes will be in the TBB Developer Guide)			

GNU C library (glibc) specific functions:
 	
`malloc_usable_size, __libc_malloc,`
`__libc_calloc, __libc_memalign, __libc_free,`
`__libc_realloc, __libc_pvalloc, __libc_valloc`
	YES		

Microsoft C run-time library functions:
 	
`_msize, _aligned_malloc, _aligned_realloc,`
`_aligned_free, _aligned_msize`
			YES

`valloc`	YES	YES	
`malloc_size`		YES	
`memalign, pvalloc, mallopt`	YES		

Figure 7-4. *List of routines replaced by proxy*

	Release version library	**Debug version library**
Linux	`libtbbmalloc_proxy.so.2`	`libtbbmalloc_proxy_debug.so.2`
macOS	`libtbbmalloc_proxy.dylib`	`libtbbmalloc_proxy_debug.dylib`
Windows	`tbbmalloc_proxy.dll`	`tbbmalloc_proxy_debug.dll`

Figure 7-5. *Names of the proxy library*

Linux: malloc/new Proxy Library Usage

On Linux, we can do the replacement either by loading the proxy library at program load time using the LD_PRELOAD environment variable or by linking the main executable file with the proxy library (-ltbbmalloc_proxy). The Linux program loader must be able to find the proxy library and the scalable memory allocator library at program load time. For that, we may include the directory containing the libraries in the LD_LIBRARY_PATH environment variable or add it to /etc/ld.so.conf. There are two limitations for dynamic memory replacement: (1) glibc memory allocation hooks, such as __malloc_hook, are not supported, and (2) Mono (an open source implementation of Microsoft's .NET Framework) is not supported.

Windows: malloc/new Proxy Library Usage

On Windows, we must modify our executable. We can either force the proxy library to be loaded by adding an #include in our source code or use certain linker options as shown in Figure 7-6. The Windows program loader must be able to find the proxy library and the scalable memory allocator library at program load time. For that, we may include the directory containing the libraries in the PATH environment variable.

Include tbbmalloc_proxy.h (which causes it to load during application startup):

```
#include <tbb/tbbmalloc_proxy.h>
```

Or add the following parameters to the linker options for the binary (which is loaded during application startup). They can be specified for the EXE file or a DLL that is loaded upon application startup:

```
For win32 (note the triple underscore):
    tbbmalloc_proxy.lib /INCLUDE:"___TBB_malloc_proxy"
For win64 (note the double underscore)::
    tbbmalloc_proxy.lib /INCLUDE:"__TBB_malloc_proxy"
```

Figure 7-6. *Ways to use the proxy library on Windows (note: win32 has an additional underscore vs. win64)*

Windows developers have two additional features to assist with debug:

1. Setting the TBB_MALLOC_DISABLE_REPLACEMENT environment variable to 1 will disable replacement for program invocation while it is set. In this case, the program will use standard dynamic memory allocation functions. Note that the oneTBB memory allocation libraries are still required for the program to start even if their usage is disabled.

2. The TBB_malloc_replacement_log function creates a log indicating if dynamic memory replacement happens or not. This is unique to Windows due to the nature of replacement on Windows (which is much different than on other operating systems). An example is shown in Figure 7-7.

```cpp
#include "tbb/tbbmalloc_proxy.h"
#include <stdio.h>

int main () {
  char **func_replacement_log;
  int func_replacement_status =
        TBB_malloc_replacement_log (&func_replacement_log);

  if (func_replacement_status != 0) {
    printf ("tbbmalloc_proxy cannot replace memory allocation routines\n");
    for (char ** log_string = func_replacement_log;
         *log_string != 0;
         log_string++)
      printf("%s\n",*log_string);
  }
  return 0;
}
```

Example output:
```
tbbmalloc_proxy cannot replace memory allocation routines
Success: free (ucrtbase.dll), byte pattern: <C74424100000000008B4424>
Fail: _msize (ucrtbase.dll), byte pattern: <E90B000000CCCCCCCCCCCC>
```

Figure 7-7. *Windows replacement log utility function TBB_malloc_replacement_log. Sample code memalloc/windows_proxy.cpp*

Testing Our Proxy Library Usage

As a simple double-check to see that our program is taking advantage of a faster allocation, we can use the test program in Figure 7-8 on a multicore machine. In Figure 7-9, we show how we run this little test and the timing differences we saw on a quadcore virtual machine running Ubuntu Linux. On Windows directly, using the Visual Studio "Performance Profiler," we saw times of 94ms without the scalable memory allocator and 50ms with it (adding #include <tbb/tbbmalloc_proxy.h> into tbb_mem. cpp). The only purpose in timing like this is to verify that we are configured correctly. All these runs show how this little test can verify that the injection of the scalable memory allocator is working (for new/delete) and yielding nontrivial performance boosts! A trivial change to use malloc() and free() instead shows comparable results. We include it as tbb_malloc.cpp in the sample programs download associated with this book.

The example programs do use a lot of stack space, so "ulimit -s unlimited" (Linux/macOS) or "/STACK:10000000" (Visual Studio: Properties ➤ Configuration Properties ➤ Linker ➤ System ➤ Stack Reserve Size) will be important to avoid immediate crashes.

```
int main() {
  double *a[N];

  tbb::parallel_for(0, N-1, [&](int i) { a[i] = new double; });
  tbb::parallel_for(0, N-1, [&](int i) { delete a[i];        });

  return 0;
}
```

Figure 7-8. *Small test program for speed of new/delete. Sample code* *memalloc/tbb_mem.cpp*

```
Default is proxy usage controlled by environment variable:
g++ -o tbb_mem tbb_mem.cpp -ltbb

time ./tbb_mem
real    0m0.090s
user    0m0.301s
sys     0m0.099s

export LD_PRELOAD=$TBBROOT/lib/libtbbmalloc_proxy.so
time ./tbb_mem
real    0m0.020s
user    0m0.188s
sys     0m0.039s

unset LD_PRELOAD
time ./tbb_mem
real    0m0.091s
user    0m0.272s
sys     0m0.102s

or… alternately (always with proxy):
g++ -o tbb_mem tbb_mem.cpp -ltbb -ltbbmalloc_proxy
time ./tbb_mem
real    0m0.025s
user    0m0.190s
sys     0m0.029s
```

Figure 7-9. *Running and timing code from Figure 7-8 – sample outputs*

F a m i l y 1	`void *scalable_malloc (size_t size)`	`malloc` analogue.
	`void scalable_free (void *ptr)`	free analogue.
	`void *scalable_realloc (void *ptr, size_t size)`	realloc analogue.
	`void *scalable_calloc (size_t nobj, size_t size)`	calloc analogue complementing `scalable_malloc`.
	`int scalable_posix_memalign (void **memptr, size_t alignment, size_t size)`	`posix_memalign` analogue.
F a m i l y 2	`void *scalable_aligned_malloc (size_t size, size_t alignment)`	`posix_memalign` analogue.
	`void *scalable_aligned_realloc (void *ptr, size_t size, size_t alignment)`	realloc analogue complementing `scalable_malloc`
	`void scalable_aligned_free (void *ptr)`	free analogue for a previously allocated by `scalable_aligned_malloc` or `scalable_aligned_remalloc`
A l l F a m i l i e s	`size_t scalable_msize (void *ptr)`	msize/malloc_size/malloc_us able_size analogue. Returns the usable size of a memory block previously allocated by scalable_x, or 0 (zero) if ptr does not point to such a block.
	`int scalable_allocation_mode (int param, intptr_t value)`	Set TBB allocator-specific allocation modes. *Discussed in a section titled "Performance Tuning: some control knobs" near the end of this chapter.*
	`int scalable_allocation_command (int cmd, void *param)`	Call TBB allocator-specific commands. *Discussed in a section titled "Performance Tuning: some control knobs" near the end of this chapter.*

Figure 7-10. *Functions offered by the TBB scalable memory allocator*

C Functions: Scalable Memory Allocators for C

A set of functions, listed in Figure 7-10, provide a C-level interface to the scalable memory allocator. Since TBB programming uses C++, these interfaces are not here for TBB users – they are here for use with C code.

Each allocation routine scalable_x behaves analogously to a library function x. The routines form the two families shown in Figure 7-11. Storage allocated by a scalable_x function in one family must be freed or resized by a scalable_x function in the same family and not by a C standard library function. Similarly, any storage allocated by a C standard library function, or C++ new, should not be freed or resized by a scalable_x function.

These functions are defined by the specific #include <tbb/scalable_allocator.h>.

Family	Allocation Routine	Deallocation Routine	Analogous Library

1	`scalable_malloc`
	`scalable_calloc`
	`scalable_realloc`
		`scalable_free`	C standard library

	`scalable_posix_memalign`		POSIX
2	`scalable_aligned_malloc` `scalable_aligned_realloc`	`scalable_aligned_free`	Microsoft C run-time

Figure 7-11. *Coupling of allocate–deallocate functions by families*

`tbb::cache_aligned_allocator< T >`	Scalable memory allocation, aligned to begin on a cache line. Helps avoid false sharing, but alignment can come at some cost in additional memory consumption.
`tbb::scalable_allocator< T >`	Scalable memory allocation. Calling this directly will fail if the TBBmalloc library is not available.
`tbb::tbb_allocator< T >`	The class selects `tbb::scalable_allocator` when available, and falls back on standard `malloc` when the TBBmalloc library is not available. Calling this will work even if the TBBmalloc library is not available.

Figure 7-12. *Classes offered by the TBB scalable memory allocator*

C++ Classes: Scalable Memory Allocators for C++

While the proxy library offers a blanket solution to adopting scalable memory allocation, it is all based on specific capabilities that we might choose to use directly. TBB offers C++ classes for allocation in three ways: (1) allocators with the signatures needed by the C++ STL `std::allocator<T>`, (2) memory pool support for STL containers, and (3) a specific allocator for aligned arrays.

Allocators with `std::allocator<T>` Signature

A set of classes, listed in Figure 7-12, provide a C++-level interface to the scalable memory allocator. TBB has three template classes (`tbb_allocator`, `cache_aligned_allocator`, and `scalable_allocator`) that support the same signatures as `std::allocator<T>` per the C++ standards. This includes supporting `<void>` in addition to <T>, per the C++11 and prior standards, which was deprecated in C++17. This means they can be passed as allocation routines to be used by STL class templates such as vector. All four classes model an allocator concept that meets all the "allocator requirements" of C++, but with additional guarantees required by the standard for use with ISO C++ containers.

scalable_allocator

The scalable_allocator class template allocates and frees memory in a way that scales with the number of processors. Using a scalable_allocator in place of std::allocator may improve program performance. Memory allocated by a scalable_allocator should be freed by a scalable_allocator, not by a std::allocator.

The scalable_allocator allocator class template requires that the TBBmalloc library be available. If the library is missing, calls to the scalable_allocator will fail. In contrast, if the memory allocator library is not available, the other allocators (tbb_allocator or cache_aligned_allocator) fall back on malloc and free.

This class is defined with #include <tbb/scalable_allocator.h> and is notably not included by the (usually) all-inclusive tbb/tbb.h.

tbb_allocator

The tbb_allocator class template allocates and frees memory via the TBBmalloc library if it is available; otherwise, it reverts to using malloc and free. The cache_aligned_allocator and zero_allocator use tbb_allocator; therefore, they offer the same fallback on malloc, but scalable_allocator does not and therefore will fail if the TBBmalloc library is unavailable. This class is defined with #include <tbb/tbb_allocator.h>.

cache_aligned_allocator

The cache_aligned_allocator class template offers both scalability and protection against false sharing. It addresses false sharing by making sure each allocation is done on a separate cache line.

Use cache_aligned_allocator only if false sharing is likely to be a real problem (see Figure 7-2). The functionality of cache_aligned_allocator comes at some cost in space because it allocates in multiples of cache-line-size memory chunks, even for a small object. The padding is typically 128 bytes. Hence, allocating many small objects with cache_aligned_allocator may increase memory usage.

Trying both tbb_allocator and cache_aligned_allocator and measuring the resulting performance for a particular application is a good idea.

Note that protection against false sharing between two objects is guaranteed only if both are allocated with cache_aligned_allocator. For instance, if one object is allocated by cache_aligned_allocator<T> and another object is allocated some other way, there is no guarantee against false sharing because cache_aligned_allocator<T> starts an allocation on a cache line boundary but does not necessarily allocate to the end of a cache line. If an array or structure is being allocated, since only the start of the allocation is aligned, the individual array or structure elements may land together on cache lines with other elements. An example of this, along with padding to force elements onto individual cache line, is show in Figure 7-3.

This class is defined with #include <tbb/cache_aligned_allocator.h>.

Replacing new and delete Selectively

There are several reasons one might develop custom new/delete operators, including error checking, debugging, optimization, and usage statistics gathering.

We can think of new/delete as coming in variations for individual objects and for arrays of objects. Additionally, C++11 defines throwing, nonthrowing, and placement versions of each of these: either the global set (::operator new, ::operator new[], ::operator delete, and ::operator delete[]) or the class-specific sets (for class X, we have X::operator new, X::operator new[], X::operator delete, and X::operator delete[]). Finally, C++17 adds an optional alignment parameter to all versions of new.

If we want to globally replace all the new/delete operators and do not have any custom needs, we will use the proxy library. This also has the benefit of replacing malloc/free and related C functions.

For custom needs, it is most common to overload the class-specific operators rather than the global operators. This section shows how to replace the global new/delete operators as an example, which can be customized for particular needs. We show throwing and nonthrowing versions, but we did not override the placement versions since they do not actually allocate memory. We also did not implement versions with

212

alignment (C++17) parameters. It is also possible to replace new/delete operators for individual classes using the same concepts, in which case you may choose to implement placement versions and alignment capabilities. All these are managed by TBB if the proxy library is used.

Figure 7-13 shows a way to replace new and delete. All versions of new and delete should be replaced at once, which amounts to four versions of new and four versions of delete. Of course, it is necessary to link with the scalable memory library.

Our example chooses to ignore any new handler because there are thread safety issues. Our variation of the basic signature includes the additional parameter const std::nothrow_t& that means that this operator will not throw an exception but will return NULL if the allocation fails. These nonthrowing exception operators can be used for C runtime libraries.

```cpp
#include <tbb/scalable_allocator.h>

// No retry loop because we assume that
// scalable_malloc does all it takes to allocate
// the memory, so calling it repeatedly
// will not improve the situation at all

void* operator new (size_t size, const std::nothrow_t&)
{
  if (size == 0) size = 1;
  if (void* ptr = scalable_malloc (size))
    return ptr;
  return NULL;
}

void* operator new[] (size_t size, const std::nothrow_t&)
{
  return operator new (size, std::nothrow);
}
void operator delete (void* ptr, const std::nothrow_t&)
{
  if (ptr != 0) scalable_free (ptr);
}

void operator delete[] (void* ptr, const std::nothrow_t&)
{
  operator delete (ptr, std::nothrow);
}
```

Figure 7-13. *Demonstration of replacement of new and delete operators. Sample code memalloc/replace_new_n_delete.cpp*

Performance Tuning: Some Control Knobs

TBB offers some special controls regarding allocations from the OS, huge page support, and flushing of internal buffers. Each of these is provided to fine-tune performance.

Huge pages (*large pages* on Windows) are used to improve the performance for programs that utilize a very large amount of memory. In order to use huge pages, we need a processor and an operating system with support, and then we need to do something so our application takes advantage of huge pages. Fortunately, most systems meet these requirements, and TBB includes built-in support for huge pages.

What Are Huge Pages?

In most cases, a processor allocates memory 4K bytes at a time in what are commonly called pages. Virtual memory systems use page tables to map addresses to actual memory locations. Without diving in too deep, suffice to say that the more pages of memory that an application uses, the more page descriptors are needed, and having a lot of page descriptors flying around causes performance issues for a variety of reasons. To help with this issue, modern processors support additional page sizes that are much larger than 4K (e.g., 2MB). For a program using 2GB of memory, 524,288 page descriptors are needed to describe the 2GB of memory with 4K pages. Only 1,024 page descriptors are needed using 2MB descriptors and only two if 1GB descriptors are available. Of course, nothing is perfect, and large pages can reduce performance in some cases. On multi-socket systems, enabling huge pages can cause memory migration between sockets (NUMA targets) to become more expensive if using certain techniques (e.g., auto-NUMA, memory tiering), since the OS now needs to copy a whole large page (e.g., 2MB). As always, some attention is needed when tuning to verify actual results based on the behavior of particular applications.

TBB Support for Huge Pages

To use huge pages with TBB memory allocation, it should be explicitly enabled by calling `scalable_allocation_mode(TBBMALLOC_USE_HUGE_PAGES,1)` or by setting the `TBB_MALLOC_USE_HUGE_PAGES` environment variable to 1. The environment variable is useful when substituting the standard malloc routines with the `tbbmalloc_proxy` library.

These provide ways to tweak the algorithms used for all usages of the TBB scalable memory allocator (regardless of the method of usage: proxy library, C functions, or C++ classes). The functions take precedence over any environment variable settings. These are definitely not for casual use; they are here for self-proclaimed "control freaks" and offer great ways to optimize performance for particular needs. We recommend careful evaluation of the performance impact on an application, in the target environment, when using these features.

Of course, both methods assume that the system/kernel is configured to allocate huge pages. The TBB memory allocator also supports pre-allocated and transparent huge pages, which are automatically allocated by the Linux kernel when suitable. Huge pages are not a panacea; they can have negative impact on performance if their usage is not well considered.

The functions, as listed in Figure 7-14, are defined with #include <tbb/tbb_allocator.h>.

int scalable_allocation_mode (int mode, intptr_t value) mode = TBBMALLOC_USE_HUGE_PAGES or TBBMALLOC_SET_SOFT_HEAP_LIMIT	Set TBB allocator-specific allocation modes.
Environment variable: TBB_MALLOC_USE_HUGE_PAGES	A value of "1" (one) will enable the use of huge pages by the allocator if supported by the operating system.
int scalable_allocation_command (int cmd, void *reserved) reserved should be zero	Call TBB allocator-specific commands.

Figure 7-14. *Ways to refine TBB scalable memory allocator behaviors*

scalable_allocation_mode(int mode, intptr_t value)

The scalable_allocation_mode function may be used to adjust the behavior of the scalable memory allocator. The arguments, described in the following two paragraphs, control aspects of behavior of the TBB allocators. The function returns TBBMALLOC_OK if the operation succeeded or TBBMALLOC_INVALID_PARAM if mode is not one of those described in the following subsections or if value is not valid for the given mode. A return value of TBBMALLOC_NO_EFFECT is possible for conditions described when they apply (see explanation of each function).

TBBMALLOC_USE_HUGE_PAGES

`scalable_allocation_mode(TBBMALLOC_USE_HUGE_PAGES,1)`

This function enables the use of huge pages by the allocator if supported by the operating system; a zero as the second parameter disables it. Setting the TBB_ MALLOC_USE_HUGE_PAGES environment variable to one has the same effect as calling `scalable_allocation_mode` to enable this mode. The mode set with `scalable_ allocation_mode` takes priority over the environment variable. The function will return `TBBMALLOC_NO_EFFECT` if huge pages are not supported on the platform.

TBBMALLOC_SET_SOFT_HEAP_LIMIT

`scalable_allocation_mode(TBBMALLOC_SET_SOFT_HEAP_LIMIT, size)`

This function sets a threshold of `size` bytes on the amount of memory the allocator takes from the operating systems. Exceeding the threshold will urge the allocator to release memory from its internal buffers; however, it does not prevent the TBB scalable memory allocator from requesting more memory when needed.

int scalable_allocation_command(int Cmd, void *param)

The `scalable_allocation_command` function may be used to command the scalable memory allocator to perform an action specified by the first parameter. The second parameter is reserved and must be set to zero. The function returns `TBBMALLOC_OK` if the operation succeeded or `TBBMALLOC_INVALID_PARAM` if `reserved` is not equal to zero or if `cmd` is not a defined command (`TBBMALLOC_CLEAN_ALL_BUFFERS` or `TBBMALLOC_CLEAN_ THREAD_BUFFERS`). A return value of `TBBMALLOC_NO_EFFECT` is possible as we describe next.

TBBMALLOC_CLEAN_ALL_BUFFERS

`scalable_allocation_command(TBBMALLOC_CLEAN_ALL_BUFFERS, 0)`

This function cleans internal memory buffers of the allocator and possibly reduces memory footprint. It may result in increased time for subsequent memory allocation requests. The command is not designed for frequent use, and careful evaluation of the performance impact is recommended. The function will return `TBBMALLOC_NO_EFFECT` if no buffers were released.

TBBMALLOC_CLEAN_THREAD_BUFFERS

`scalable_allocation_command(TBBMALLOC_CLEAN_THREAD_BUFFERS, 0)`

This function cleans internal memory buffers but only for the calling thread. It may result in increased time for subsequent memory allocation requests; careful evaluation of the performance impact is recommended. The function will return `TBBMALLOC_NO_EFFECT` if no buffers were released.

Summary

Using a scalable memory allocator is an essential element in any parallel program. The performance benefits can be incredibly significant. Without a scalable memory allocator, serious performance issues often arise due to contention for allocation, false sharing, and other useless cache-to-cache transfers. The TBB scalable memory allocation (TBBmalloc) capabilities include use of `new` as well as explicit calls to `malloc` and so on, all of which can be used directly or they can all be automatically replaced via the proxy library capability of TBB. The scalable memory allocation in TBB can be used regardless of whether we use any other part of TBB; the rest of TBB can be used regardless of which memory allocator is used (TBBmalloc, `tcmalloc`, `jemalloc`, `llalloc`, `malloc`, etc.).

CHAPTER 8

Synchronization

The three key things to know about synchronization are as follows:

1. Use it when needed; otherwise, some algorithms will not work reliably.

2. Find ways to avoid it as much as possible, in order to maximize the potential for performance from parallelism.

3. Algorithm choice has a lot to do with how much synchronization is needed.

In this chapter, we cover synchronization mechanisms and alternatives to achieve mutual exclusion. This prepares us to use them as needed.

An effective parallel algorithm hinges on its synchronization strategy and implementation. In this chapter, we will review many synchronization options – all of which have their time and place to use in the world. With a simple histogram example, we will see that some are fantastic options and others are absolutely terrible (assuming we want speedup!).

Equally important, we illustrate the process of rethinking an algorithm in our quest to minimize the need for synchronization. In our example, we start with a simple code following from a naïve approach that resorts to mutexes, evolve it to exploit atomic operations, and then further reduce the synchronization between threads, thanks to privatization and reduction techniques. In the latter of these, we show how to leverage thread-local storage (TLS) as a way to avoid highly contended mutual exclusion overhead. In this chapter, we assume you are, to some extent, familiarized with the concepts of "lock," "shared mutable state," "mutual exclusion," "thread safety," "data race," and other synchronization-related terminology. If not, a gentle introduction to them is provided in the Preface of this book.

© Michael J. Voss, James R. Reinders 2025
M. J. Voss and J. R. Reinders, *Today's TBB*, https://doi.org/10.1007/979-8-8688-1270-5_8

TBB no longer offers atomic operations (learn more on how to update legacy code in Chapter 12), because modern C++ supports portable atomic operations that are more than adequate. We discuss `std::atomic` in this chapter. TBB does offer scalable mutexes of various styles because the standard offerings of modern C++ can definitely be improved upon for serious parallel programming work. We discuss both `tbb::` and `std::` mutexes in this chapter. Nevertheless, we will endeavor to motivate why we should avoid using them if we can.

Regardless of how you do synchronization (`std::`, `tbb::`, etc.), the gem from this chapter is this: careful rethinking of our algorithms can often result in cleaner implementations that perform much better. We highly recommend reading this chapter until this lesson is deeply internalized.

Our Running Example: Histogram of an Image

Let us start with a simple example that can be implemented with different kinds of mutual exclusion (mutex) objects or atomics or even by avoiding most of the synchronization operations altogether. We will describe all these possible implementations with their pros and cons and use them to illustrate the use of mutexes, locks, atomic variables, and thread-local storage.

There are different kinds of histograms, but an image histogram is probably the most widely used, especially in image and video devices and image processing tools. For example, in almost all photo editing applications, we can easily find a palette that shows the histogram of any of our pictures, as we see in Figure 8-1.

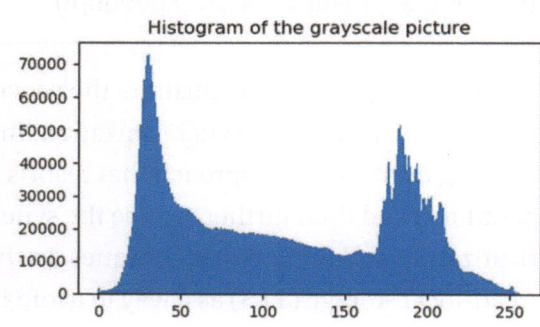

Figure 8-1. *Grayscale picture (of Ronda, Málaga) and its corresponding image histogram*

For the sake of simplicity, we will assume grayscale images. In this case, the histogram represents the number of pixels (y-axis) with each possible brightness value (x-axis). If image pixels are represented as bytes, then only 256 tones or brightness values are possible, with zero being the darkest tone and 255 the lightest tone. In Figure 8-1, we can see that the most frequent tone in the picture is a dark one: out of the 5M pixels, more than 70,000 have the tone 30 as we see at the spike around $x = 30$. Photographers and image professionals rely on histograms as an aid to quickly see the pixel tone distribution and identify whether or not image information is hidden in any blacked-out, or saturated, regions of the picture.

In Figure 8-2, we illustrate the histogram computation for a 4×4 image where the pixels can only have eight different tones from 0 to 7. The bidimensional image is usually represented as a unidimensional vector that stores the 16 pixels following a row-major order. Since there are only eight different tones, the histogram only needs eight elements, with indices from 0 to 7. The elements of the histogram vector are sometimes called "bins" where we "classify" and then count the pixels of each tone. Figure 8-2 shows the histogram, hist, corresponding to that particular image. The "4" we see stored in bin number 1 is the result of counting the four pixels in the image with tone 1. Therefore, the basic operation to update the value of the bins while traversing the image is hist[<tone>]++.

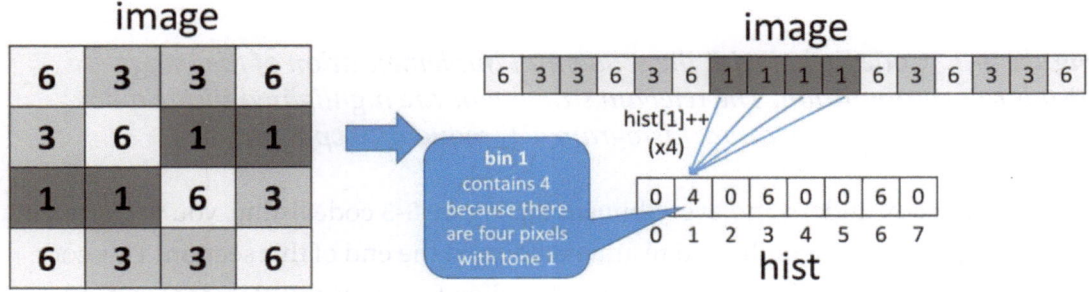

Figure 8-2. *Computing the histogram, hist, from an image with 16 pixels (each value of the image corresponds to the pixel tone)*

From an algorithmic point of view, a histogram is represented as an array of integers with enough elements to account for all possible tone levels. Assuming the image is an array of bytes, there are now 256 possible tones; thus, the histogram requires 256 elements or bins. The sequential code that computes the histogram of such an image is presented in Figure 8-3.

```cpp
int main() {
  constexpr long int n = 1000000;
  constexpr int num_bins = 256;

  // Initialize random number generator
  std::random_device seed;        // Random device seed
  std::mt19937 mte{seed()};       // mersenne_twister_engine
  std::uniform_int_distribution<> uniform{0,num_bins};
  // Initialize image
  std::vector<uint8_t> image; // empty vector
  image.reserve(n);                // image vector prealocated
  std::generate_n(std::back_inserter(image), n,
                  [&] { return uniform(mte); }
              );

  // Initialize histogram
  std::vector<int> hist(num_bins);

  // Serial execution
  tbb::tick_count t0 = tbb::tick_count::now();
  std::for_each(image.begin(), image.end(),
      [&hist] (uint8_t i) { hist[i]++; }
  );
  tbb::tick_count t1 = tbb::tick_count::now();
  double t_serial = (t1 - t0).seconds();

  std::cout << "Serial time: " << t_serial << std::endl;
  return 0;
}
```

Figure 8-3. *Code listing with the sequential implementation of the image histogram computation. The relevant statements are highlighted inside a box. Sample code synchronization/histogram_01_sequential.cpp*

If you already understand everything in the Figure 8-3 code listing, you will probably want to skip a few paragraphs and resume reading at the end of this section. This code first declares the vector image of size n (say 1 million for a megapixel image) and, after initializing the random number generator, it populates the image vector with random numbers in the range [0,255] of type uint8_t. For this, we use a mersenne_twister_engine, mte, which generates random numbers uniformly distributed in the range [0, num_bins) and inserts them into the image vector. Next, the hist vector is constructed with num_bins positions (initialized to zero by default). Note that we declared an empty vector image for which we later reserved n integers instead of constructing image(n). That way we avoid traversing the vector first to initialize it with zeros and once again to insert the random numbers.

The actual histogram computation could have been written in C/C++ using a more traditional approach

```
for (int i = 0; i < N; ++i) hist[image[i]]++;
```

which counts in each bin of the histogram vector the number of pixels of every tonal value. However, in the example of Figure 8-3, we fancied showing you a C++ alternative that uses the STL for_each algorithm and may be more natural for C++ programmers. Using the for_each STL approach, each actual element of the image vector (a tone of type uint8_t) is passed to the lambda expression, which increments the bin associated with the tone. For the sake of expediency, we rely on the tbb::tick_count class in order to account for the number of seconds required in the histogram computation. The member functions now and seconds are self-explanatory, so we do not include further explanation here.

An Unsafe Parallel Implementation

The first naïve attempt to parallelize the histogram computation consists of using a tbb::parallel_for as shown in Figure 8-4.

```
// Parallel execution
std::vector<int> hist_p(num_bins);
t0 = tbb::tick_count::now();
tbb::parallel_for(tbb::blocked_range<size_t>{0, image.size()},
                  [&](const tbb::blocked_range<size_t>& r)
                  {
                      for (size_t i = r.begin(); i < r.end(); ++i)
                        hist_p[image[i]]++;
                  });
t1 = tbb::tick_count::now();
double t_parallel = (t1 - t0).seconds();

std::cout << "Serial:  "   << t_serial   << ", ";
std::cout << "Parallel: " << t_parallel << ", ";
std::cout << "Speed-up: " << t_serial/t_parallel << std::endl;

if (hist != hist_p)
    std::cerr << "Parallel computation failed!!" << std::endl;
return 0;
```

Figure 8-4. *Code listing with the unsafe parallel implementation of the image histogram computation. Sample code synchronization/histogram_02_unsafe_parallel.cpp*

In order to compare the histogram resulting from the sequential implementation of Figure 8-3 and the result of the parallel execution, we declare a new histogram vector hist_p. Next, the crazy idea here is to traverse all the pixels in parallel … Why not? Aren't they independent pixels? To that end, we rely on the parallel_for template that was covered in Chapter 2 to have different threads traverse different chunks of the iteration space and, therefore, read different chunks of the image. However, this is not going to work: the comparison of vectors hist and hist_p (yes, hist!=hist_p does the right thing in C++), at the end of Figure 8-4, reveals that the two vectors are different due to a problem in our logic (of course, it is randomly possible they could be the same despite the error in our logic, but that is unlikely and did not happen when we ran it):

```
./histogram_02_unsafe_parallel
Serial: 0.253051, Parallel: 9.39047, Speed-up: 0.0269477
Parallel computation failed!!
```

As is the case for all examples in this book, we share some timings that we saw when preparing the book only so we can see relative changes between examples. All the example codes are available for you to try on any system you wish. We wish to instill a sense of relative changes that can (and should) happen in general with the programming techniques we are teaching in this book. The reader is always advised to check the timings they see on their preferred system configurations!

A problem arises because, in the parallel implementation, different threads are likely to increment the same shared bin at the same time. In other words, our code is not thread-safe. More formally, as it is, our parallel unsafe code exhibits "undefined behavior," which also means that our code is not correct. In Figure 8-5, we illustrate the problem supposing that there are two threads, A and B, running on cores 0 and 1, each one processing half of the pixels. Since there is a pixel with brightness 1 in the image chunk assigned to Thread A, it will execute hist_p[1]++. Thread B also reads a pixel with the same brightness and will also execute hist_p[1]++. If both increments coincide in time, one executed on core 0 and the other on core 1, it is highly likely that we will miss an increment.

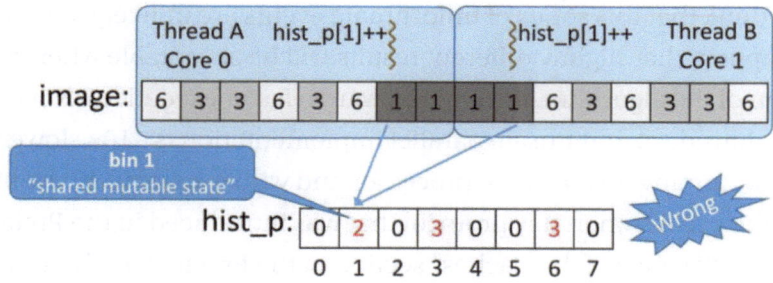

Figure 8-5. *Unsafe parallel update of the shared histogram vector*

This happens because the increment operation is not atomic (or indivisible). Instead, it usually consists of three operations: load the variable from memory into a register, increment the register, and store the register back into memory.[1] Using a more formal jargon, this kind of operation is known as a read–modify–write or RMW operation. Having concurrent writes to a shared variable is formally known as shared mutable state. In Figure 8-6, we illustrate a possible sequence of machine instructions corresponding to the C++ instruction hist_p[1]++.

hist_p[1]++ →	R1 on Core 0	R1 on Core 1	Time or cycle
load R1, @(hist_p+1)	1	1	X
add R1, R1, #1	2	2	X+1
store R1, @(hist_p+1)	2	2	X+2

Figure 8-6. *Unsafe update of a shared variable or shared mutable state*

If at the time of executing these two increments we have already found one previous pixel with brightness 1, hist_p[1] contains a value of one. This value could be read and stored in private registers by both threads, which will end up writing two in this bin instead of three, which is the correct number of pixels with brightness 1 that have been encountered thus far. Thinking about this case is somehow oversimplified, since it did not consider caches and cache coherence, but serves us to illustrate the data race issue. A more elaborate example is included in the Preface (see Figures 16 and 17).

---

[1] Due to the very essence of the von Neumann architecture, the computational logic is separated from the data storage so the data must be moved into where it can be computed, then computed, and finally moved back out to storage again.

We might think that this series of unfortunate events are unlikely to happen or, even if they happen, that slightly different results will be acceptable when running the parallel version of the algorithm. Is not the reward a faster execution? Not quite: as we saw in the previous page, our unsafe parallel implementation is ~10× slower than the sequential one (running on a 16-core processor and with n equal to 1,000 million pixels). The culprit is the cache coherency protocol that was introduced in the Preface (see "Locality and the Revenge of the Caches" section in the Preface). In the serial execution, the histogram vector is likely to be fully cached in the L1 cache of the core running the code. Since there are a million pixels, there will be a million increments in the histogram vector, most of them served at cache speed.

Note   On most x86 64-bit processors, a cache line can hold 16 integers (64 bytes). The histogram vector with 256 integers will need just 16 cache lines if the vector is adequately aligned. Therefore, after 16 cache misses (or much fewer if prefetching is exercised), all histogram bins are cached, and each one is accessed in only around three cycles (that's *very* fast!) in the serial implementation (assuming a large enough L1 cache and that the histogram cache lines are never evicted by other data).

On the other hand, in the parallel implementation, all threads will fight to cache the bins in per-core private caches, but when one thread writes in one bin on one core, the cache coherence protocol invalidates the 16 bins that fit in the corresponding cache line in all the other cores. This invalidation causes the subsequent accesses to the invalidated cache lines to cost an order of magnitude more time than the much-desired L1 access time. The net effect of this ping-pong mutual invalidation is that the threads of the parallel implementation end up incrementing un-cached bins, whereas the single thread of the serial implementation almost always increments cached bins. Remember once again that the one-megapixel image requires 1 million increments in the histogram vector, so we want to create an increment implementation that is as fast as possible. In this parallel implementation of the histogram computation, we find both false sharing (e.g., when Thread A increments hist_p[0] and Thread B increments hist_p[15], due to both bins landing in the same cache line) and true sharing (when both threads, A and B, increment hist_p[i]). We will deal with false and true sharing in subsequent sections.

A First Safe Parallel Implementation: Coarse-Grained Locking

Let's first solve the problem of parallel access to a shared data structure. We need a mechanism that prevents other threads from reading and writing in a shared variable when a different thread is already in the process of writing the same variable. In more layman terms, we want a fitting room where a single person can enter, see how the clothes fit, and then leaves the fitting room for the next person in the queue. Figure 8-7 illustrates that a closed door on the fitting room excludes others. In parallel programming, the fitting room door is called a mutex: when a person enters the fitting room, they acquire and hold a lock on the mutex by closing and locking the door, and when the person leaves, they release the lock by leaving the door open and unlocked. In more formal terms, a mutex is an object used to provide mutual exclusion in the execution of a protected region of code. This region of code that needs to be protected with mutual exclusion is usually known as a "critical section." The fitting room example also illustrates the concept of contention, a state where the resource (a fitting room) is wanted by more than one person at a time, as we can see in Figure 8-7(c). Since the fitting room can be occupied just by a single person at a time, the use of the fitting room is "serialized." Similarly, anything protected by a mutex can reduce the performance of a program: first, due to the extra overhead introduced by managing the mutex object and, second and more importantly, because the contention and serialization it can elicit. A key reason we want to reduce synchronization as much as possible is to avoid contention and serialization, which in turns limits scaling in parallel programs.

The fitting room analogy

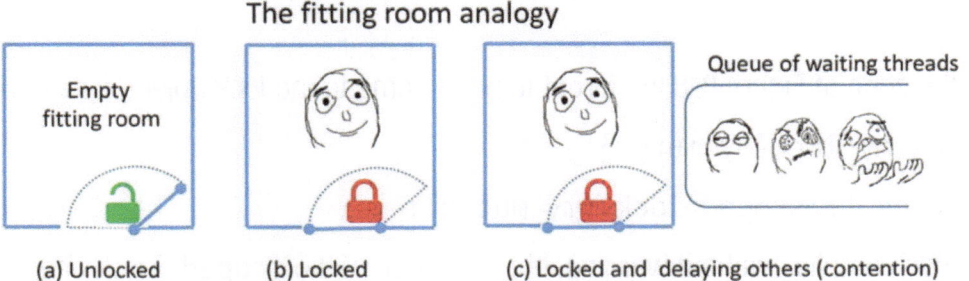

(a) Unlocked   (b) Locked   (c) Locked and delaying others (contention)

Figure 8-7. *Closing a door on a fitting room excludes others*

In this section, we focus on the TBB mutex classes and related mechanisms for synchronization. While TBB predates C++11, it is worth noting that C++11 did standardize support for a mutex class, although it is not as customizable as the ones in the TBB library. In TBB, the simplest mutex is the `spin_mutex` that can be used after including `tbb/spin_mutex.h` or the all-inclusive `tbb.h` header file. With this new tool in our hands, we can implement a safe parallel version of the image histogram computation as we can see in Figure 8-8.

```
#include <tbb/spin_mutex.h>

// Parallel execution
using my_mutex_t=tbb::spin_mutex;
my_mutex_t my_mutex;

parallel_for(tbb::blocked_range<size_t>{0, image.size()},
             [&](const tbb::blocked_range<size_t>& r)
             {
                 my_mutex_t::scoped_lock my_lock{my_mutex};
                 for (size_t i = r.begin(); i < r.end(); ++i)
                     hist_p[image[i]]++;
             });
```

Figure 8-8. *Code listing with our first safe parallel implementation of the image histogram computation that uses coarse-grained locking. Sample code synchronization/histogram_03_1st_safe_parallel.cpp*

The object `my_lock` that acquires a lock on `my_mutex` when it is created automatically unlocks (or releases) the lock in the object destructor, which is called when leaving the object scope. It is therefore advisable to enclose the protected regions with additional braces, {}, to keep the lifetime of the lock as short as possible, so that the other waiting threads can take their turn as soon as possible.

Note

If in the code of Figure 8-8 we forget to put a name to the lock object, for example

`// was my_lock{my_mutex}`

`my_mutex_t::scoped_lock {my_mutex};`

the code compiles without warning, but the scope of the `scoped_lock` ends at the semicolon. Without the name of the object (`my_lock`), we are constructing an anonymous/unnamed object of the `scoped_lock` class, and its lifetime ends at the semicolon because no named object outlives the definition. This is not useful, and the critical section is *not* protected with mutual exclusion.

A more explicit, but *not recommended*, alternative of writing the code of Figure 8-8 is presented in Figure 8-9.

```
parallel_for(tbb::blocked_range<size_t>{0, image.size()},
             [&](const tbb::blocked_range<size_t>& r)
             {
                 my_mutex_t::scoped_lock my_lock;
                 my_lock.acquire(my_mutex);
                 for (size_t i = r.begin(); i < r.end(); ++i)
                   hist_p[image[i]]++;
                 my_lock.release();
             });
```

Figure 8-9. *A discouraged alternative (best to do as in Figure 8-8) for acquiring a lock on a mutex. Sample code synchronization/histogram_03_1st_safe_parallel.cpp*

C++ pundits favor the alternative of Figure 8-8, known as "Resource Acquisition Is Initialization" (RAII), because it frees us from remembering to release the lock because it is tied to the object lifetime. More importantly, using the RAII version, the lock object destructor, where the lock is released, is also called in case of an exception so that we avoid leaving the lock acquired due to the exception. If in the version of Figure 8-9 an exception is thrown before the my_lock.release() member function is called, the lock is also released regardless, because the destructor is invoked and, there, the lock is released. If a lock leaves its scope but was previously released with the release() member function, then the destructor does nothing.

Back to our code of Figure 8-8, you may be wondering, "But wait. Haven't we serialized our parallel code with a coarse-grained lock?" Yes, you are right! As we can see in Figure 8-10, each thread that wants to process its chunk of the image first tries to acquire the lock on the mutex, but only one will succeed and the rest will impatiently wait for the lock to be released. Not until the thread holding the lock releases it can a different thread execute the protected code. Therefore, the parallel_for ends up being executed serially! The good news is that, now, there are no concurrent increments of the histogram bins, and the result is finally correct. Yeah!

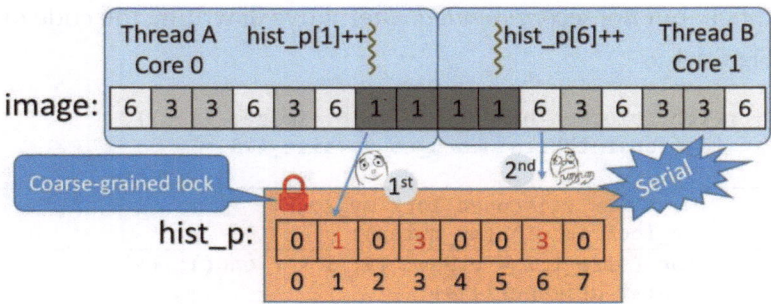

Figure 8-10. *Thread A holds the coarse-grained lock to increment bin number 1, while Thread B waits because the whole histogram vector is locked*

If we compile and run our new version, what we get is a parallel execution that is slower than the sequential one:

```
./histogram_03_1st_safe_parallel
Serial: 0.274083, Parallel: 0.488502, Speed-up: 0.561068
```

This approach is called coarse-grained locking because we are protecting a coarse-grained data structure (actually the whole data structure – the histogram vector – in this case). We could partition the histogram vector into several sections and protect each section with its own lock. That way, we would increase the concurrency level (different threads accessing different sections can proceed in parallel), but we would have increased the complexity of the code and the memory required for each of the mutex objects.

A word of caution is in order! Figure 8-11 shows a common mistake of parallel programming newbies.

```
// my_mutex_t my_mutex; NOT here! Moved to the body! Yikes!
parallel_for(tbb::blocked_range<size_t>{0, image.size()},
  [&](const tbb::blocked_range<size_t>& r)
  {
    my_mutex_t my_mutex;
    my_mutex_t::scoped_lock my_lock{my_mutex};
    for (size_t i = r.begin(); i < r.end(); ++i)
      hist_p[image[i]]++;
});
```

Figure 8-11. *Common mistake made by parallel programming newbies*

This code compiles without errors or warnings, so what is wrong with it? Back to our fitting room example, our intention was to avoid several people entering the fitting room at the same time. In Figure 8-11, my_mutex is defined inside the parallel section, and there will be a mutex object per task, each one locking its own mutex, which does not prevent concurrent access to the critical section. As we can see in Figure 8-12, the newbie code essentially has a separate door for each person into the same fitting room! That is not what we want! The solution is to declare my_mutex once (as we did in Figure 8-8) so that all accesses have to enter the fitting room through the same door.

Wrong fitting room

More than one door!

Figure 8-12. *A fitting room with more than one door*

Before tackling a fine-grained locking alternative, let's discuss two aspects that deserve a comment. First, the execution time of the "parallelized-then-serialized" code of Figure 8-8 is greater than the time needed by the serial implementation. This is due to the "parallelization-then-serialization" overhead, but also due to a poorer exploitation of the caches. Of course, there is no false sharing nor true sharing, because in our serialized implementation there is no "sharing" whatsoever! Or is there? In the serial implementation, only one thread accesses a cached histogram vector. In the coarse-grained implementation, when one thread processes its chunk of the image, it will cache the histogram in the cache of the core where the thread is running. When the next thread in the queue can finally process its own chunk, it may need to cache the histogram in a different cache (if the thread is running on a different core). The threads are still sharing the histogram vector, and more cache misses will likely occur with the proposed implementation than with the serial one.

The second aspect that we want to mention is the possibility of configuring the mutex behavior by choosing one of the possible mutex flavors that are shown in Figure 8-13. It is therefore recommended to use

```
using my_mutex_t = <mutex_flavor>
```

and then use my_mutex_t onward. That way, we can easily change the mutex flavor in a single program line and experimentally evaluate easily which flavor suits us best. It may be necessary to also include a different header file, as indicated in Figure 8-13, or use the all-inclusive tbb.h.

Mutex flavor	Scalable	Fair	Recursive	Long Wait	Size
tbb::mutex <tbb/mutex.h>	✔	✘	✘	blocks	1 byte
tbb::null_mutex <tbb/null_mutex.h>	✔	✔	✔	never	empty
tbb::rw_mutex <tbb/rw_mutex.h>	✔	✘	✘	blocks	1 word
tbb::null_rw_mutex <tbb/null_rw_mutex.h>	✔	✔	✔	never	empty
tbb::queuing_mutex <tbb/queuing_mutex.h>	✔	✔	✘	yields	1 word
tbb::queuing_rw_mutex <tbb/queuing_rw_mutex.h>	✔	✔	✘	yields	1 word
tbb::speculative_spin_mutex <tbb/spin_mutex.h>	HW depend. (yes if H/W support, no if not)	✘	✘	yields	2 cache lines
tbb::speculative_spin_rw_mutex <tbb/spin_rw_mutex.h>	HW depend.	✘	✘	yields	3 cache lines
tbb::spin_mutex <tbb/spin_mutex.h>	✘	✘	✘	yields	1 byte
tbb::spin_rw_mutex – if using try_lock() <tbb/spin_rw_mutex.h>	✘	✘	✘	yields	1 word
tbb::spin_rw_mutex – if using lock() <tbb/spin_rw_mutex.h>	✔	✘	✘	blocks	1 word
std::mutex <mutex>	✘	✘	✘	blocks	≥ 3 words
std::recursive_mutex <mutex>	✘	✘	✔	blocks	≥ 3 words
std::recursive_timed_mutex <mutex>	✘	✘	✔	blocks	≥ 3 words
std::shared_mutex <shared_mutex>	✘	✘	✘	blocks	≥ 3 words
std::shared_timed_mutex <shared_mutex>	✘	✘	✘	blocks	≥ 3 words
std::timed_mutex <mutex>	✘	✘	✘	blocks	≥ 3 words

Figure 8-13. *Different mutex flavors and their properties: 7 from* tbb:: *and 6 from* std::. *For* std::, *it is possible some implementations will do better than indicated, but the C++ standard does not guarantee we can count on that*

Mutex Flavors

In order to understand the different flavors of mutex, we have to first describe the properties that we use to classify them:

1. **Scalable** mutexes do not consume excessive core cycles nor memory bandwidth while waiting to have their turn. The motivation is that a waiting thread should avoid consuming the hardware resources that may be needed by other nonwaiting threads.

2. **Fair** mutexes use a FIFO policy for the threads to take their turn. The term "fair" for mutexes refers to mutexes that prioritize giving the lock to the thread that has waited the longest. When a lock is unfair, a thread can potentially be starved (never given the lock as long as other threads are requesting it).

3. **Recursive** mutexes allow a thread already holding a lock on a mutex to acquire another lock on the same mutex. Rethinking your code to avoid mutexes is great; doing it to avoid recursive mutexes is almost a must! Then, why does the standard C++ library provide them? There may be corner cases in which recursive mutexes are unavoidable. They may also come in handy when we can't be bothered or have no time to rethink a more efficient solution. Note: The original TBB had a recursive mutex for the same reason as the standard C++ library does now – convenience. It was dropped when updating for modern C++ since the standard C++ library can now be used in the rare case when we leave a recursive mutex in our code.

In the table in Figure 8-13, we also include the size of the mutex object and the behavior of the thread if it must wait for a long time to get a lock on the mutex. With regard to the last point, when a thread is waiting its turn, it can busy-wait, block, or yield. A thread that blocks will be changed to the blocked state so that the only resource required by the thread is the memory that keeps its sleeping state. When the thread can finally acquire the lock, it wakes up and moves back to the ready state where all the ready threads wait for their next turn. The OS scheduler assigns time slices to the ready threads that are waiting in a ready-state queue. A thread that yields while waiting its turn to hold a lock is kept in the ready state. When the thread reaches the top of the ready-state queue, it is dispatched to run, but if the mutex is still locked by other thread, it again gives away its time slice (it has nothing else to do!) and goes back to the ready-state queue.

Note

Note that in this process there may be two queues involved: (i) the ready-state queue managed by the OS scheduler, where ready threads are waiting, not necessarily in FIFO order, to be dispatched to an idle core and become running threads, and (ii) the mutex queue managed by the OS or by the mutex library in user space, where threads wait their turn to acquire a lock on a queueing mutex.

If the core is not oversubscribed (there is only one thread running in this core), a thread that yields because the mutex is still locked will be the only one in the ready-state queue and be dispatched right away. In this case, the yield mechanism is virtually equivalent to a busy-wait.

Now that we understand the different properties that can characterize the implementation of a mutex, let's delve into the particular mutex flavors that `tbb::` and `std::` offer.

`mutex` is offered by modern C++ and TBB. The advantages of the TBB version are evident in the Figure 8-13 table. Any `mutex` blocks on long waits, which can lead to longer response times when the mutex is released.

`tbb::spin_mutex`, on the contrary, never blocks the thread. It spins, busy-waiting in user space while waiting to hold a lock on a mutex. The waiting thread will yield after a number of tries to acquire the loop, but if the core is not oversubscribed, this thread keeps the core wasting cycles and power. On the other hand, once the mutex is released, the response time to acquire it is the fastest possible (no need to wake up and wait to be dispatched to run). This mutex is not fair, so no matter for how long a thread has been waiting its turn, a quicker thread can overtake it and acquire the lock if it is the first to find the mutex unlocked. A free-for-all prevails in this case, and in extreme situations, a weak thread can starve, never getting the lock. Nonetheless, this is the recommended mutex flavor under light contention situations because it can be the fastest one.

`tbb::queueing_mutex` is the scalable and fair version of the `spin_mutex`. It still spins, busy-waiting in user space, but threads waiting on that mutex will acquire the lock in FIFO order, so starvation is not possible.

tbb::speculative_spin_mutex is built on top of Hardware Transactional Memory (HTM) that is available in some processors. On systems without HTM, it simply behaves as a spin_mutex. The HTM philosophy is to be optimistic! HTM lets all threads enter a critical section at the same time hoping that there will be no shared memory conflicts! But what if there are? In this case, the hardware detects the conflict and rolls back the execution of one of the conflicting threads, which has to retry the execution of the critical section. In the coarse-grained implementation shown in Figure 8-8, we could add this simple line

```
using my_mutex_t = tbb::speculative_spin_mutex;
```

and, then, the parallel_for that traverses the image becomes parallel once again. Now, all threads are allowed to enter the critical section (to update the bins of the histogram for a given chunk of the image), but only if there is an actual conflict updating one of the bins, one of the conflicting threads has to retry the execution. For this to work efficiently, the protected critical section must be small enough so that conflicts and retries are rare, which is not the case in the code of Figure 8-8.

tbb::spin_rw_mutex, tbb::queueing_rw_mutex, and tbb::speculative_spin_rw_mutex are the reader–writer mutex counterparts of the previously covered flavors. These implementations allow multiple readers to read a shared variable at the same time. The lock object constructor has a second argument, a Boolean, that we set to false if we will only read (not write) inside the critical section:

```
using my_mutex_t=tbb::spin_mutex;
rwmutex_t my_mutex;
{
  rwmutex_t::scoped_lock my_lock{my_mutex, /*is_writer =*/false};
  // A reader lock is acquired so multiple
  // concurrent reads are allowed
}
```

If, for any reason, a reader lock has to be promoted to a writer lock, TBB provides an upgrade_to_writer() member function that can be used as follows

```
bool success=my_lock.upgrade_to_writer();
```

which returns true if the my_lock is successfully upgraded to a writer lock without releasing the lock or false otherwise.

Finally, we have `null_mutex` and `null_rw_mutex` that are just dummy objects that do nothing. So what's the point? Well, we can find these mutexes useful if we pass a mutex object to a function template that may or may not need a real mutex. In case the function does not really need the mutex, just pass the dummy flavor.

When Scalable Is Most Important

The term *scalable* is used for implementations that perform well when there is a lot of contention for the lock. This characteristic for TBB mutexes is obtained in the implementation (algorithm) for all the mutexes except the `speculative_spin_mutex`, which relies on a scalable hardware mechanism available in some x86 implementations.

We need scalable locks when contention is not light or a critical section (the duration for which the lock is held) is not very quick. Put another way, we need to avoid non-scalable locks unless two conditions are met: (1) contention for the lock is light, *and* (2) the critical section is very quick. If a non-scalable lock is chosen, the scalability of our application can be profoundly reduced if these two conditions are not met.

However, we should never forget that using a scalable mutex does not mean that our application itself will magically scale. If a lock is highly contended, we have a serializing bottleneck in our code. A scalable mutex itself performs well in that situation compared with a non-scalable alternative, adding as little additional overhead as possible in contended cases. But that doesn't mean that the application's algorithm results in useful parallelism. As we described earlier, a `tbb::spin_mutex` actively spins, but yields if it does not quickly acquire the lock. Yielding reduces contention by giving opportunities for other threads to make progress, but it does not change the fact that the thread failed to get the lock it needed and is now stuck waiting for its turn. Using a non-scalable mutex would simply make this bad situation worse!

A Second Safe Parallel Implementation: Fine-Grained Locking

Now that we know a lot about the different flavors of mutexes, let us think about an alternative implementation of the coarse-grained locking one in Figure 8-8. One alternative is to declare a mutex for every bin of the histogram so that instead of locking the whole data structure with a single lock, we only protect the single memory position that we are actually incrementing. To do that, we need a vector of mutexes, `fine_m`, as the one shown in Figure 8-14.

```cpp
using my_mutex_t=tbb::spin_mutex;
std::vector<my_mutex_t> fine_m(num_bins);
std::vector<int> hist_p(num_bins);
parallel_for(tbb::blocked_range<size_t>{0, image.size()},
            [&](const tbb::blocked_range<size_t>& r)
            {
              for (size_t i = r.begin(); i < r.end(); ++i){
                int tone=image[i];
                my_mutex_t::scoped_lock my_lock{fine_m[tone]};
                hist_p[tone]++;
              }
            });
```

Figure 8-14. *Code listing with a second safe parallel implementation of the image histogram computation that uses fine-grained locking. Sample code synchronization/histogram_04_2nd_safe_parallel.cpp*

As we see in the lambda used inside the `parallel_for`, when a thread needs to increment the bin `hist_p[tone]`, it will acquire the lock on `fine_m[tone]`, preventing other threads from touching the same bin. Essentially "you can update other bins, but not this particular one." This is illustrated in Figure 8-15 where Threads A and B are updating in parallel different bins of the histogram vector.

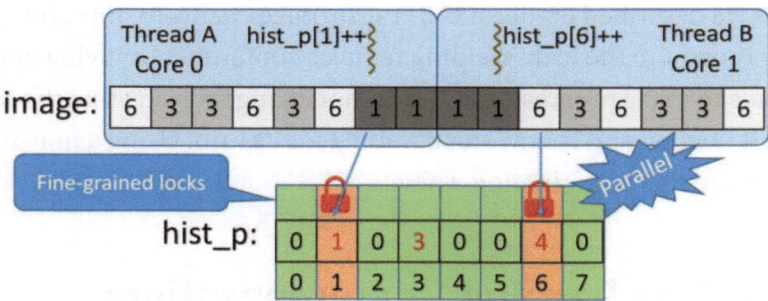

Figure 8-15. *Thanks to fine-grained locking, we exploit more parallelism. Yet, as we will see, this is the worst-performing example so far! There is more to discuss and learn*

However, from a performance standpoint, this alternative is not really an optimal one (actually it is the slowest alternative up to now):

```
./histogram_04_2nd_safe_parallel
Serial: 0.266333, Parallel: 108.981, Speed-up: 0.00244386
```

Now we need not only the histogram array but also an array of mutex objects of the same length. This means a larger memory requirement and, moreover, more data that will be cached and that will suffer from false sharing and true sharing. Bummer!

Convoying and Deadlocks

In addition to the lock inherent overhead, locks are at the root of two additional problems: convoying and deadlock. Let's cover first "convoying." This name comes from the mental image of all threads convoying one after the other at the lower speed of the first one. We need an example to better illustrate this situation, as the one depicted in Figure 8-16. Let's suppose we have threads 1, 2, 3, and 4 executing on the same core the same code, where there is a critical section protected by a spin mutex A. If these threads hold the lock at different times, they run happily without contention (situation 1). But it may happen that thread 1 runs out of its time slice before releasing the lock, which sends A to the end of the ready-state queue (situation 2).

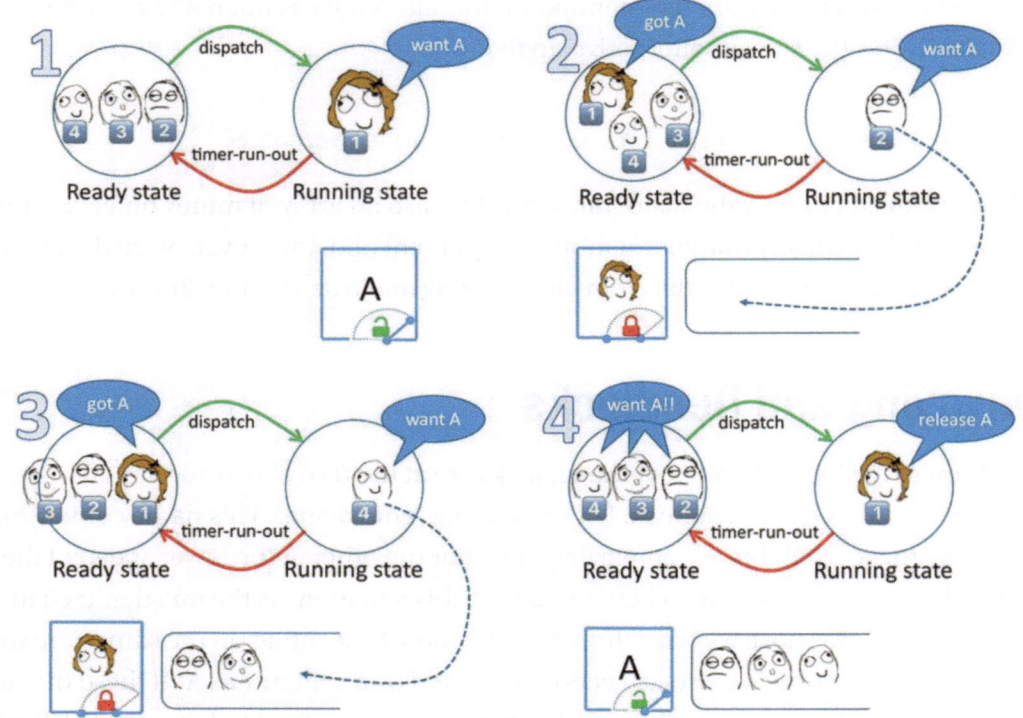

Figure 8-16. *Convoying in the case of oversubscription (a single core running four threads, all of them wanting the same mutex A)*

Threads 2, 3, and 4 will now get their corresponding time slices, but they cannot acquire the lock because 1 is still the owner (situation 3). This means that 2, 3, and 4 can now yield or spin, but in any case, they are stuck behind a big truck in first gear. When 1 is dispatched again, it will release lock A (situation 4). Now 2, 3, and 4 are all poised to fight for the lock, with only one succeeding and the others waiting again. This situation is recurrent, especially if now threads 2, 3, and 4 need more than a time slice to run their protected critical section. Moreover, threads 2, 3, and 4 are now inadvertently coordinated, all running in step the same region of the code, which leads to a higher probability of contention on the mutex! Note that convoying is especially acute when the cores are oversubscribed (as in this example where four threads compete to run on a single core), which also reinforces our recommendation to avoid oversubscription.

An additional well-known problem arising from locks is "deadlock." Figure 8-17(a) shows a nightmare-provoking situation in which nobody can make progress even when there are available resources (empty lines that no car can use). This is deadlock in real life, but get this image out of your head (if you can!) and come back to our virtual world of parallel programming. If we have a set of N threads that are holding a lock and also waiting to acquire a lock already held by any other thread in the set, our N threads are deadlocked. An example with only two threads is presented in Figure 8-17(b): thread 1 holds a lock on mutex A and is waiting to acquire a lock on mutex B, but thread 2 is already holding the lock on mutex B and waiting to acquire the lock on mutex A. Clearly, no thread will progress, forever doomed in a deadly embrace! We can avoid this unfortunate situation by not requiring the acquisition of a different mutex if the thread is already holding one – or, at least, by having all threads always acquire the locks in the same order.

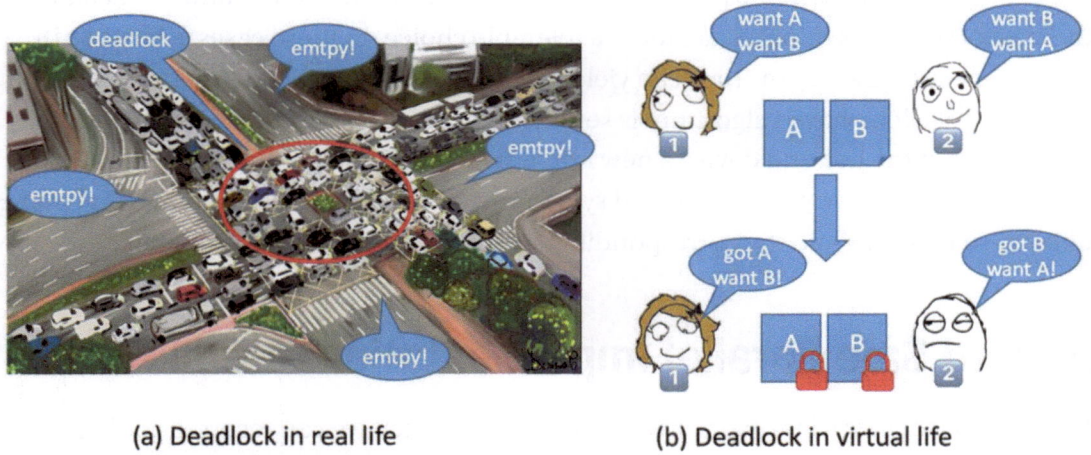

(a) Deadlock in real life   (b) Deadlock in virtual life

Figure 8-17. *Deadlock situations*

We can inadvertently provoke deadlock if a thread already holding a lock calls a function that also acquires a different lock. The recommendation is to eschew calling a function while holding a lock if we don't know what the function does (usually advised as *don't call other people's code while holding a lock*). Alternatively, we should carefully check that the chain of subsequent function calls won't induce deadlock. Ah! And we should also avoid locks whenever possible!

Since C++11, the function std::lock can be used to avoid deadlock when locking multiple *Lockable* objects (https://en.cppreference.com/w/cpp/named_req/Lockable). std::lock applies a deadlock avoidance algorithm to ensure that the set of objects passed to it are locked without deadlocking by using a series of calls to lock, try_lock, and unlock. You can learn more details about std::lock at https://en.cppreference.com/w/cpp/thread/lock. This function works with the standard mutex types but also any type that models the Lockable named requirements. The tbb::mutex, tbb::spin_mutex, tbb::rw_mutex, and tbb::spin_rw_mutex satisfy the requirements in the [thread.mutex.requirements] section of the ISO C++ standard, making them *Lockable* objects and therefore usable with std::lock and any other C++ functions and classes that work with Lockable objects or C++ mutexes.

Although convoying and deadlock are not really hitting our histogram implementation, they should have helped convince us that locks often bring more problems than they solve and that they are not the best alternative to get high parallel performance. Only when the probability of contention is low and the time to execute the critical section is minimal are locks a tolerable choice. In these cases, a basic spin_lock or speculative_spin_lock can yield some speedup. But in any other cases, the scalability of a lock-based algorithm is seriously compromised, and the best advice is to think out of the box and devise a new implementation that does not require a mutex altogether. But can we get fine-grained synchronization without relying on several mutex objects, so that we avoid the corresponding overheads and potential problems?

A Third Safe Parallel Implementation: Atomics

Fortunately, there is a less expensive mechanism to which we can resort to getting rid of mutexes and locks in many cases. We can use atomic variables to perform atomic operations. As was illustrated in Figure 8-6, the increment operation is not atomic but divisible into three smaller operations (load, increment, and store). However, we can declare an atomic variable and do the following:

```
#include <atomic>
std::atomic<int> counter;
counter++;
```

Note that for atomics, we can rely on C++ std::atomic (see https://en.cppreference.com/w/cpp/atomic). The original TBB had to supply atomic operations as C++ did not define them. Today's TBB still offers beneficial high-performance mutexes, but for atomics we rely on standard C++. See Chapter 12 for more information and advice regarding moving older programs that relied on TBB for everything forward to today's TBB and C++.

In the case we just showed, the increment of the atomic variable *is* an atomic operation. This means that any other thread accessing the value of counter will "see" the operation as if the increment is done in a single step (not as three smaller operations, but as a single one). That is, any other "sharp-eyed" thread will either observe the operation completed or not, but it will never observe the increment half-complete.

Atomic operations do not suffer from convoying or deadlock[2] and are faster than mutual exclusion alternatives. However, not all operations can be executed atomically, and those that can are not applicable to all data types. The `std::atomic` template can be instantiated for any type that is *TriviallyCopiable* and is also both *CopyConstructible* and *CopyAssignable* (refer to `std::atomic` in cppreference to see the exact meaning of these named requirements). Luckily, `std::atomic<T>` supports atomic operations for many of the most commonly used types, including when T is an integral, enumeration, or pointer data type. The most important atomic operations supported on a variable x of such a type `std::atomic<T>` are listed in Figure 8-18.

---

[2] Atomic operations cannot be nested, so they cannot provoke deadlock.

`=x` `x.load()`	read the value of x
`x=` `x.store(y)`	write the value of x, and return it do $x=y$ *(no result – is void)*
`x.fetch_add(y)` `x++`	do $x+=y$ and return the old value of x do $x+=1$ and return the old value of x
`x+=y` `x.fetch_sub(y)`	do $x+=y$ and return the old value of x do $x-=y$ and return the old value of x
`x--` `x-=y`	do $x-=1$ and return the old value of x do $x-=y$ and return the old value of x
`x.fetch_and(y)` `x&=y`	do $x\&=y$ and return the old value of x
`x.fetch_or(y)` `x|=y`	do $x\|=y$ and return the old value of x
`x.fetch_xor(y)` `x^=y`	do $x^=y$ and return the old value of x
`x.compare_exchange_weak(z,y)` `x.compare_exchange_strong(z,y)`	if x equals z, then do $x=y$. Result (bool) indicates if swap occurred. Strong version is preferred outside loops, and weak is used in loops.

Figure 8-18. *Fundamental operations on atomic variables. Additionally, C++ offers* `std::memory_order` *as a parameter to some operations*

Another useful idiom based on atomics is the one already used in the wavefront example presented in Figure 2-16 (Chapter 2). Having an atomic integer `refCount` initialized to "y" and several threads executing this code

```
if (--refCount == 0) { ... /* body */ ... };
```

will result in only the y-th thread executing the previous line entering in the "body."

Of these fundamental operations, `compare_exchange_strong` (Compare Exchange) can be considered as the mother of all atomic read–modify–write (RMW) operations. This is because all atomic RMW operations can be implemented on top of the Compare Exchange operation. In the table, there are two variants of Compare Exchange listed: `compare_exchange_strong` and `compare_exchange_weak`. The difference is that `compare_exchange_weak` is allowed to "fail spuriously." That is, it might return `false` and not perform the exchange even though x did in fact equal z. The weak variant exists because it might be more efficient to implement on some systems. If we use the weak variant, we need to write our code to account for these spurious failures.

Atomic and Happens-Before

It is important to know that constructs in TBB exist for us to hint that parallelism can be used while allowing that they do *not* have to run in parallel. We call this *relaxed sequential semantics*. That has implications on how we think about synchronization. We should never assume that two tasks generated by a TBB algorithm will definitely execute concurrently – maybe TBB will choose to use a single thread to execute all of the tasks. We shouldn't, for example, have one TBB task wait for the result of another TBB task by repeatedly checking an atomic variable. This pattern might work when multiple threads are assigned to execute tasks, but deadlock if only one thread is executing all tasks. In general, atomics should not be used as synchronizing operations across TBB tasks.

Regarding atomicity, we must remember that while a single atomic operation is atomic, two consecutive atomic operations are not atomic together – only individually. This is a common misconception, as it's easy to mistakenly assume that a series of atomic operations will behave atomically as a whole.

All is not lost though. C++ provides `std::memory_order` parameters for some atomic operations to ensure specific ordering guarantees. These parameters determine how memory accesses, including non-atomic memory accesses, are ordered around an atomic operation. The C++ standard is very detailed about memory order, and a summary can be found in cppreference (`https://en.cppreference.com/w/cpp/atomic/memory_order`), alongside an in-depth discussion of this topic. So we only touch on the subject here.

The `std::atomic` operations default to `std::memory_order_seq_cst`. In brief, this ordering means that all memory operations that are done in a thread before an atomic store marked as `std::memory_order_seq_cst` will be visible to another thread that does an atomic `std::memory_order_seq_cst` load from that same variable. On top of this, there is a single total modification order for all atomic operations tagged as `std::memory_order_seq_cst` across all threads. This means that all threads see the modifications of atomic variables in the same order. This is a good, safe default.

But other orderings exist because they may increase flexibility and therefore potential performance. One example is release–acquire ordering. If one thread stores a value into an atomic variable with `memory_order_release` and a second thread loads that value from the same atomic variable with `memory_order_acquire`, the store in the first thread synchronizes with the load in the second thread. Any memory written in the first thread that happened before the atomic store is guaranteed to be visible in the second thread once the atomic load completes. In some sense, this may seem like `std::memory_order_seq_cst` except that we need to remember which one to acquire and which one to release. But it also does not create a total modification across all atomic operations, so threads may see updates to different atomic variables in different orders. Again, cppreference has a good discussion of the complications that can arise, and we refer interested readers there.

TBB focuses on high performance by guiding us to use scalable techniques, specifically through a *relaxed sequential semantics* model, that is, optional parallelism. If we want to ensure that memory operations performed by one TBB task are visible to another TBB task in a specific order, we need to use atomics and mutexes to accomplish that. And if we want to increase flexibility, we can consider using orderings that are more relaxed than the default `std::memory_order_seq_cst`.

NOTES ON CONSIDERING A SMALL CRITICAL SECTION

Just in case you need to protect a small critical section, and you are already convinced to avoid locks, let's dip our toes into the details of the Compare Exchange operation a little bit. Say that our code requires to atomically multiply a shared integer variable, v, by 3. We are aiming for a lock-free solution, though we know that multiplication is not included as one of the atomic operations. Here is where Compare Exchange comes in. First thing is to declare v as an atomic variable

```
std::atomic<uint32_t> v;
```

so now we can call v.compare_exchange_weak(old_v, new_v), which atomically does

```
ov=v; if (ov == old_v) v=new_v; return ov;
```

That is, if and only if v is equal to old_v, we can update v with the new value. In any case, we return ov (the shared v used in the "==" comparison). Now, the trick to implement our "times 3" atomic multiplication is to code what is dubbed Compare Exchange loop:

```
void fetch_and_triple(std::atomic<uint32_t>& v)
{
  uint32_t old_v;
  do {
    old_v=v; //take a snapshot
  } while (!v.compare_exchange_weak(old_v, old_v * 3));
}
```

Our new `fetch_and_triple` is thread-safe (can be safely called by several threads at the same time) even when it is called passing the same shared atomic variable. This function is basically a do-while loop in which we first take a snapshot of the shared variable (which is key to later compare if other thread has managed to modify it). Then, atomically, if no other thread has changed v (v==old_v), we do update it (v=old_v*3) and return v. Since in this case v == old_v (again, no other thread has changed v), we leave the do-while loop and return from the function with our shared v successfully updated.

However, after taking the snapshot, it is possible that another thread updates v. In this case, v!=old_v, which implies that (i) we do not update v and (ii) we stay in the do-while loop hoping that lady luck will smile on us next time (when no other greedy thread dares to touch our v in the interim between the moment we take the snapshot and we succeed updating v). Figure 8-19 illustrates how v is always updated either by thread 1 or thread 2. It is possible that one of the threads has to retry (as thread 2 that ends up writing 81 when initially it was about to write 27) one or more times, but this shouldn't be a big deal in well-devised scenarios.

The two caveats of this strategy are (i) it scales badly and (ii) it may suffer from the "A-B-A problem" (there is background on the classic A-B-A problem in Chapter 3). Regarding the first one, consider P threads contending for the same atomic, only one succeeds with P-1 retrying, then another succeeds with P-2 retrying, then P-3 retrying, and so on, resulting in a quadratic work. This problem can be ameliorated resorting to an "exponential back-off" strategy that multiplicatively reduces the rate of consecutive retries to reduce contention. On the other hand, the A-B-A problem happens when, in the interim time (between the moment we take the snapshot and we succeed updating v), a different thread changes v from value A to value B and back to value A. Our Compare Exchange loop can succeed without noticing the intervening thread, which can be problematic. Double-check that you understand this problem and its consequences if you need to resort to a Compare Exchange loop in your developments.

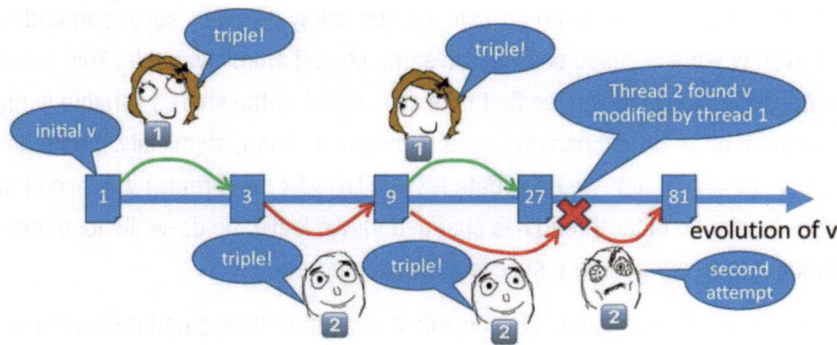

Figure 8-19. *Two threads concurrently calling to our fetch_and_triple atomic function implemented on top of a Compare Exchange loop*

But now it is time to get back to our running example. A re-implementation of the histogram computation can now be expressed with the help of atomics as shown in Figure 8-20.

```
#include <atomic>

std::vector<std::atomic<int>> hist_p(num_bins);
parallel_for(tbb::blocked_range<size_t>{0, image.size()},
             [&](const tbb::blocked_range<size_t>& r)
             {
               for (size_t i = r.begin(); i < r.end(); ++i)
                 hist_p[image[i]]++;
             });
```

Figure 8-20. *Code listing with a third safe parallel implementation of the image histogram computation that uses atomic variables. Sample code synchronization/histogram_06_3rd_safe_parallel.cpp*

In this implementation, we get rid of the mutex objects and locks and declare the vector so that each bin is a std::atomic<int> (initialized to 0 by default). Then, in the lambda, it is safe to increment the bins in parallel. The net result is that we get parallel increments of the histogram vector, as with the fine-grained locking strategy, but at a lower cost both in terms of mutex management and mutex storage.

However, performance-wise, this implementation is still way too slow:

```
./histogram_06_3rd_safe_parallel
Serial: 0.282609, Parallel: 10.4025, Speed-up: 0.0271674
```

In addition to the atomic increment overhead, false sharing and true sharing are issues that we have not addressed yet. False sharing is tackled in Chapter 7 by leveraging aligned allocators and padding techniques. False sharing is a frequent showstopper that hampers parallel performance, so we highly encourage you to read in Chapter 7 the recommended techniques to avoid it.

Great, assuming that we have fixed the false sharing problem, what about the true sharing one? Two different threads will eventually increment the same bin, which will be ping-pong from one cache to another. We need a better idea to solve this one!

A Better Parallel Implementation: Privatization and Reduction

The real problem posed by the histogram reduction is that there is a single shared vector to hold the 256 bins that all threads are eager to increment. So far, we have seen several implementations that are functionally equivalent, like the coarse-grained, fine-grained, and atomic-based ones, but none of those are totally satisfactory if we also consider nonfunctional metrics such as performance and energy.

The common solution to avoid sharing something is to privatize it. Parallel programming is not different in this respect. If we give a private copy of the histogram to each thread, each one will happily work with its copy, cache it in the private cache of the core in which the thread is running, and therefore increment all the bins at the cache speed (in the ideal case). No more false sharing nor true sharing nor anything, because the histogram vector is not shared any more.

Okay, but then …each thread will end up having a partial view of the histogram because each thread has only visited some of the pixels of the full image. No problem, now is when the reduction part of this implementation comes into play. The final step after computing a privatized partial version of the histogram is to reduce all the contributions of all the threads to get the complete histogram vector. There is still some synchronization in this part because some threads have to wait for others that have not finished their local/private computations yet, but in the general case, this solution ends up being much less expensive than the other previously described implementations. Figure 8-21 illustrates the privatization and reduction technique for our histogram example.

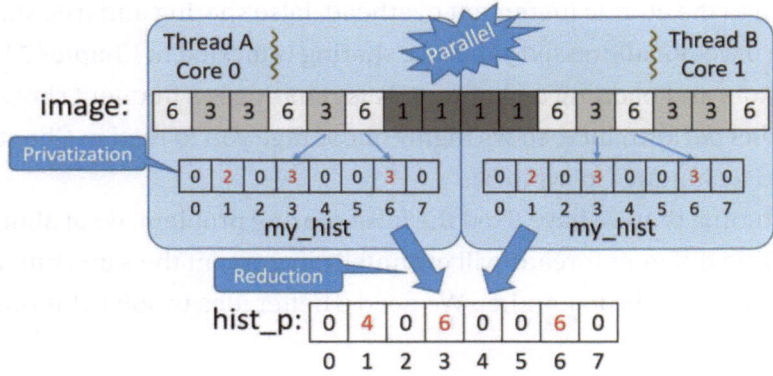

Figure 8-21. *Each thread computes its local histogram,* my_hist, *that is later reduced in a second step*

TBB offers several alternatives to accomplish privatization and reduction operations, some based on thread-local storage (TLS) and a more user-friendly one based on the reduction template. Let's go first to the TLS version of the histogram computation.

Thread-Local Storage (TLS)

Thread-local storage, for our purposes here, refers to having a per-thread privatized copy of data. Using TLS, we can reduce accesses to shared mutable state between threads and also exploit locality because each private copy can be (sometimes partially) stored in the local cache of the core on which the thread is running. Of course, copies take up space, so they should not be used to excess.

An important aspect of TBB is that we do not know how many threads are being used at any given time. Even if we are running on a 64-core system, and we use parallel_for for 64 iterations, we cannot assume there will be 64 threads active. This is a critical factor in making our code composable, which means it will work even if called inside a parallel program or if it calls a library that runs in parallel. Therefore, we do not know how many thread-local copies of data are needed even in our example of a parallel_for with 64 iterations. The template classes for thread-local storage in TBB are here to give an abstract way to ask TBB to allocate, manipulate, and combine the right number of copies without us worrying about how many copies that is. This lets us create scalable, composable, and portable applications.

TBB provides two template classes for thread-local storage. Both provide access to a local element per thread and create the elements (lazily) on demand. They differ in their intended use models:

Class enumerable_thread_specific (ETS) provides thread-local storage that acts like an STL container with one element per thread. The container permits iterating over the elements using the usual STL iteration idioms. Any thread can iterate over all the local copies, seeing the other threads' local data.

Class combinable provides thread-local storage for holding per-thread subcomputations that will later be reduced to a single result. Each thread can only see its local data or, after calling enumerable_thread_specific::combine, the combined data.

enumerable_thread_specific (ETS)

Let's see, first, how our parallel histogram computation can be implemented, thanks to the enumerable_thread_specific class. In Figure 8-22, we see the code needed to process in parallel different chunks of the input image and have each thread write on a private copy of the histogram vector.

```
#include <tbb/enumerable_thread_specific.h>
// Parallel execution
using vector_t = std::vector<int>;
using priv_h_t = tbb::enumerable_thread_specific<vector_t>;
priv_h_t priv_h{num_bins};
parallel_for(tbb::blocked_range<size_t>{0, image.size()},
             [&](const tbb::blocked_range<size_t>& r)
             {
                 priv_h_t::reference my_hist = priv_h.local();
                 for (size_t i = r.begin(); i < r.end(); ++i)
                     my_hist[image[i]]++;
             });
//Sequential reduction of the private histograms
vector_t hist_p(num_bins);
for(auto i=priv_h.begin(); i!=priv_h.end(); ++i){
  for (int j=0; j<num_bins; ++j)
      hist_p[j]+=(*i)[j];
}
```

Figure 8-22. *Parallel histogram computation on private copies using class* enumerable_thread_specific. *Sample code synchronization/ histogram_08_4th_safe_parallel_private.cpp*

We declare first an enumerable_thread_specific object, priv_h, of type std::vector<int>. The constructor indicates that the vector size is num_bins integers. Then, inside the parallel_for, an undetermined number of threads will process chunks of the iteration space, and for each chunk, the body (a lambda in our example) of the parallel_for will be executed. The thread taking care of a given chunk calls my_hist = priv_h.local() that works as follows. If it is the first time this thread calls the local() member function, a new private vector is created for this thread. If, on the contrary, it is not the first time, the vector was already created, and we just need to reuse it. In both cases, a reference to the private vector is returned and assigned to my_hist, which is used inside the parallel_for to update the histogram counts for the given chunk. That way, a thread processing different chunks will create the private histogram for the first chunk and reuse it for the subsequent ones. Quite neat, right?

At the end of the parallel_for, we end up with an undetermined number of private histograms that need to be combined to compute the final histogram, hist_p, accumulating all the partial results. But how can we do this reduction if we do not even know the number of private histograms? Fortunately, an enumerable_thread_specific not only provides thread-local storage for elements of type T but also can be iterated across like an STL container, from beginning to end. This is carried out at the end of Figure 8-22, where variable i sequentially traverses the different private histograms and the nested loop j takes care of accumulating on hist_p all the bin counts.

If we would rather show off our outstanding C++ programming skills, we can take advantage of that fact that priv_h is yet another STL container and write the reduction as we show in Figure 8-23.

```
for (const auto& i:priv_h) { // i traverses all private vectors
    std::transform(hist_p.begin(),    // source 1 begin
                   hist_p.end(),      // source 1 end
                   i.begin(),         // source 2 begin
                   hist_p.begin(),    // destination begin
                   std::plus<int>() );// binary operation
}
```

Figure 8-23. *A more stylish way of implementing the reduction. Sample code synchronization/histogram_09_5th_safe_parallel_private.cpp*

Since the reduction operation is a frequent one, enumerable_thread_specific also offers two additional member functions to implement the reduction: combine_each() and combine(). In Figure 8-24, we illustrate how to use the member function combine_each in a code snippet that is completely equivalent to the one in Figure 8-23.

```
priv_h.combine_each([&](const vector_t& a)
  { // for each priv histogram a
    std::transform(hist_p.begin(),     // source 1 begin
                   hist_p.end(),       // source 1 end
                   a.begin(),          // source 2 begin
                   hist_p.begin(),     // destination begin
                   std::plus<int>() ); // binary operation
});
```

Figure 8-24. *Using* combine_each() *to implement the reduction. Sample code synchronization/histogram_10_6th_safe_parallel_private.cpp*

As we see in Figure 8-24, Func f is provided as a lambda, where the STL transform algorithm oversees accumulating the private histograms into hist_p. In general, the member function combine_each calls a unary functor for each element in the enumerable_thread_specific object. This combine function, with signature void(T) or void(const T&), usually reduces the private copies into a global variable.

The alternative member function combine() does return a value of type T. In Figure 8-25, we show the reduction implementation using the T(T,T) signature that, for each pair of private vectors, computes the vector addition into vector a and return it for possible further reductions. The combine() member function takes care of visiting all local copies of the histogram to return a pointer to the final hist_p.

```
vector_t hist_p = priv_h.combine([](vector_t a,
                                    vector_t b) -> vector_t
  {// for each priv histogram
    std::transform(a.begin(),         // source 1 begin
                   a.end(),           // source 1 end
                   b.begin(),         // source 2 begin
                   a.begin(),         // destination begin
                   std::plus<int>() ); // binary operation
    return a;
});
```

Figure 8-25. *Using* combine() *to implement the same reduction. Sample code synchronization/histogram_11_7th_safe_parallel_combine.cpp*

And what about the parallel performance?

```
./histogram_08_4th_safe_parallel_private
Serial: 0.318113, Parallel: 0.0355086, Speed-up: 8.95876
```

Now we are talking!

VICTORY AT LAST – AND MORE TO COME!

For this simple histogram, we finally see a performance gain from parallelism. The key was we needed an effective way to allow the parallelism to happen! It is especially important to know we need to find the right fit and not assume that just any technique should work well. In the remainder of this chapter, we have even better things to learn as we improve more. Step-by-step we are reviewing options in synchronization so that we can apply them effectively to our other algorithms and applications in the future.

The three equivalent reductions shown in Figures 8-23, 8-24, and 8-25 are executed sequentially, so there is still room for performance improvement if the number of private copies to be reduced is large (say that 64 threads are computing the histogram) or the reduction operation is computationally intensive (e.g., private histograms have 1,024 bins). We will also address this issue, but before then we need to cover a second alternative to implement thread-local storage.

Combinable

A combinable<T> object provides each thread with its own local instance, of type T, to hold thread-local values during a parallel computation. Contrary to the previously described ETS class, a combinable object cannot be iterated as we did with priv_h in Figures 8-22 and 8-23. However, combine_each() and combine() member functions are available because this combinable class is provided in TBB with the sole purpose of implementing reductions of local data storage.

In Figure 8-26, we re-implement once again the parallel histogram computation, now relying on the combinable class.

```
#include <tbb/combinable.h>

// Parallel execution
using vector_t = std::vector<int>;
tbb::combinable<vector_t> priv_h{[num_bins](){return vector_t(num_bins);}};

parallel_for(tbb::blocked_range<size_t>{0, image.size()},
             [&](const tbb::blocked_range<size_t>& r)
             {
               vector_t& my_hist = priv_h.local();
               for (size_t i = r.begin(); i < r.end(); ++i)
                 my_hist[image[i]]++;
             });

//Sequential reduction of the private histograms
vector_t hist_p(num_bins);
priv_h.combine_each([&](const vector_t& a)
  { // for each priv histogram a
    std::transform(hist_p.begin(),     // source 1 begin
                   hist_p.end(),       // source 1 end
                   a.begin(),          // source 2 begin
                   hist_p.begin(),     // destination begin
                   std::plus<int>() );// binary operation
});
```

Figure 8-26. *Re-implementing the histogram computation with a combinable object. Sample code synchronization/histogram_12_8th_safe_parallel_combine.cpp*

In this case, priv_h is a combinable object where the constructor provides a lambda with the function that will be invoked each time priv_h.local() is called. In this case, this lambda just creates an initial vector of num_bins integers. The parallel_for, which updates the per-thread private histograms, is quite similar to the implementation shown in Figure 8-22 for the ETS alternative, except that my_hist is just a reference to a vector of integers. As we said, now we cannot iterate the private histograms by hand as we did in Figure 8-22, but to make up for it, member functions combine_each() and combine() work pretty much the same as the equivalent member functions of the ETS class that we saw in Figures 8-24 and 8-25. Note that this reduction is still carried out sequentially, so it is only appropriate when the number of objects to reduce and/or the time to reduce two objects is small.

The Easiest Parallel Implementation: Reduction Template

As we covered in Chapter 2, TBB already comes with a high-level parallel algorithm to easily implement a `parallel_reduce`. Then, if we want to implement a parallel reduction of private histograms, why don't we just rely on this `parallel_reduce` template? In Figure 8-27, we see how we use this template to code an efficient parallel histogram computation.

```
#include <tbb/parallel_reduce.h>
  // Parallel execution
  using vector_t = std::vector<int>;
  using image_iterator = std::vector<uint8_t>::iterator;
  vector_t hist_p = parallel_reduce (
      /*range*/
      tbb::blocked_range<image_iterator>{image.begin(), image.end()},
      /*identity*/
      vector_t(num_bins),

      // 1st Lambda: Parallel computation on private histograms
      [](const tbb::blocked_range<image_iterator>& r, vector_t v) {
          std::for_each(r.begin(), r.end(),
              [&v](uint8_t i) {v[i]++;});
          return v;
      },
      // 2nd Lambda: Parallel reduction of the private histograms
      [](vector_t a, const vector_t& b) -> vector_t {
          std::transform(a.begin(),          // source 1 begin
                         a.end(),            // source 1 end
                         b.begin(),          // source 2 begin
                         a.begin(),          // destination begin
                         std::plus<int>() );// binary operation
          return a;
  });
```

Figure 8-27. *Code listing with a better parallel implementation of the image histogram computation that uses privatization and reduction. Sample code synchronization/histogram_13_9th_safe_parallel_reduction.cpp*

The first argument of `parallel_reduce` is just the range of iterations that will be automatically partitioned into chunks and assigned to threads. Somewhat oversimplifying what is really going on under the hood, the threads will get a private histogram initialized with the identity value of the reduction operation, which in this case is a vector of bins initialized to 0. The first lambda is taking care of the private and local computation of the partial histograms that results from visiting just some of the chunks of the image. Finally, the second lambda implements the reduction operation, which in this case could have been expressed as

```
[num_bins](vector_t a, const vector_t & b) -> vector_t {
    for(int i=0; i<num_bins; ++i) a[i] += b[i];
    return a;
});
```

which is exactly what the std::transform STL algorithm is doing. The execution time is similar to the one obtained with ETS and combinable:

```
./histogram_13_9th_safe_parallel_reduction
Serial: 0.269894, Parallel: 0.0324757, Speed-up: 8.31066
```

In order to shed more light on the practical implications of the different implementations of the histogram we have discussed so far, we collect in Figure 8-28 all the speedups obtained on our system. The exact machine or timings are not the key concern here; this simply helps give us a perspective on the variations we could expect to encounter.

Implementation:	Unsafe	Coarse	Fine	Atomic	TLS	Reduction
Speedup:	0.027	0.561	0.002	0.027	8.959	8.310

Figure 8-28. *Example speedups of the different histogram implementations*

We clearly identify three different sets of behaviors. Unsafe, fine-grained locking, and atomic solutions are way slower with four cores than in sequential (way slower here means more than one order of magnitude slower!). As we said, frequent synchronization due to locks and false sharing/true sharing is a real issue, and having histogram bins going back and forth from one cache to the other results in very disappointing speedups. The fine-grained solution is the worst because we have false sharing and true sharing for both the histogram vector and the mutex vector. As a single representative of its own kind, the coarse-grained solution is just slightly worse than the sequential one. Remember that this one is just a "parallelized-then-serialized" version in which a coarse-grained lock obliges the threads to enter the critical section one by one. The small performance degradation of the coarse-grained version is actually measuring the overhead of the parallelization and mutex management, but we are free from false sharing or true sharing now. Finally, privatization+reduction solutions (TLS and parallel_reduce) are leading the pack. They scale pretty well, even more than linearly, since the parallel_reduction, being a bit slower due to the tree-like reduction, does not pay off in this problem. The number of cores is small, and the time required for the reduction (adding to 256 int vectors) is negligible. For this tiny problem, the sequential reduction implemented with TLS classes is good enough.

Recap of Our Options

For the sake of backing up all the different alternatives that we have proposed to implement just a simple algorithm like the histogram computation one, let's recap and elaborate on the pros and cons of each alternative. Figure 8-29 illustrates some of our options with an even simpler vector addition of 800 numbers using eight threads. The corresponding sequential code would be similar to

```
sum = 0;
for (int i = 0; i < N; ++i) sum += vec[i];
```

For our casting in this chapter (if you care about our humor here, check out the sidebar "Laurel and Hardy"), we have chosen "The Mistaken, the Hardy, the Laurel, the Nuclear, the Local, and the Wise":

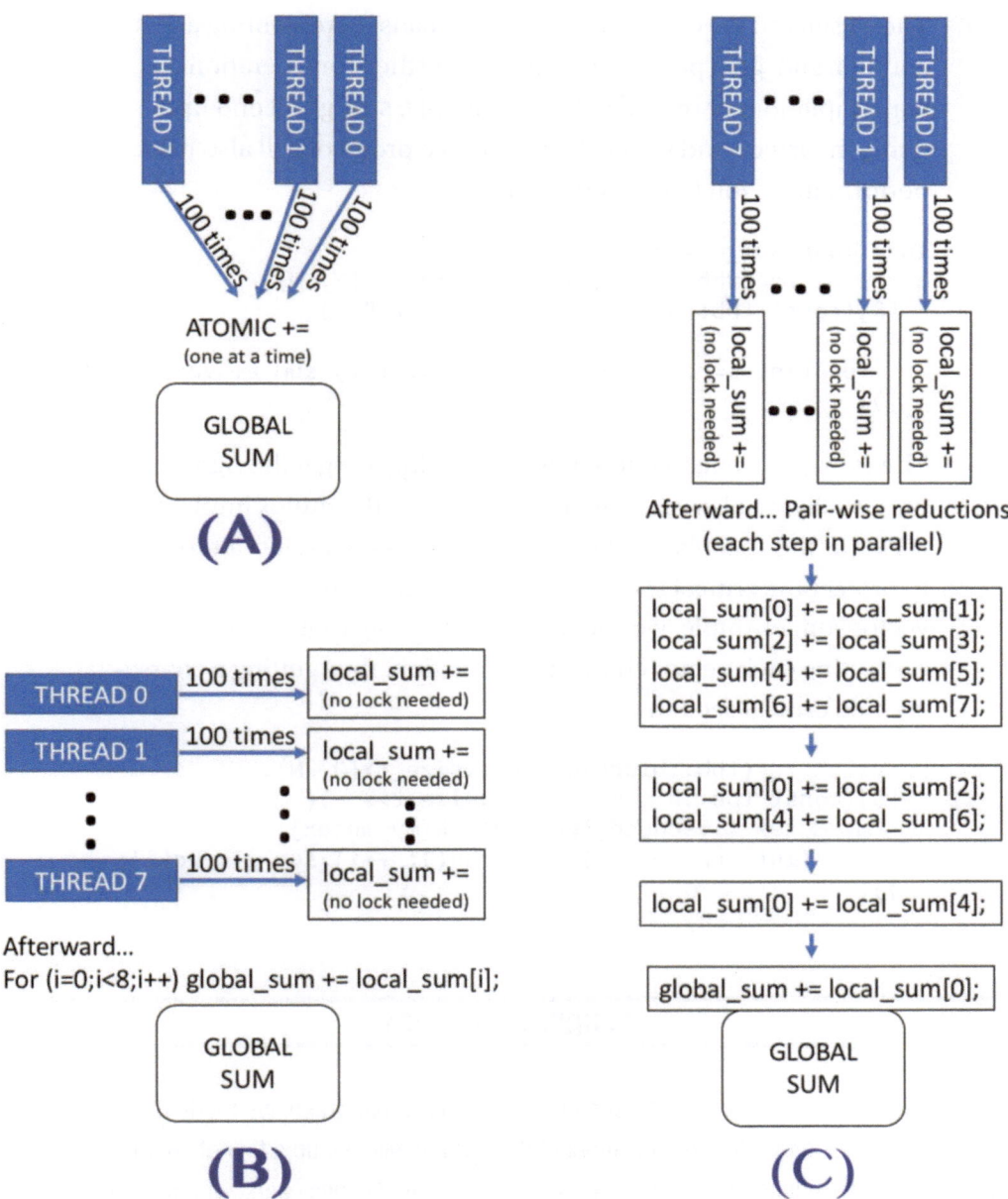

Figure 8-29. *Avoid contention when summing 800 numbers with eight threads: (A) atomic, protecting a global sum with atomic operations; (B) local, using* enumerable_thread_specific; *(C) wise, using* parallel_reduce

- The Mistaken: We can have the eight threads incrementing a global counter, sum_g, in parallel without any further consideration, contemplation, or remorse! Most probably, sum_g will end up being incorrect, and the cache coherence protocol will also ruin performance. You have been warned.

```
long long sum_g = 0;
parallel_for(tbb::blocked_range<size_t>{0, N},
  [&](const tbb::blocked_range<size_t>& r)
  {
    for (int i=r.begin(); i<r.end(); ++i) sum_g+=vec[i];
  });
```

- The Hardy: If we use coarse-grained locking, we get the right result, but usually we also serialize the code unless the mutex implements HTM (as the speculative flavor does). This is the easiest alternative to protect the critical section, but not the most efficient one. For our vector sum example, we will illustrate the coarse-grained locking by protecting each vector chunk accumulation, thus getting a coarse-grained critical section.

```
parallel_for(tbb::blocked_range<size_t>{0, N},
  [&](const tbb::blocked_range<size_t>& r){
    my_mutex_t::scoped_lock mylock{my_mutex};
    for (int i=r.begin(); i<r.end(); ++i) sum_g+=vec[i];
  });
```

LAUREL AND HARDY

Rather than delete a humorous reference not everyone would grasp, we made the questionable choice to offer an educational tidbit, which will use up a few of your precious neurons forever. Suppose for a moment that one wants to discuss coarse-grained locking and fine-grained locking with a little humor.

Also suppose one has enjoyed the famous comic duo from the early days of cinema known as Laurel and Hardy. Hardy played the coarser individual and Laurel played the fine individual. Throw in the fact that Laurel was decidedly English and Hardy staunchly American – one can imagine how hilarity unfolds. Hopefully you can see why Hardy (coarse) and Laurel (fine) seemed logical for us to cast alongside the Mistaken (bad news), the Nuclear (all in), the Local (timid), and the Wise (our favorite) in our tale of synchronized programming. If you find that you have even more spare neurons to use up, please note that their works are readily available for your entertainment when you are not too busy programming in C++.

- The Laurel: Fine-grained locking is more laborious to implement and typically requires more memory to store the different mutexes that protect the fine-grained sections of the data structure. The silver lining though is that the concurrency among threads is increased. We may want to assess different mutex flavors to choose the best one in the production code. For the vector sum, we don't have a data structure that can be partitioned so that each part can be independently protected. Let's consider a fine-grained implementation (the following one) in which we have a lighter critical section (in this case is as serial as the coarse-grained one, but threads compete for the lock at finer granularity).

```
parallel_for(tbb::::blocked_range<size_t>{0, N},
  [&](const tbb::blocked_range<size_t>& r){
      for (int i=r.begin(); i<r.end(); ++i){
        my_mutex_t::scoped_lock mylock{my_mutex};
        sum_g+=vec[i];
      }
  });
```

- The Nuclear: In some cases, atomic variables can come to our rescue, for example, when the shared mutable state can be stored in an integral type and the needed operation is simple enough. This is less expensive than the fine-grained locking approach, and the concurrency level is on par. The vector sum example (see Figure 8-29(A)) would be as follows, in this case, as sequential as the two previous approaches and with the global variable as highly contended as in the finer-grained case.

```cpp
std::atomic<long long> sum_a{0};
parallel_for(tbb::blocked_range<size_t>{0, N},
  [&](const tbb::blocked_range<size_t>& r)
  {
    for (int i=r.begin(); i<r.end(); ++i) sum_a+=vec[i];
  });
```

- The Local: Not always can we come up with an implementation in which privatizing local copies of the shared mutable state saves the day. But in such a case, thread-local storage (TLS) can be implemented, thanks to enumerate_thread_specific (ETS) and combinable classes. They work even when the number of collaborating threads is unknown and convenient reduction methods are provided. These classes offer enough flexibility to be used in different scenarios and can suit our needs when a reduction over a single iteration space does not suffice. To compute the vector sum, we present in the following an alternative in which the private partial sums, priv_s, are later accumulated sequentially, as in Figure 8-29(B).

```cpp
using priv_s_t = tbb::enumerable_thread_specific<long long>;
priv_s_t priv_s{0};
parallel_for(tbb::blocked_range<size_t>{0, N},
  [&](const tbb::blocked_range<size_t>& r)
  { priv_s_t::reference my_s = priv_s.local();
    for (int i=r.begin(); i<r.end(); ++i) my_s+=vec[i];
  });
  long long sum_p = 0;
  for (auto& i:priv_s) {sum_p+=i;}
```

- The Wise: When our computation fits into a reduction pattern, it is highly recommendable to relay on the `parallel_reduction` template instead of hand-coding the privatization and reduction using the TBB thread-local storage features. The following code may look more intricate than the previous one, but wise software architects devised clever tricks to fully optimize this common reduction operation. For instance, in this case the reduction operation follows a tree-like approach with complexity $O(n/p + \log n)$ instead of $O(n)$, as we see in Figure 8-29(C). Note: It is not uncommon to just say the complexity of a parallel reduction diminishes to $O(\log n)$ for parallel operations, but this is only roughly true when n/p becomes relatively small, where p is the number of parallel working threads. Take advantage of what the library puts in your hands instead of reinventing the wheel. This is certainly the method that scales best for a large number of cores and a costly reduction operation.

```
sum_p = parallel_reduce(tbb::blocked_range<size_t>{0, N}, 0,
[&](const tbb::blocked_range<size_t>& r, const long long& mysum)
  {
    long long res = mysum;
    for (int i=r.begin(); i<r.end(); ++i) res+=vec[i];
    return res;
  },
[&](const long long& a, const long long& b)
  {
    return a+b;
  });
```

As with the histogram computation, we also evaluate the performance of the different implementations of the vector addition of size 10^9 on an Intel Core Ultra processor-based system with threads set to eight, as we can see in Figure 8-30. Now the computation is an even finer-grained one (just incrementing a variable), and the relative impact of 10^9 lock–unlock operations or atomic increments is higher, as can be seen in the speedup (deceleration more properly speaking!) of the atomic (Nuclear) and fine-grained (Laurel) implementations. The coarse-grained (Hardy) implementation takes a slightly larger hit now than in the histogram case. Unsafe (Mistaken) is now 5.75× faster than sequential. The real winners both come in at 6.3× faster than the sequential code:

the TLS (Local) and the `parallel_reduction` (Wise) implementations. Try the code with various configurations – and you'll see the reduction code (Wise) can sometimes be much faster than TLS (Local) depending on the hardware, but sometimes they are close to equivalent. They are always many orders of magnitude faster than the Laurel and Hardy bad examples, and they are thread-safe too.

Implementation:	Mistaken	Hardy	Laurel	Nuclear	Local	Wise
Speedup:	5.7536	0.8140	0.0008	0.0095	6.2983	6.3107

Figure 8-30. *Example speedups of the different implementations of the vector addition for N=10⁹*

You might wonder why we went through all these different alternatives to end up recommending the last one. Why did we not just go directly to the `parallel_reduce` solution if it is the best one? Well, unfortunately, parallel life is hard, and not all parallelization problems can be solved with a simple reduction. In this chapter, we provide you with the devices to leverage synchronization mechanisms if they are really necessary but also show the benefits of rethinking the algorithm and the data structure if at all possible.

Summary

The TBB library provides support for mutual exclusion to help us synchronize threads when we need to access shared data safely. The library also provides thread-local storage (TLS) classes (as ETS and `combinable`) and algorithms (as `parallel_reduction`) that help us avoid the need for synchronization. In this chapter, we walked through the epic journey of parallelizing an image histogram computation. All of these capabilities rely on and interact with modern C++ capabilities such as atomic variables. We have treated them as one combined topic in order to best illustrate how to use them together for maximum benefit.

Never forget that the best strategy is finding an algorithm to solve our problem that has the least need for synchronization (the least contention).

For the running example used in this chapter, we saw different parallel implementations starting from an incorrect one and then iterated through different synchronization alternatives, like coarse-grained locking, fine-grained-locking, and atomics, to end up with some alternative implementations that do not use locks at all. On the way, we stopped at some remarkable spots, presenting the properties that allow us to characterize mutexes, the different kinds of mutex flavors available in the standard C++ library together with the TBB library, and common problems that usually arise when relying on mutexes to implement our algorithms.

Hopefully we will all remember that careful rethinking of our algorithms can often result in cleaner implementations that perform much better. If not, perhaps we should read the chapter again? It is a very important lesson.

For More Information

Here are some additional reading materials we recommend related to this chapter:

C++ Concurrency in Action, second edition, Anthony Williams, Manning Publications, 2018.

A Primer on Memory Consistency and Cache Coherence, Daniel J. Sorin, Mark D. Hill, and David A. Wood, Morgan & Claypool Publishers, 2011.

Special Thanks

Photo of Ronda, Málaga, in Figure 8-1, taken by Rafael Asenjo, used with permission.

Memes shown within our figures are used with permission from 365psd.com "33 Vector meme faces."

Traffic jam in Figure 8-17 drawn by Denisa-Adreea Constantinescu while a PhD student at the University of Malaga, used with permission.

CHAPTER 9

Cancellation and Exception Handling

In previous chapters, we explored how to create numerous tasks to achieve parallelism. In this chapter, we will focus on two essential aspects of task management: canceling tasks and handling exceptions that may arise within them.

C++ provides robust exception handling, which is crucial for building resilient applications. TBB ensures that we can effectively access and manage exceptions occurring in the tasks we create using TBB.

While using our application, we may initiate tasks that we later want to cancel before they are completed. This can occur due to exceptions, where an issue in one task diminishes our interest in receiving the results of other tasks. For example, if we are processing a flow graph and one stage fails in a way that invalidates the entire computation, we may choose to cancel the remaining tasks. Additionally, we might wish to cancel tasks when a solution has already been found, rendering the other tasks unnecessary. For instance, we may start multiple search tasks and decide to terminate the search as soon as any task reports a match.

TBB exception and cancellation support addresses the complexities arising from several factors:

- Exceptions may be thrown within tasks executed by multiple threads.

- Task cancellation must be implemented to promptly terminate any work causing an exception.

- Composability must be preserved throughout the process.

- Exception management should not affect performance when no exceptions occur.

© Michael J. Voss, James R. Reinders 2025
M. J. Voss and J. R. Reinders, *Today's TBB*, https://doi.org/10.1007/979-8-8688-1270-5_9

The implementation of exceptions within TBB meets all the necessary requirements, including task cancellation support. Task cancellation is essential because throwing an exception may necessitate halting the execution of the parallel algorithm that generated it. For instance, if a `parallel_for` algorithm encounters an out-of-bounds or division-by-zero exception, the library may need to cancel the entire `parallel_for`. This requires TBB to terminate all tasks processing chunks of the parallel iteration space and then transition to the exception handler. TBB's task cancellation seamlessly handles the cancellation of tasks involved in the problematic `parallel_for` without affecting unrelated parallel tasks.

Task cancellation is valuable not only for exception handling but also in its own right. In this chapter, we begin by demonstrating how cancellation can be leveraged to accelerate some parallel algorithms. Although TBB algorithms handle cancellation out of the box, advanced developers may want to gain full control over task cancellation and understand its implementation in TBB. We aim to address such needs in this chapter.

The other part of this chapter focuses on exception handling. Exception handling "just works" without added complexity: using the familiar try–catch construct, as in sequential code, is sufficient to capture standard C++ exceptions and additional TBB-specific ones. We also go beyond the basics by explaining how to create custom TBB exceptions and exploring the interplay between TBB exception handling and cancellation.

Even if you are skeptical of exception handling and prefer the "error code" approach, please keep reading to discover the advantages of TBB exception handling in developing dependable, fault-tolerant parallel applications.

How to Cancel Collective Work

In certain situations, it's necessary to cancel a task. This can be due to external factors (such as a user canceling the operation via a GUI button) or internal ones (like finding an item that eliminates the need for further searching). While these scenarios are common in sequential code, they also occur in parallel applications. For example, some computationally intensive global optimization algorithms use a branch-and-bound parallel pattern. In this pattern, the search space is organized as a tree, and it may be desirable to cancel tasks traversing certain branches if the solution is likely elsewhere.

Let's see how we can put cancellation to work with a somewhat contrived example: we want to find the position of the single -2 in a vector of integers, data. The example is contrived because we set data[500]=-2, so we do know the output beforehand (i.e., where –2 is stored). The implementation uses a parallel_for algorithm as we see in Figure 9-1.

```cpp
std::vector<int> data(n);
data[500] = -2;
int index = -1;
auto t1 = tbb::tick_count::now();
tbb::parallel_for(tbb::blocked_range<int>{0, n},
  [&](const tbb::blocked_range<int>& r){
      for(int i=r.begin(); i!=r.end(); ++i){
        if(data[i] == -2) {
          index = i;
          // commenting out the following line, can increase run time
          tbb::task::current_context()->cancel_group_execution();
          break;
        }
      }
});
auto t2 = tbb::tick_count::now();
std::cout << "Index "      << index;
std::cout << " found in " << (t2-t1).seconds() << " seconds!\n";
```

Figure 9-1. *Finding the index in which –2 is stored. Sample code* cancellation/cancel_group_execution1.cpp

The goal is to cancel all concurrent tasks in the parallel_for once one task finds that data[500]==-2. How does task::current_context()->cancel_group_execution() work? Well, task::current_context() returns a reference to the innermost task group context (TGC).

A task group context (TGC) represents a group of tasks that can be canceled. A TGC is represented by a tbb::task_group_context object. While the naming might be confusing, tbb::task_group_context is not the same thing as the tbb::task_group introduced in Chapter 6. The tbb::task_group introduced in Chapter 6 is used to run and wait for tasks, while a tbb::task_group_context represents a set of properties used by the task scheduler during execution. To prevent confusion, we use TGC in this chapter as a reminder of this distinction.

As its name suggests, task::current_context()->cancel_group_execution() cancels not just the calling task but *all* tasks in the same group.

In this example, the group consists of all tasks participating in the `parallel_for` algorithm. By canceling this group, we halt all tasks and effectively interrupt the parallel search. Imagine the task that finds `data[500]==-2` announcing to its siblings, "Hey, I found it! Stop searching!" Typically, each TBB algorithm creates its own TGC, and any task in this group can cancel the entire algorithm.

For a vector of size `n=1,000,000,000`, this loop consumes `0.0004` seconds, and the output can appear as

```
Index 500 found in 0.000368532 seconds!
```

However, if `task::current_context()->cancel_group_execution()` is omitted, the execution time increases several hundred times as long (to 0.1 seconds) on the system used for writing this chapter and testing this example.

That's all it takes for basic TBB algorithm cancellation. With a compelling reason to cancel tasks (achieving more than 200× speedup in this example!), we can also delve into how task cancellation operates and consider strategies for controlling which tasks are canceled.

Advanced Task Cancellation

We can optionally pass a TGC object to high-level algorithms like `parallel_for` or a flow graph. For example, an alternative approach to the code in Figure 9-1 is shown in Figure 9-2.

```cpp
tbb::task_group_context tg;
...
tbb::parallel_for(tbb::blocked_range<int>{0, n},
  [&](const tbb::blocked_range<int>& r){
      for(int i=r.begin(); i!=r.end(); ++i){
        if(data[i] == -2) {
          index = i;
          // commenting out the following line, can increase run time
          tg.cancel_group_execution();
          break;
        }
      }
}, tg); // our new parameter to parallel_for
```

Figure 9-2. *Alternative implementation of the code in Figure 9-1. Sample code cancellation/cancel_group_execution2.cpp*

In this code, we see that a TGC, `tg`, is created and passed as the last argument of the `parallel_for` and used to call `tg.cancel_group_execution()` (now using a member function of the `task_group_context` class).

Note that the codes of Figures 9-1 and 9-2 are completely equivalent. The optional TGC parameter, `tg`, passed as the last argument of the `parallel_for` just opens the door to more elaborate developments. For example, say that we also pass the same TGC variable, `tg`, to a `parallel_pipeline` that we launch in a parallel thread. Now, any task collaborating either in the `parallel_for` or in the `parallel_pipeline` can call `tg.cancel_group_execution()` to cancel both parallel algorithms.

When a task triggers the cancellation of the whole TGC, spawned tasks waiting in the queues are finalized without being run, but already running tasks will not be canceled by the TBB scheduler because the scheduler is non-preemptive. Therefore, before passing the control to the task's body, the scheduler checks the cancellation flag of the task's TGC and then decides if the task should be executed or the whole TGC canceled. But if the task already has the control, it has the control until it decides to return it to the scheduler.

Next question: to which TGC are the new tasks assigned? While we have the tools to fully control this mapping, it's important to understand the default behavior as well. First, let's explore how to manually map tasks to a TGC.

Explicit Assignment of TGC

As we have seen, we can create TGC objects and pass them to the high-level parallel algorithms (`parallel_for` and others) and to the lower-level tasking API (`tbb::task_group`). All the tasks launched using the same `task_group::run()` member function will belong to the same TGC, enabling any task in the group to cancel the entire set.

For example, consider the code of Figure 9-3, where we rewrite the parallel search for a specific value "hidden" in a `data` vector to find its index. This time, we use a manually implemented divide-and-conquer approach using the `task_group` features (similar to what `parallel_for` does internally, even if it's not visible to us). The class `task_group` provides a function `cancel` that cancels its underlying TGC. Note that while in Figure 9-3, we call `g.cancel()` and `g` is a `task_group`, that call cancels the underlying TGC.

```cpp
int grainsize = 100;
std::vector<int> data;
int myindex=-1;
tbb::task_group g;

void SerialSearch(long begin, long end) {
  for(int i=begin; i<end; ++i){
    if(data[i]==-2){
      myindex=i;
      g.cancel();
      break;
} } }

void ParallelSearch(long begin, long end) {
  // UNCOMMENT after initial run
  // if(tbb::is_current_task_group_canceling()) return;
  if((end-begin) < grainsize) { //cutoof equivalent
    return SerialSearch(begin, end);
  }else{
    long mid=begin+(end-begin)/2;

    g.run([&]{ParallelSearch(begin, mid);}); // spawn a task
    g.run([&]{ParallelSearch(mid, end);});    // spawn another task
  }
}

int main(int argc, char** argv)
{
  int n = 100000000;
  data.resize(n);
  data[n/2] = -2;

  auto t0 = tbb::tick_count::now();
  SerialSearch(0,n);
  auto t1 = tbb::tick_count::now();
  ParallelSearch(0,n);
  g.wait();       // wait for all spawned tasks
  auto t2 = tbb::tick_count::now();
  double t_s = (t1 - t0).seconds();
  double t_p = (t2 - t1).seconds();

  std::cout << "SerialSearch:   " << myindex << " Time: " << t_s << std::endl;
  std::cout << "ParallelSearch: " << myindex << " Time: " << t_p
            << " Speedup: "        << t_s/t_p << std::endl;
  return 0;
}
```

Figure 9-3. *Manual implementation of the parallel search using* task_group *class. Sample code cancellation/cancel_group_execution3.cpp*

For expediency, the vector data, the resulting myindex, and the task_group g are global variables. This code recursively divides the search space until it reaches a certain grainsize. The function ParallelSearch(begin,end) is used for this parallel partitioning. When the grain size becomes sufficiently small (100 iterations in our example), SequentialSearch(begin,end) is invoked. If the target value, –2, is found within any range checked by SequentialSearch, all spawned tasks are canceled using g.cancel(). On our laptop with four cores, and for N equal to 10 million, this is the output of our algorithm:

```
SerialSearch:   50000000 Time: 0.0201569
ParallelSearch: 50000000 Time: 0.00018978 Speedup: 106.212
```

5000000 is the index of the -2 value we have found.

Considering the speedup, it's surprising that the parallel version runs 119 times faster than the sequential code. This occurs because the parallel implementation often performs less work than its sequential counterpart: once a task finds the key, further traversal of the vector data is unnecessary. In our run, the key is in the middle of the vector, at N/2. The sequential version must reach this point, while the parallel version searches simultaneously at different positions, such as 0, N/4, N/2, and N·3/4.

If you were impressed by the achieved speedup, there's even more potential for improvement. Keep in mind that cancel() cannot terminate tasks that are already running. However, a running task can check if another task in the TGC has canceled the execution. To implement this with the task_group class, simply add (by uncommenting in the supplied code) the following check within your running task

```
if(tbb::is_current_task_group_canceling()) return;
```

at the beginning of the ParallelSearch() function. This apparently minor mod results in these execution times:

```
SerialSearch:   50000000 Time: 0.0217766
ParallelSearch: 50000000 Time: 0.000181158 Speedup: 120.208
```

Cancellation is definitely worthwhile to implement; the effects can be much more dramatic at times depending on the exact algorithm and data. Be careful not to overuse, as the cost of the cancellation check can be nontrivial. As always, test your performance when trying new techniques to verify the impact and let real performance results guide us for our particular needs.

Default Assignment of TGC

What happens if we don't explicitly specify the TGC? The default behavior follows these rules:

- A top-level (root) thread implicitly creates its own TGC when it uses an algorithm, and it is tagged as "**isolated**." The first task executed by this thread belongs to that TGC and subsequent child tasks inherit the same parent's TGC.

- When one of these tasks invokes a parallel algorithm without explicitly passing a TGC as optional argument (e.g., parallel_for, parallel_reduce, parallel_pipeline, task_group, flow graph, etc.), a new TGC, labeled as "**bound**," is implicitly created for the new tasks collaborating in this nested algorithm. This TGC is therefore a child *bound* to the isolated parent TGC.

- If tasks of a parallel algorithm invoke a nested parallel algorithm, a new bound child TGC is created for this new algorithm, where the parent is now the TGC of the invoking task.

An example of a forest of TGC trees automatically built by a hypothetical TBB code is depicted in Figure 9-4.

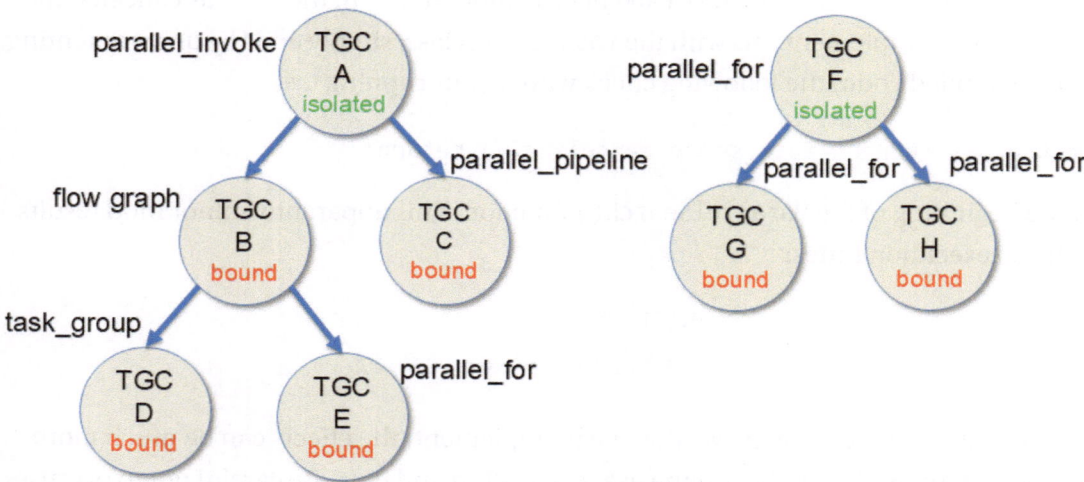

Figure 9-4. *A forest of TGC trees automatically created when running a hypothetical TBB code*

In our hypothetical TBB code, the user wants to nest several TBB algorithms but knows nothing about TGCs so they just call the algorithms without passing the optional and explicit TGC object. In one master thread, there is a call to a parallel_invoke, which automatically initializes the scheduler creating one arena and the first isolated TGC, A. Then, inside the parallel_invoke, two TBB algorithms are created, a flow graph and a parallel_pipeline. For each of these algorithms, a new TGC, B and C in this case, is automatically created and bound to A. Inside one of the flow graph nodes, a task_group is created, and a parallel_for is instantiated in a different flow graph node. This results in two newly created TGCs, D and E, which are bound to B. This forms the first tree of our TGC forest, with an isolated root and where all the other TGCs are bound, that is, they have a parent. The second tree is built in a different master thread that creates a parallel_for with just two parallel ranges, and for each one a nested parallel_for is called. Again, the root of the tree is an isolated TGC, F, and the other TGCs, G and H, are bound.

Note that the user simply wrote TBB code, nesting some algorithms within others. TBB automatically constructs the forest of TGCs. Remember, multiple tasks share each TGC.

Now, what happens if a task gets canceled? Easy. The rule is that the whole TGC containing this task is canceled, but the cancellation also propagates downward. For example, if we cancel a task of the flow graph (TGC B), we will also cancel the task_group (TGC D) and the parallel_for (TGC E), as shown in Figure 9-5. It makes sense: we are canceling the flow graph and everything created from there on.

The example is somewhat contrived, as finding a real application with this level of algorithm nesting might be challenging. However, it effectively illustrates how different TGCs are automatically linked to support TBB's renowned composability.

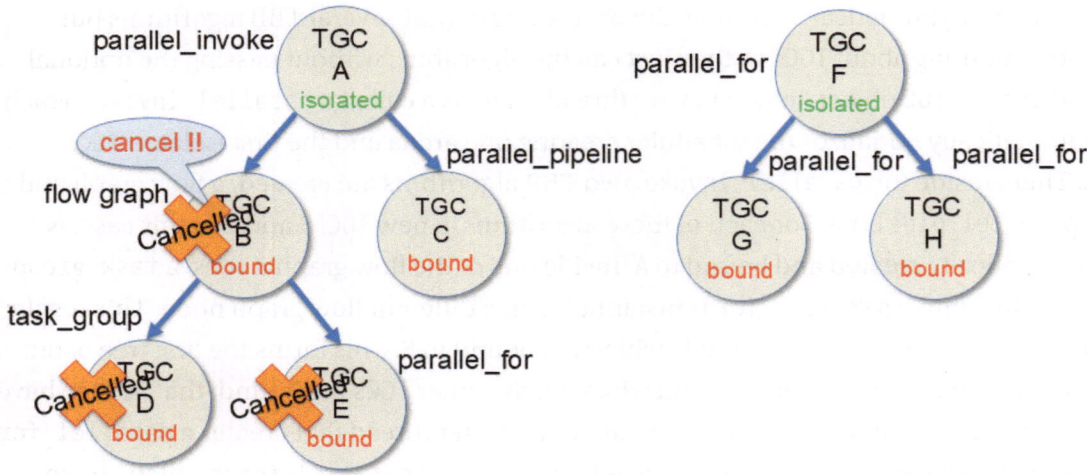

Figure 9-5. *Cancel is called from a task belonging to TGC B.*

If we want to cancel the flow graph and the task_group while keeping the parallel_for (TGC E) active, we can achieve this by manually creating an isolated TGC object and passing it as the last argument of the parallel_for. This can be done with code like that in Figure 9-6, where a function_node of the flow graph, g, takes advantage of this feature.

```
tbb::flow::function_node<float,float> node{g,…,[&](float a){
    tbb::task_group_context TGC_E(tbb::task_group_context::isolated);
    // nested parallel_for
    tbb::parallel_for(0, N, 1,[&](…){ /*loop body*/ }, TGC_E);
    return a;
}};
```

Figure 9-6. *Alternative to detach a nested algorithm from the tree of TGCs. Sample code* cancellation/cancel_group_execution4.cpp

The isolated TGC object, TGC_E, is created on the stack and passed as the last argument to the parallel_for. Now, as depicted in Figure 9-7, even if a task of the flow graph cancels its TGC B, the cancellation propagates downward till TGC D but cannot reach TGC E because it has been created detached from the tree.

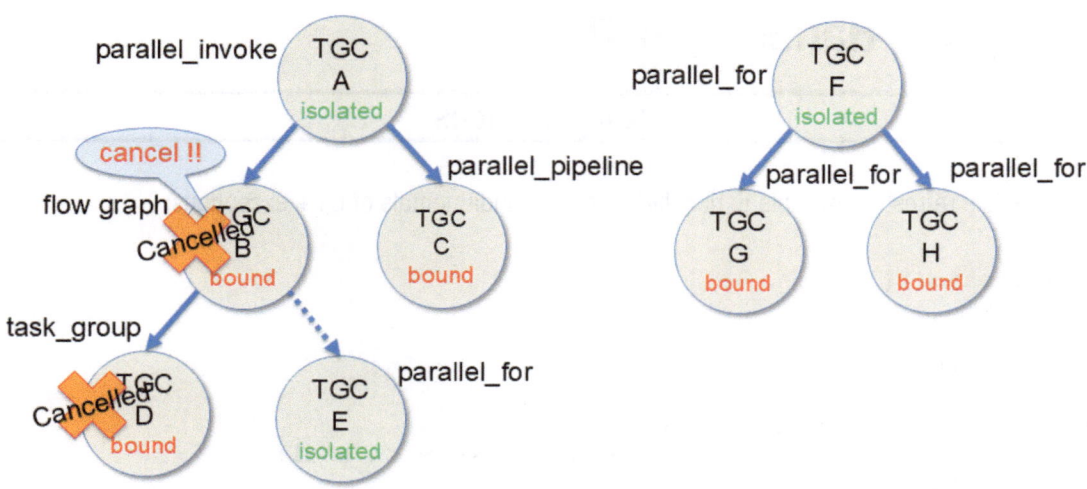

Figure 9-7. *TGC E is now isolated and won't be canceled*

More precisely, the isolated TGC E can now be the root of another tree in our forest of TGCs because it is an isolated TGC and it can be the parent of new TGCs created for deeper nested algorithms. We will see an example of this in the next section.

To summarize, if we nest TBB algorithms without explicitly passing a TGC object to them, the default TGC forest will produce the expected behavior in case of cancellation. However, this behavior can be controlled at our will by creating the necessary number of TGC objects and passing them to the desired algorithms. For example, we can create a single TGC, A, and pass it to all the parallel algorithms invoked in the first thread of our hypothetical TBB example. In such a case, all tasks collaborating in all algorithms will belong to that TGC A, as depicted in Figure 9-8. If now a task of the flow graph gets canceled, not only the nested task_group and parallel_for algorithms are also canceled, but all the algorithms sharing the TGC A.

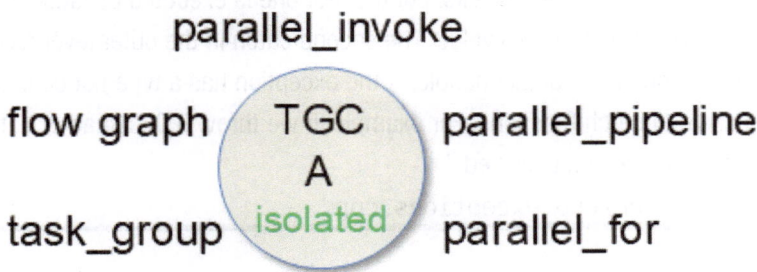

Figure 9-8. *After modifying our hypothetical TBB code so that we pass a single TGC A to all the parallel algorithms*

Exception Handling in TBB

C++ EXCEPTIONS

Here is a refresher example to help illustrate the fundamentals of C++ exceptions:

```cpp
int main(){
  try{
    try{
      throw 5;
    }
    catch (const int& n){
      cout << "Re-throwing value: " << n << endl;
      throw;
    }
  }
  catch(int& e){
    cout << "Value caught: " << e << endl;
  }
  catch (...){
    cout << "Exception occurred\n";
  }
}
```

The output after running this code is

```
Re-throwing value: 5
Value caught: 5
```

As we can see, the first try block includes a nested try–catch. This one throws as an exception as an integer with value 5. Since the catch block matches the type, this code becomes the exception handler. Here, we only print the value received and rethrow the exception upward. At the outer level there are two catch blocks, but the first one is executed because the argument type matches the type of the thrown value. The second catch in the outer level receives an ellipsis (…) so it becomes the actual handler if the exception has a type not considered in the preceding chain of catch functions. For example, if we throw 5.0 instead of 5, the output message would be "Exception occurred."

Sample code `exception/cpp_exceptions.cpp`.

Now that we understand cancellation as the keystone mechanism supporting TBB exception management, let's consider exceptions and including how they behave in the presence of cancellations. Note that we are not diving into `std::exception_ptr` in this book, as it is simply equivalently useful with TBB as with just C++ when writing exception handlers. Our goal now is to master the development of bulletproof code that exercise exceptions, as the one in Figure 9-9.

```cpp
int main(){
  std::vector<int> data(1000);
  try{
    tbb::parallel_for(0, 2000, [&] (int i) { data.at(i)++; });
  }
  catch(const std::out_of_range& ex) {
    std::cout << "Out_of_range: " << ex.what() << std::endl;
  }
  return 0;
}
```

Figure 9-9. *Basic example of TBB exception handling. Sample code* `exception/exception_catch1.cpp`

Okay, maybe it is not completely bulletproof yet, but for a first example it is good enough. The thing is that the vector `data` has only 1000 elements, but the `parallel_for` algorithm insists on walking till position 2000-1. To add insult to injury, `data` is not accessed using `data[i]`, but using `Data.at(i)`, which, contrary to the former, adds bound-checking and throws `std::out_of_range` objects if we don't toe the line. Therefore, when we compile and run the code of Figure 9-9, we will get

```
Out_of_range: vector::_M_range_check: __n (which is 1500) >= this->size() (which is 1000)
```

Several tasks will be spawned to increment `data` elements in parallel. Some of them will try to increment at positions beyond 999. The task that first touches an out-of-range element, for example, `data.at(1003)++`, clearly must be canceled. Then, the `std::vector::at()` member function instead of incrementing the inexistent 1003 position throws `std::out_of_range`. Since the exception object is not caught by the task, it is rethrown upward, getting to the TBB scheduler. Then, the scheduler catches the exception and proceeds to cancel all concurrent tasks of the corresponding TGC (we already know how the whole TGC gets canceled). In addition, a pointer to the exception object is stored in the TGC data structure. When all TGC tasks are canceled, the TGC is finalized, which rethrows the exception in the thread that started the TGC execution. In our example, this is the thread that called `parallel_for`. But the `parallel_for` is in a `try` block with a `catch` function that receives an `out_of_range` object. This means that the `catch` function becomes the exception handler, which finally prints the exception message. The `ex.what()` member function is responsible of returning a string with some verbose information about the exception.

Note   **Implementation detail.** The compiler is not aware of the threading nature of a TBB parallel algorithm. This means that enclosing such algorithm in a try block results in only the calling thread (master thread) being guarded, but the worker threads will be executing tasks that can throw exceptions too. To solve this, the scheduler already includes try–catch blocks so that every worker thread is able to intercept exceptions escaping from its tasks.

We recommend that the argument of the `catch()` function should be passed by const reference. That way, a single catch function capturing a base class can capture objects of all derived types. For example, in Figure 9-9, we could have written `catch(const std::exception& ex)` instead of `catch(const std::out_of_range& ex)` because `std::out_of_range` is derived from `std::logic_failure` that in turn is derived from the base class `std::exception` and capturing by reference captures all related classes.

Final Notes on Exception Handling

Since TBB fully supports C++ exceptions, the remaining challenge is considering how our exception handling (or lack thereof) affects our final program. A single exception will propagate upward in a dependency chain of tasks. Eventually, no matter at what level it is thrown, this will gracefully do away with the whole parallel algorithm (as it would do with a serial one). We can prevent the chain of cancellations by either catching the exception at the desired level or by configuring the required nested algorithm in an isolated TGC. The choice is ours. It's no different from C++ exception handling in a program without TBB, other than our need to consider the many parallel sources of issues that are possible when threads execute in parallel.

Summary

In this chapter, we explored how canceling a TBB parallel algorithm and using exception handling for runtime errors are straightforward processes. Both features work seamlessly out of the box with default settings. We also discussed an important aspect of TBB: the task group context (TGC). This element is crucial for implementing cancellation and exception handling in TBB and can be manually utilized for greater control over these features.

We began by covering the cancellation process, explaining how a task can cancel its entire TGC. We then reviewed how to manually assign a TGC to a task and the rules that apply when the developer does not explicitly define this mapping. The default rules ensure expected behavior: if a parallel algorithm is canceled, all nested parallel algorithms are also canceled.

Next, we discussed exception handling. TBB exceptions behave similarly to exceptions in sequential code, although considering the implications of parallelism makes our job more complex. An exception thrown in one task by one thread may be caught by a different thread depending on lifetimes. Thanks to modern C++ features, an exact copy of the exception can be transferred between threads. TBB and C++ together give us all the functionality needed to address any situation that may arise in our parallel application.

For More Information

Here is additional reading material we recommend related to this chapter:

Deb Haldar, Top 15 C++ Exception handling mistakes and how to avoid them. `www.acodersjourney.com/2016/08/top-15-c-exception-handling-mistakes-avoid/`

CHAPTER 10

Performance: Pillars of Composability

The Types of Composability

The TBB library is designed to provide *composable performance*. Ultimately, when we say that TBB is a composable parallel library, we mean that developers can mix and match code that uses TBB freely anywhere they want. These uses of TBB can be serial, one after the other; they can be nested; and they can be concurrent. And if TBB code is combined in any of these ways, the program will still work correctly, and the performance will be good.

It might not be obvious that parallel programming models have often had restrictions that were difficult to manage in complex applications. Imagine if we could not use "while" statements within an "if" statement, even indirectly in functions we call. Before TBB, equally difficult restrictions existed for some parallel programming models, such as OpenMP. Even the newer SYCL standard lacks full composability (the most obvious example is that while SYCL is a single-source model, not all SYCL commands can be used inside SYCL kernels). Similarly, CUDA is highly restricted in what type of code can be run from kernels.

The most frustrating aspect of non-composable parallel programming models is that there is such a thing as requesting too much parallelism or introducing parallelism in the wrong place or at the wrong time. This is horrible and something TBB avoids. In our experience, naïve users of non-composable models often overuse parallelism – and their programs crash from explosions in memory use, or they slow down to a crawl due to unbearable synchronization overheads. Concern about these issues can lead experienced programmers to expose too little parallelism, resulting in load imbalances

© Michael J. Voss, James R. Reinders 2025
M. J. Voss and J. R. Reinders, *Today's TBB*, https://doi.org/10.1007/979-8-8688-1270-5_10

and poor scaling. Using a composable programming model avoids the need to worry about this difficult balancing act.

Composability makes TBB extraordinarily dependable to use in both simple and complex applications. Composability is a design philosophy that allows us to create programs that are more scalable because we can expose parallelism without fear.

Composability is, unfortunately, not a simple yes-or-no property of a programming model. Even though OpenMP has known composability issues for nested parallelism, it would be incorrect to label OpenMP as a non-composable programming model. If an application invokes one OpenMP construct after another OpenMP construct in series, this serial composition works just fine. It would likewise be an overstatement to say that TBB is a fully composable programming model that works well with all other parallel programming models in all situations. Composability is more accurately thought of as a measure of how well two programming models, or even a single programming model mixed with itself, perform when composed in a specific way.

For example, let's consider two parallel programming models: model A and model B. Let's define T_A as the throughput of a kernel when it uses model A to express outer-level parallelism and T_B as the throughput of the same kernel when it uses model B (without using model A) to express inner-level parallelism. If the programming models are composable, we would expect the throughput of the kernel using both outer and inner parallelism to be T_{AB} >= $\max(T_A, T_B)$. How much more T_{AB} is than $\max(T_A, T_B)$ depends both on how efficiently the models compose with each other and on the physical properties of the targeted platform, such as the number of cores, the size of the memory, etc. But most developers would be surprised if adding more parallelism by combining outer and inner parallelism would decrease the amount of work you can get done in a fixed period of time. Unfortunately for non-composable models, that is often the case.

Figure 10-1 shows the three general types of composition that we can use to combine software constructs: nested execution, concurrent execution, and serial execution. We say that TBB is a composable threading library because when a TBB parallel algorithm is composed with other TBB parallel algorithms in one of the three ways shown in Figure 10-1, the resulting code performs well, that is, the throughput $T_{TBB1+TBB2}$ >= $\max(T_{TBB1}, T_{TBB2})$. If TBB is combined with another parallel model that coordinates through a shared arbitrator, then likewise $T_{TBB+Other}$ >= $\max(T_{TBB}, T_{Other})$. We discuss TBB's arbitrator later in this chapter.

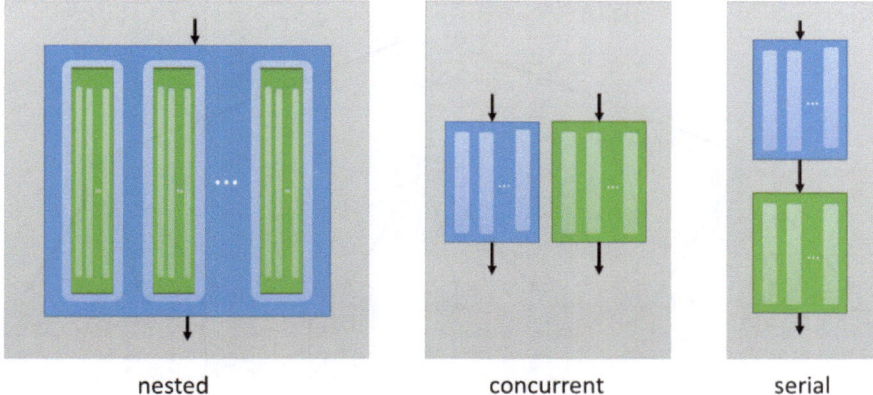

Figure 10-1. *The ways in which software constructs can be composed*

However, if TBB is combined with a different parallel model that does not coordinate with TBB through a shared arbitrator, there is no guarantee that $T_{TBB+Other} >= max(T_{TBB}, T_{Other})$, because the other model may behave greedily. Even so, the TBB library is designed to be a good citizen, and it has properties that make it more likely to compose well even with libraries that do not coordinate with it. We cover these properties in more detail throughout this chapter.

Nested Composition

In a nested composition, the machine executes one parallel algorithm inside of another parallel algorithm. The intention of a nested composition is almost always to add more parallelism, and it can even exponentially increase the amount of work that can be executed in parallel as shown in Figure 10-2. Handling nested parallelism effectively was a primary goal in the design of TBB.

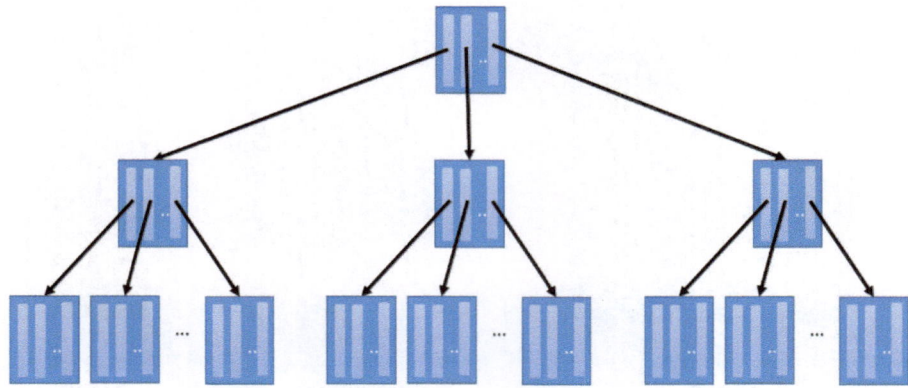

Figure 10-2. *Nested parallelism can lead to an exponential growth in the number of available parallel tasks (or, when using a non-composable library, threads)*

In fact, the algorithms provided by the TBB library in many cases depend on nested composition to create scalable parallelism. For example, in Chapter 2, we discussed how nested invocations of TBB's `parallel_invoke` can be used to create a scalable parallel version of quicksort. TBB is designed from the ground up to be an effective executor of nested parallelism.

In contrast to TBB, other parallel models may perform catastrophically bad in the presence of nested parallelism. A concrete example is the OpenMP API. OpenMP is a widely used programming model for shared memory parallelism – and it is very effective for single-level parallelism. However, its basic parallel loop constructs use a notoriously bad model for nested parallelism because mandatory parallelism is an integral part of their definition. In applications that have multiple levels of parallelism, each OpenMP parallel construct creates an additional team of threads. Each thread allocates stack space and needs to be scheduled by the OS's thread scheduler. If the number of threads is very large, the application can run out of memory. If there are more threads than the number of logical cores, the threads must share cores, and so these extra threads tend to offer little benefit due to the oversubscription of the hardware resources, adding only overhead.

The most practical choice for nested parallelism with OpenMP is typically to turn off the nested parallelism completely. In fact, the OpenMP API provides an environment variable, `OMP_NESTED`, for the purpose of turning on or off nested parallelism. Because TBB has relaxed sequential semantics and uses tasks to express parallelism instead of threads, it can flexibly adapt parallelism to the available hardware resources. We can safely leave nested parallelism on with TBB – there's no need for a mechanism to broadly turn off a type of parallelism in TBB! In fact, as stated before, nested parallelism is a key design principle for many TBB algorithms.

Later in this chapter, we discuss the key features of TBB that make it very effective at executing nested parallelism, including its thread pool and work-stealing task scheduler.

Concurrent Composition

As shown in Figure 10-3, concurrent composition is when the executions of parallel algorithms overlap in time. Concurrent composition can be used to intentionally add more parallelism, or it can arise by happenstance when two unrelated applications (or constructs in the same program) execute concurrently on the same system. Concurrent and parallel execution are not always the same thing! As shown in Figure 10-3, concurrent execution is when two constructs execute during the same time period, while parallel execution is when those two constructs execute simultaneously. This means that parallel execution is a form of concurrent execution, but concurrent execution is not always parallel execution. Concurrent composition improves performance when it is effectively turned into parallel execution.

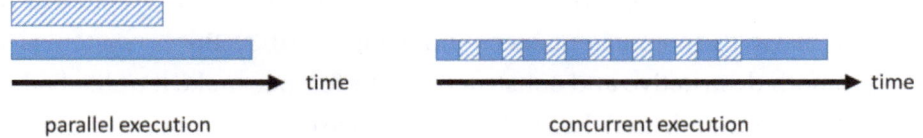

Figure 10-3. *Parallel vs. concurrent execution*

Note   It is sometimes confusing because the C++ standard defines *forward progress guarantees*, which include terms such *as concurrent forward progress guarantees, parallel forward progress guarantees,* and *weakly parallel forward progress guarantees.* The C++ standard also defines execution policies that include `sequenced_policy, unsequenced_policy, parallel_policy,` and `parallel_unsequenced_policy.` Unless otherwise stated, when we use the terms parallel and concurrent, we mean them as defined in this section. When we refer to the specific terms in the C++ standard, we will refer to those terms explicitly.

A concurrent composition of the two loops in Figure 10-4 is when a parallel implementation of loop 1 executes concurrently with a parallel implementation of loop 2, whether in two different processes or in two different threads in the same process.

```
// loop 1                          // loop 2
for (int i = 0; i < N; ++i)        for (int i = 0; i < M; ++i)
{                                  {
    b[i] = f(a[i]);                    d[i] = g(c[i]);
}                                  }
```

Figure 10-4. *Two loops that may be executed concurrently*

When executing constructs concurrently, an arbitrator (a runtime library like TBB, the operating system, or some combination of systems) is responsible for assigning system resources to the different constructs. If the two constructs require access to the same resources at the same time, then access to these resources must be interleaved.

Good performance for a concurrent composition might mean that the wall-clock execution time is as short as the time to execute the longest-running construct, since all the other constructs can execute in parallel with it (like in the parallel execution in Figure 10-3). Or good performance might mean that the wall-clock execution time is no longer than the sum of the execution times of all the constructs if the executions need to be interleaved (like in the concurrent execution in Figure 10-3). But no system is ideal, and sources of both destructive and constructive interference make it unlikely that we get performance that exactly matches either of these cases.

TBB's thread pool and its work-stealing task scheduler, discussed later in this chapter, help with concurrent composition as well, reduce arbitration overheads, and in many cases lead to task distributions that optimize resource usage. If TBB's default behaviors are not satisfactory, the features described in Chapter 11 can be used to mitigate negative impacts of resource sharing as needed.

Serial Composition

The final way to compose two constructs is to execute them serially, one after the other without overlapping them in time. This may seem like a trivial kind of composition with no implications on performance, but (unfortunately) it is not. When we use serial composition, we typically expect good performance to mean that there is no interference between the two constructs.

For example, if we consider the loops in Figure 10-5, the serial composition is to execute loop 3 followed by loop 4. We might expect that the time to complete each parallel construct when executed in series is no different than the time to execute that same construct alone. If the time it takes to execute loop 3 alone after parallelism is added using a parallel programming model A is $t_{3,A}$ and the time to execute loop 4 alone using a parallel programming model B is $t_{4,B}$, then we would expect the total time for executing the constructs in series is no more than the sum of the times of each construct, $t_{3,A} + t_{4,B}$.

```
// loop 3
for (int i = 0; i < N; ++i) {
    b[i] = f(a[i]);
}

// loop 4
for (int i = 0; i < N; ++i) {
    c[i] = f(b[i]);
}
```

Figure 10-5. *Two loops that are executed one after the other*

In serial composition, the application must transition from one parallel construct to the next. Figure 10-6 shows ideal and non-ideal transitions between constructs when using the same or different parallel programming models. In both ideal cases, there is no overhead, and we move immediately from one construct to the next. In practice, there is often some time required to clean up resources after executing a construct in parallel as well as some time required to prepare resources before the execution of the next construct.

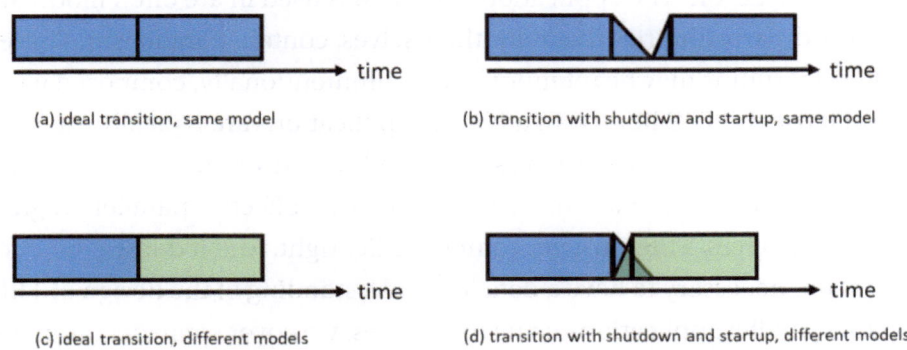

(a) ideal transition, same model

(b) transition with shutdown and startup, same model

(c) ideal transition, different models

(d) transition with shutdown and startup, different models

Figure 10-6. *Transitioning between the executions of different constructs*

When the same model is used, as shown in Figure 10-6(b), a runtime library may do work to shut down the parallel runtime only to have to immediately start it back up again. In Figure 10-6(d), we see that if two different models are used for the constructs, they may be unaware of each other, and so the shutdown of the first construct and the startup, and even execution, of the next construct can overlap, perhaps degrading performance. Both cases can be optimized – and TBB is designed with these transitions in mind.

And as with any composition, performance can be impacted by the sharing resources between the two constructs. Unlike with the nested or concurrent compositions, the constructs do not share resources simultaneously or in an interleaved fashion, but still, the ending state of the resources after one construct finishes can affect the performance of the next construct. For example, in Figure 10-5, we can see that loop 3 writes to array b and then loop 4 reads from array b. Assigning the same iterations in loops 3 and 4 to the same core might increase data locality resulting in fewer cache misses. In contrast, an assignment of the same iterations to different cores can result in unnecessary cache misses. Using two runtimes that are not aware of each other, and therefore do not know where iterations are placed, might lead to incompatible assignments and poorer performance.

Why TBB Is a Composable Library

The TBB library is a composable library by design. When it was first introduced, there was a recognition that as a parallel programming library targeted at all developers – not just developers of flat, monolithic applications – it had to address the challenges of composability head-on. The applications that TBB is used in are often modular and make use of third-party libraries that may, themselves, contain parallelism. These other parallel algorithms may be intentionally, or unintentionally, composed with algorithms that use the TBB library. In addition, applications are typically executed in multiprogrammed environments, such as on shared servers or on personal laptops, where multiple processes execute concurrently. To be an effective parallel programming library for all developers, TBB must get composability right. And it does!

While it is not necessary to have a detailed understanding of the design of TBB to create scalable parallel applications using its features, we cover some details in this section for interested readers. And, if we start using the performance features described in the next chapter, we must understand the composability trade-offs we are making whenever we constrain or change TBB's default behavior. If you are happy enough to trust that TBB does the right thing and are not too interested in the how or are not interested in changing its defaults, then you can safely skip the rest of this chapter. But if not, read on to learn more about why TBB is so effective at composability.

The TBB Thread Pool and Task Arenas

The features of the TBB library that are primarily responsible for its composability are its *global thread pool* and *arenas*, as well as the *arbitrator* that determines how to allot threads to arenas. Figure 10-7 shows how the global thread pool and a single default arena interact in an application that has a single main thread; for simplicity, we will assume that there are P=4 logical cores on the target system.

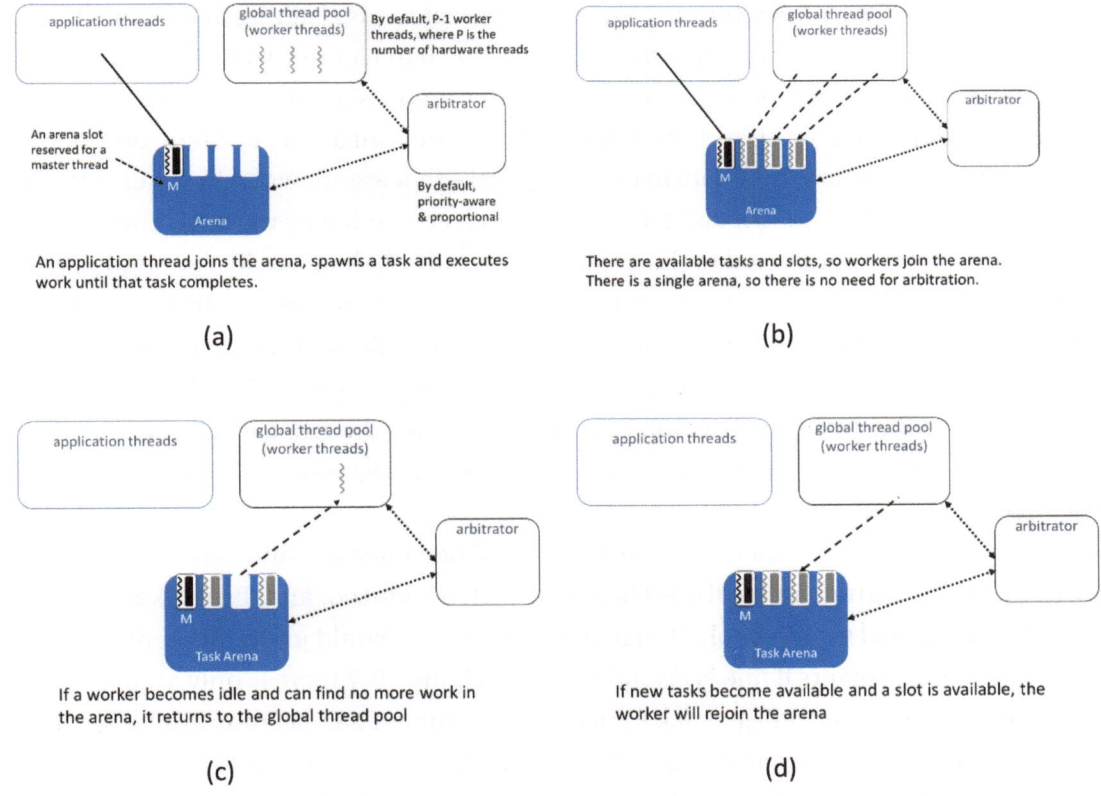

Figure 10-7. *In many applications, there is a single main thread and a single default arena. Worker threads are created by the TBB library to participate in executing work.*

Figure 10-7(a) shows that the application has 1 application thread (the main thread) and a global thread pool of workers that is initialized with P-1 threads. Initially each thread in the global thread pool sleeps while waiting for an opportunity to participate in parallel work. Figure 10-7(a) shows that a single default task arena is created. Each application thread that uses TBB is given its own task arena to isolate its work from the work of the other application threads. In Figure 10-7, there is only a single task arena since there is only a single application thread. When the application thread executes a TBB parallel algorithm, it executes a dispatcher tied to that task arena until the algorithm is complete. The dispatchers are represented by the boxes that contain a wavy line and solid box. While waiting for the algorithm to complete, the master thread can participate in executing tasks that are spawned into the arena. The main thread is shown filling the slot reserved for a master thread and being paired with a dispatcher.

When a master thread joins an arena and first spawns a task, the arena is given an allotment of threads by the arbitrator, and the worker threads sleeping in the global thread pool wake up and migrate to the arena as shown in Figure 10-7(b). In this example, there are no competing arenas, and so this arena is granted an allotment equal to the number of its open slots. When a thread joins an arena, by filling one of its slots, its dispatcher can participate in executing tasks that are spawned by other threads in that arena, as well as spawn tasks that can be seen and stolen by the other threads' dispatchers that are connected to the arena. In Figure 10-7, there are just enough threads to fill the slots in the task arena since the global thread pool creates P-1 threads and the default task arena has enough slots for P-1 threads. Typically, this is exactly the number of threads we want, since the main thread plus P-1 worker threads will fully occupy the cores in the machine without oversubscribing them. Once the arena is fully occupied, the spawning of tasks does not wake up additional threads waiting in the global thread pool.

Figure 10-7(c) shows that when a worker thread becomes idle and can find no more work to do in its current arena, the arena's allotment is reduced, and the worker thread returns to the global thread pool. At that point, the worker could join a different task arena that needs workers if one is available, but in Figure 10-7 there is only a single task arena, so the thread will go back to sleep. If later more tasks become available, the arena's allotment will be adjusted, and threads that have returned to the global thread pool will wake back up and rejoin the arena to assist with the additional work as shown in Figure 10-7(d).

The scenario outlined in Figure 10-7 represents the very common case of an application that has a single main thread and no additional application threads and where no advanced features of TBB are used to change any defaults. In Chapter 11, we discuss advanced TBB features that will allow us to create more complicated examples that include multiple task arenas with varying priorities and numbers of slots. When there are more task arena slots than worker threads, the arbitrator must decide how many threads to allot to each arena. At the time of the writing of this book, by default, TBB uses a priority-aware, proportional arbitration policy. In this book, when we describe the arbitration choices made by TBB, we will assume this policy is in effect.

Figure 10-8 shows two simple cases to highlight the key characteristics of this arbitration policy. In Figure 10-8(a) there are two competing arenas, with equal priorities, which have a total of six slots for workers, but there are only three worker threads available. The arbitrator will proportionally divide the workers between them, so each will get roughly half of the three workers. In Figure 10-8(b), the two arenas have different priorities. The arbitrator will fully populate the higher-priority arena before providing any workers to the lower-priority arena.

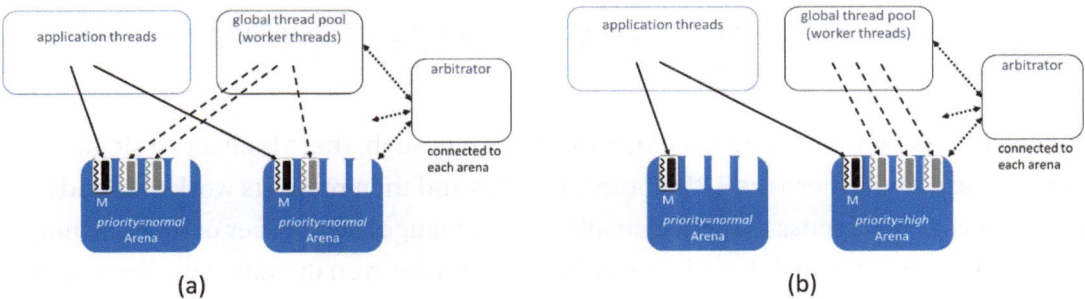

Figure 10-8. *Competing arenas receive worker threads based on the allotment determined by the arbitrator. When using the default priority-aware, proportional arbitrator, (a) arenas with the same priority will receive threads proportional to their worker slots, and (b) arenas with higher priorities will be fully populated before any threads are allotted to arenas with lower priorities.*

In Chapter 11, we discuss advanced TBB features that will allow us to create more complicated examples like the one shown in Figures 10-8 and 10-9. In Figure 10-9, there are many application threads and several arenas, which highlights a few other interesting points about arenas. By default, there is one slot reserved for an application thread, like in Figures 10-7 and 10-8. However, as shown by the right two task arenas in Figure 10-9, a task arena can be created that reserves multiple slots for application threads or no slots at all for application threads. An application thread can fill any slot, while worker threads that migrate to an arena from the global thread pool cannot fill slots reserved for application threads. The arbitrator is aware of the number of slots that are available for worker threads in each arena and makes its decisions accordingly.

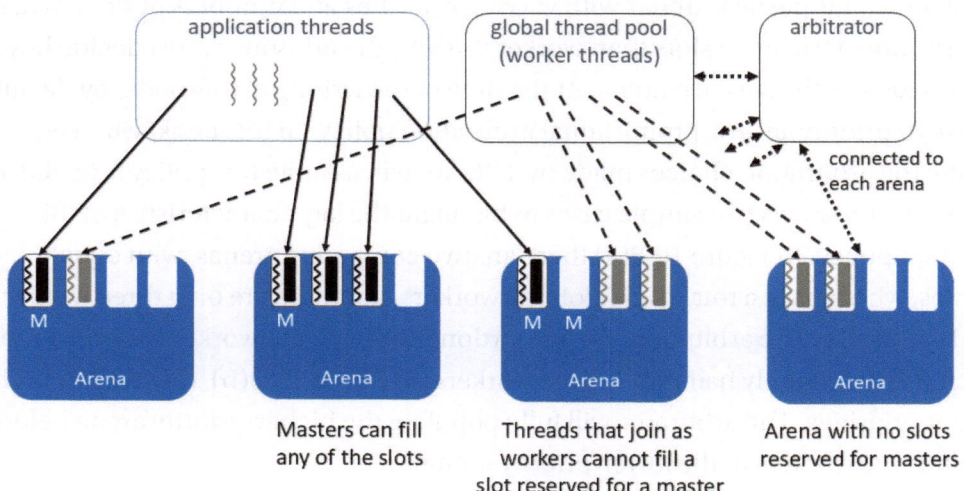

Figure 10-9. *Arenas may have varying numbers of slots reserved for master threads, including none at all*

Regardless of how complicated our application though, there is always a single global thread pool where the TBB library allocates and then requests worker threads. In Chapter 11, we discuss features that allow us to change the number of threads that are allocated to the global thread pool at initialization or even dynamically, if we need to. But this limited set of worker threads is one reason that TBB is composable, since it prevents unintended oversubscription of the platform's cores.

Each application thread also gets its own implicit arena. A thread cannot steal a task from a thread that is in another task arena, so this nicely isolates the work done by different application threads by default.

The design of TBB makes applications and algorithms that use TBB tasks compose well when executed nested, concurrently, or serially. When nested, TBB tasks generated at all levels are executed within the same arena using only the limited set of worker threads assigned to the arena by the TBB library, preventing an exponential explosion in the number of threads. When run concurrently by different master threads, the worker threads are split between the arenas. And when executed serially, the worker threads are reused across the constructs.

The TBB Task Dispatcher: Work Stealing and More

The Threading Building Blocks scheduling strategy is often described as *work stealing*. And this is mostly true. Work stealing is a strategy that is designed to work well in dynamic environments and applications, where tasks are spawned dynamically and execution occurs on a multiprogrammed system. When tasks are distributed by work stealing, threads actively look for new tasks when they become idle, instead of having work passively assigned to them. This pay-as-you-go approach to work distribution is efficient because it does not force threads to stop doing useful work just so they can distribute part of their work to other idle threads. Work stealing moves these overheads on to the idle threads – which have nothing better to do anyway! Work-stealing schedulers stand in contrast to *work-sharing* schedulers, which assign tasks to worker threads up front when tasks are first spawned. In a dynamic environment, where tasks are spawned dynamically and some hardware threads may be more loaded or less capable than others (for example e-cores and p-cores), work-stealing schedulers are more reactive, resulting in better load balancing and higher performance.

In a TBB application, a thread participates in executing TBB tasks by executing a task dispatcher that is attached to a specific task arena. Figure 10-10 shows some of the important data structures that are maintained in each arena and others that are maintained separately by each thread that participates in an arena.

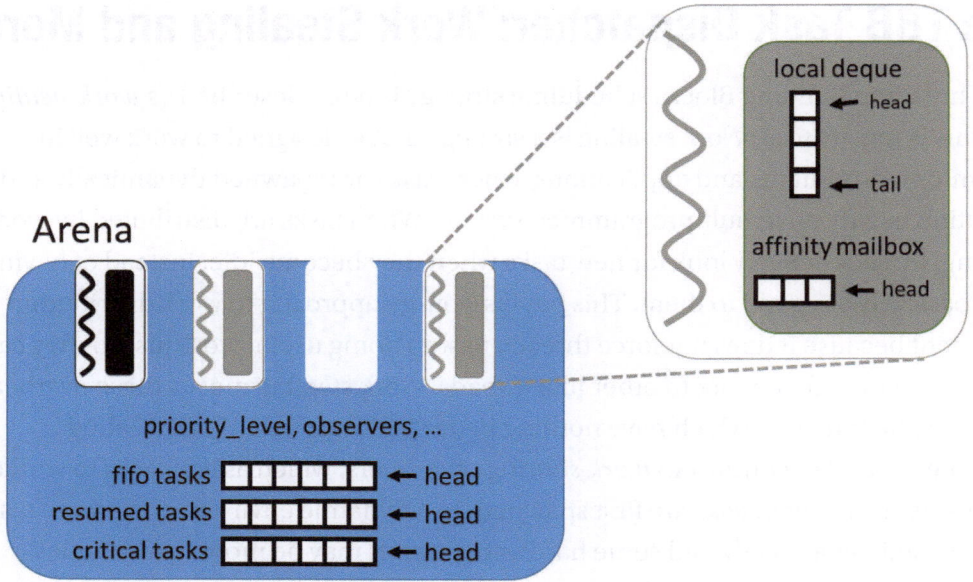

Figure 10-10. *The queues in an arena and the per-thread data structures. It should be noted that while shown as simple queues in the diagram, TBB uses scalable queue implementations.*

For the moment, let us ignore the shared queues in the task arena and the affinity mailbox in the per-thread data and focus only on the local deque[1] in the task dispatcher. It is the local deque that is used to implement the work-stealing scheduling strategy in TBB. The other data structures are used to implement extensions to work stealing, and we will come back to those later.

In Chapter 2, we discussed the different kinds of loops that are implemented by the generic parallel algorithms included in the TBB library. Many of them depend on the concept of a Range, a recursively divisible set of values that represent the iteration space of the loop. These algorithms recursively divide a loop's Range, using *split tasks* to create subranges, until they reach a good size to pair with the loop body to execute as a *body task*. Figure 10-11 shows an example distribution of tasks that implement a loop pattern. The top-level task t0 represents the splitting of the complete Range, which is recursively split down to the leaves where the loop body is applied to each given subrange. With the distribution shown in Figure 10-11, each thread executes body tasks across a contiguous

---

[1] Deque means *double ended queue*, a data structure, not to be confused with dequeue, which is the action to remove an item from a queue.

set of iterations. Since nearby iterations often access nearby data, this distribution tends to optimize for locality. And because threads execute tasks within isolated task trees, once a thread gets an initial subrange to work on, it can execute on that tree without interacting much with the other threads.

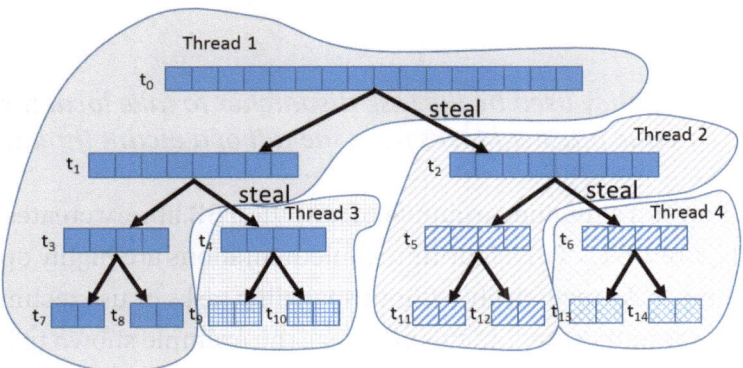

Figure 10-11. *A distribution of tasks that implements a loop pattern*

The TBB loop algorithms are examples of *cache-oblivious* algorithms. Perhaps ironically, cache-oblivious algorithms are designed to highly optimize the use of CPU data caches – they just do this without knowing the details about cache or cache line sizes. As with the TBB loop algorithms, these algorithms are typically implemented using a divide-and-conquer approach that recursively divides data sets into smaller and smaller pieces that eventually fit into the data caches regardless of their sizes. We cover cache-oblivious algorithms in more detail in Chapter 11.

The TBB library task dispatchers use their local deques to implement a scheduling strategy that is optimized to work with cache-oblivious algorithms and create distributions like the one in Figure 10-11. This strategy is sometimes called a depth-first work, breadth-first steal policy. Whenever a thread *spawns* a new task – that is, makes it available to its task arena for execution – that task is placed at the head of its task dispatcher's local deque. Later when it finishes the task it is currently working on and needs a new task to execute, it attempts to take work from the head of its local deque, taking the task it most recently spawned as shown in Figure 10-12. If, however, there is no task available in a task dispatcher's local deque, it looks for non-local work by randomly selecting another worker thread in its task arena. We call the selected thread a *victim* since the dispatcher is planning to steal a task from it. If the victim's local deque is not empty, the dispatcher takes a task from the tail of the victim thread's local deque, as shown in Figure 10-12, taking the task that was least-recently-spawned by that thread.

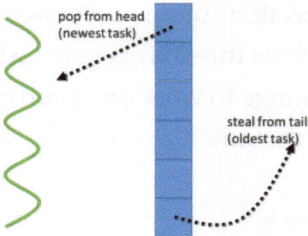

Figure 10-12.   *The policy used by the task dispatcher to take local tasks from the head of the local deque but steal tasks from the tail of a victim thread's deque*

Figure 10-13 gives a simplified example of how the TBB library creates a distribution like the one in Figure 10-11. TBB algorithm implementations are highly optimized and so may divide some tasks recursively without spawning tasks or use techniques like scheduler bypass (described later in this chapter); the example shown in Figure 10-13 assumes that each split and body task is spawned into the task arena. This is not really the case for the optimized TBB algorithms; however, this assumption is useful for illustrative purposes here.

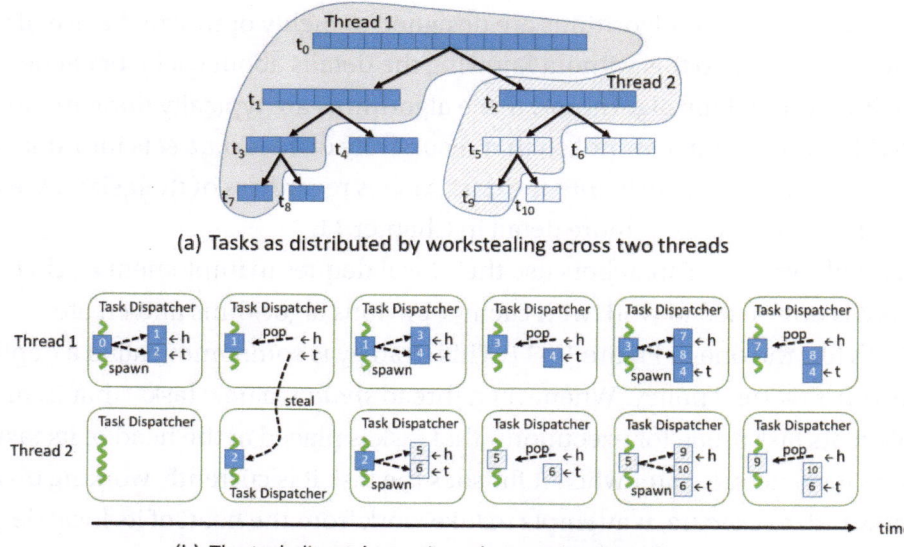

Figure 10-13.   *A snapshot of how tasks may be distributed across two threads and the actions the two task dispatchers took to acquire the tasks. Note: The actual implementations of TBB loop patterns use scheduler bypass and other optimizations that remove some spawns. Even so, the stealing and execution order will be similar to this figure.*

In Figure 10-13, thread 1 starts with the root task and initially splits the Range into two large pieces. It then goes depth-first down one side of the task tree, splitting tasks until it reaches the leaf where it applies the body to a final subrange. Thread 2, which is initially idle, steals from the tail of thread 1's local deque, providing itself with the second large piece that Thread 1 created from the original Range. Figure 10-13(a) is a snapshot in time, for example, tasks t_4 and t_6 have not yet been taken by any thread. If two more worker threads are available, we can easily imagine that we get the distribution shown in Figure 10-11. At the end of the timeline in Figure 10-13(b), threads 1 and 2 still have tasks in their local deques. When they pop the next task, they will grab the leaves that are contiguous with the tasks they just completed.

We shouldn't forget when looking at Figures 10-11 and 10-13 that the distribution shown is only one possibility. If the work per iteration is uniform and none of the cores are oversubscribed, we will likely get the equal distributions shown. Work stealing, however, means that if one of the threads is executing on an overloaded core, it will steal less often and subsequently acquire less work. The other threads will then pick up the slack. A programming model that only provides a static, equal division of iterations to cores would be unable to adapt to such a situation.

As we noted earlier, the TBB task dispatchers however are not just work-stealing schedulers. Figures 10-14 and 10-15 provide simplified pseudo-code representations of the entire TBB task dispatch loop.

```
try_to_get_next_task:
  t_next = try to get a critical task
    else try to pop from end of thread's local deque
  if t_next is not valid
    do
      do
        t_next = try to get critical task
          else try to get from thread's affinity mailbox
          else try to get from arena's resumed tasks
          else try to get from arena's fifo tasks
          else try to steal task from random victim thread in same arena
      while t_next is not valid and the thread should stay in this arena
    while thread must stay in this arena
  end if

return t_next
```

Figure 10-14. *Pseudo-code for how a dispatcher finds a next task for a thread in an arena. A thread "should stay in this arena" if it is a worker thread, the arena's allotment has not been reduced, and it has spent a reasonably small time looking for new tasks. The reasonable time to spend looking for work is an implementation detail and is not under the control of TBB users. A thread "must stay in arena" if it is a master and its work is not yet done.*

Figure 10-14 shows the logic for how a thread finds a next task to execute when it has become idle. From Figure 10-14, we can see that there is a preference for critical tasks. Currently, there is no public API for developers to submit critical tasks directly, but the implementation of some TBB features uses critical tasks when they need to prioritize work for task scheduling. If there is ever a critical task, it is given priority over all other ways to find a next task. Since we, as application developers, are not submitting critical tasks directly, and the way they are used in the implementation of specific features might change, we won't discuss them in detail in this book.

Next in Figure 10-14, the local deque is checked. The local deque holds tasks that were spawned by this thread, tasks that likely exhibit temporal and spatial locality since they were spawned by the thread looking for a next task.

If there is nothing in the local deque, then the thread repeatedly attempts to find work. The inner loop checks first for a critical task, then in the shared mailbox (see Chapter 11 to learn more about affinity mailboxes), then for resumed tasks (see Chapter 6 to learn about resumable tasks), and then for FIFO enqueued tasks (see Chapter 11 to learn about enqueued tasks), and finally it attempts to steal from another thread's local deque.

This inner loop repeats these steps until a task is found or the thread decides it should leave the arena. A worker decides to leave the arena if the arena's allotment has decreased or if it has tried to look for work for some time but has failed to find any valid next task. The exact time or number of attempts the thread makes to find work is an implementation detail of the library. The outer loop in Figure 10-14 simply prevents a master thread from prematurely leaving the arena until all the work that relates to its initial task is done.

A simplified description of the whole task dispatcher, which calls the function in Figure 10-14, is shown in Figure 10-15.

```
dispatcher:
  if is master
    t_next = starting task
  else
    t_next = try_to_get_next_task()
  end if

  while t_next is valid

    do // innermost execute and bypass loop
      t = t_next
      if t's task group context has been canceled
        t_next = t->cancel()
      else
        t_next = t->execute()
      end if
      t_crit = try to get critical task
      if t_crit is valid
        spawn t_next
        t_next = t_crit
      end if
    while t_next is a valid task // end bypass loop

    if I'm a master and work is done
      break
    else if I'm a worker, arena allotment has changed and I should leave
      break
    end if

    t_next = try_to_get_next_task()

  end while

  // couldn't find valid t_next

  if I'm a worker thread
    return myself to the global thread pool
  else I'm a master thread
    return
  end if
```

Figure 10-15. *Pseudo-code for an approximation of the TBB task dispatch loop*

A master thread joins an arena with a task to execute, and so it has a first task when it enters the dispatcher. A worker that joins an arena calls `try_to_get_next_task()` to find its first task to execute. As shown in Figure 10-15, the thread then enters the outer loop that keeps it in the arena as long as it can and should do more work. Next, it enters the "innermost execute and bypass loop." There, the thread either executes or cancels the `t_next` that it has identified, depending on the state of its `task_group_context`. Cancellation is described more in Chapter 9.

The call to `t->execute()` may return a next task, a technique called *scheduler bypass*. This is the fastest way for a task to provide a next task since it short-circuits the dispatcher's selection logic. However, even if the task returns a next task, the thread first checks to see if there are any critical tasks that should be executed instead. If so, it spawns the task that was returned from the call to execute and instead executes the critical task. As described previously, critical tasks are used in the implementation of TBB features and not something we submit into an arena directly. The thread repeats this innermost loop until there is no critical task or its call to execute does not return a next task. When it leaves this innermost loop, if it is a master thread and its work is done, or if it's a worker thread and the arena allotment has been reduced, the thread leaves the arena.

If the thread does not leave the arena, it looks for more work to do by again calling `try_to_get_next_task()`. If `try_to_get_next_task` returns without finding a valid next task, the outer while-loop ends, and the thread leaves the arena.

There are a few ways that the dispatch loop described in Figures 10-14 and 10-15 differs from the very simple model described in Figure 10-13. First, the TBB implementation can inject critical tasks that are prioritized over all other kinds of work. Second, there are conditions under which a worker thread will leave an arena, either so it can be migrated to another arena of higher priority or with greater need or because there is simply no more work to do in the arena. Third, there are other kinds of tasks, such as affinitized tasks (described in Chapter 11), enqueued tasks (described in Chapter 11), and resumable tasks (described in Chapter 6) that are not distributed through work stealing. We talk about these other kinds of tasks as they are introduced throughout this book.

TBB Interoperability with Other Models, Frameworks, and Libraries

Interoperability Achieved by Using TBB As a Common CPU Threading Layer

So far in this chapter, we have described why TBB composes well with itself. Developers can mix and match TBB algorithms and libraries that use TBB and rely on TBB to do sensible things to maintain good performance. The impact of this self-composability is further amplified when TBB is used as the threading layer in the implementation of other libraries.

For example, many of the oneAPI math and AI libraries such as oneDPL, oneMKL, oneDNN, and oneDAL either use oneTBB by default when launching work onto CPUs or have the option to use oneTBB as the CPU backend. Similarly, the SYCL CPU device in Intel's SYCL implementation uses oneTBB to implement SYCL parallel constructs for CPUs. The Intel OpenVINO inferencing framework uses oneTBB to schedule work on CPUs. Beyond oneAPI and Intel libraries, some third-party libraries and frameworks have likewise chosen TBB as their default, or at least an optional backend. As an example, the VFX Reference Platform has settled on TBB as its common threading layer. Nvidia's Thrust library has a TBB backend.

So, if these libraries are configured to use TBB, we can mix and match them together along with explicit TBB code, knowing that all these uses of TBB will compose well with each other.

It is this desire for composability that has led both the oneAPI Toolkits and the Unified Acceleration (UXL) Foundation to promote oneTBB as a common backend. Other frameworks, libraries, and efforts have made this same choice for similar reasons.

Interoperability Between TBB and Other CPU Threading Models

The composability properties of TBB described in this chapter even help when TBB code is combined with other models for CPU threading. Let's reconsider the types of composition that we introduced earlier in Figure 10-1.

If TBB is nested within threads from another model, the use of TBB will create oversubscription, but that oversubscription will be limited. If we execute TBB parallel_ for loops concurrently inside of 1,000 native C++ threads, the TBB library will still only add a limited number of worker threads since the number of threads in the global thread pool is limited. So, if these 1,000 threads execute on a platform with 8 cores, there will *not* be 1,000 + 1,000 × 7 = 8,000 worker threads but only 1,000 + 7 = 1,007 threads. TBB will add to the oversubscription, but only to a limited degree.

Similarly, if a TBB parallel algorithm is executed concurrently with another non-TBB parallel algorithm, again TBB will only add at most the number of threads in its global thread pool. So, for example, if ten TBB parallel loops are executed concurrently with ten OpenMP parallel loops on a platform with eight cores, TBB will again only add seven additional worker threads. So the ten OpenMP loops may (or perhaps likely) use 10 × 8 = 80 threads (OpenMP has teams with mandatory parallelism), but TBB will add only 7 more on top of that, yielding a total of 80 + 7 = 87 threads. Again, there's added oversubscription due to TBB, but to a limited degree.

Finally, if TBB is serially composed with another non-TBB parallel algorithm, TBB will quickly shut down its threads to limit competition for resources. As described in Figure 10-14, TBB worker threads only look for work for a short period of time before leaving the arena, returning to the global thread pool, and going to sleep. TBB worker threads do not endlessly, greedily spin looking for work.

And we get all these limits when TBB is unaware of the other libraries. But we might remember that back in Figure 10-9, there was an arbitrator that determines the allotment for each TBB arena. By default, the arbitration policy is a priority-aware, proportional policy that only manages TBB arenas. However, the arbitrator can be made aware of non-TBB runtimes. In the oneAPI Toolkits, there is (at the time of the writing of this book) an experimental Thread Composability Manager (TCM) that can be used as an arbitrator across oneAPI parallel runtimes, allowing the arbitrator to be aware of CPU threads used by oneTBB, OpenMP, OpenCL, and SYCL. In the future, this arbitrator may become a public feature that will allow additional models to opt in to arbitration.

Interoperability Between TBB Threading and Vectorization

There are other forms of parallelism beyond CPU threading, including vectorization. Figure 10-16 shows an analogy for the types of parallelism supported on many modern CPUs that are supported as the standard execution policies in std::execution. In

Figure 10-16, a highway is used as an analogy for CPU parallelism, and each car represents a piece of work, each person within a car represents an execution resource applied to the work, and each highway lane represents a hardware thread.

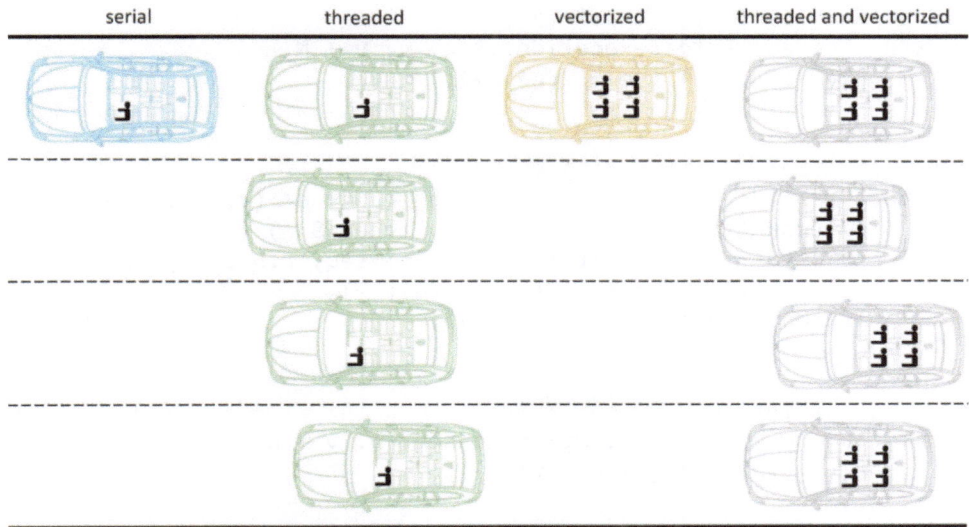

Figure 10-16. *The different kinds of parallelism on CPUs. From left to right in the figure, these correspond to the C++ Standard Template Library (STL) execution policies:* std::execution::seq, std::execution::par, std::execution::unseq, *and* std::execution::par_unseq

In Figure 10-16, a serial execution uses only a single core and does not use the SIMD/vector units on that core for parallel execution. A threaded execution uses multiple cores (and therefore highway lanes) but does not take advantage of SIMD execution. And a threaded and vectorized execution uses all parallel resources, the cores + the SIMD units.

The TBB library adds parallelism through threading. So, using the analogy in Figure 10-16, it places cars with a driver into all the lanes. But how do we get additional people into all the seats? Luckily TBB composes well with vectorization, so it is easy to use vectorized or vectorizable loops with TBB algorithms to enable all the SIMD units. Figure 10-17 shows an example of the various kinds of parallel execution and how they can be composed within a TBB parallel_for. The uses of std::for_each in Figure 10-17 that are passed execution::seq operate without vectorization as a usual serial loop. Those calls that are passed std::execution::unseq may add vectorization – the execution policies are always just a hint that tells the implementation that is legal to apply that type of parallelism. In the function pfor_unseq_f, we can see that adding vectorization inside of the TBB parallel algorithm body is as simple as using an unseq policy to iterate over the blocked_range.

```
void serial_f(int N, v_type* v) {
    std::for_each(std::execution::seq, v, v + N,
        [](v_type& e) { e = f(e); });
}

void pfor_f(int N, v_type* v) {
    tbb::parallel_for(tbb::blocked_range<v_type*>(v, v + N),
        [=](const tbb::blocked_range<v_type*>& r) {
            std::for_each(std::execution::seq, r.begin(), r.end(),
                [](v_type& e) { e = f(e); });
        }, tbb::static_partitioner());
}

void unseq_f(int N, v_type* v) {
    std::for_each(std::execution::unseq, v, v + N,
        [](v_type& v) { v = f(v); });
}

void pfor_unseq_f(int N, v_type* v) {
    tbb::parallel_for(tbb::blocked_range<v_type*>(v, v + N),
        [=](const tbb::blocked_range<v_type*>& r) {
            std::for_each(std::execution::unseq, r.begin(), r.end(),
                [](v_type& e) { e = f(e); });
        }, tbb::static_partitioner());
}
```

Figure 10-17. *The different kinds of parallelism on CPUs*

Interoperability Between TBB Threading and Accelerator Offload

Just like with vectorization, TBB does not directly introduce offload to an accelerator, but instead it is designed to work seamlessly with offload. The two primary support mechanisms for this are resumable tasks (you can see an example in Chapter 6 that interacts with a SYCL offload to a GPU) and the flow graph API's async_node (you can see an example of these features used with SYCL in Chapters 5 and 6). Both features allow the introduction of asynchrony that prevents a TBB worker thread from blocking while waiting for asynchronous work to complete. Without these features, a TBB task that submits work to a GPU might need to wait for it to be completed. Stretching the analogy in Figure 10-16, this would be like parking a car in the middle of a highway lane whenever work is offloaded to a non-CPU device; the work might be accelerated on the other device, but the CPU (highway lane) is blocked until it completes.

Interoperability Between TBB Threading and Future C++ Features

It is difficult to predict the future, but there are several features that are on track for inclusion in C++26 that may interact and overlap with functionality provided by TBB, such as the additional features in `std::execution` (see `https://en.cppreference.com/w/cpp/experimental/execution`).

The Execution Library proposed for C++26 provides a framework for managing asynchronous execution on generic execution resources. Among other abstractions, this framework introduces schedulers that the proposal describes as "a lightweight handle that represents a strategy for scheduling work onto an execution resource." TBB is an example of an existing library that can be supplied as a scheduler that maps work onto a pool of CPU threads.

Interoperability with Process-Based Parallelism

The TBB library respects the process affinity masks set by OS calls and tools like numactl. When used with MPI (Message Passing Interface) libraries or Python libraries that implement parallelism using processes, the TBB library views the machine according to those settings. For example, when TBB calculates the default number of threads for the global thread pool, the number of workers created will be based on those settings and not the underlying physical machine.

Summarizing TBB's Composability and Interoperability

Figure 10-18 provides a summary of the composability and interoperability of TBB when used with itself, other parallel programming approaches, and expected, future C++ features.

Type of Composition	Notes
TBB and itself when combined serially, concurrently, or nested.	The design of TBB uses a global thread pool, arenas and an arbitrator that prevents over-subscription and allows TBB code to be mixed-and-matched without fear.
TBB and other CPU threading models	By design, TBB is a good citizen that limits its oversubscription, even if it is nested within other models or is used concurrently within other non-TBB threads.
TBB and other CPU threading models with a joint arbitrator	The design of TBB allows a common arbitrator between threading models. The oneAPI Toolkits currently have an experimental arbitrator, the Thread Composability Manager (TCM), that can be used across TBB, OpenMP, OpenCL and SYCL to limit oversubscription on the CPUs.
TBB and TBB-based library and frameworks	Parallel libraries and frameworks that use TBB as an underlying engine can be mixed-and-matched with each other and explicit TBB code without fear. Examples include oneAPI / UXL libraries such as oneDPL, oneDNN, oneMKL as well as OpenVINO and libraries in the VFX platform.
TBB and SIMD / vectorization	SIMD / vectorization can be cleanly nested within TBB code to further improve performance.
TBB and offload to accelerators	TBB features such as resumable tasks and `async_node` enable efficient asynchronous offload to accelerators.
TBB and future C++ features	The team working on TBB is well aware of the direction of the C++ standard and continues to make TBB work well with new features. It is expected that TBB will provide a scheduler that aligns with the upcoming C++26 execution facilities, including a way to replace the default C++ parallel scheduler with TBB.
TBB and process-based parallelism	TBB library views the machine topology according to the OS settings for affinity masks set by tools such as numactl. ThereforeTBB will limit its default concurrency to match those settings.

Figure 10-18. *A summary of the composability and interoperability of the TBB library*

Summary

This chapter delved into the concept of composability within TBB, categorizing it into nested, concurrent, and serial execution. We established TBB's composability as a design philosophy that enhances scalability, enabling developers to expose parallelism without fear of over- or underutilization.

We contrasted TBB's approach to nested parallelism with that of OpenMP, highlighting how TBB's relaxed sequential semantics and task-based model allow for efficient execution without the need to disable nested parallelism. This distinction is critical for C++ programming and less critical for straightforward loop-oriented C and Fortran code.

We clarified that composability is not a binary attribute; rather, it varies based on how programming models interact. The chapter illustrates this through examples of nested and concurrent compositions, highlighting how TBB effectively manages nested parallelism to optimize throughput. We discussed concurrent composition, where parallel algorithms can overlap in execution, further enhancing performance.

Composability is ours to understand and preserve; TBB gives us a model that supports composability. It is up to us to understand that and not lose it.

Hopefully, this chapter not only explained the concept of composability, but it instilled a strong desire to always create composable code ourselves.

CHAPTER 11

Performance Tuning

Earlier in this book, we explored various ways to express parallelism with TBB, such as algorithms, flow graphs, and task groups. In those chapters, we highlighted how TBB delivers strong performance across a range of systems, regardless of core count or memory size. In Chapter 10, we discussed how the combination of TBB's global thread pool, arbitrator, arenas, and task scheduler contributes to its composability, allowing it to effectively adapt to typical conditions.

However, parallel programming is inherently about performance; if we weren't concerned with performance, we likely wouldn't bother with any of the additional complexity required to add parallelism. There are times when we may want to add a boost to performance by providing hints or extra constraints to help the TBB runtime do a better job. The availability of these performance controls is one of the key differences between TBB and other higher-level algorithm libraries such as the C++ parallel algorithms. The downside to performance tuning, though, is that when we provide extra hints and constraints, we may make our application a little less composable and a little less portable since we're constraining the library's choices by tuning for a specific platform. So we need to be very cautious if we decide to use the features discussed in this chapter.

In this chapter, we discuss two broad categories of tuning: (1) constraining the number of threads and hardware resources used by the library and (2) optimizing the TBB algorithms for granularity and affinity. We cover constraining first, by covering four topics: `global_control`, `task_arena`, hardware-aware scheduling, and `task_scheduler_observer`. We then cover algorithm optimization in three sections that address granularity and locality, determinism, and pipeline tuning.

© Michael J. Voss, James R. Reinders 2025
M. J. Voss and J. R. Reinders, *Today's TBB*, https://doi.org/10.1007/979-8-8688-1270-5_11

Controlling What Resources Are Used by TBB

One of the key controls we have for impacting performance is influencing what kind of compute resources and how many of them are used for executing tasks.

TBB makes a few assumptions that inform its default settings. The defaults assume the following:

1. We want to use all the logical CPU cores available to the application, regardless of the memory hierarchy or capabilities of the cores.

2. We want to use the default stack size for any worker threads that TBB creates.

3. We *do not* want to oversubscribe the platform's logical cores, and instead we want to have a single software thread servicing tasks per logical core.

4. All tasks have equal priority.

These inform the defaults used by the TBB library and its algorithms and typically lead to good performance. So the general guidance is that, unless you must, it's best to keep these defaults.

Even so, Figure 11-1 summarizes the features that let us override these defaults. As application developers, we may know that some of the assumptions listed above do not hold for our use case. As described in Chapter 10, the TBB library offers composable performance because of the interplay between its global thread pool, arbitration policy, the default implicit task arenas, and its work-stealing task scheduler. When we use the features described in this chapter, we are meddling with these finely balanced interactions – so we should be careful.

With these caveats in mind, the remainder of this section discusses the features in Figure 11-1 in more detail so we can use them if we decide to try to outperform the defaults.

Feature	Description
`tbb::global_control`	Intended for use at the application level, instances of this object can control maximum allowed parallelism, the stack size of created worker threads, and termination behaviors.
`tbb::task_arena`	Instances of `task_arena` can create new TBB arenas or act as lightweight handles to existing arenas. Arenas can be created with different numbers of slots, different numbers of slots reserved for master threads and can be created with constraints that pin threads to NUMA nodes or to particular processor types, such as efficiency or performance cores.
`tbb::info`	The `tbb::info` namespace provides functions for querying the number of NUMA nodes, the types of cores available and the default concurrency on the platform or on specific NUMA nodes. The results of these queries can be used to constrain explicitly initialized `task_arena` instances.
`tbb::task_scheduler_observer`	Instances of `task_scheduler_observer` execute user defined code when a thread joins or leaves a specific TBB arena. The user-defined code can be used, for example, to have precise control over thread placement.

Figure 11-1. *The features in TBB that are used to control the execution resources used by TBB*

Figure 11-2 reintroduces a figure from Chapter 10. Figure 11-2 reminds us that there is a limited set of threads in the global thread pool; these are allotted to TBB arenas based on the policy of the arbitrator and the number and type of slots in the arenas.

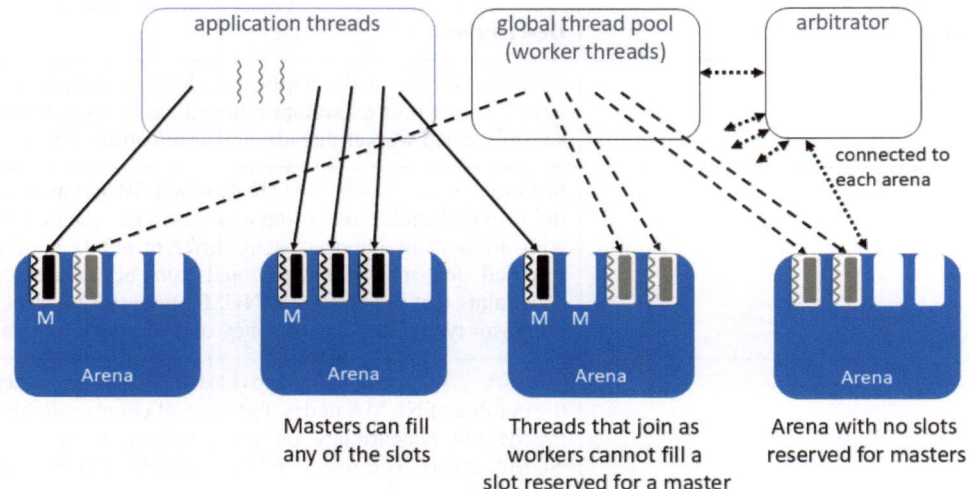

Figure 11-2. *A more complicated example that uses multiple TBB arenas*

The features listed in Figure 11-1 let us change the maximum number of threads available to the global thread pool, the number of slots in the arenas, the number of slots that are reserved for master threads, and the priorities of arenas and even let us provide hardware-aware preferences for how an arena assigns its threads to the logical cores on the platform.

Using `global_control` to Set Application-Level Properties

There are three application-level properties that can be set for TBB. The first is the maximum number of threads that can be actively executing tasks; we can think of this as changing the size of the global thread pool. The second is the stack size for worker threads. And the last relates to error handling.

We create `global_control` objects to change these application-level properties. The class definition for `class global_control` is shown in Figure 11-3. There are three parameters defined in `global_control`: `max_allowed_parallelism`, `thread_stack_size`, and `terminate_on_exception`.

Each `global_control` object can modify only a single parameter, and so we need to create multiple instances to set multiple parameters. The impact of a `global_control` object ends when the lifetime of the object ends. If there is more than one `global_control` object alive that sets the same parameter, conflicting requests are settled by a parameter-specific *selection rule*.

```
namespace tbb {
    class global_control {
    public:
        enum parameter {
            max_allowed_parallelism,
            thread_stack_size,
            terminate_on_exception
        };

        global_control(parameter p, size_t value);
        ~global_control();

        static size_t active_value(parameter param);
    };
} // namespace tbb
```

Figure 11-3. *The* `global_control` *class interface as described in [scheduler.
global_control]*

A `global_control` instance (Figure 11-3) affects the whole process; it is a crude tool, and we should use it sparingly and (likely) only from the top level of the application. For example, most developers would not expect a third-party library to set the number of threads in the global thread pool, impacting all other parts of the application. *That would be rude.*

Using `max_allowed_parallelism`

The global `max_allowed_parallelism` parameter sets a *ceiling* on the number of worker threads that can be actively executing tasks at the same time. TBB assumes that there is one master thread, and so the actual number of workers is limited to `max_allowed_parallelism - 1`, leaving room for the master thread to join and participate.

The ceiling set by `max_allowed_parallelism` can have a huge impact on all aspects of parallel execution. If we reduce this ceiling, we may not be able to take full advantage of the available hardware. If we increase the ceiling, we may allow the TBB library to oversubscribe the hardware resources by assigning more than one software thread to the same logical core. The arbitrator, shown in Figure 11-2, distributes threads to arenas based on a proportional, priority-aware policy, and so when there are competing arenas, `max_allowed_parallelism` affects how populated each arena can be.

Why change this global parameter at all? Since it is a ceiling, we might want to decrease it to prevent the library from using *too many threads* or increase it because we want the library to use more than one thread per logical core. We might choose to decrease max_allowed_parallelism if we know we need to allocate a lot of per-thread memory. Perhaps we'd run out of memory on a system with many cores. Or perhaps we know that our computation simply doesn't scale well enough to take advantage of all the logical cores on our system. By limiting the value, we avoid the overheads of managing threads that we, as developers, know will only add overheads. But again, we should remember this is a global setting, so we shouldn't be rude and change global values if we don't fully understand the ramifications on other parts of the code.

Similarly, there may be valid cases for increasing the max_allowed_parallelism. For example, perhaps the tasks do some I/O and allowing some oversubscription hides the system time spent waiting for results.

Figure 11-4 shows a simple example that creates a global_control object and then executes a parallel_for. In this example, the value for max_allowed_parallelism is p, which is passed as an argument. The default concurrency on the platform is stored in default_P.

```cpp
#include <tbb/tbb.h>

const int default_P = tbb::info::default_concurrency();
void noteParticipation(); /* record info for participation vector */
void dumpParticipation(int p); /* display participation vector */

void doWork(double seconds) {
  noteParticipation();
  tbb::tick_count t0 = tbb::tick_count::now();
  while ((tbb::tick_count::now() - t0).seconds() < seconds);
}

void arenaGlobalControlImplicitArena(int p) {
  tbb::global_control gc(tbb::global_control::max_allowed_parallelism, p);
  tbb::parallel_for(0,
                    10*tbb::info::default_concurrency(),
                    [](int) { doWork(0.01); });
}

int main() {
  arenaGlobalControlImplicitArena(default_P);
  dumpParticipation(default_P);
  arenaGlobalControlImplicitArena(default_P/2);
  dumpParticipation(default_P/2);
  arenaGlobalControlImplicitArena(2*default_P);
  dumpParticipation(2*default_P);
  return 0;
}
```

Figure 11-4. *In the function arenaGlobalControlImplicitArena, a global_ control object is used to set max_allowed_parallelism and then a tbb::parallel for is called. The noteParticipation function increments a thread-local sum, which is later used to create an output vector displayed by dumpParticipation. Sample code performance_tuning/global_control_and_implicit_arena.cpp*

The example prints a vector that shows how many iterations of the parallel_for loop are executed by each thread that participates in executing tasks in the implicit arena. In the main function, arenaGlobalControlImplicitArena is called with p = default_P, p = default_P/2, and p = 2*default_P. The code to store and display the vectors is provided in Figure 11-5.

```cpp
#include <atomic>
#include <iostream>
#include <vector>

std::atomic<int> next_tid;
tbb::enumerable_thread_specific<int> my_tid(-1);
std::vector<std::atomic<int>> tid_participation(2*default_P);

void noteParticipation() {
  auto& t = my_tid.local();
  if (t == -1) {
    t = next_tid++;
  }
  ++tid_participation[t];
}

void clearParticipation() {
  next_tid = 0;
  my_tid.clear();
  for (auto& p : tid_participation)
    p = 0;
}

void dumpParticipation(int p) {
  int sum = tid_participation[0];
  std::cout << "[" << tid_participation[0];
  for (int i = 1; i < std::min(p, default_P); ++i) {
    sum += tid_participation[i];
    std::cout << ", " << tid_participation[i];
  }
  for (int i = p; i < default_P; ++i)
    std::cout << ", -";
  std::cout << "]\n"
            << "sum == " << sum  << "\n"
            << "expected sum " << 10*default_P << "\n\n";
  clearParticipation();
}
```

Figure 11-5. *The functions that create and display the participation vector from Figure 11-4. Sample code* performance_tuning/global_control_and_implicit_arena.cpp

When the example in Figure 11-4 is run on a system with eight logical cores and arenaGlobalControlImplicitArena is called with p=8, the thread allotment will be similar to Figure 11-6.

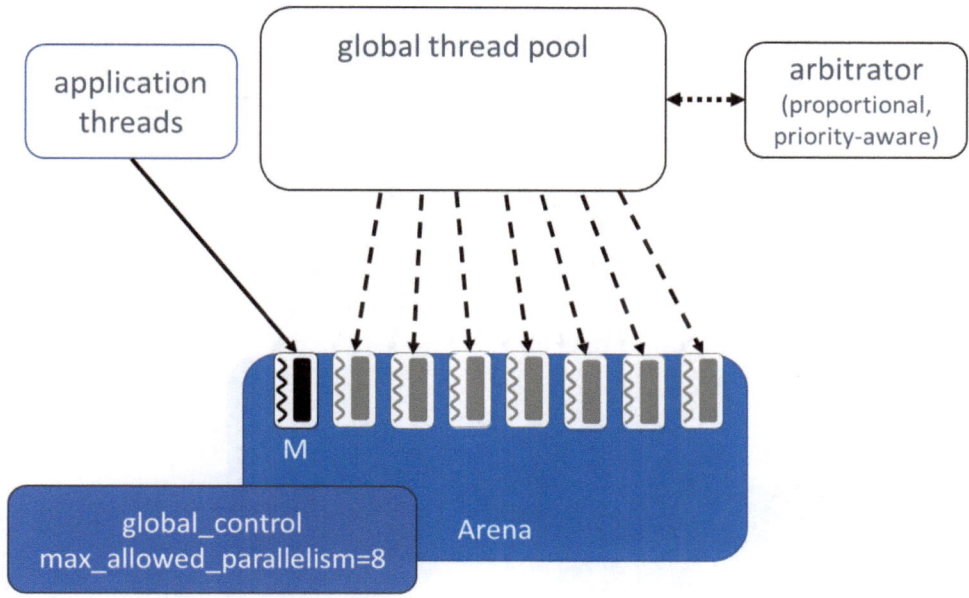

Figure 11-6. *An example allotment of threads when* max_allowed_
parallelism=8 *on a system with eight logical cores when running sample code*
performance_tuning/global_control_and_implicit_arena.cpp

When the example in Figure 11-4 is executed using p = default_P, the output we
record shows that each of the 8 threads executes 10 of the 80 iterations (although work
stealing would not guarantee this exact distribution):

```
[10, 10, 10, 10, 10, 10, 10, 10]
sum == 80
expected sum 80
```

A key point to remember when setting max_allowed_parallelism is that it has no
direct effect on the number of slots in arenas. All implicitly created arenas will still have
1 slot reserved for a master thread and P-1 other slots available for workers. So, when
arenaGlobalControlImplicitArena is called with p = default_P/2, thread allotment
will look like Figure 11-7.

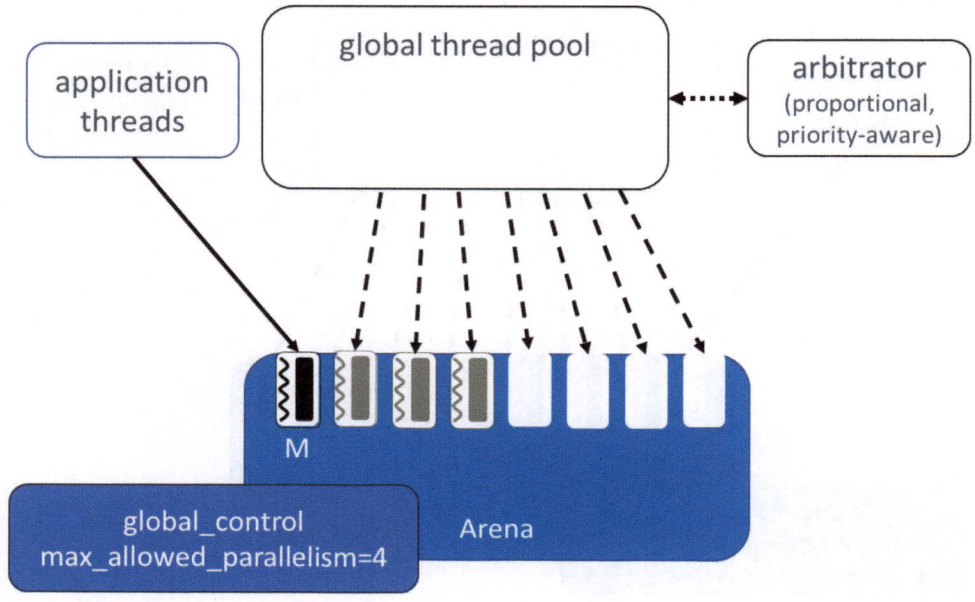

Figure 11-7. *An example allotment of threads when* `max_allowed_`
`parallelism=4` *on a system with eight logical cores when running sample code*
`performance_tuning/global_control_and_implicit_arena.cpp`

And when executed, the output of the extended example shows

```
[20, 20, 20, 20, -, -, -, -]
sum == 80
expected sum 80
```

If we set `max_allowed_parallelism` to a value that is smaller than the number of
slots, there will not be enough threads to fill the slots in a default arena – but the slots
are still there! And that's okay. Finally, when calling `arenaGlobalControlImplicitArena`
with `p = 2*default_P`, but when still using the implicit arena, we see an allotment
similar to Figure 11-8.

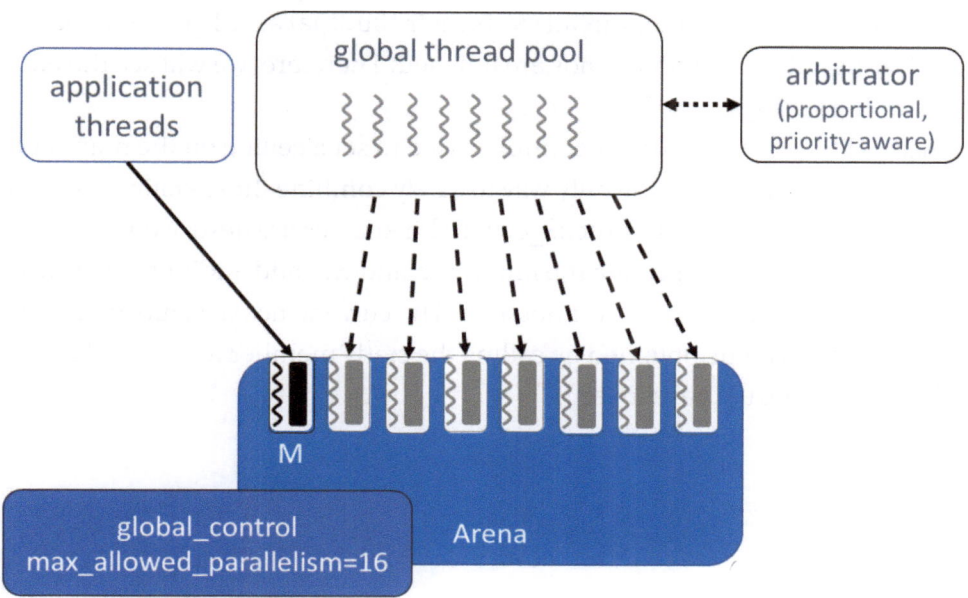

Figure 11-8. *An example allotment of threads when* max_allowed_
parallelism=16 *on a system with eight logical cores when running sample code*
performance_tuning/global_control_and_implicit_arena.cpp

As expected by Figure 11-8, the output shows that while the max_allowed_
parallelism value allows there to be more threads available to distribute to arenas,
there are still only default_P=8 slots in the implicit arena and so still only eight threads
can participate in that arena. We should note that when TBB has a choice of threads to
provide to an arena, threads that have recently left that arena will be more likely chosen
by TBB to return to it. The output for p = 16 will look like

```
[10, 10, 10, 10, 10, 10, 10, 10]
sum == 80
expected sum 80
```

Do not worry though; we will soon describe how to create explicit arenas that can
have as many or as few slots as we like. Before we do that though, let's consider examples
where there is more than one global_control.

In Figure 11-9, arenaGlobalControlImplicitArena is called in parallel from two
different C++ standard threads. In each thread, there is a conflicting request to set max_
allowed_parallelism. The waitUntil function ensures that both tbb::global_control

objects are created before either thread starts their `tbb::parallel_for` and that neither object is destroyed before both threads are finished. Therefore, we will see the effect of two overlapping settings.

The `max_allowed_parallelism` control is used to set a ceiling on the number of threads that are active, and so the only way to safely combine these ceilings is to use the smallest value. Of course, as `global_control` instances are destroyed, the TBB library can (and it does) recalculate the minimum and will add additional threads to the global pool for distribution whenever possible. The current, active value for a `global_control` parameter can be obtained by calling the static member function `global_control::active_value(parameter)`.

```cpp
#include <thread>
#include <tbb/tbb.h>

const int default_P = tbb::info::default_concurrency();

void waitUntil(int N);
void noteParticipation(int offset);
void dumpParticipation()
void doWork(int offset, double seconds) {
  noteParticipation(offset);
  tbb::tick_count t0 = tbb::tick_count::now();
  while ((tbb::tick_count::now() - t0).seconds() < seconds);
}

counter_t counter1 = 0, counter2 = 0;

void arenaGlobalControlImplicitArena(int p, int offset) {
  tbb::global_control gc(tbb::global_control::max_allowed_parallelism, p);

  waitUntil(2, counter1);
  tbb::parallel_for(0,
                    10*default_P,
                    [=](int) {
                      doWork(offset, 0.01);
                    });
  waitUntil(2, counter2);
}

void runTwoThreads(int p0, int p1) {
  std::thread t0([=]() { arenaGlobalControlImplicitArena(p0, 1); });
  std::thread t1([=]() { arenaGlobalControlImplicitArena(p1, 10000); });
  t0.join();
  t1.join();
}

int main() {
  runTwoThreads(default_P/2, default_P);
  dumpParticipation();
  return 0;
}
```

Figure 11-9. *Two conflicting global_control objects set max_allowed_ parallelism. The implementations of the functions waitUntil and noteParticipation are provided in Figure 11-10. Sample code performance_ tuning/global_control_and_implicit_conflict.cpp*

```
void noteParticipation(int offset) {
  auto& t = my_tid.local();
  if (t == -1) {
    t = next_tid++;
  }
  tid_participation[t] += offset;
}

void waitUntil(int N, counter_t& c) {
  ++c;
  while (c != N);
}
```

Figure 11-10. *The updated noteParticipation function that increments by an offset and a simple waitUntil implementation. C++20 introduced std::barrier and std::latch, which could be used to replace waitUntil when using a standard library that supports C++20. Sample code performance_tuning/global_control_ and_implicit_conflict.cpp*

To make the output of our extended example more discernible, Figure 11-9 increments the profiling counter differently for each of the two standard threads (for the t0 it increments by 1 for each iteration a thread executes, and for the t1 call it increments the counter by 10,000).

So calling runTwoThreads with p0 = default_P/2 and p1 = default_P on our system with eight logical cores, we see an output of

```
[340000, 27, 60027, 70026, 330000, 0, 0, 0, 0]
sum == 800080
expected sum == 800080
```

Let's take apart these numbers. First, we should expect the sum of the per-thread counters, given that both loops execute 80 iterations, to be $10 \times 8 \times 1 + 10 \times 8 \times 10,000$ = 800,080, and it is. Next, we can see that a total of five different threads execute some work. We stated that the rule for conflicting requests is to use the minimum value. And we see $\min(8/2, 8) - 1 = 3$ worker threads plus the two master threads, for a total of five threads.

Change the Stack Size for New Threads

The two other global_control parameters are thread_stack_size and terminate_on_ exception.

As the name suggested, the thread_stack_size impacts the stack size for worker threads created by TBB library. Key points for thread_stack_size are that

1. Setting this parameter does not affect application threads since they are already created; only worker threads created by TBB are affected.

2. The value must be set before the worker threads are created, which is typically before the first use of TBB for executing tasks.

The selection rule for multiple, conflicting global_control setting values for thread_stack_size is to use the maximum value. In this case the maximum value is used to ensure that threads have enough stack space to accommodate the largest demand. And just as with max_allowed_parallelism, the value is dynamically updated based on the lifetimes of the global_control objects. If the object that sets the largest value is destroyed, the second largest value becomes the new active value. Whenever a new worker thread is created, the current active value is used.

Change Exception Handling

The final parameter is terminate_on_exception. This parameter is a Boolean value, with a value of 0 or 1, and the selection rule is logical disjunction (it is only false if all values are 0). Setting the parameter to 1 causes termination in any condition that would throw or rethrow an exception.

Using task_arena to Constrain Resources and Set Priorities

As shown in Figure 11-2, threads must move into an arena before they participate in executing TBB tasks. We further control resource usage by setting the number of slots in arenas.

The definition for class task_arena is shown in Figure 11-11.

```cpp
namespace tbb {
    class task_arena {
    public:
        static const int automatic = /* unspecified */;
        static const int not_initialized = /* unspecified */;

        enum class priority : { /* See Figure 11-14 */ };
        struct constraints { /* See Figure 11-18 */ };

        task_arena(int max_concurrency = automatic,
                   unsigned reserved_for_masters = 1,
                   priority a_priority = priority::normal);
        task_arena(constraints a_constraints,
                   unsigned reserved_for_masters = 1,
                   priority a_priority = priority::normal);
        task_arena(const task_arena &s);
        explicit task_arena(tbb::attach);
        ~task_arena();

        void initialize();
        void initialize(int max_concurrency,
                        unsigned reserved_for_masters = 1,
                        priority a_priority = priority::normal);
        void initialize(constraints a_constraints,
                        unsigned reserved_for_masters = 1,
                        priority a_priority = priority::normal);
        void initialize(tbb::attach);

        void terminate();
        bool is_active() const;
        int max_concurrency() const;

        template<typename F> auto execute(F&& f) -> decltype(f());
        template<typename F> void enqueue(F&& f);

        void enqueue(task_handle&& h);
    };
} // namespace tbb
```

Figure 11-11. *The class definition for tbb::task_arena as described in [scheduler. task_arena]*

An *arena*, as shown in Figure 11-2, is an internal object managed by the TBB library and represents where threads go to participate in work. We can explicitly create new arenas or get access to existing arenas by creating tbb::task_arena objects that act as a handle to arenas. We should remember, from Chapter 10, that whenever any application thread starts parallel work without spawning or enqueuing it into an explicitly created task_arena, an implicit arena is used for that thread, and if one does not yet exist for that thread, a new one is created. As we saw in the previous sections, implicit arenas always have P slots with one slot reserved for a master thread, so they can be occupied by up to P-1 worker threads plus a master thread.

Creating an Explicit Arena with a Non-default Number of Slots

In Figure 11-11, there are several constructors shown. For now, let's ignore the priority and constraints arguments – we'll get back to those later.

If we want to create an arena with four slots, we can construct an arena and simply pass 4:

```
tbb::task_areana a(4);
```

In this case, there will be a newly created arena with four total slots and one of those slots will be reserved for a master thread. We can make all the slots available to workers by providing 0 as the second argument (reserved_for_masters):

```
tbb::task_areana a(4, 0);
```

Now there will be four total slots and none reserved for a master. This doesn't mean that an application thread cannot participate. It just means that if there are enough worker threads available, all the slots are *allowed* to be filled by workers. But perhaps there are not enough worker threads, or perhaps an application thread tries to join the arena first; in those cases, the application thread will still be able to fill any open slot.

There are also two special ways to construct an arena:

```
tbb::task_arena a(tbb::attach);
tbb::task_arena b(a);
```

If we pass tbb::attach, a task_arena is constructed that is connected to the internal arena used by the calling thread. The calling thread could be a master thread with an implicit arena, a master thread that has joined an explicit arena, or a worker thread. If the calling thread is a master thread and no internal arena exists yet, this constructor creates a task_arena with default parameters.

The task_arena copy constructor copies the settings from the provided arena – but it does not represent a handle to the same internal arena. It creates a new one with the same settings.

Submitting Work to an Explicit **task_arena**

task_arena has two primary interfaces for submitting work: execute and enqueue. Both receive a function object as an argument and create a task to execute the function object within the arena.

When a thread calls task_arena::execute, it tries to join the arena and execute the task. If it cannot join the arena (since there are no slots for it to occupy), it enqueues the task into the arena and then waits until the task has been completed. If the thread cannot immediately find a slot, it might join later when one becomes available. But, in any case, execute only returns when the submitted work is done.

In contrast, when a thread calls task_arena::enqueue, it enqueues the task to the arena without trying to join the arena and then immediately returns, likely before the task is done.

Let's revisit our earlier examples in Figures 11-4 and 11-5 but now use explicit task arenas to get tighter control over the number of threads that can participate in work. Figure 11-12 shows an example that has a single instance of a global_control object and a task_arena that is created with 2*default_P slots. When run with p=default_P/2 or p=default_P, the number of threads is less than or equal to the number of slots, and so all available threads can participate.

```
#include <tbb/tbb.h>

const int default_P = tbb::info::default_concurrency();
void doWork(double seconds);

void arenaGlobalControlExplicitArena(int p) {
  tbb::global_control gc(tbb::global_control::max_allowed_parallelism, p);

  tbb::task_arena a{2*tbb::info::default_concurrency()};

  a.execute([]() {
    tbb::parallel_for(0,
                      10*tbb::info::default_concurrency(),
                      [](int) { doWork(0.01); });
  });
}

int main() {
  arenaGlobalControlExplicitArena(default_P);
  dumpParticipation(default_P);
  arenaGlobalControlExplicitArena(default_P/2);
  dumpParticipation(default_P/2);
  arenaGlobalControlExplicitArena(2*default_P);
  dumpParticipation(2*default_P);
  return 0;
}
```

Figure 11-12. *An example that uses* global_control *and* tbb::task_arena. *Sample code performance_tuning/ performance_tuning/global_control_and_ explicit_arena.cpp*

The interesting case for Figure 11-12 is when p=2*default_P. Executing this on a system with eight hardware threads results in

```
[7, 9, 9, 6, 5, 5, 9, 5, 3, 4, 3, 3, 4, 4, 3, 1]
sum == 80
expected sum 80
```

We can see that there are now more slots in the explicit arena a and so all threads can participate. With the larger number of threads and the need for threads to move into this explicit arena, we can also see that work is not as evenly distributed among the threads. This uneven distribution is partly due to this being a toy example. In a regular, compute-intensive workload, where the same arena is used repeatedly, the threads will be more likely to settle into an arena, stay there, and be ready to execute new work as it arrives.

We can also revisit the example in Figure 11-9 in which there was a conflict between two global_control instances. Figure 11-13 shows an updated example.

```cpp
void arenaGlobalControlExplicitArena(int p, int offset) {
  tbb::global_control gc(tbb::global_control::max_allowed_parallelism, p);

  // we use waitUntil to force overlap of the gc lifetimes
  waitUntil(2, counter1);
  tbb::task_arena a{2*tbb::info::default_concurrency()};

  a.execute([=]() {
    tbb::parallel_for(0,
                      10*tbb::info::default_concurrency(),
                      [=](int) { doWork(offset, 0.01); });
  });

  // we prevent either gc from being destroyed until both are done
  waitUntil(2, counter2);
}

void runTwoThreads(int p0, int p1) {
  std::thread t0([=]() { arenaGlobalControlExplicitArena(p0, 1); });
  std::thread t1([=]() { arenaGlobalControlExplicitArena(p1, 10000); });
  t0.join();
  t1.join();
}

int main() {
  runTwoThreads(default_P/2, 2*default_P);
  dumpParticipation();
  return 0;
}
```

Figure 11-13. *Two conflicting global_control objects set max_allowed_ parallelism before explicit arenas with many slots are created. Sample code performance_tuning/global_control_and_explicit_conflict.cpp*

When we execute Figure 11-13 with p0=default_P/2 and p1=2*default_P on our system with eight hardware threads, we see

```
[27, 340000, 330000, 60027, 70026, 0, 0, 0, 0, 0, 0, 0, 0, 0, 0, 0, 0]
sum == 800080
expected sum == 800080
```

Again, we see only five threads participate even though there are now many open slots in the two arenas. While it might seem disappointing that the p1 = 16 case only had four threads participate in execution, we should remember that there were conflicting requests to limit `max_allowed_parallelism`! We might take this result as a reminder that changing global values should be done with extreme care and a global application view.

Setting the Priority for a `task_arena`

Until now, we've ignored the `priority` arguments for the `task_arena` constructors shown in Figure 11-11. Figure 11-14 shows the possible values for priority: `low`, `normal`, and `high`.

```
enum class priority : /* unspecified type */ {
    low =     /* unspecified */,
    normal = /* unspecified */,
    high =    /* unspecified */
};
```

Figure 11-14. *The definition of priorities in* `class tbb::task_arena` *as described in [scheduler.task_arena]*

As described in Chapter 10, the arbitrator, by default, uses a priority-aware, proportional allotment policy. We can set the priority for an arena by providing one of the values shown in Figure 11-14. The demand for worker threads from `high`-priority arenas will be fully satisfied before any worker threads are allotted to `normal`- or `low`-priority arenas, and likewise the demand from all `normal`-priority arenas will be fully satisfied before any worker threads are allotted to `low`-priority arenas. We should note that the "demand for worker threads" is a function of both the number of unfilled worker slots and the availability of work in the arena. If there are no tasks available to steal from other threads or to take from any of the shared queues, the arena will be considered to have no demand for worker threads, even if it has unfilled slots. TBB smartly does not provide worker threads to an arena if there would be nothing for them to do once they get there.

Figure 11-15 shows an example that again creates two different `task_arena` instances within two different standard C++ threads. The main function that drives the example is provided in Figure 11-16. Each arena uses the default number of slots, with one slot reserved for a master, but one uses `priority0` and the other `priority1`. First, we should note that since each arena is used from a different C++ thread, they each will have at least one thread (the C++ thread) that joins the arena as a master thread when `execute` is called.

```
#include <thread>
#include <tbb/tbb.h>

void printArrival(tbb::task_arena::priority priority);

using counter_t = std::atomic<int>;
counter_t counter = 0;
void waitUntil(int N, counter_t& c) {
  ++c;
  while (c != N);
}

void explicitArenaWithPriority(tbb::task_arena::priority priority) {
  tbb::task_arena a{tbb::info::default_concurrency(),
                    /* reserved for master */ 1, priority};
  a.execute([=]() {
    tbb::parallel_for(0,
                      2*tbb::info::default_concurrency(),
                      [=](int) { printArrival(priority); });
  });
}

void runTwoThreads(tbb::task_arena::priority priority0,
                   tbb::task_arena::priority priority1) {
  std::thread t0([=]() {
    waitUntil(2, counter);
    explicitArenaWithPriority(priority0);
  });
  std::thread t1([=]() {
    waitUntil(2, counter);
    explicitArenaWithPriority(priority1);
  });
  t0.join();
  t1.join();
}
```

Figure 11-15. *Two arenas are created with different priorities. The* waitUntil *function implements a barrier to increase the chance the threads conflict with each other. The main function and the* printArrival *function are provided in Figure 11-16. Sample code* performance_tuning/priorities_and_conflict.cpp

```cpp
#include <cstdio>

int main() {
  counter = 0;
  std::printf("\n\nrunTwoThreads with low (.) and high (|)\n");
  runTwoThreads(tbb::task_arena::priority::low,
                tbb::task_arena::priority::high);

  counter = 0;
  std::printf("\n\nrunTwoThreads with low (.) and normal (:)\n");
  runTwoThreads(tbb::task_arena::priority::low,
                tbb::task_arena::priority::normal);

  counter = 0;
  std::printf("\n\nrunTwoThreads with normal (:) and high (|)\n");
  runTwoThreads(tbb::task_arena::priority::normal,
                tbb::task_arena::priority::high);
  std::printf("\n");
  return 0;
}

void printArrival(tbb::task_arena::priority priority) {
  switch (priority) {
    case tbb::task_arena::priority::low:
      std::printf(".");
      break;
    case tbb::task_arena::priority::normal:
      std::printf(":");
      break;
    case tbb::task_arena::priority::high:
      std::printf("|");
      break;
    default:
      break;
  }
  std::fflush(stdout);
  tbb::tick_count t0 = tbb::tick_count::now();
  while ((tbb::tick_count::now() - t0).seconds() < 0.01);
}
```

Figure 11-16. *The main function and the printArrival function used by Figure 11-15. Sample code performance_tuning/priorities_and_conflict.cpp*

The main function in Figure 11-16 calls runTwoThreads in three different configurations: t0 is low priority and t1 is high priority, t0 is low priority and t1 is normal priority, and t0 is normal priority and t1 is high priority. The printArrival function prints a message as each task executes an iteration of the parallel_for. If the calling thread is in a high-priority arena, it prints "|"; if it is in a normal-priority arena, it prints ":"; and if it is in a low-priority arena, it prints ".". Roughly, the larger and denser the character is, the higher the priority it represents. From the output, we will see that the higher-priority work items occur first – but since each arena has at least one thread (the C++ thread/master) that called execute, the lower-priority arena still makes some progress.

The output we obtained from the example looked like

```
runTwoThreads with low (.) and high (|)
|.||||||||.|||||||||..............

runTwoThreads with low (.) and normal (:)
:.:::::::.:::::::::...:.........

runTwoThreads with normal (:) and high (|)
|||:||||||||:||||||:::::::::::::::
```

The higher-priority arenas were favored for execution, that is, they received the worker threads first. We should note that if a higher-priority arena has fewer available slots than the number of worker threads, the remaining threads will be used to satisfy the demand of lower-priority arenas. The priority setting does not exclude lower-priority arenas; but it fully satisfies the demand of the highest-priority arenas first.

Using Constraints to Create Hardware-Aware Task Arenas

In addition to setting the number of slots in an explicit arena, we can set preferences for an arena to execute work on a specific NUMA node or to limit the arena to use only certain types of cores, such as only performance cores or only efficiency cores. These settings are hints, and there is no guarantee that TBB will respect our suggestion, although it typically does when it can. TBB relies on OS support for implementing these constraints, and different OSes have different types of support – some provide guarantees, and some do not.

We make our preferences known to TBB by using the task_arena constructor (or matching initialize function) that takes a constraints parameter (see Figure 11-11). Passing a constraints parameter lets us set hardware-oriented preferences for the arena. These include numa_id, core_type, and max_threads_per_core.

tbb::info Namespace and tbb::task_arena::constraints

There are several free functions in the info namespace that can help us pick appropriate values for a platform. These functions are shown in Figure 11-17.

```cpp
namespace tbb {
    using numa_node_id = /*implementation-defined*/;
    using core_type_id = /*implementation-defined*/;

    namespace info {
        std::vector<numa_node_id> numa_nodes();
        std::vector<core_type_id> core_types();

        int default_concurrency(task_arena::constraints c);
        int default_concurrency(numa_node_id id =
                                task_arena::automatic);
    }
} // namespace tbb
```

Figure 11-17. *The free functions in the info namespace from tbb/info.h as described in [info_namespace]*

The TBB library uses hwloc when available to determine the topology of the platform. hwloc is a software package that provides a portable way to query information about the topology of a system, as well as to apply some NUMA controls, like data placement and thread affinity. hwloc was not distributed as part of TBB at the time this book was written, but it is widely available for Windows, Linux, and macOS, and TBB will use the latest version of hwloc it finds on the system to support the functions in Figure 11-17.

Figure 11-18 shows those details of the constraints type nested in the task_arena class, including the constructor, setter functions, and member variables.

```
struct constraints {
    constraints(numa_node_id numa_node_      = task_arena::automatic,
                int             max_concurrency_ = task_arena::automatic);
    constraints& set_numa_id(numa_node_id id);
    constraints& set_max_concurrency(int maximal_concurrency);
    constraints& set_core_type(core_type_id id);
    constraints& set_max_threads_per_core(int threads_number);

    numa_node_id numa_id = task_arena::automatic;
    int max_concurrency = task_arena::automatic;
    core_type_id core_type = task_arena::automatic;
    int max_threads_per_core = task_arena::automatic;
};
```

Figure 11-18. *The definition of constraints found in* tbb/info.h *as described in* *[scheduler.task_arena]*

Limiting an Arena to a Single NUMA Node

Advanced programmers who care about performance know that exploiting locality is paramount. When it comes to locality, cache locality is the one that immediately springs to mind, but in many cases, for heavy-duty applications running on large shared memory architectures, Non-uniform Memory Access (NUMA) locality should also be considered. As you certainly know, NUMA conveys the message that memory is organized in different banks and some cores have faster access to some of the "close" banks than to "far" banks. More formally, a *NUMA node* is a grouping of the cores, caches, and local memory in which all cores share the same access time to the local shared caches and memory. Access time from one NUMA node to a different one can be significantly larger. Some questions arise, such as how the program data structures are allocated on the different NUMA nodes and where the threads that process these data structures are running (are they close to or far from the data).

Tuning for performance on NUMA systems comes down to four activities:

1. Discovering your platform topology

2. Understanding the costs associated with accessing memory

3. Controlling where your data is stored (data placement)

4. Controlling where your work executes (thread or task affinity)

The TBB library greatly simplifies activities (1) and (4). The function numa_nodes in the info namespace returns a vector of numa_node_id elements. These ids correspond to the NUMA nodes on the platform. We can set the numa_node_id in a constraints object and pass it to create a task_arena that masks all threads that enter the underlying arena so they can only be scheduled on that NUMA node.

TBB chooses to not aid with activity (2) since it may require subtle, platform-specific knowledge that is outside of the scope of TBB's responsibilities. And while TBB does not directly assist with activity (3), its features can be used on platforms that support first-touch (such as Linux) to execute loops that will cause data to reside on NUMA nodes that are later used to process the data.

Figure 11-19 shows an example of how we might use tbb::info and tbb::task_ arena to perform activities (1) and (4). This example starts by using tbb::info to detect the number of NUMA nodes on the platform. Next, two vectors are created: one for task_arena objects and one for task_group objects. In a loop, the task_arena objects are initialized so that each one is constrained to a different NUMA node. We should note that there are no slots reserved for masters in these arenas (we explicitly pass a 0). We do this because there is only a single application thread, but perhaps several arenas. Since TBB by default creates P-1 worker threads, there will be enough worker threads to fully populate all but one of the arenas. For example, if there are 4 NUMA nodes, each with 8 cores, TBB creates 4 × 8 – 1 = 31 worker threads. In the example, the application thread will join one of the arenas as a master thread.

After the arenas are initialized, we use a loop to enqueue tasks to execute parallel_ for loops into all but one of the arenas. We create the task by calling task_group::defer; this function is introduced in Chapter 6. By using task_group::defer, a task is created, and the reference count is incremented in the task_group. Any call to wait on this task_ group will not return until this task has been executed. tbb::task_arena::enqueue submits a task to the arena, but the calling thread does not join the arena to participate in the work. By using this combination of task_group::defer and tbb::task_ arena::enqueue, our main application thread is able to submit work to each arena and task_group safely without joining the arena.

After that loop, the application thread calls execute on the remaining arena. This submits a task to the arena and causes the calling thread to join the arena or, if all the slots are full, to block until the submitted task is finished. The application thread stays in that arena until the parallel_for is done.

Finally, to wait for all the work in the other arenas (NUMA nodes), the application thread enters the final loop that submits a task to each of the remaining arenas using execute. Very likely these arenas are fully populated, but even so, the calling thread will block until the task_group[i].wait() task is done.

The example in Figure 11-19 is just one possible way of using the tbb::info and tbb::task_group support for NUMA systems. TBB provides basic facilities that can be used to query platform properties and constrain arenas. How these features are used is up to us.

```cpp
#include <vector>
#include <tbb/tbb.h>

int N = 1000;
double w = 0.01;
double f(double v);

void constrain_for_numa_nodes() {
  std::vector<tbb::numa_node_id> numa_nodes = tbb::info::numa_nodes();
  std::vector<tbb::task_arena> arenas(numa_nodes.size());
  std::vector<tbb::task_group> task_groups(numa_nodes.size());

  // initialize each arena, each constrained to a different NUMA node
  for (int i = 0; i < numa_nodes.size(); i++)
    arenas[i].initialize(tbb::task_arena::constraints(numa_nodes[i]), 0);

  // enqueue work to all but the first arena, using task_group to track work
  // by using defer, the task_group reference count is incremented immediately
  for (int i = 1; i < numa_nodes.size(); i++)
    arenas[i].enqueue(
      task_groups[i].defer([] {
        tbb::parallel_for(0, N, [](int j) { f(w); });
      })
    );

  // directly execute the work to completion in the remaining arena
  arenas[0].execute([] {
    tbb::parallel_for(0, N, [](int j) { f(w); });
  });

  // join the other arenas to wait on their task_groups
  for (int i = 1; i < numa_nodes.size(); i++)
    arenas[i].execute([&task_groups, i] { task_groups[i].wait(); });
}
```

Figure 11-19. *Using* info::numa_nodes *to create one* task_group *and one* task_ *arena per NUMA node. Sample code* performance_tuning/constraints.cpp

Limiting an Arena to Certain Core Types

With the introduction of Intel's hybrid cores and Arm's big.LITTLE technology, a single CPU may now have a diverse set of cores with different efficiencies and processing power. For example, the 12th Gen Intel Core processors introduced in 2021 (known by the codename Alder Lake) are CPUs that contain both performance cores (p-cores) and efficiency cores (e-cores). In most cases, the operating system should be trusted to dynamically move threads onto the appropriate core types, and we shouldn't intervene. In fact, there are complex software and hardware systems in place, such as Intel Thread Director, which work with the operating system to maximize performance per watt. But, if we think we know better (which we probably don't), we can use features in TBB to create arenas that will execute work on specific core types, circumventing these carefully co-designed, intelligent systems.

A function in the info namespace used alongside task_arena constraints lets us meddle. The function core_types (Figure 11-20) in the tbb::info namespace returns a vector of core_type_id elements. This vector is sorted in order from the least performant to the most performant core type available on the system. So, on the previously mentioned Alder Lake platforms with e-cores and p-cores, the vector would contain two elements, the first an id that represents e-cores and the second that represents p-cores. We can set the core_type_id in a constraints object and pass it to create a task_arena that binds all threads that enter the underlying arena to that core type.

```
void constrain_for_core_type() {
    std::vector<tbb::core_type_id> core_types = tbb::info::core_types();
    tbb::task_arena arena(
      tbb::task_arena::constraints{}.set_core_type(core_types.back())
    );

    arena.execute([] {
        tbb::parallel_for(0, N, [](int) { f(w); });
    });
}
```

Figure 11-20. *Using info::core_types to create a task_arena that uses the most performant core type on the system. Sample code performance_tuning/constraints.cpp*

Setting the Maximum Number of Threads per Core

Some processors may have more logical cores than physical cores. This technology is sometimes referred to as hyperthreading (HT) or simultaneous multithreading (SMT). Processors that support this share some resources between the logical cores that are located on the same physical core. By default, TBB assumes that we want to use one thread per logical core and so creates arena slots in arenas and worker threads in the global thread pool under that assumption. Sometimes, based on performance measurements, we may want to limit the number of logical cores that are used per physical core to avoid the overheads of sharing resources between the logical cores. To do so, we can set the `max_threads_per_core` value in a `constraints` object and pass it to create a `task_arena` to limit the number of threads that will be allowed to run on each physical core. A common choice, when limiting is desirable, is to set the value to 1 as shown in Figure 11-21.

In Figure 11-21, we first use `tbb::info` to obtain the vector of `core_type_id`. We then create a constraint that uses the most performant core type but also uses `c.set_max_threads_per_core(1)` to limit the number of threads per physical core to 1, turning off HT or SMT if present on that core type.

```
void constrain_for_no_hyperthreading() {
    tbb::task_arena::constraints c;
    std::vector<tbb::core_type_id> core_types = tbb::info::core_types();
    c.set_core_type(core_types.back());
    c.set_max_threads_per_core(1);
    tbb::task_arena no_ht_arena(c);

    no_ht_arena.execute( [] {
        tbb::parallel_for(0, N, [](int) { f(w); });
    });
}
```

Figure 11-21. *Setting the maximum threads to use per core to 1. Sample code* performance_tuning/constraints.cpp

A possibly more composable way to limit the number of threads executing on cores is by setting the maximal concurrency of the `tbb::task_arena` as shown in Figure 11-22. In this example, we create the same constraint object as in Figure 11-21, but instead of using it to constrain a `task_arena`, we pass it to the function `tbb::info::default_concurrency`. When we pass a constraint to this function, it returns the default concurrency under those constraints. Let's consider a platform with 2 p-cores, each p-core supporting 2 hardware threads (HT), plus 8 e-cores, each supporting only 1 hardware thread. This platform has a total of $2 \times 2 + 8 = 12$ hardware threads. But given the tbb::task_arena::constraints c in Figure 11-22, tbb::info::default_concurrency(c) will return 2, not 12. There are 2 p-cores and if we only want to use 1 thread per p-core, then we have a default concurrency of 2.

```
void limit_concurrency_for_no_hyperthreading() {
    tbb::task_arena::constraints c;
    std::vector<tbb::core_type_id> core_types = tbb::info::core_types();
    c.set_core_type(core_types.back());
    c.set_max_threads_per_core(1);
    int no_ht_concurrency = tbb::info::default_concurrency(c);
    tbb::task_arena arena( no_ht_concurrency );

    arena.execute( [] {
        tbb::parallel_for(0, N, [](int) { f(w); });
    });
}
```

Figure 11-22. *Reducing the number of threads in an arena so that there are only enough slots to have one thread per core without explicitly preventing use of hyperthreading. Sample code performance_tuning/constraints.cpp*

Using task_scheduler_observer to Execute Your Own Code

If using constraints is not sufficient to configure threads exactly as we like, there's still one more fallback option, task_scheduler_observer. A task_scheduler_observer observes when a thread starts and stops processing tasks in an arena. To use this feature, we derive our own class from task_scheduler_observer, overriding on_scheduler_entry or on_scheduler_exit to introduce our own code. Observation is disabled at creation, and so observe() must be called to enable observation. Figure 11-23 shows the class declaration for task_scheduler_observer.

```
namespace tbb {

    class task_scheduler_observer {
    public:
        task_scheduler_observer();
        explicit task_scheduler_observer( task_arena& a );
        virtual ~task_scheduler_observer();

        void observe( bool state=true );
        bool is_observing() const;

        virtual void on_scheduler_entry( bool is_worker ) {}
        virtual void on_scheduler_exit( bool is_worker } {}
    };

} // namespace tbb
```

Figure 11-23. *The* `task_scheduler_observer` *class as described in [scheduler.task_scheduler_observer]*

Figure 11-24 shows an example class `PinningObserver` that inherits from `tbb::task_scheduler_observer` and could be used to call OS-specific functions to set the thread affinity mask directly for each thread as they enter and leave the `task_arena` a. In this figure, we provide functions that print when a thread enters and leaves the arena, but we do not include any OS-specific pinning calls.

```cpp
#include <iostream>
#include <sstream>
#include <thread>
#include <tbb/tbb.h>

// these are placeholder for where we would put OS-specific types and calls
using affinity_mask_t = std::string;
void set_thread_affinity( int tid, const affinity_mask_t& mask ) {
  std::ostringstream buffer;
  buffer << std::this_thread::get_id()
         << " -> (" << tid
         << ", " << mask << ")\n";
  std::cout << buffer.str();
}
void restore_thread_affinity() {
  std::ostringstream buffer;
  buffer <<  std::this_thread::get_id()
         << " -> (restored)\n";
  std::cout << buffer.str();
}

// observer class
class PinningObserver : public tbb::task_scheduler_observer {
public:
    // HW affinity mask to be used for threads in an arena
    affinity_mask_t m_mask;
    PinningObserver( tbb::task_arena &a, const affinity_mask_t& mask )
        : tbb::task_scheduler_observer(a), m_mask(mask) {
        observe(true); // activate the observer
    }
    void on_scheduler_entry( bool worker ) override {
        set_thread_affinity(
            tbb::this_task_arena::current_thread_index(), m_mask);
    }
    void on_scheduler_exit( bool worker ) override {
        restore_thread_affinity();
    }
};
```

Figure 11-24. *A* `PinningObserver` *that calls user-provided functions for setting and restoring thread affinity as threads enter and leave an area. In this example, we provide placeholder functions* `set_thread_affinity` *and* `restore_thread_affinity` *where OS-specific code can be placed. The function* `current_thread_index` *returns the number of the slot that the thread occupies in the arena. Sample code* `performance_tuning/task_scheduler_observer.cpp`

Figure 11-25 uses our `PinningObserver` to observe threads as they enter and leave two task arenas. Each arena is initialized to have `tbb::info::default_concurrency()`/2 slots.

```cpp
void observeTwoArenas() {
  int P = tbb::info::default_concurrency();

  // two arenas, each with half the hw threads
  tbb::task_arena a0(P/2);
  tbb::task_arena a1(P/2);

  PinningObserver obs0(a0, "mask_zero");
  PinningObserver obs1(a1, "mask_one");

  // Execute consecutive loops
  std::cout << "Execute a0 loop\n";
  a0.execute([] {
    tbb::parallel_for(0, N, [](int j) { f(w); });
  });
  std::cout << "Execute a1 loop\n";
  a1.execute([] {
    tbb::parallel_for(0, N, [](int j) { f(w); });
  });

  // Execute concurrent loops
  std::cout << "Execute a0 and a1 concurrently\n";
  std::thread t0([&]() {
    waitUntil(2, counter);
    a0.execute([] {
      tbb::parallel_for(0, N, [](int j) { f(w); });
    });
  });
  std::thread t1([&]() {
    waitUntil(2, counter);
    a1.execute([] {
      tbb::parallel_for(0, N, [](int j) { f(w); });
    });
  });
  t0.join();
  t1.join();
}
```

Figure 11-25. *Using the PinningObserver to observe the entry and exit of threads from two arenas. Sample code performance_tuning/task_scheduler_ observer.cpp*

When we ran this example on a platform with eight hardware threads, we saw the following output:

```
Execute a0 loop
139781604495104 -> (0, mask_zero)
139781564798720 -> (1, mask_zero)
139781568997120 -> (2, mask_zero)
139781560600320 -> (3, mask_zero)
139781560600320 -> (restored)
139781564798720 -> (restored)
139781568997120 -> (restored)
139781604495104 -> (restored)
Execute a1 loop
139781604495104 -> (0, mask_one)
139781564798720 -> (1, mask_one)
139781568997120 -> (2, mask_one)
139781560600320 -> (3, mask_one)
139781604495104 -> (restored)
Execute a0 and a1 concurrently
139781560600320 -> (restored)
139781568997120 -> (restored)
139781564798720 -> (restored)
139781556401920 -> (0, mask_zero)
139781564798720 -> (1, mask_zero)
139781568997120 -> (2, mask_zero)
139781560600320 -> (3, mask_zero)
139781548009216 -> (0, mask_one)
139781535418112 -> (3, mask_one)
139781539616512 -> (2, mask_one)
139781531219712 -> (1, mask_one)
139781556401920 -> (restored)
139781564798720 -> (restored)
139781560600320 -> (restored)
139781568997120 -> (restored)
139781548009216 -> (restored)
```

On the left of each line is the unique thread id for each thread that participates. If the thread is entering an arena, the right-hand side shows a pair (arena slot, mask) that shows which slot the thread is occupying in the arena and what mask it would apply if we had real OS-specific pinning code in our example. When a thread leaves an arena, the right-hand side is (restored).

There are some interesting points to notice from this output. First, when the loops are executed consecutively, we see threads migrate between the arenas; for example, thread 139781564798720 joins a0 and then later moves to a1. When the loops execute concurrently, we see more workers participating across the two arenas.

Features for Granularity and Locality

So far in this chapter we have focused on controlling resource allocation using `global_control` or explicit `task_arena` objects.

In Chapter 2, we described the generic parallel algorithms provided by the TBB library and gave a few examples to show how they can be used. While doing so, we noted that the default behavior of the algorithms was often good enough but claimed that there were ways to tune performance if needed. In this section, we back up that claim by revisiting some TBB algorithms and talk about important features that can be used to change their default behaviors.

There are three concerns that will dominate our discussions. The first is ***granularity*** – the amount of work that a task does. The TBB library is efficient at scheduling tasks, but we need to think about the size of the tasks that our algorithms will create since task size can have a significant impact on performance, especially if the tasks are extremely small or extremely large. The second issue is ***data locality***. As discussed in detail in the Preface, how an application uses caches and memory can make or break an application's performance. And the third issue is ***available parallelism***. Our goal when using TBB is to introduce parallelism of course, but we cannot do it blindly without considering granularity and locality. Tuning an application's performance is often an exercise in balancing the trade-offs between these three concerns.

One of the key differences between the TBB algorithms and other interfaces like Parallel STL is that the TBB algorithms provide hooks and features that let us influence their behavior around these three concerns. The TBB algorithms are not just black boxes over which we have no control!

In this section, we first discuss task granularity and arrive at a rule of thumb about how big is big enough when it comes to task size. We will then focus on the simple loop algorithms and how to use Ranges and Partitioners to control task granularity and data locality. We also have a brief discussion about determinism and its impact on flexibility when tuning for performance. We conclude the chapter by turning our attention to the TBB pipeline algorithm and discussing how its features affect granularity, data locality, and maximum parallelism.

OUR TEST MACHINES

In this chapter, we collect some performance measurements to assist in discussions of performance-related features. These are not rigorously collected benchmark results, but instead are used to demonstrate key performance concerns or the impact of particular TBB features.

We use two test machines.

The first machine we refer to as our *Linux Server System*. It is a system with two Intel Xeon Platinum 8580 processors (formerly codename Emerald Rapids) running Ubuntu 22.04.4 LTS. This system has two sockets, each with two NUMA nodes. Each socket has 60 physical cores, and each core supports 2 logical cores (using Intel Hyper-Threading Technology). The total system therefore has $2 \times 60 \times 2 = 240$ logical cores. In almost all our experiments, we reduce the number of threads used by our examples to make the discussion easier or to allow us to use smaller data set sizes. Each of the two processors has a 300 MB cache and the system has a total of 528MB of memory.

The second system we refer to as our *Laptop System*. It is a system with an Intel Core Ultra 7 165U processor (formerly codename Meteor Lake) running Windows 11 in "Best Performance" mode. This processor has two performance cores (p-cores) and eight efficiency cores (e-cores). Each of the two p-cores supports two logical cores (using Intel Hyper-Threading Technology). The total system therefore has $2 \times 2 + 8 = 12$ logical cores. This system has a 12MB Intel Smart Cache and 32GB of memory.

Task Granularity: How Big Is Big Enough?

To let the TBB library have maximum flexibility in balancing the load across threads, we want to divide the work done by an algorithm into as many pieces as possible. At the same time, to minimize the overheads of work stealing and task scheduling, we want to create tasks that are as large as possible. Since these forces oppose each other, the best performance for an algorithm is found somewhere in the middle.

To complicate matters, the exact best task size varies by platform and application, and therefore there is no exact guideline that applies universally. Still, it is useful to have a ballpark number that we can use as a crude guideline. With these caveats in mind, we therefore offer the following rule of thumb.

Rule of Thumb on Task Size

TBB tasks should be on average greater than 1 microsecond to effectively hide the overheads of work stealing.

It's important to keep in mind that not every task needs to be greater than 1 microsecond – in fact, that's often not possible. In divide-and-conquer algorithms, for example, we might use small tasks to divide up the work and then use larger tasks at the leaves. This is how the TBB `parallel_for` algorithm works. TBB tasks are used to both split the range and to apply the body to the final subranges. The split tasks typically do very little work, while the loop body tasks are much larger. In this case, we can't make all the tasks larger than 1 microsecond, but we can aim to make the average of the task sizes larger than 1 microsecond.

When we use algorithms like `parallel_invoke` or use TBB tasks directly, we are in complete control of the size of our tasks. For example, in Chapter 2, we implemented a parallel version of quicksort using a `parallel_invoke` and directed the recursive parallel implementation to a serial implementation once the array size (and therefore task execution time) fell below a cutoff threshold:

```
if (end - begin < cutoff) {
    serialQuicksort(begin, end);
}
```

When we use simple loop algorithms, like `parallel_for`, `parallel_reduce`, and `parallel_scan`, their range and partitioner arguments provide us with the control we need. We will talk about these in more detail in the next section.

Choosing Ranges and Partitioners for Loops

As introduced in Chapter 2, a Range represents a recursively divisible set of values – typically a loop's iteration space. We use Ranges with the simple loop algorithms: `parallel_for`, `parallel_reduce`, `parallel_deterministic_reduce`, and `parallel_scan`. A TBB algorithm partitions its range and applies the algorithm's body object(s) to these subranges using TBB tasks. Combined with Partitioners, Ranges provide a simple but powerful way to represent iteration spaces and control how they should be partitioned into tasks and assigned to worker threads. This partitioning can be used to tune task granularity and data locality.

To be a Range, a class must match the set of requirements for the named requirement Range in the TBB specification [req.range], shown in Figure 11-26. A Range can be copied, can be split using a *splitting constructor*, and may optionally provide a *proportional splitting constructor*. It also must provide methods to check if it is empty or divisible.

Pseudo-Signature	Semantics
R::R(const R&)	Copy constructor.
R::~R()	Destructor.
bool R::empty() const	True if range is empty.
bool R::is_divisible() const	True if range can be partitioned into two subranges.
R::R(R &r, split)	Basic splitting constructor. Splits r into two subranges.
R::R(R &r, proportional_split proportion)	**Optional**. Proportional splitting constructor. Splits r into two subranges in accordance with proportion.

Figure 11-26. *The Range named requirement [req.range]*

While we can define our own Range types, the TBB library provides the blocked ranges shown in Figure 11-27, which will cover most situations. For example, we can represent the iteration space of the following nested loop with a blocked_range2d<int, int> r(i_begin, i_end, j_begin, j_end):

```
for (int i = i_begin; i < i_end, ++i )
  for (int j = j_begin; j < j_end; ++j )
    /* loop body */
```

Range Type	Constructor Arguments	Description
blocked_range	Value begin, Value end, size_type grainsize	Models a 1-dimensional range.
blocked_range2d	RowValue row_begin, RowValue row_end, [size_type row_grainsize], ColValue col_begin, ColValue col_end, [size_type col_grainsize]	Models a 2-dimensional range. After repeated splitting, the subranges approach the aspect ratio of the row and column grain sizes.
blocked_range3d	PageValue page_begin, PageValue page_end, [size_type page_grainsize], RowValue row_begin, RowValue row_end, [size_type row_grainsize], ColValue col_begin, ColValue col_end, [size_type col_grainsize]	Models a 3-dimensional range. After repeated splitting, the subranges approach the aspect ratio of the page, row, and column grain sizes.
blocked_nd_range	const dim_range_type& dim0, /*, ... N parameters of the same type*/ const Value (&dim_size)[N], size_type grainsize = 1	Models an N-dimensional range. Unlike the other blocked range types in this table, all dimensions are over the same Value type. The dim_range_type is blocked_range<Value>. There are two constructors. The first constructor takes exactly N dim_range_type objects, one per dimension. The second constructor takes an array of N Value type elements where each element is the size of the corresponding dimension and assumes the ranges start at 0. The second constructor also takes a single common grain size for all dimensions.

Figure 11-27. *The different predefined range types provided by TBB as described in [algorithms.blocked_range], [algorithms.blocked_range2d], [algorithms. blocked_range3d], and [algorithms.blocked_nd_range]*

An Overview of Partitioners

Along with Ranges, TBB algorithms support Partitioners that specify how an algorithm should partition its Range. The different Partitioner types are shown in Figure 11-28.

Partitioner	Description	When used with `blocked_range` with grain size of g
`simple_partitioner`	Chunk size determined by grain size.	$g/2 \leq$ chunksize $\leq g$
`auto_partitioner`	Automatic chunk size with grain size acting as floor.	$g/2 \leq$ chunksize
`affinity_partitioner`	Automatic chunk size with grain size acting as floor. Cache affinity and initial uniform distribution of iterations.	
`static_partitioner`	Deterministic chunk size. Cache affinity and uniform distribution of iterations without any further subdivision possible. A uniform distribution is created unless the grain size prevents P chunks from being created.	$\max(g/3, N/P) \leq$ chunksize where: N is problem size P is number of threads that can participate in task execution.

Figure 11-28. *The partitioner types provided by TBB as described in [algorithms. simple_partitioner], [algorithms.auto_partitioner], [algorithms.affinity_ partitioner], and [algorithms.static_partitioner]*

A `simple_partitioner` is used to recursively divide a Range until its `is_divisible` method returns false. For the blocked range types, this means the range will be divided until its size is less than or equal to its grainsize. If we have highly tuned our grainsize (and we will talk about this in the next section), we want to use a `simple_partitioner` since it ensures that the final subranges respect the provided grainsizes.

An `auto_partitioner` uses a dynamic algorithm to sufficiently split a range to balance load, but it does not necessarily divide a range as finely as `is_divisible` allows. When used with the blocked range classes, the grainsize still provides a lower bound on the size of the final chunks but is much less important since the `auto_partitioner` can decide to use larger grainsizes. It is therefore commonly acceptable to use a grainsize of 1 and just let the `auto_partitioner` determine the best grainsize. In oneTBB, the default Partitioner type used for `parallel_for`, `parallel_reduce`, and `parallel_scan` is an `auto_partitioner`.

A `static_partitioner` distributes the range over the worker threads as uniformly as possible without the possibility for further load balancing. The work distribution and mapping to threads is deterministic and only depends on the number of iterations, the grainsize, and the number of threads. The `static_partitioner` has the lowest overhead of all partitioners since it makes no dynamic decisions. Using a `static_partitioner` can also result in improved cache behavior since the scheduling pattern will be repeated across executions of the same loop. A `static_partitioner` however severely restricts load balancing, so it needs to be used judiciously. In section "Using a `static_partitioner`," we will highlight the strengths and weaknesses of `static_partitioner`.

The `affinity_partitioner` combines the best from `auto_partitioner` and `static_partitioner` and improves cache affinity if the same partitioner object is reused when a loop is reexecuted over the same data set. The `affinity_partitioner`, like `static_partitioner`, initially creates a uniform distribution but allows for additional load balancing. It also keeps a history of which thread executes which chunk of the range and tries to recreate this execution pattern on subsequent executions. If a data set fits completely within the processors' caches, repeating the scheduling pattern can result in significant performance improvements.

Choosing a Grainsize (or Not) to Manage Task Granularity

At the beginning of this section, we talked about how important task granularity can be. When we use a blocked range type, we should always then highly tune our grainsize, right? Not necessarily. Selecting the right grainsize when using a blocked range can be extremely important or almost irrelevant – it all depends on the Partitioner being used.

If we use a `simple_partitioner`, the grainsize is the sole determinant of the size of the ranges that will be passed to the body. When a `simple_partitioner` is used, the range is recursively subdivided until `is_divisible` returns false. In contrast, all the other Partitioners have their own internal algorithms for deciding when to stop dividing ranges. Choosing a grainsize of 1 is typically sufficient for these other partitioners that use `is_divisible` as only a lower bound.

To demonstrate the impact of grainsize on the different Partitioners, we can use a simple `parallel_for` microbenchmark (Figure 11-29) and vary the number of iterations in the loop (N), the grainsize (gs), the execution time per loop iteration (tpi), and the Partitioner (p).

```
template< typename P >
static inline double executePfor(int num_trials, int N,
                                 int gs, P &p, double tpi) {
  tbb::tick_count t0;
  for (int t = -1; t < num_trials; ++t) {
  if (!t) t0 = tbb::tick_count::now();
    tbb::parallel_for (
        tbb::blocked_range<int>{0, N, gs},
        [tpi](const tbb::blocked_range<int> &r) {
            for (int i = r.begin(); i < r.end(); ++i) {
                spinWaitForAtLeast(tpi);
            }
        },
        p // The partitioner
    );
  }
  tbb::tick_count t1 = tbb::tick_count::now();
  return (t1 - t0).seconds()/num_trials;
}
```

Figure 11-29. *A function used to measure the time to execute a* parallel_for *with N iterations using a partitioner (p), a grainsize (gs), and time per iteration (tpi). Sample code performance_tuning/parallel_for_partitioners_timed.cpp*

Figure 11-30 shows the results of the program shown in Figure 11-29, when executed for N=2^{18} using each of the Partitioner types available in TBB and with a range of grainsizes.

tbb::task_arena constraints were used to limit the computation to a single NUMA node with only one thread per core and a total of eight threads.

We can see that for a very small time_per_iteration of 100ns, the simple_ partitioner approaches the other partitioner's maximum performance when the grainsize is $\geq$ 16. As the time per iteration increases, the simple_partitioner approaches the maximum performance more quickly since fewer iterations are needed to overcome scheduling overheads.

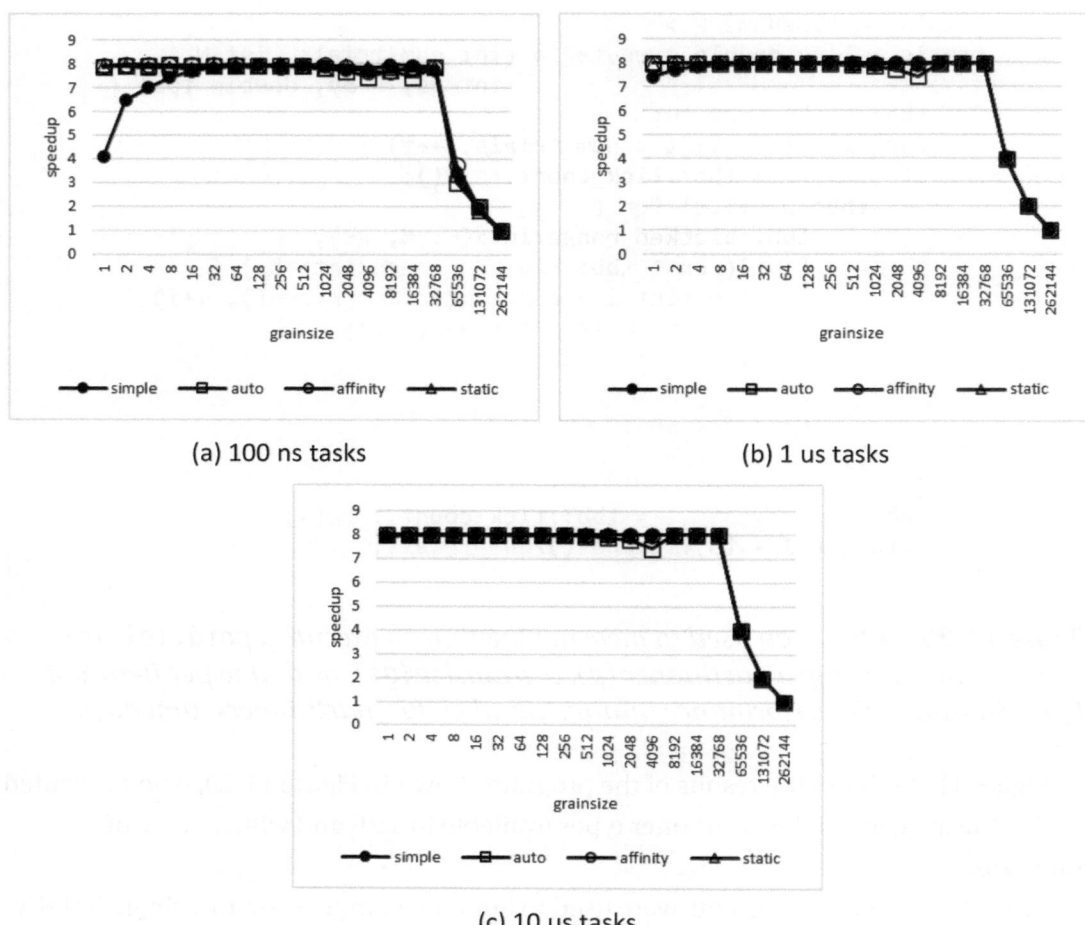

(a) 100 ns tasks   (b) 1 us tasks

(c) 10 us tasks

Figure 11-30. *Speedup for different Partitioner types and increasing grainsizes compared with a serial execution. The total number of iterations in the loop being tested is $2^{18} = 262,144$. We collected these results on the Linux Server System described earlier in this chapter.* tbb::task_arena *constraints were used to limit the computation to a single NUMA node with only one thread per core and maximum concurrency of eight hardware threads*

For all the Partitioner types shown in Figure 11-30 except simple_partitioner, we see maximum performance from a grainsize of 1 until 4,096. Our application is configured to use eight threads, and therefore we need a grainsize less than or equal to $2^{18}/8 = 32,768$ to provide at least one chunk to each thread; consequently, all the Partitioners begin to tail off after a grainsize of 32,768. We might also note that at a grainsize of 4,096, the auto_partitioner and affinity_partitioner show drops in performance in all figures. This is because picking large grainsizes limits the choices available to these algorithms, interfering with their ability to complete their automated partitioning.

This small experiment confirms that the grainsize is critically important for `simple_partitioner`. We can use a `simple_partitioner` to manually select the size of our tasks, but when we do so, we need to be more accurate in our choices.

A second takeaway is that efficient execution, with a speedup close to the linear upper bound, is seen when the body size approaches 1us (100ns × 16 = 1.6us). This result reinforces the rule of thumb we presented earlier in this book! This should not be surprising since experience and experiments like these are the reason for our rule of thumb in the first place.

Ranges, Partitioners, and Data Cache Performance

Ranges and Partitioners can improve data cache performance by enabling cache-oblivious algorithms or by enabling cache affinity. Cache-oblivious algorithms are useful when a data set is too large to fit into the data caches but reuse of data within the algorithm can be exploited if it is solved using a divide-and-conquer approach. In contrast, cache affinity is useful when the data set completely fits into the caches. Cache affinity is used to repeatedly schedule the same parts of a range onto the same processors – so that the data that fits in the cache can be accessed again from the same cache.

Cache-Oblivious Algorithms

A cache-oblivious algorithm is an algorithm that achieves good (or even optimal) use of data caches without depending upon knowledge of the hardware's cache parameters. The concept is similar to loop tiling or loop blocking but does not require an accurate tile or block size. Cache-oblivious algorithms often recursively divide problems into smaller and smaller subproblems. At some point, these small subproblems begin to fit into a machine's caches. The recursive subdivision might continue all the way down to the smallest possible size, or there may be a cutoff point for efficiency – but this cutoff point is *not* related to the cache size and typically creates patterns that access data sized well below any reasonable cache size.

Because cache-oblivious algorithms are not at all disinterested in cache performance, we've heard many other suggested names, such as *cache agnostic*, since these algorithms optimize for whatever cache they encounter, and *cache paranoid*, since they assume there can be infinite levels of caches. But cache-oblivious is the name used in the literature, and it has stuck.

Here, we will use matrix transposition as an example of an algorithm that can benefit from a cache-oblivious implementation. A non-cache-oblivious serial implementation of matrix transposition is shown in Figure 11-31.

```cpp
void serialTranspose(int N, double *a, double *b) {
  for (int i = 0; i < N; ++i) {
    for (int j = 0; j < N; ++j) {
      b[j*N+i] = a[i*N+j];
    }
  }
}
```

Figure 11-31. *A serial implementation of a matrix transposition. Sample code*
performance_tuning/parallel_for_transpose_partitioners.cpp

For simplicity, let's assume that four elements fit in a cache line in our machine. Figure 11-32 shows the cache lines that will be accessed during the transposition of the first two rows of the N × N matrix a. If the cache is large enough, it can retain all of the cache lines accessed in b during that transposition of the first row of a and not need to reload these during that transposition of the second row of a. But if it is not large enough, these cache lines will need to be reloaded – resulting in a cache miss at each access to the matrix b. In the figure, we show a 16 × 16 array, but imagine if it was very large.

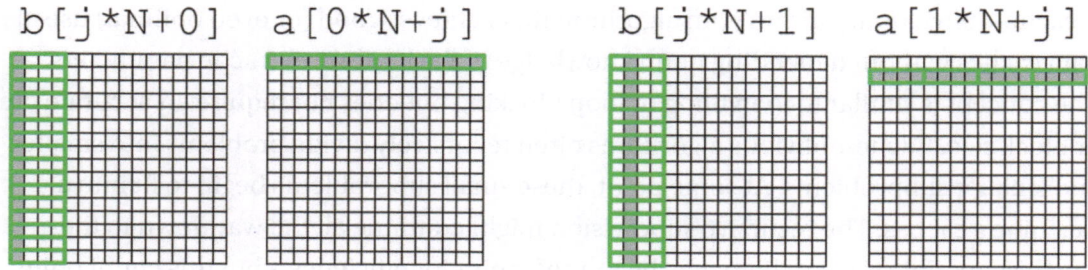

Figure 11-32. *The cache lines accessed when transposing the first two rows of the*
matrix a. For simplicity, we show four items in each cache line

A cache-oblivious implementation of this algorithm reduces the amount of data accessed between reuses of the same cache line or data item. As shown in Figure 11-33, if we focus on transposing only a small block of matrix a before moving on to other blocks of matrix a, we can reduce the number of cache lines that hold elements of b that need to be retained in the cache to get performance gains due to cache line reuse regardless of how big the whole matrix is.

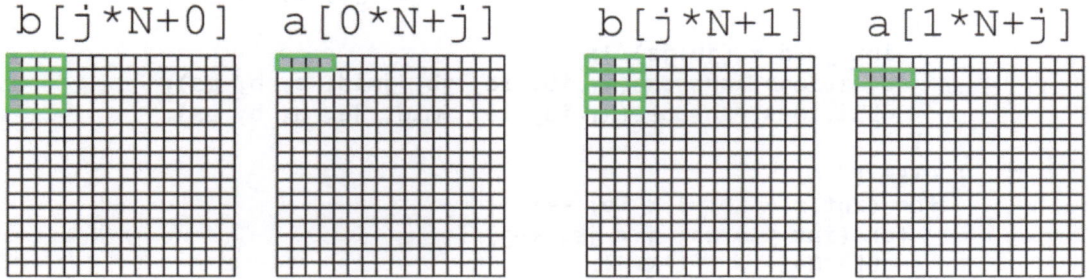

Figure 11-33. *Transposing a block at a time reduces the number of cache lines that need to be retained to benefit from reuse*

A serial implementation of a cache-oblivious implementation of matrix transposition is shown in Figure 11-34. It recursively subdivides the problem along the i and j dimensions and uses a serial for-loop when the range drops below a threshold.

```
void obliviousTranspose(int N, int ib, int ie, int jb, int je,
                        double *a, double *b, int gs) {
    int ilen = ie-ib;
    int jlen = je-jb;
    if (ilen > gs || jlen > gs) {
        if ( ilen > jlen ) {
            int imid = (ib+ie)/2;
            obliviousTranspose(N, ib, imid, jb, je, a, b, gs);
            obliviousTranspose(N, imid, ie, jb, je, a, b, gs);
        } else {
            int jmid = (jb+je)/2;
            obliviousTranspose(N, ib, ie, jb, jmid, a, b, gs);
            obliviousTranspose(N, ib, ie, jmid, je, a, b, gs);
        }
    } else {
        for (int i = ib; i < ie; ++i) {
            for (int j = jb; j < je; ++j) {
                b[j*N+i] = a[i*N+j];
            }
        }
    }
}
```

Figure 11-34. *A serial cache-oblivious implementation of a matrix transposition. Sample code performance_tuning/parallel_for_transpose_partitioners.cpp*

Because the implementation alternates between dividing in the i and the j direction, the matrix a is transposed using the traversal pattern shown in Figure 11-35, first completing block 1, then 2, then 3, and so on. If gs is 4 and our cache line size is 4, we get the reuse within each block that we showed in Figure 11-33. But if our cache line is 8 items instead of 4 (which is much more likely for real systems), we would get reuse not only within the smallest blocks but also across blocks. For example, if the data cache can retain all the cache lines loaded during blocks 1 and 2, these will be reused when transposing blocks 3 and 4.

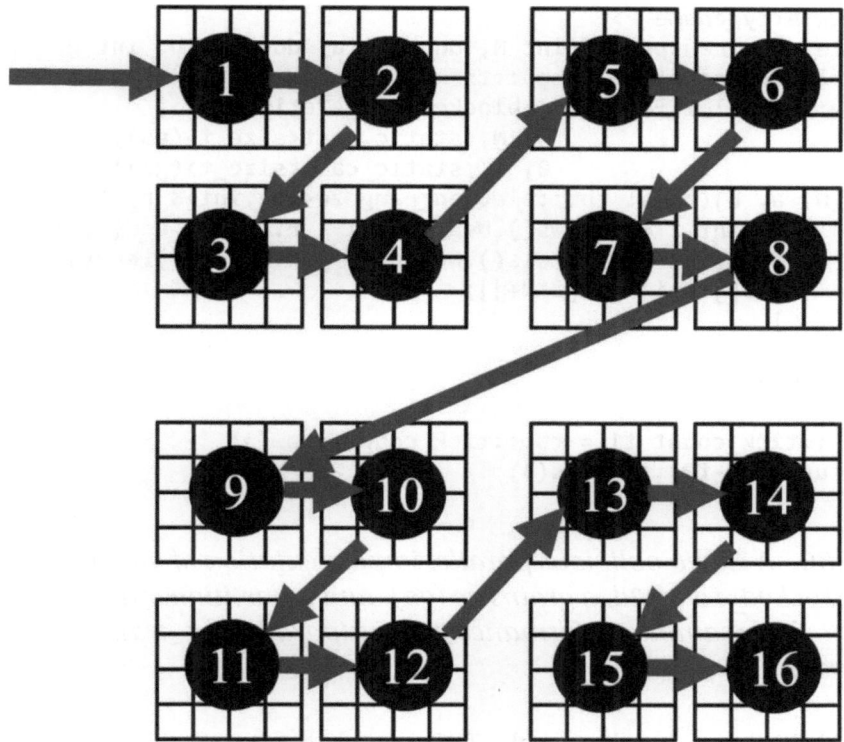

Figure 11-35. *A traversal pattern that computes the transpose for sub-blocks of a before moving on to other blocks*

This is the true power of cache-oblivious algorithms – we don't need to exactly know the sizes of the levels of the memory hierarchy. As the subproblems get smaller, they fit in progressively smaller parts of the memory hierarchy, improving reuse at each level.

The TBB loop algorithms and the TBB scheduler are designed to specifically support cache-oblivious algorithms. We can therefore quickly implement a cache-oblivious parallel implementation of matrix transposition using a `parallel_for`, a `blocked_range2d`, and a `simple_partitioner` as shown in Figure 11-36. We use a `blocked_range2d` because we want the iteration space subdivided into two-dimensional blocks. And we use a `simple_partitioner` because we only get the benefits from reuse if the blocks are subdivided down to sizes smaller than the cache size; the other Partitioner types optimize load balancing and so may choose larger range sizes if those are sufficient to balance load.

```
template<typename P>
double pforTranspose2d(int N, double *a, double *b, int gs) {
  tbb::tick_count t0 = tbb::tick_count::now();
  tbb::parallel_for( tbb::blocked_range2d<int,int>{
                        0, N, static_cast<size_t>(gs),
                        0, N, static_cast<size_t>(gs)},
    [N, a, b](const tbb::blocked_range2d<int,int>& r) {
      for (int i = r.rows().begin(); i < r.rows().end(); ++i) {
        for (int j = r.cols().begin(); j < r.cols().end(); ++j) {
          b[j*N+i] = a[i*N+j];
        }
      }
    }, P()
  );
  tbb::tick_count t1 = tbb::tick_count::now();
  return (t1-t0).seconds();
}
```

Figure 11-36. *A cache-oblivious parallel implementation of matrix transposition that uses* blocked_range2d, *a grainsize (*gs*), and a partitioner as a template argument P. Code sample performance_tuning/parallel_for_transpose_partitioners.cpp*

Figure 11-37 shows that the way the TBB parallel_for recursively subdivides ranges creates the same blocks that we want for our cache-oblivious implementation. The depth-first work and breadth-first stealing behavior of the TBB scheduler also mean that the blocks will execute in an order similar to the one shown in Figure 11-35.

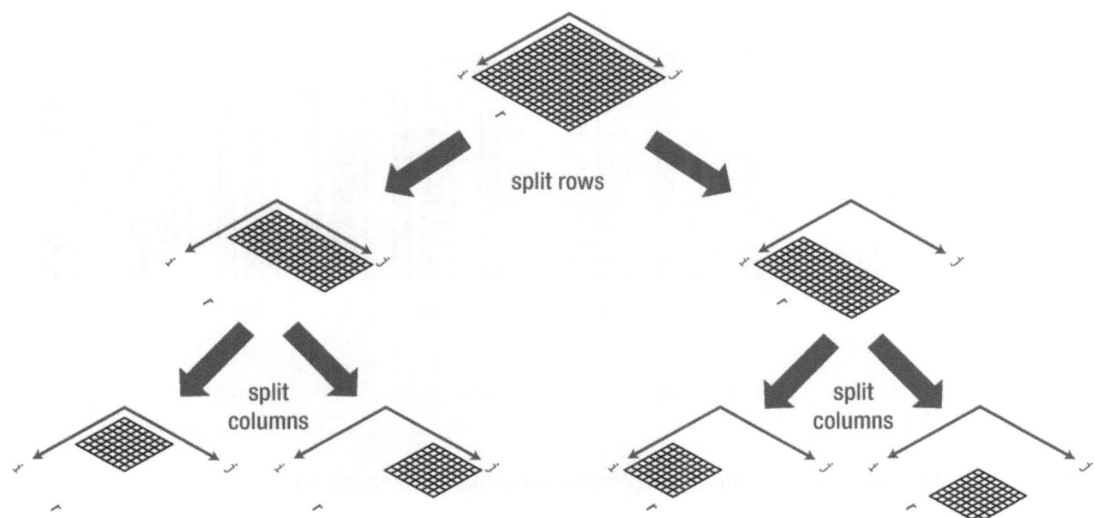

Figure 11-37. *The recursive subdivision of the blocked_range2d provides a division that matches the blocks we want for our cache-oblivious parallel implementation*

Figure 11-38 shows the performance of the serial cache-oblivious implementation in Figure 11-34, the performance of an implementation using a 1D blocked_range, and the performance of a blocked_range2d implementation similar to the one in Figure 11-36. We implemented our parallel versions so that we could change the grainsize and partitioner easily as was shown in Figure 11-36.

In Figure 11-38, we show the speedup of our implementations on our Linux Server System using a 32768 × 32768 matrix compared with the simple serial implementation from Figure 11-31.

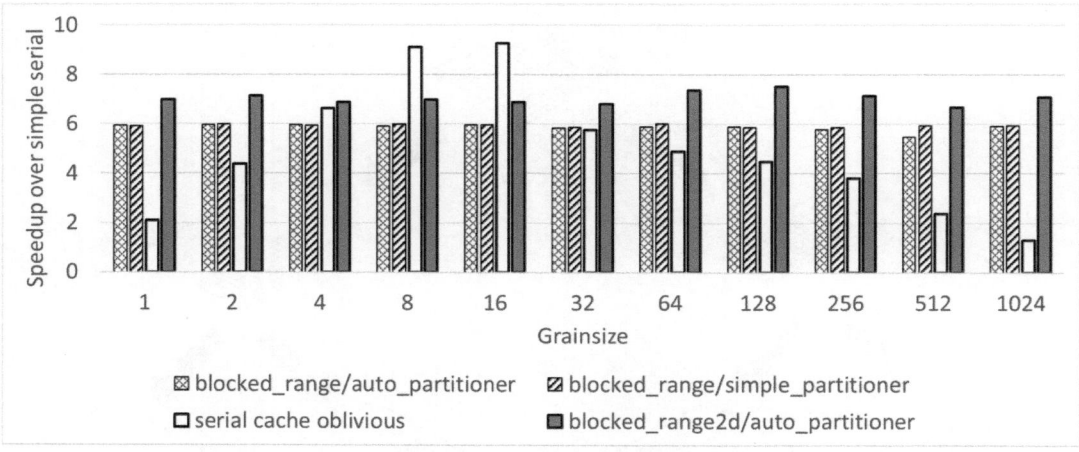

(a) The serial cache-oblivious algorithm outperforms most parallel versions

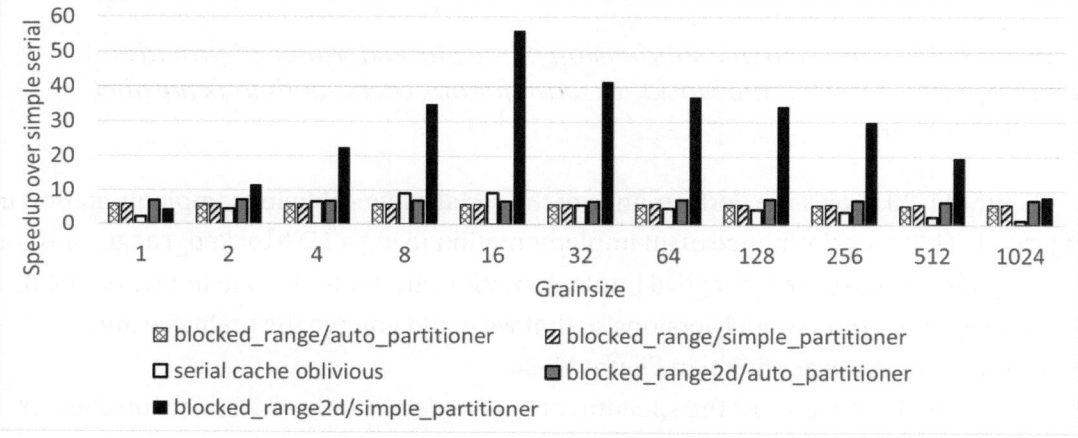

(b) But blocked_range2d with simple partitioner shows better performance

Figure 11-38. *The speedup on our test machine for N = 32,768 with various grainsizes and partitioners. We collected these results on the Linux Server System described earlier in this chapter.* tbb::task_arena *constraints were used to limit the computation to a single NUMA node with only one thread per core and maximum concurrency of eight hardware threads*

Matrix transposition is limited by the speed at which we can read and write data – there is no compute whatsoever. We can see from Figure 11-38 that most of the parallel implementations never reach a speedup of 8 on 8 threads, regardless of the grainsize we use. The speedup is limited by the memory bandwidth.

Our serial cache-oblivious algorithm reorders memory accesses, reducing the number of cache misses. It significantly outperforms the simple version and even most of the parallel implementations. When we use a `blocked_range2d` in our parallel implementation, we similarly get 2D subdivisions. But as we see in Figure 11-38, only when we use a `simple_partitioner` does it fully behave like a cache-oblivious algorithm. In fact, our cache-oblivious parallel algorithm with a `blocked_range2d` and a `simple_partitioner` reduces pressure on the memory hierarchy to such a degree that it reaches speedups in excess of 50× over the serial implementation when using only eight threads.

Not all problems have cache-oblivious solutions, but many common problems do. It is worth the time to research problems to see if a cache-oblivious solution is possible and worthwhile. If so, the blocked range types and the `simple_partitioner` will make it very easy to implement one with TBB algorithms.

Cache Affinity

Cache-oblivious algorithms improve cache performance by breaking problems, which have data locality but do not fit into the cache, down into smaller problems that do fit into the cache. In contrast, cache affinity addresses the repeated execution of ranges across data that already fit in the cache. Since the data fits in the cache, if the same subranges are assigned to the same processors on subsequent executions, the cached data can be accessed more quickly. We can use either an `affinity_partitioner` or a `static_partitioner` to enable cache affinity for the TBB loop algorithms. Figure 11-39 shows a simple microbenchmark that adds a value to each element in a 1D array. The function receives a reference to the Partitioner because we need to receive the Partitioner as a reference to record history in the `affinity_partitioner` object.

```
template <typename Partitioner>
void parForAdd(double v, int N, double *a, Partitioner& p) {
  tbb::parallel_for( tbb::blocked_range<int>(0, N, 1),
    [v, a](const tbb::blocked_range<int>& r) {
      for (int i = r.begin(); i < r.end(); ++i) {
        a[i] += v;
      }
    }, p
  );
}
```

Figure 11-39. A function that uses a TBB parallel_for to add a value to all of the elements of a 1D array. Sample code performance_tuning/parallel_for_addition_partitioners.cpp

To see the impact of cache affinity, we can execute this function repeatedly, sending in the same value for N and the same array a. When using an `auto_partitioner`, the scheduling of the subranges to threads will vary from invocation to invocation. Even if array a completely fits into the processors' caches, the same region of a may not fall on the same processor in subsequent executions:

```cpp
for (int i = 0; i < M; ++i) {
  parForAdd(v[i], N, a,
  tbb::auto_partitioner{});
}
```

If we use an `affinity_partitioner`, however, the TBB library will record the task scheduling and try to recreate it on each execution. Because the history is recorded in the Partitioner, we must pass the same Partitioner object on subsequent executions and cannot simply create a temporary object like we did with `auto_partitioner`:

```cpp
tbb::affinity_partitioner aff_p;
for (int i = 0; i < M; ++i) {
  parForAdd(v[i], N, a, aff_p);
}
```

Finally, we can also use a `static_partitioner` to create cache affinity. Because the scheduling is deterministic when we use a `static_partitioner`, we do not need to pass the same partitioner object for each execution:

```cpp
for (int i = 0; i < M; ++i) {
  parForAdd(v[i], N, a,
  tbb::static_partitioner{});
}
```

We executed this microbenchmark on our test machine configured to use only eight threads with N = 1,000,000 and M = 10,000. Our array of doubles is 1,000,000 × 8 = 8MB in size. Our test machine had 2MB L2 data caches, one per core. When using an `affinity_partitioner`, the test completed 1.5 times faster than when using the `auto_partitioner`. When using a `static_partitioner`, the test completed three times faster than when using the `auto_partitioner`!

Because the data was able to fit into the aggregate L2 cache size ($8 \times 2MB = 16MB$), replaying the same scheduling had a significant impact on the execution time. In the next section, we'll discuss why the `static_partitioner` outperformed the `auto_partitioner` in this case and why we shouldn't be too surprised or excited about that. If we increase N to 10,000,000 elements, we no longer see a large difference in the execution times since array a is now too large to fit in the caches of our test system – in this case, rethinking the algorithm to implement tiling/blocking to exploit cache locality is necessary.

Using a `static_partitioner`

The `static_partitioner` is the lowest-overhead partitioner, and it quickly provides a uniform distribution of a blocked range across the threads in an arena. Since the partitioning is deterministic, it also can improve cache behavior when a loop or a series of loops are executed repeatedly on the same range. In the previous section, we saw that it outperformed `affinity_partitioner` significantly for our microbenchmark. However, because it creates just enough chunks to provide one to each thread in the arena, there is no opportunity for work stealing to balance the load dynamically. In effect, the `static_partitioner` disables the TBB library's work-stealing scheduling approach.

There is a good reason though for TBB to include `static_partitioner`. As the number of cores increases, random work stealing becomes costlier, especially when transitioning from a serial part of an application to a parallel part. When the master thread first spawns new work into the arena, all the worker threads wake up and as a *thundering herd* try to find work to do. To make matters worse, they don't know where to look and start randomly peeking into not only the master thread's deque but each other's local deques too. Some worker thread will eventually find the work in the master and subdivide it, and another worker will eventually find this subdivided piece, subdivide it, and so on. And after a while, things will settle down, and all the workers will find something to do and will happily work from their own local deques.

But, if we already know that the workload is well balanced, the system is not oversubscribed, and all our cores are equally powerful, do we really need all this work-stealing overhead to just get a uniform distribution across the workers? Not if we use a `static_partitioner`! It is designed for just this case. It pushes tasks that uniformly distribute the range to the worker threads so that they don't have to steal tasks at all. When it applies, `static_partitioner` is the most efficient way to partition a loop.

But don't get too excited about static_partitioner! If the workload is not uniform or any of the cores are oversubscribed with additional threads, then using a static_partitioner can wreck performance. For example, Figure 11-40 shows the same microbenchmark configuration we used in Figure 11-29 to examine the impact of grainsize on performance. But shows what happens when we run on our Laptop System while running other desktop apps.

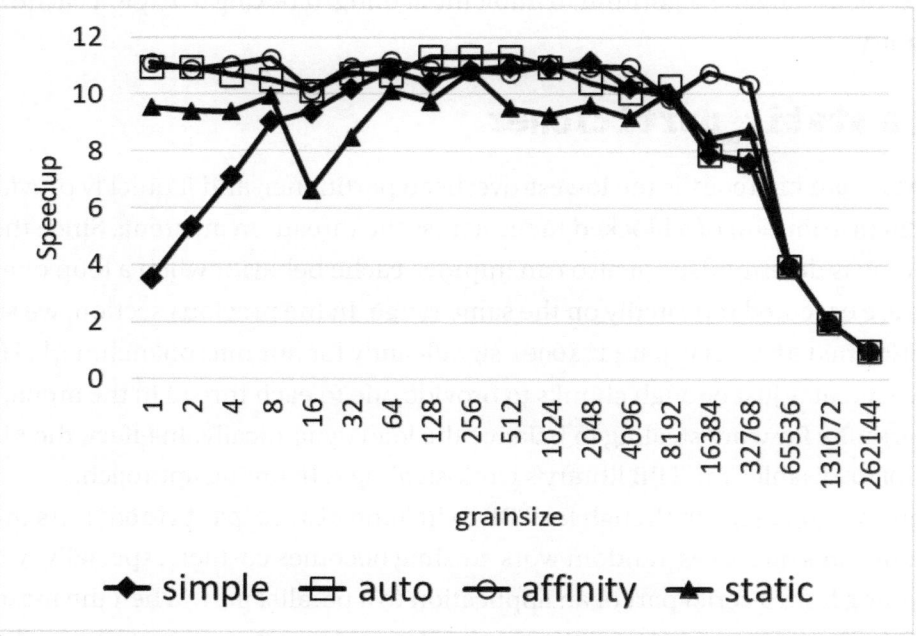

Figure 11-40. *Speedup relative to the serial implementation for different Partitioner types and increasing grainsizes when an additional thread executes a spin loop in the background. The time per iteration is set to 100ns*

In Figure 11-40, the simple_partitioner shows the usual improvement as the grainsize grows. And the partitioners that flexibly choose a grainsize automatically so that load can be balanced, auto_partitioner and affinity_partitioner, are very tolerant of the extra load on the system, providing speedups close to 12 on our 12–logical core system. The static_partitioner does not do as well. It assumes that all the cores are equally capable and equally available to participate in work and therefore uniformly distributes the work among them. On our Laptop System, we have other applications running, and we also have a mix of e-cores and p-cores. In this scenario, our cores are not equally capable, and because of the load they may not be equally available. As a result, speedup for static_partitioner is lower and less stable than the other partitioners.

It is not just the system that a static_partitioner is sensitive to. Figure 11-41 shows a loop where the work increases with each iteration. If a static_partitioner is used, the thread that gets the lowest set of iterations will have much less work to do than the unlucky thread that gets the highest set of iterations.

```cpp
void doWork(double usec) {
  double sec = usec*1e-06;
  tbb::tick_count t0 = tbb::tick_count::now();
  while ((tbb::tick_count::now() - t0).seconds() <= sec);
}

template <typename Partitioner>
void buildingWork(int N, Partitioner& p) {
  tbb::parallel_for( tbb::blocked_range<int>(0, N, 1),
    [](const tbb::blocked_range<int>& r) {
      for (int i = r.begin(); i <  r.end(); ++i) {
        doWork(i);
      }
    }, p
  );
}
```

Figure 11-41. *A loop where the work increases in each iteration. Sample code performance_tuning/partitioners_imbalanced_loops.cpp*

We ran the loop in Figure 11-41 ten times using each partitioner type with N = 1,000 on our Linux Server System. As usual, we limited the application by using task_arena constraints to eight threads. The results, as expected, show the static_partitioner underperforming on this example:

```
auto_partitioner = 0.629797 seconds
affinity_partitioner = 0.629912 seconds
static_partitioner = 1.17187 seconds
```

The auto_partitioner and affinity_partitioner rebalance the load across the threads, while the static_partitioner is stuck with its initial uniform but unfair distribution.

The `static_partitioner` is therefore almost exclusively useful in High-Performance Computing (HPC) applications. These applications run on systems with many cores and often in batch mode, where a single application is run at a time. If the workload does not need *any* dynamic load balancing, then `static_partitioner` will almost always outperform the other partitioners. Well-balanced workloads and single-user, batch-mode systems are the exception and not the rule.

Restricting the Scheduler for Determinism

In Chapter 2, we discussed associativity and floating-point types. We noted that any implementation of floating-point numbers is an approximation, and so parallelism can lead to different results when we depend on properties like associativity or commutativity. Those results aren't necessarily wrong; they are just different. Still, in the case of reduction, TBB provides a `parallel_deterministic_reduce` algorithm if we want to ensure that we get the same results for each execution on the same input data when executed on the same machine.

As we might guess, `parallel_deterministic_reduce` only accepts `simple_partitioner` or `static_partitioner`, since the number of subranges is deterministic for both partitioner types. The `parallel_deterministic_reduce` also always executes the same set of split and join operations on a given machine no matter how many threads dynamically participate in execution and how tasks are mapped to threads – the `parallel_reduce` algorithm may not. The result is that `parallel_deterministic_reduce` will always return the same result when run on the same machine – but sacrifices some flexibility to do so.

Figure 11-42 shows the speedup for the pi calculation example from Chapter 2 when implemented using `parallel_reduce` and `parallel_deterministic_reduce`. For this example, we collected measurements on our Laptop System. We configured the application, using `tbb::task_arena` constraints, to execute this application using only the eight e-cores. We did not close all our other applications, allowing several desktop applications to remain active. We did this to, again, highlight the limitations of static partitioning.

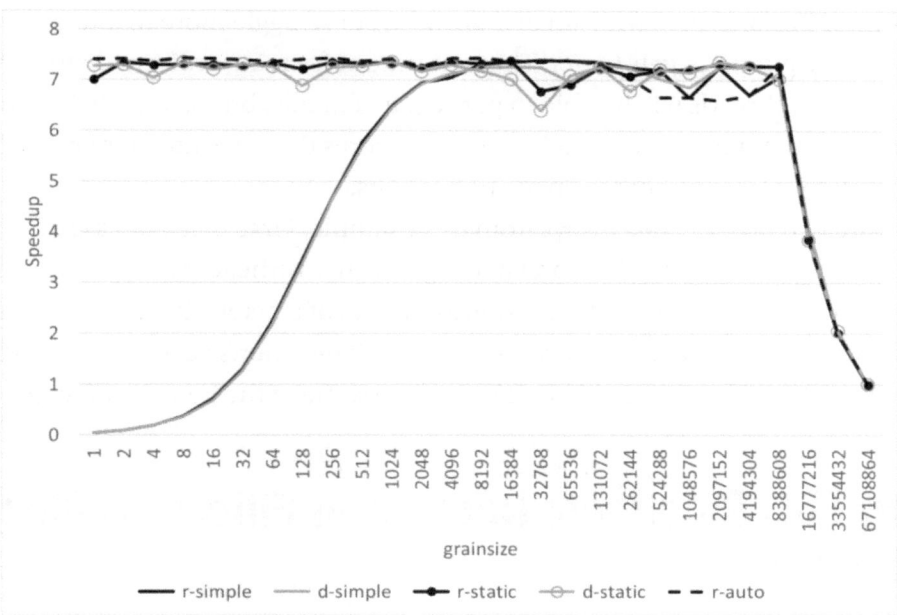

Figure 11-42. *Speedup for the pi example from Chapter 2 using* parallel_reduce *with an* auto_partitioner *(r-auto), a* simple_partitioner *(r-simple), and a* static_partitioner *(r-static) and* parallel_deterministic_reduce *with a* simple_partitioner *(d-simple) and a* static_partitioner *(d-static)*

The maximum speedup is similar for both the deterministic and nondeterministic versions of reduce; however, the auto_partitioner performs very well for parallel_ reduce, and that is simply not an option with parallel_deterministic_reduce. While parallel_deterministic_reduce will have some additional overhead because it must perform all the splits and joins, this overhead is typically small. The bigger limitation is that we cannot use any of the partitioners that automatically find a chunk size for us.

On our system, which was slightly loaded with other applications, we can see that r-auto (parallel_reduce with the auto_partitioner) stays close to the peak speedup until it reaches a point where the large grainsize limits its flexibility. As we should expect by now, both r-simple (parallel_reduce with the simple_partitioner) and d-simple (parallel_deterministic_reduce with the simple_partitioner) start performing well once a sufficient grainsize is used. We can note that the difference between these two is negligible; adding determinism did not impact performance significantly. We should notice that both r-static (parallel_reduce with the static_partitioner) and d-static (parallel_deterministic_reduce with the static_partitioner) do not show poor performance with small grainsizes but struggle more to maintain peak speedups as the grainsize gets larger. These partitioners create uniform distributions, assuming that all threads will be able to participate equally, but on our slightly loaded system they cannot participate equally, since the cores they execute on may be involved in other work related to our other open applications.

There are two primary takeaways from this example. First, using `parallel_deterministic_reduce` typically won't add significant overhead. Second, the use of `parallel_deterministic_reduce` requires the use of a deterministic partitioner, which means we either need to select a sufficiently large grainsize for use with `simple_partitioner` or use `static_partitioner` and lose some of the benefits of work stealing.

Tuning TBB Pipelines: Number of Filters, Modes, and Tokens

Just as with the loop algorithms, the performance of TBB pipelines is impacted by granularity, locality, and available parallelism. Unlike the loop algorithms, TBB pipelines do not support Ranges and Partitioners. Instead, the controls used to tune pipelines include the number of filters, the filter execution modes, and the number of tokens passed to the pipeline when it is run.

TBB pipeline filters are spawned as tasks and scheduled by the TBB library, and therefore, just as with the subranges created by the loop algorithms, we want the filter bodies to execute long enough to mitigate overheads, but we also want ample parallelism. We balance these concerns by how we break our work into filters. The filters should also be well balanced in execution time since the slowest serial stage will be a bottleneck.

As described in Chapter 2, pipeline filters are also created with an execution mode: `serial_in_order`, `serial_out_of_order`, or `parallel`. When using `serial_in_order` mode, a filter can process at most one item at a time, and it must process them in the same order that the first filter generated them in. A `serial_out_of_order` filter is allowed to execute the items in any order. A `parallel` filter is allowed to execute on different items in parallel. We will look at how these different modes limit performance later in this section.

When run, we need to provide a `max_number_of_live_tokens` argument to a TBB pipeline, which constrains the number of items that are allowed to flow through the pipeline at any given time.

Figure 11-43 shows the structure of the microbenchmarks we will use to explore these different controls. In the figure, both pipelines are shown with eight filters – but we will vary this number in our experiments. The top pipeline has filters that use the same execution mode, and all have the same spin_time – so this represents a very well-balanced pipeline. The bottom pipeline has one filter that spins for imbalance * spin_time – we will vary this imbalance factor to see the impact of imbalance on speedup.

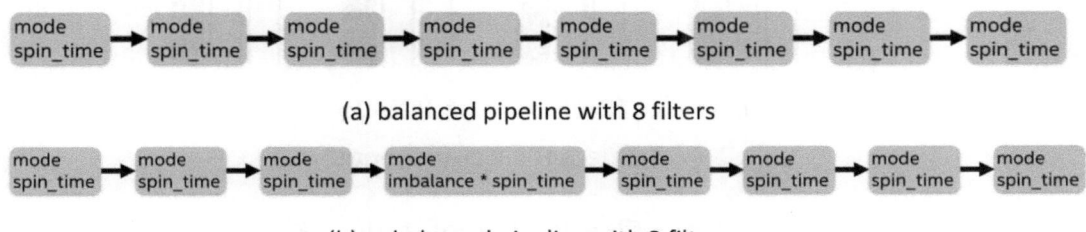

(a) balanced pipeline with 8 filters

(b) unbalanced pipeline with 8 filters

Figure 11-43. *A balanced pipeline microbenchmark and an imbalanced pipeline microbenchmark*

Understanding a Balanced Pipeline

Let's first consider how well our rule of thumb for task sizes applies to pipelines. Is a filter body of 1 microsecond sufficient to mitigate overheads? Figure 11-44 shows the speedup of our balanced pipeline microbenchmark when fed 8,000 items while using only a single token. The results are shown for various filter execution times. Since there is only a single token, only a single item will be allowed to flow through the pipeline at a time. The result is a serialized execution of the pipeline (even when the filter execution mode is set to parallel).

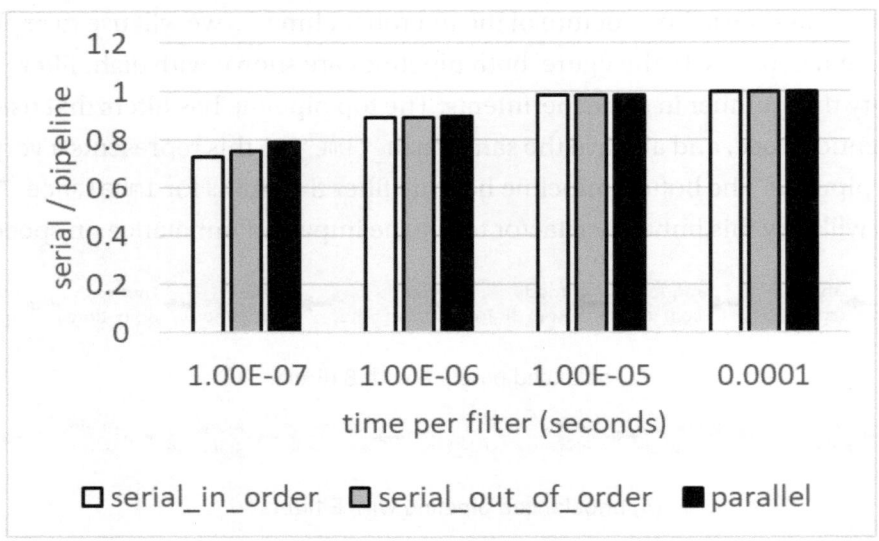

Figure 11-44. *The overhead seen by different filter execution modes when executing a balanced pipeline with eight filters, a single token, and 8,000 items on our Linux Server System. Sample code performance_tuning/parallel_pipeline_ timed.cpp*

When compared with a true serial execution, where we execute the proper number of spins in a for-loop, we see the impact of managing the work as a TBB pipeline. In Figure 11-44, we see that when the spin_time approaches 1 microsecond, the overhead is fairly low, and we get very close to the execution time of the true serial execution. It seems that our rule of thumb applies to a TBB pipeline too!

Now, let's look at how the number of filters affects performance. In a serial pipeline, the parallelism comes only from overlapping different filters. In a pipeline with parallel filters, parallelism is also obtained by executing the parallel filters simultaneously on different items. Our target platform supports eight threads, so we should expect at most a speedup of 8 for a parallel execution.

Figure 11-45 shows the speedup of our balanced pipeline microbenchmark when setting the number of tokens to 8. For both serial modes, the speedup increases with the number of filters. This is important to remember, since the speedup of a serial pipeline does not scale with the data set size like the TBB loop algorithms do. The balanced pipeline that contains all parallel filters however has a speedup of 8 even with only a single filter. This is because the 8,000 input items can be processed in parallel in that single filter – there is no serial filter to become a bottleneck.

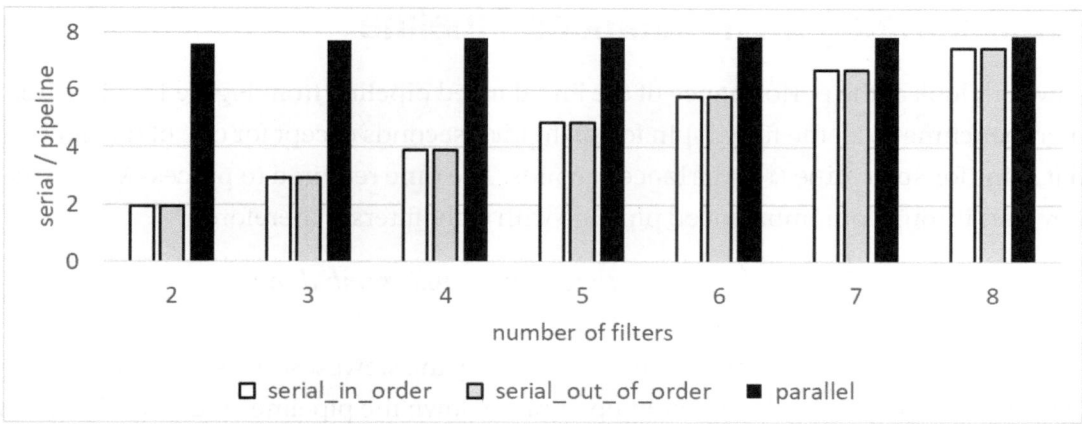

Figure 11-45. *The speedup achieved by the different filter execution modes when executing a balanced pipeline with eight tokens, 8,000 items, and an increasing number of filters. The filters spin for 100 microseconds. Collected on our Linux Server System. Sample code performance_tuning/parallel_pipeline_timed.cpp*

In Figure 11-46, we see the speedup for our balanced pipeline when using eight filters but with varying numbers of tokens. Because our platform has eight threads, if we have fewer than eight tokens, there are not enough items in flight to keep all the threads busy. Once we have at least eight items in the pipeline, all threads can participate. Increasing the number of tokens past eight has little impact on performance.

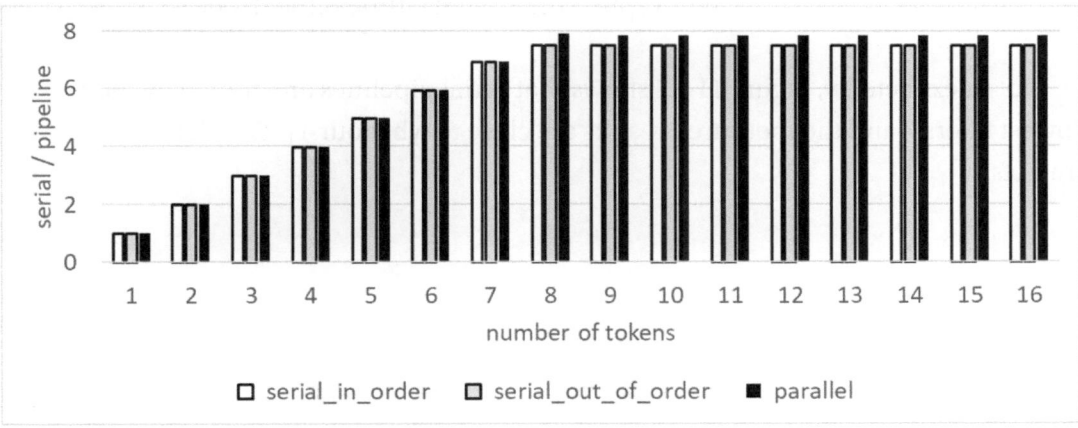

Figure 11-46. *The speedup achieved by the different filter execution modes when executing a balanced pipeline with eight filters, 8,000 items, and an increasing number of tokens. The filters spin for 100 microseconds. Collected on our Linux Server System. Sample code performance_tuning/parallel_pipeline_timed.cpp*

Understanding an Imbalanced Pipeline

Now, let's look at the performance of the imbalanced pipeline from Figure 11-43. In this microbenchmark, all the filters spin for `spin_time` seconds except for one of the filters that spins for `spin_time * imbalance` seconds. The time required to process N items as they pass through our imbalanced pipeline with eight filters is therefore

$$T_1 = N * (7 * spin\_time + spin\_time * imbalance)$$

In the steady state, a serial pipeline is limited by the slowest serial stage. The steady state ignores the time it takes to ramp up or ramp down the pipeline, and so each filter is executing at its maximum rate. We can model the steady state time of this same pipeline when the imbalanced filter executes with serial mode but there are enough threads to overlap the execution of all filters as

$$T_\infty = N * \max(spin\_time, spin\_time * imbalance)$$

Figure 11-47 shows the results of our imbalanced pipeline when executed on our test platform with different imbalance factors. We also include the theoretical maximum speedup, labeled as T_1/T_∞, calculated as

$$Speedup_{max} = \frac{7 * spin\_time + spin\_time * imbalance}{\max(spin\_time,\ spin\_time * imbalance)}$$

Not unexpectedly, Figure 11-47 shows that serial pipelines are limited by their slowest filters – and the measured results are close to what our T_1/T_∞ calculation predicts.

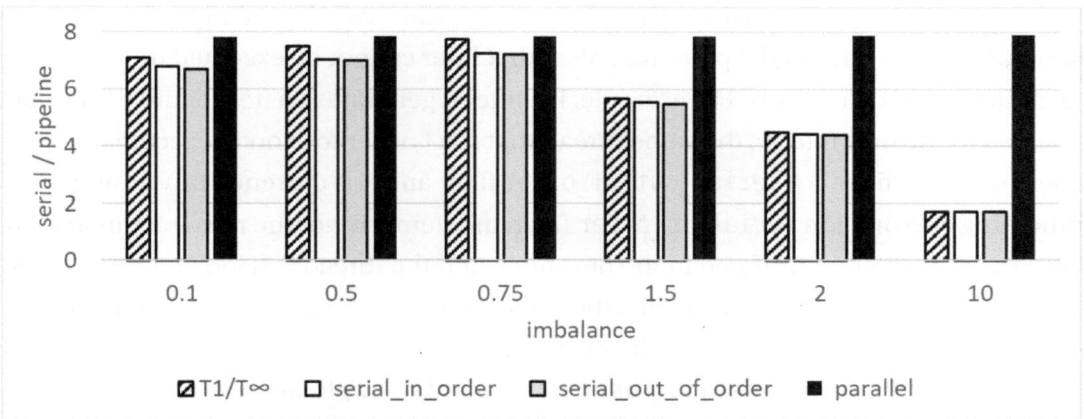

Figure 11-47. *The speedup achieved by the different filter execution modes when executing an imbalanced pipeline with eight filters, 8,000 items, and different imbalance factors. Seven of the filters spin for 100 microseconds, and the other spins for* imbalance *x 100 microseconds*

In contrast, the parallel_pipeline that use parallel mode for its filters is shown to not be limited by the slowest stage because the TBB scheduler can overlap the execution of the slowest filter with other invocations of that same filter. You may be wondering if increasing the number of tokens beyond eight will help, but in this case, no. Our test system has only eight threads, so we can at most overlap eight instances of the slowest filter. While there may be cases where a temporary load imbalance can be smoothed out by having more tokens than the number of threads, in our microbenchmark where the imbalance is a constant factor, we are in fact limited by the slowest stage and the number of threads – and any number of additional tokens will not change that.

However, there are algorithms in which an insufficient number of tokens will hamper the automatic load balancing feature of the work-stealing TBB scheduler. This is the case when the stages are not well balanced and there are serial stages stalling the pipe.

Pipelines and Data Locality and Thread Affinity

With the TBB loop algorithms, we used the blocked range types, affinity_partitioner, and static_partitioner to tune cache performance. The TBB parallel_pipeline function has no similar options. But all is not lost! The execution order built into TBB parallel_pipeline is designed to enhance temporal data locality without the need to do anything special.

When a TBB master or worker thread completes the execution of a TBB filter, it executes the next filter in the pipeline unless that filter cannot be executed due to execution mode constraints. For example, if a filter f_0 generates an item i and its output is passed to the next filter f_1, the same thread that ran f_0 will move on to execute f_1 – unless that next filter is a `serial_out_of_order` filter and it is currently processing something else or it is a `serial_in_order` filter and item i is not the next item in line. In those cases, the item is buffered in the next filter, and the thread will look for other work to do. Otherwise, to maximize locality, the thread will follow the data it just generated and process that item by executing the next filter.

Internally, the processing of one item in the filter f_0 is implemented as a task executed by a thread/core. When the filter is done, the task recycles itself to execute the next filter f_1. Essentially, the dying task f_0 reincarnates into the new f_1 task, bypassing the scheduler – the same thread/core that executed f_0 will also execute f_1. In terms of data locality and performance, this is way better than what a regular/naive pipeline implementation would do: filter f_0 (served by one or several threads) enqueuing the item in filter f_1's queue (where f_1 is also served by one or several threads). This naive implementation wrecks locality because the item processed by filter f_0 on one core is likely to be processed on a different core by filter f_1. In TBB, if f_0 and f_1 fulfill the conditions mentioned previously, this will never happen. As a result, the TBB pipeline is biased toward finishing items that are already in flight before injecting more items at the beginning of the pipeline; this behavior not only exploits data locality but uses less memory by reducing the size of the queues that are necessary for serial filters.

Summary

In this chapter, we discussed two ways that we can use to tune the performance of parallelism expressed using TBB: (1) constrain the number of threads and hardware resources used by the library and (2) optimize the TBB algorithms for granularity and affinity.

For constraining resources, we introduced `global_control`, explicit `task_arena` objects, and `task_scheduler_observer` objects. `global_control` instances are used to set global parameters such as a ceiling on the number of worker threads that can execute concurrently. Explicit `task_arena` objects let us control how many threads may be used for specific work and provide hints on how threads that join an arena should be mapped to the hardware platform. And, lastly, `task_scheduler_observer` objects let us run our own code whenever a thread joins into parallel execution.

We then turned our attention to the performance hooks for the TBB algorithms. These hooks let us control granularity, affinity, and concurrency.

CHAPTER 12

Migrating TBB to oneTBB

Today's TBB (oneTBB) relies on modern C++, in particular C++11 and later, and therefore has shed interfaces that were needed in a pre-C++11 world. In addition, interfaces to the scheduler were cleaned up to improve usability based on more than a decade of user experience.

While oneTBB is mostly source compatible with TBB, some interfaces have disappeared. This chapter discusses these changes and what to do when migration from the *older TBB* to the new *oneTBB* is needed. We hope both to provide a guide to migrating code and to explain why things have changed for those of us that have been using TBB a long time. Migrating is important because bug and security fixes as well as new features and improvements are only being added to oneTBB. So, to continue to get the best of TBB, we need to migrate to oneTBB.

Long Live tbb:: – No Need to Migrate Code to oneapi::

Consistent with our assertion that "It's still TBB to me," the use or non-use of the oneapi namespace is optional. We suggest that we don't bother making any changes to TBB code to mention oneapi namespaces or header paths. Simply using the tbb namespace and the tbb in header paths has always worked and continues to work. There is no requirement to recode tbb:: into oneapi::tbb:: or change <tbb/...> into <oneapi/tbb/...>.

For those that are curious about how this all works, the files in include/tbb include the matching headers from include/oneapi/tbb. For example, other than the copyright info, the file include/tbb/parallel_for.h includes a single line:

```
#include "../oneapi/tbb/parallel_for.h"
```

M. J. Voss and J. R. Reinders, *Today's TBB*, https://doi.org/10.1007/979-8-8688-1270-5_12

All public classes and functions are defined in the tbb namespace but then *injected* into the oneapi::tbb namespace. Each header in the include/oneapi/tbb has code like

```
namespace oneapi {
    namespace tbb = ::tbb;
}
```

It is not important to completely understand how this all works, but rest assured that everything in the tbb namespace is in the oneapi::tbb namespace (and vice versa) and that all the headers in include/tbb redirect to the headers in the include/oneapi/tbb directory.

We love oneAPI and all that it does – but we do not recommend changing code that works just fine without the oneapi name being added. The use of oneapi::tbb:: is a convenience feature that simply connects to tbb::. Likewise, <oneapi/tbb/...> is equivalent to <tbb/...>.

What Changed

We can separate the motivations for changes from TBB to oneTBB into two categories: (1) alignment with modern C++ and (2) improved interfaces. We conclude this chapter with some notes on old TBB vs. new TBB (oneTBB) runtime compatibility when used together (spoiler alert: they work together, but migrating to the new library completely has advantages).

Change: Modern C++ Alignment

The C++ standard committee has released new standards at a three-year cadence since 2011. That first update, C++11, is often recognized as the start of *modern C++*. While it is expected that oneAPI and its C++ libraries will increase the required version of the C++ standard over time, the current version only requires C++11. C++11 introduced a whole host of important features, such as rvalue references, lambda expressions, auto, atomic variable types, unique_ptr, shared_ptr, and more.

If we compile our applications with an even more recent version of the C++ standard, we may unlock additional features in oneTBB such as deduction guides (introduced in C++17). Deduction guides may allow us to drop explicit template arguments in some cases. If we compile with a C++11 compiler (or flag), the support that depends on features in newer C++ standards is simply not available.

Removal of tbb::atomic

One significant change in the move from TBB to oneTBB is that the TBB atomic interfaces were dropped in favor of the newer standard atomic interfaces that modern C++ has added. The developers of TBB confirmed that the implementation of the standard atomic interfaces is comparable in performance to the TBB atomics, so there was no need to maintain these hand-rolled implementations. The implementation of the TBB library was simultaneously moved to use these standard interfaces internally, making the TBB library itself more portable.

Changing a TBB program from TBB atomics to modern C++ atomics is mostly a mechanical replacement exercise. This includes changing the namespace tbb to std and using the <atomic> header. Many names are exactly the same, but some are not. For example, we need to replace calls to compare_and_swap with compare_exchange_weak or compare_exchange_strong. tbb::atomic provides a copy constructor (that creates a new independent copy), while std::atomic does not.

Synchronization, including atomics, has an entire chapter in this book since it is such a critical topic in parallel programming. In Chapter 8, we discuss the synchronization support of TBB and modern C++ together in order to do justice to the high-level topic of making sure our synchronization supports efficient scaling of our algorithms (a.k.a. "do not let the synchronization get in the way any more than necessary").

For the running example used in Chapter 8, we see different parallel implementations starting from an incorrect one and then iterated through different synchronization alternatives, including coarse-grained locking, fine-grained-locking, atomics, and some alternative implementations that do not use locks at all. On the way, we stopped at some remarkable spots, presenting the properties that allow us to characterize mutexes, the different kinds of mutex flavors available in the standard C++ library and extensions in the TBB library, and common problems that usually arise when relying on mutexes to implement our algorithms.

Figure 12-1 shows the example from Chapter 8 as it would have been expressed using the old TBB atomics and how it is shown in Chapter 8 with standard atomics. As shown, the change in this specific case is minimal.

```
#include <tbb/tbb.h>
  // Parallel execution
  std::vector<tbb::atomic<int>> hist_p(num_bins);
  parallel_for(tbb::blocked_range<size_t>{0, image.size()},
              [&](const tbb::blocked_range<size_t>& r)
              {
                for (size_t i = r.begin(); i < r.end(); ++i)
                  hist_p[image[i]]++;
              });
```

(a) Using the old TBB atomics

```
#include <atomic>
  // Parallel execution
  std::vector<std::atomic<int>> hist_p(num_bins);
  parallel_for(tbb::blocked_range<size_t>{0, image.size()},
              [&](const tbb::blocked_range<size_t>& r)
              {
                for (size_t i = r.begin(); i < r.end(); ++i)
                  hist_p[image[i]]++;
              });
```

(b) Using a standard atomic

Figure 12-1. *The example from Chapter 8 showing the "before" and "after" migrating from tbb::atomic to std::atomic. Sample code migration/migrate_atomics*

tbb::tbb_exception, tbb::captured_exception, tbb::movable_exception

As mentioned before, oneTBB requires C++11 support, including the ability to capture exceptions using std::exception_ptr. Before C++11 could be relied on, TBB provided the machinery for capturing, summarizing, and rethrowing exceptions. Exceptions are described in more detail in Chapter 9.

Other Changes

The other changes related to advances in the C++ standard simply make TBB easier to use, such as support for lambda expressions as an additional way to provide bodies for algorithms, or make TBB code more efficient, such as using rvalue references and std::move where appropriate. But these other changes only affect newly written code and do not require existing code to be modified.

Change: Removing Redundant or Problematic Interfaces

A decade of experience with TBB strongly suggested that some interfaces were simply not necessary or were error-prone.

Controls Accessed via `task_scheduler_init`

When TBB was first released, there was no support for explicit task arenas (explicit arenas are described in Chapter 11). Originally, there was only a single arena that was shared across all threads. During this time, there was no need to separate controls into global controls and those that affected specific arenas. The class `task_scheduler_init` was the single interface for setting the maximum number of threads in the thread pool, the number of slots in the singular arena, and the thread stack sizes. Its lifetime also controlled the initialization and termination of the overall TBB scheduler.

But, as the library evolved and support for multiple implicit and then explicit task arenas was introduced, it became useful to separate controls into those that would affect overall library properties and those that affected specific arenas. The `task_scheduler_init` class was left out of the modern version of the library because it simply conflated too many separate concerns that are now addressed by cleaner, separated controls.

Class `task_scheduler_init` was deprecated prior to the first release of oneTBB and not included at all in the modernized library. The `tbb::info::default_concurrency()` function has replaced `tbb::task_scheduler_init::default_num_threads()` as the way to query the default number of threads. The class `tbb::global_control`, described in Chapter 11, is the oneTBB approach for setting global parameters such as maximum concurrency, thread stack size, and error handling approaches. And class `task_arena`, also described in Chapter 11, is the new way to control the number of slots available for threads to participate in work.

The `task_arena` class continued to evolve far beyond what was supported by `task_scheduler_init` and now supports priority levels and hardware-aware constraints, as described in Chapter 11. A simple example of replacing `task_scheduler_init` with these new interfaces is shown in Figure 12-2.

```
const int N = tbb::task_scheduler_init::default_num_threads();

void setThreadsAndSlots() {
  tbb::task_scheduler_init init(N);

  tbb::parallel_for(0,
                    10*N,
                    [](int) { doWork(0.01); });
}
```

(a) The old interfaces

```
const int N = tbb::info::default_concurrency();

void setThreadsAndSlots() {
  tbb::global_control gc(tbb::global_control::max_allowed_parallelism, N);

  tbb::task_arena a{N};

  a.execute([]() {
    tbb::parallel_for(0,
                      10*N,
                      [](int) { doWork(0.01); });
  });
}
```

(b) The new interfaces

Figure 12-2. *Migrating from the old* tbb::task_scheduler_init *interface to the new* tbb::info, tbb::global_control, *and* tbb::task_arena *interfaces. Sample code migration/migrate_task_scheduler_init.cpp*

While Figure 12-2 may be more verbose, there is little room to confuse what the setting is for the number of available threads in the global thread pool as opposed to the number of available slots in the arena. We also know exactly which arena is being used, which is important if we are constraining arenas. In Chapter 11, we show how to combine uses of tbb::global_control and tbb::task_arena to precisely control the maximum allowed concurrency.

Finally, the lifetime of the TBB scheduler is now controlled with class task_scheduler_handle and the free function: void finalize(task_scheduler_handle &handle).

The table in Figure 12-3 summarizes how these conflated concerns are now more cleanly separated in oneTBB.

Concern controlled by `task_scheduler_init`	Replacement
Query default number of threads	`int tbb::info::default_concurrency();`
Global parameters such as `max_concurrency` and thread stack sizes.	`tbb::global_control`
The number of slots available for worker and master threads to populate for specific work.	`tbb::task_arena`
Lifetime of the TBB scheduler, the global thread pool, and data structures.	`tbb::task_scheduler_handle` `void tbb::finalize(task_scheduler_handle &handle);`

Figure 12-3. *A summary of how the concerns handled by* `task_scheduler_init` *have been more cleanly separated in oneTBB*

Removal of `parallel_do`

Another interface that has been dropped from the library is `parallel_do`. This was done not because it was confusing, but because it was redundant. There was a time during TBB's evolution when two very similar algorithms were included in the library, `parallel_do` and `parallel_for_each`. Both created tasks by traversing from a `begin` to an end iterator or by iterating across the elements in a container. The difference between the two interfaces was that `parallel_do` included an optional feeder argument used by the body to feed additional items to process in parallel. As TBB was modernized, these two algorithms were fused into one, a revised `parallel_for_each`. The updated version of this algorithm, described in Chapter 2, supports the optional feeder argument to the body. Once this addition was made, there was simply no reason to maintain two very similar algorithms.

The path to migrate from `parallel_do` to `parallel_for_each` is a simple replacement as shown in Figure 12-4.

```
tbb::parallel_do( &top_left, &top_left+1,
  [&](const BlockIndex& bi, tbb::parallel_do_feeder<BlockIndex>& f) {
    auto [r, c] = bi;
    computeBlock(N, r, c, x, a, b);
    // add successor to right if ready
    if (c + 1 <= r && --ref_count[r*num_blocks + c + 1] == 0) {
      f.add(BlockIndex(r, c + 1));
    }
    // add successor below if ready
    if (r + 1 < (size_t)num_blocks &&
        --ref_count[(r+1)*num_blocks + c] == 0) {
      f.add(BlockIndex(r+1, c));
    }
  }
);
```

(a) The old interfaces

```
tbb::parallel_for_each( &top_left, &top_left+1,
  [&](const BlockIndex& bi, tbb::feeder<BlockIndex>& f) {
    auto [r, c] = bi;
    computeBlock(N, r, c, x, a, b);
    // add successor to right if ready
    if (c + 1 <= r && --ref_count[r*num_blocks + c + 1] == 0) {
      f.add(BlockIndex(r, c + 1));
    }
    // add successor below if ready
    if (r + 1 < (size_t)num_blocks &&
        --ref_count[(r+1)*num_blocks + c] == 0) {
      f.add(BlockIndex(r+1, c));
    }
  }
);
```

(b) The new interfaces

Figure 12-4. *Migrating from the old tbb::parallel_do interface to the new tbb::parallel_for_each interface. Sample code migration/migrate_parallel_do.cpp*

Removal of Class **pipeline**

Another tidying up of the library was the removal of the class tbb::pipeline. The TBB developers learned that the type-safe tbb::parallel_pipeline function, described in detail in Chapter 2, was significantly more user-friendly and sufficient for the key use cases required by TBB users. While a good replacement, the class tbb::pipeline did cover one additional use case that is not covered by the tbb::parallel_pipeline function, *thread-bound filters*.

Thread-bound filters were not processed by a TBB worker thread at all. Instead, those filters are explicitly processed by calling the `process_item` or `try_process_item` function on the filter from a non-TBB controlled thread. When introduced in the older version of TBB, this feature was designed to be used in the implementation of communication or offload libraries that needed to invoke functions from specific threads – the only threads that were allowed to access specific resources. Over time, these restrictions became less and less common. Now, this feature has become simply unnecessary.

The path to migrate from the older class `tbb::pipeline` to the new type-safe `tbb::parallel_pipeline` function is not a simple search-and-replace, but even so, the concepts for most use cases are a straightforward mapping. There are still filters (which can be `parallel`, `serial_out_of_order`, and `serial_in_order`). There is still a `max_number_of_live_tokens` argument that limits the total number of items that can be in flight. And there are still interfaces for expressing a linear order for applying the filters to items as they flow through the pipeline. But the syntax of the interface has changed. Chapters 2 and 11 provide more detail on using the interfaces in today's TBB.

Removal of Task-Oriented Priorities in Favor of Arena Priorities

Chapter 11 describes the interface for creating a priority-aware `task_arena`. Prior to oneTBB, there were interfaces in TBB for setting priorities on a task-by-task basis for enqueued tasks or through `task_group_context` for groups of tasks. As TBB evolved, explicit `task_arena` objects became the abstraction for isolating work that should be constrained in different ways. In Chapter 11, we described how to add hardware-aware constraints to a `task_arena` as well as set priorities on a `task_arena` basis. `task_arena` has both an `execute` and an `enqueue` method and is the natural place to group related tasks.

The path to migration for priorities is the same, whether the old code uses enqueued tasks or `task_group_context`. In both cases, an explicit `task_arena` can be created with the needed priority and work executed in that specific arena. `task_arena` provides an enqueue function to replace uses where a single task was enqueued. And an algorithm can be nested inside of a call to `task_arena::execute` to migrate cases where `task_group_context` had been used.

Let's first start by looking at so-called *fire-and-forget* tasks. In the old version of TBB, these were tasks that were enqueued using the lowest-level tasking interface. In Figure 12-5(a), a new class is defined that inherits from `tbb::task` and overrides the virtual function `execute`. Then in the main loop, tasks of this type are enqueued using the lowest-level tasking API. The final argument to the function is the priority, such as `tbb::priority_low`, `tbb::priority_normal`, or `tbb::priority_high`.

```
auto P = tbb::task_scheduler_init::default_num_threads();

class MyTask : public tbb::task {
public:
  MyTask(const char *m, int i) : msg(m), messageId(i) { }
  tbb::task *execute() override {
    taskFunction(msg, messageId);
    return NULL;
  }
private:
  std::string msg;
  int messageId;
};

void enqueueSeveralTasks(int num_iterations) {
  for (int i = 0; i < num_iterations; ++i) {
    tbb::task::enqueue(*new( tbb::task::allocate_root() )
                       MyTask( "L", i ), tbb::priority_low);
    tbb::task::enqueue(*new( tbb::task::allocate_root() )
                       MyTask( "N", i ), tbb::priority_normal);
    tbb::task::enqueue(*new( tbb::task::allocate_root() )
                       MyTask( "H", i ), tbb::priority_high);
  }
  doWork(1.0);
}
```

(a) The old interfaces

```
auto P = tbb::info::default_concurrency();

void enqueueSeveralTasks(int num_iterations) {
  tbb::task_arena low_arena{P, 0, tbb::task_arena::priority::low};
  tbb::task_arena normal_arena{P, 0, tbb::task_arena::priority::normal};
  tbb::task_arena high_arena{P, 0, tbb::task_arena::priority::high};

  for (int i = 0; i < num_iterations; ++i) {
    low_arena.enqueue([i]() { taskFunction("L", i); });
    normal_arena.enqueue([i]() { taskFunction("N", i); });
    high_arena.enqueue([i]() { taskFunction("H", i); });
  }
  doWork(1.0);
}
```

(b) The new interfaces

Figure 12-5. *Migrating from the old enqueue interface to the new* tbb::task_
arena interface for enqueuing single tasks. Sample code migration/migrate_
priorities.cpp

Figure 12-5(b) shows that this pattern can be migrated to oneTBB by using task_arena objects that have used constraints to set priorities. Each task is now enqueued into a different task arena.

The older versions of TBB also supported priorities as part of task_group_context. A priority could be set for a task_group_context object, and that object could then set the priority for all of the work related to that algorithm.

Consistently, oneTBB uses task_arena objects instead when constraints, such as priorities, need to be set. Figure 12-7 shows how the example from Figure 12-6 is expressed using oneTBB.

```
void runParallelForWithHighPriority() {
  std::thread t0([]() {
    waitUntil(2);
    tbb::task_group_context tgc;
    tgc.set_priority(tbb::priority_normal);
    tbb::parallel_for(0, 10,
          [](int i) {
              std::printf("N");
              std::this_thread::sleep_for(std::chrono::milliseconds(10));
          }, tgc);
  });
  std::thread t1([]() {
    waitUntil(2);
    tbb::task_group_context tgc;
    tgc.set_priority(tbb::priority_high);
    tbb::parallel_for(0, 10,
          [](int i) {
              std::printf("H");
              std::this_thread::sleep_for(std::chrono::milliseconds(10));
          }, tgc);
  });
  t0.join();
  t1.join();
  std::printf("\n");
}
```

Figure 12-6. *An example of the old interface that set priorities using task_group_context. Sample code migration/migrate_priorities.cpp*

```
void runParallelForWithHighPriority() {
  std::thread t0([]() {
    waitUntil(2);
    tbb::task_arena normal_arena{P, 0, tbb::task_arena::priority::normal};
    normal_arena.execute([]() {
      tbb::parallel_for(0, 10, [](int i) {
        std::printf("N");
        std::this_thread::sleep_for(std::chrono::milliseconds(10));
      });
    });
  });
  std::thread t1([]() {
    waitUntil(2);
    tbb::task_arena high_arena{P, 0, tbb::task_arena::priority::high};
    high_arena.execute([]() {
      tbb::parallel_for(0, 10, [](int i) { std::printf("H"); });
        std::this_thread::sleep_for(std::chrono::milliseconds(10));
    });
  });
  t0.join();
  t1.join();
  std::printf("\n");
}
```

Figure 12-7. *Setting priorities with oneTBB using* `task_arena`. *Sample code* `migration/migrate_priorities.cpp`

Removal of Lowest-Level Task/Scheduler APIs

Perhaps the biggest change in oneTBB is the removal of the lowest-level tasking API as a public interface.

It is important to bear in mind that TBB aims to help us maximize *thread composability* and scalability in our application. We want our application to work correctly and efficiently, even after we assemble it from multiple codes, some of which we wrote and some of which we did not. The original interfaces exposed low-level knobs that turned out to be unnecessary, confusing, and overly constraining. This combination led to non-optimal code that, in turn, reduced scaling unless they were corrected.

Newer features in TBB, such as flow graphs, `task_group`, and task arenas, have evolved to offer the right interfaces for applications. Migrating applications to these interfaces and retiring the original interfaces has proven beneficial. This chapter helps us understand the finer points when migrating our code.

In case you are curious, there are new low-level scheduler interfaces that are purely internal to be used for the internal implementation of algorithms. These interfaces do not try to serve both the TBB implementors and application writers. As such, they are even less suitable for non-expert use, but they offer more control and flexibility to the expert TBB implementors. These interfaces seek to solve only one problem: the internal implementation of TBB itself. Keeping it that way has proven important. Likewise, the application-level interfaces now can focus on serving their purpose well.

While today's TBB does help maximize our success in writing scalable and composable code, refinements and additions will continue in the future. In addition, the TBB developers continue to refine the task_group, as described in Chapter 6, to simplify the expression of even more use cases, continuing to up-level the older low-level tasking interface.

Migrating from Low-Level Task API

The low-level task API of Threading Building Blocks (TBB) was considered complex and hence error-prone, which was the primary reason it had been removed from oneAPI Threading Building Blocks (oneTBB). This guide helps with the migration from TBB to oneTBB (today's TBB) for the use cases where the low-level tasking API is used.

Task Blocking

For most use cases, the spawning of a few individual, independent tasks can be replaced with the use of either tbb::task_group or tbb::parallel_invoke.

For example, in Figure 12-8(a), the old TBB interfaces are used to create and schedule tasks. RootTask, ChildTask1, and ChildTask2 are the user-provided functors that inherit from tbb::task and implement its interface. The spawning of the ChildTask1 and ChildTask2 tasks lets them (possibly) execute in parallel with each other. The RootTask is then executed after they both were complete.

```cpp
class MyTask : public tbb::task {
  double my_time;
public:
  MyTask(double t=0.0) : my_time(t) {}
  virtual tbb::task* execute() {
    doWork(my_time);
    return nullptr;
  }
};

void taskBlocking() {
  MyTask& root = *new(tbb::task::allocate_root()) MyTask{};

  MyTask& child1 =
    *new(root.allocate_child()) MyTask{0.1};
  MyTask& child2 =
    *new(root.allocate_child()) MyTask{0.2};

  root.set_ref_count(3);

  tbb::task::spawn(child1);
  tbb::task::spawn(child2);
  root.wait_for_all();
}
```

(a) The old interfaces

```cpp
void taskBlocking() {
  tbb::task_group g;
  g.run([]() { doWork(0.1); });
  g.run([]() { doWork(0.2); });
  g.wait();
}
```

(b) The new interfaces

Figure 12-8. *Migrating from the old task interface to the new* tbb::task_group *interface for simple blocking tasks. Sample code* migration/migrate_task_blocking.cpp

Even in this most simple example, we can already see just how low level the old tasking API really was. Classes that inherited from tbb::task, such as RootTask, ChildTask1, and ChildTask2, override the virtual function execute. Then the user needs to allocate the object, using in-place new, getting the space from special functions such as tbb::task::allocate_root() and root.allocate_child(). The use of functions, such as allocate_child(), initializes the memory in special ways to create parent–child relationships. Even so, reference counting needs to be done explicitly, as shown by the call to `root.set_ref_count(3)`. "Why 3?" you might ask. Because the developer must add an additional reference count to ensure that the root task will not finish prematurely before the call to `wait_for_all` (which implicitly decremented the reference count). Doesn't seem error-prone at all, does it?

In contrast in Figure 12-8(b), the code is rewritten to `tbb::task_group`. The code is more concise. It also enables lambda functions and does not require us to implement the `tbb::task` interface that overrides the `tbb::task* tbb::task::execute()` virtual method. With this new approach, we work with functors in a C++-standard way.

Since this example is quite simple, there is even a simpler solution that is supported by both the old TBB and the newer oneTBB, `parallel_invoke`, as shown in Figure 12-9.

```
void parallelInvoke() {
  tbb::parallel_invoke([]() { doWork(0.1); },
                       []() { doWork(0.2); } );
}
```

Figure 12-9. *Using* `parallel_invoke` *to launch two tasks and wait. Sample code* `migration/migrate_task_blocking.cpp`

Adding More Work from a Task

In the older versions of TBB, the `tbb::parallel_do` algorithm is often used for cases where the amount of work is not known in advance and the work needs to be added during the execution of the parallel algorithm. Earlier in this chapter, we described how uses of the `tbb::parallel_do` algorithm can be migrated to the `tbb::parallel_for_each` algorithm. Some older application however may have used the lowest-level task API directly as shown in Figures 12-10, 12-11, and 12-12 to add work dynamically.

```
const int block_size = 512;
using BlockIndex = std::pair<size_t, size_t>;

void parallelFwdSub(std::vector<double>& x,
                    const std::vector<double>& a,
                    std::vector<double>& b) {
  const int N = x.size();
  const int num_blocks = N / block_size;

  // create reference counts
  std::vector<std::atomic<char>> ref_count(num_blocks*num_blocks);
  ref_count[0] = 0;
  for (int r = 1; r < num_blocks; ++r) {
    ref_count[r*num_blocks] = 1;
    for (int c = 1; c < r; ++c) {
      ref_count[r*num_blocks + c] = 2;
    }
    ref_count[r*num_blocks + r] = 1;
  }

  BlockIndex top_left(0,0);
```

```
  RootTask& root = *new(tbb::task::allocate_root()) RootTask{};
  root.set_ref_count(2);
  FwdSubTask& top_left_task =
      *new(root.allocate_child()) FwdSubTask(root, N, num_blocks,
                                          top_left, x, a, b, ref_count);
  tbb::task::spawn(top_left_task);
  root.wait_for_all();
```
```
}
```

Figure 12-10. *Using the old task interface to express the forward substitution example. Sample code* migration/migrate_tasks_adding_work.cpp

Figure 12-10 shows the creation of a root task with a single child task. We will skip the details of the low-level tasking API since we are migrating away from it, but at a high level the root task is used as a top-level handle to wait for the tasks that are spawned recursively in Figure 12-11.

Figure 12-11 shows the class FwdSubTask that inherits from tbb::task. This class has private member variables that are used from the execute function that is shown in detail in Figure 12-12. The old tasking API required developers to implement classes that inherit from tbb::task and override the execute method.

```
using RootTask = tbb::empty_task;

class FwdSubTask : public tbb::task {
public:
  FwdSubTask(RootTask& root, int N, int num_blocks,
             const std::pair<size_t, size_t>& bi, std::vector<double>& x,
             const std::vector<double>& a, std::vector<double>& b,
             std::vector<std::atomic<char>>& ref_count) :
             my_root(root), my_N(N), my_num_blocks(num_blocks), my_index(bi),
             my_x(x), my_a(a), my_b(b), my_ref_count(ref_count) {}

  tbb::task* execute() override { /* see Figure 12-12 */ }

private:
  RootTask& my_root;
  BlockIndex my_index;
  const int my_N, my_num_blocks;
  std::vector<double>& my_x;
  const std::vector<double>& my_a;
  std::vector<double>& my_b;
  std::vector<std::atomic<char>>& my_ref_count;
};
```

Figure 12-11. *The class that implements the old task interface to express the forward substitution example. Sample code migration/migrate_tasks_adding_work.cpp*

In the definition of the execute function in Figure 12-12, a left and/or right child might be added with the root task as the parent. The use of in-place new with allocate_ additional_child_of(root) handles the referencing counting necessary to ensure that the root does not exit prematurely. The new child tasks in turn may add more children to the root. Eventually, the leaf calls to FwdSubTask::execute return without adding any new children.

```cpp
tbb::task* execute() override {
    auto [r, c] = my_index;
    computeBlock(my_N, r, c, my_x, my_a, my_b);
    // add successor to right if ready
    if (c + 1 <= r && --my_ref_count[r*my_num_blocks + c + 1] == 0) {
        FwdSubTask& child =
          *new(allocate_additional_child_of(my_root))
                FwdSubTask(my_root, my_N, my_num_blocks, {r, c+1},
                            my_x, my_a, my_b, my_ref_count);
        tbb::task::spawn(child);
    }
    // add successor below if ready
    if (r + 1 < (size_t)my_num_blocks
        && --my_ref_count[(r+1)*my_num_blocks + c] == 0) {
        FwdSubTask& child =
          *new(allocate_additional_child_of(my_root))
                FwdSubTask(my_root, my_N, my_num_blocks, {r+1, c},
                            my_x, my_a, my_b, my_ref_count);
        tbb::task::spawn(child);
    }
    return nullptr;
}
```

Figure 12-12. *The implementation of execute that enables the old task interface to express the forward substitution example. Sample code migration/migrate_tasks_adding_work.cpp*

One possible way to migrate this example is to use tbb::parallel_for_each as is done for migration from tbb::parallel_do shown in Figure 12-4. But if we want to use a more task-oriented approach, we can use task_group as shown in Figures 12-13 and 12-14.

```cpp
const int block_size = 512;
using BlockIndex = std::pair<size_t, size_t>;

void parallelFwdSubTaskGroup(std::vector<double>& x,
                             const std::vector<double>& a,
                             std::vector<double>& b) {
  const int N = x.size();
  const int num_blocks = N / block_size;

  // create reference counts
  std::vector<std::atomic<char>> ref_count(num_blocks*num_blocks);
  ref_count[0] = 0;
  for (int r = 1; r < num_blocks; ++r) {
    ref_count[r*num_blocks] = 1;
    for (int c = 1; c < r; ++c) {
      ref_count[r*num_blocks + c] = 2;
    }
    ref_count[r*num_blocks + r] = 1;
  }

  BlockIndex top_left(0,0);
  tbb::task_group tg;
  tg.run([&]() {
    fwdSubTGBody(tg, N, num_blocks, top_left, x, a, b, ref_count);
  });
  tg.wait();
}
```

Figure 12-13. *The parallelFwdSub function from Figure 12-10 rewritten to use task_group instead of tbb::task. The implementation of the fwdSubTGBody function is shown in Figure 12-14. Sample code migration/migrate_tasks_adding_work.cpp.*

In Figure 12-14, the task_group object tg acts in a similar way to the root task in Figure 12-10. All child tasks that are recursively added are run in the same task_group tg, just like all child tasks are added as additional children to the root task in Figure 12-10.

```
void fwdSubTGBody(tbb::task_group& tg,
                  int N, int num_blocks, const std::pair<size_t, size_t> bi,
                  std::vector<double>& x, const std::vector<double>& a,
                  std::vector<double>& b,
                  std::vector<std::atomic<char>>& ref_count) {
  auto [r, c] = bi;
  computeBlock(N, r, c, x, a, b);
  // add successor to right if ready
  if (c + 1 <= r && --ref_count[r*num_blocks + c + 1] == 0) {
    tg.run([&, N, num_blocks, r, c]() {
      fwdSubTGBody(tg, N, num_blocks, BlockIndex(r, c+1), x, a, b, ref_count);
    });
  }
  // add successor below if ready
  if (r + 1 < (size_t)num_blocks && --ref_count[(r+1)*num_blocks + c] == 0) {
    tg.run([&, N, num_blocks, r, c]() {
      fwdSubTGBody(tg, N, num_blocks, BlockIndex(r+1, c), x, a, b, ref_count);
    });
  }
}
```

Figure 12-14. *The fwdSubTGBody function that implements logic that is like the execute function in Figure 12-12. Sample code migration/migrate_tasks_ adding_work.cpp*

Task Recycling

In the older versions of TBB, you could *recycle* a task object so that it could be executed again. This reduced the overheads of task allocation. Instead of allocating a new task, the member variables of the current task object were updated and then the task scheduled as if it was a new task. There were several variants of recycling in the old API, perhaps again highlighting the low-level and error-prone nature of this old API. There were functions: recycle_as_continuation, recycle_as_safe_continuation, recycle_as_ child_of, and recycle_to_reexecute. These differed in which task would become the parent of the task and, in the case of recycle_as_continuation and recycle_as_safe_ continuation, how reference counting was done to prevent premature execution. Again, we won't teach the details of a removed API in much detail here.

Figure 12-15 shows the forward substitution example that uses tbb::task when recycling is used. If the successor to the right (at c+1) is ready, recycle_as_c1 is set to true. If both successors are ready, the successor below (at r+1) is spawned as a new task, and the current task is updated to become the right successor, my_index = {r+1, c}.

If only one of the successors is ready, then no new task is spawned, and the current task is recycled as whichever task is ready, either as my_index = {r+1, c} or as my_index = {r, c+1}. If the current task is updated, recycle_to_reexecute() is called to tell the TBB scheduler to reschedule this task again after it returns.

```cpp
tbb::task* execute() override {
  auto [r, c] = my_index;
  computeBlock(my_N, r, c, my_x, my_a, my_b);
  // add successor to right if ready
  bool recycle_as_c1 = false;
  if (c + 1 <= r && --my_ref_count[r*my_num_blocks + c + 1] == 0) {
    recycle_as_c1 = true;
  }
  // add successor below if ready
  if (r + 1 < (size_t)my_num_blocks
        && --my_ref_count[(r+1)*my_num_blocks + c] == 0) {
    if (recycle_as_c1) {
      FwdSubTask& child = *new(allocate_additional_child_of(my_root))
                            FwdSubTask(my_root, my_N, my_num_blocks, {r+1, c},
                                       my_x, my_a, my_b, my_ref_count);
      tbb::task::spawn(child);
    } else {
      my_index = {r+1, c};
      recycle_to_reexecute();
    }
  }
  if (recycle_as_c1) {
    my_index = {r, c+1};
    recycle_to_reexecute();
  }
  return nullptr;
}
```

Figure 12-15. *A modified execute function that recycles tasks for the forward substitution example. Sample code* migration/migrate_recycling.cpp

In the current version of oneTBB, we can modify the members of a function object while executing its operator() function and then pass *this to tbb::task_group::run() to achieve a similar result. Figure 12-16 shows a slightly modified version of the function that was shown in Figure 12-13. In this modified version, a function object is passed to task_group::run instead of a lambda expression.

```
void parallelFwdSub(std::vector<double>& x,
                    const std::vector<double>& a,
                    std::vector<double>& b) {
  const int N = x.size();
  const int num_blocks = N / block_size;

  // create reference counts
  std::vector<std::atomic<char>> ref_count(num_blocks*num_blocks);
  ref_count[0] = 0;
  for (int r = 1; r < num_blocks; ++r) {
    ref_count[r*num_blocks] = 1;
    for (int c = 1; c < r; ++c) {
      ref_count[r*num_blocks + c] = 2;
    }
    ref_count[r*num_blocks + r] = 1;
  }

  BlockIndex top_left(0,0);

  tbb::task_group tg;
  tg.run(FwdSubFunctor{tg, N, num_blocks, top_left, x, a, b, ref_count});
  tg.wait();
}
```

Figure 12-16. *A* `task_group`*-based version of forward substitution that uses a function object in place of a lambda expression used in Figure 12-13. Sample code* `migration/migrate_recycling.cpp`

Figures 12-17 and 12-18 provide the definition of the `FwdSubFunctor` class. In place of calls to `recycle_to_reexecute` in Figure 12-15, we see calls to `tg.run(*this)`. When running on a test system, using recycling for forward substitution with either the old or current APIs, we saw a roughly 2% decrease in execution time. So, when creating many small tasks, recycling function objects might give a small performance boost in the same way that recycling tasks provided a boost with the older versions of TBB.

```cpp
class FwdSubFunctor {
public:
  FwdSubFunctor(tbb::task_group& tg,
                int N, int num_blocks,
                const std::pair<size_t, size_t>& bi,
                std::vector<double>& x,
                const std::vector<double>& a,
                std::vector<double>& b,
                std::vector<std::atomic<char>>& ref_count) :
                my_tg(tg), my_index(new BlockIndex{bi}),
                my_N(N), my_num_blocks(num_blocks),
                my_x(x), my_a(a), my_b(b), my_ref_count(ref_count) {}

  void operator()() const { /* see Figure 12-18 * / }

private:
  tbb::task_group& my_tg;
  const std::shared_ptr<BlockIndex> my_index;
  const int my_N, my_num_blocks;
  std::vector<double>& my_x;
  const std::vector<double>& my_a;
  std::vector<double>& my_b;
  std::vector<std::atomic<char>>& my_ref_count;
};
```

Figure 12-17. *The class* FwdSubFunctor. *The definition of* operator()() *is shown in Figure 12-18. Sample code* migration/migrate_recycling.cpp.

```
void operator()() const {
  auto [r, c] = *my_index;
  computeBlock(my_N, r, c, my_x, my_a, my_b);
  // add successor to right if ready
  bool recycle_as_c1 = false;
  if (c + 1 <= r && --my_ref_count[r*my_num_blocks + c + 1] == 0) {
    recycle_as_c1 = true;
  }
  // add successor below if ready
  if (r + 1 < (size_t)my_num_blocks
      && --my_ref_count[(r+1)*my_num_blocks + c] == 0) {
    if (recycle_as_c1) {
      my_tg.run(FwdSubFunctor{my_tg, my_N, my_num_blocks,
                              BlockIndex(r+1, c), my_x, my_a, my_b,
                              my_ref_count});
    } else {
      *my_index = BlockIndex{r+1,c};
      my_tg.run(*this);
    }
  }
  if (recycle_as_c1) {
    *my_index = BlockIndex{r,c+1};
    my_tg.run(*this);
  }
}
```

Figure 12-18. *The functor definition in the* task_group*-based version of forward substitution. Sample code* migration/migrate_recycling.cpp

Scheduler Bypass

Another technique used with the older TBB tasking API is *scheduler bypass*. The task::execute() method returns a pointer. In the examples shown earlier in this chapter, we always returned nullptr, as we did in Figure 12-11. Returning nullptr has no effect. But if the pointer is not null, then the scheduler uses the returned task as the next task to execute by the current thread. Just like task recycling, this technique potentially reduces overheads. Where task recycling reduces allocation overheads, scheduler bypass may reduce scheduling overheads by short-circuiting the logic to find a next task in the TBB scheduler. Figure 12-19 shows an example that uses scheduler bypass to reduce scheduling overheads for forward substitution.

```
tbb::task* execute() override {
  auto [r, c] = my_index;
  computeBlock(my_N, r, c, my_x, my_a, my_b);
  tbb::task* bypass_task = nullptr;
  // add successor to right if ready
  if (c + 1 <= r && --my_ref_count[r*my_num_blocks + c + 1] == 0) {
    bypass_task = new(allocate_additional_child_of(my_root))
                      FwdSubTask(my_root, my_N, my_num_blocks, {r, c+1},
                                 my_x, my_a, my_b, my_ref_count);
  }
  // add successor below if ready
  if (r + 1 < (size_t)my_num_blocks
      && --my_ref_count[(r+1)*my_num_blocks + c] == 0) {
    tbb::task* child_task =
      new(allocate_additional_child_of(my_root))
          FwdSubTask(my_root, my_N, my_num_blocks, {r+1, c},
                     my_x, my_a, my_b, my_ref_count);
    if (bypass_task == nullptr)
      bypass_task = child_task;
    else
      tbb::task::spawn(*child_task);
  }
  return bypass_task;
}
```

Figure 12-19. *A modified execute function that bypasses tasks using the old low-level tasking API for the forward substitution example. Sample code* `migration/ migrate_bypass_tasks.cpp`

There is an analogue for this technique that is currently a preview feature in TBB. A preview feature is not yet productized, and so this feature may change or be dropped completely. The new approach relies on deferred tasks, which are described in detail in Chapter 6. Instead of calling `task_group::run`, we call `task_group::defer` to create a `tbb::task_handle`. When a `tbb::task_handle` is returned by a functor running inside of a task started by a `task_group::run` call, the returned `task_handle` is immediately executed by the thread that executed that functor. The `defer` and `run` must be called on the same `task_group` object.

To enable this preview feature, we must define a feature-specific macro before including the TBB headers as shown in the first two lines of Figure 12-20.

```
#define TBB_PREVIEW_TASK_GROUP_EXTENSIONS 1
#include <tbb/tbb.h>
```

Figure 12-20 shows the updated task_group version of the code using scheduler bypass and a task_group.

```cpp
#define TBB_PREVIEW_TASK_GROUP_EXTENSIONS 1
#include <tbb/tbb.h>

tbb::task_handle fwdSubTGBody(tbb::task_group& tg,
                             int N, int num_blocks,
                             const std::pair<size_t, size_t> bi,
                             std::vector<double>& x,
                             const std::vector<double>& a,
                             std::vector<double>& b,
                             std::vector<std::atomic<char>>& ref_count) {
  auto [r, c] = bi;
  computeBlock(N, r, c, x, a, b);

  tbb::task_handle deferred_task;

  // add successor to right if ready
  if (c + 1 <= r && --ref_count[r*num_blocks + c + 1] == 0) {
    deferred_task = tg.defer([&, N, num_blocks, r, c]() {
                       return fwdSubTGBody(tg, N, num_blocks,
                              BlockIndex(r, c+1), x, a, b, ref_count);
                    });
  }
  // add successor below if ready
  if (r + 1 < (size_t)num_blocks && --ref_count[(r+1)*num_blocks + c] == 0) {
    if (deferred_task)
      tg.run([&, N, num_blocks, r, c]() {
        return fwdSubTGBody(tg, N, num_blocks,
                            BlockIndex(r+1, c), x, a, b, ref_count);
      });
    else
      deferred_task = tg.defer([&, N, num_blocks, r, c]() {
                         return fwdSubTGBody(tg, N, num_blocks,
                                BlockIndex(r+1, c), x, a, b, ref_count);
                      });
  }
  return deferred_task;
}
```

Figure 12-20. *A modified execute function that bypass tasks for the forward substitution example using deferred tasks. Sample code migration/migrate_bypass_tasks.cpp*

As with task recycling, the use of bypassing provides a small performance gain, regardless of which API is used. Again, for our test system the gain was about 2%.

Task Continuation

Another feature that was available in the old lowest-level TBB tasking API was continuations. Continuations are tasks that are scheduled to be executed only after another task or other tasks are completed. In oneTBB, the primary way to express dependencies like these is through the flow graph API or by doing manual reference counting, as we have done all throughout this chapter in our forward substitution example.

MANAGING TASK DEPENDENCIES

Some in the TBB community have expressed interest in having an API that reintroduces a more direct approach for creating and managing task dependencies, and there is ongoing work in that direction – stay tuned to discussions in the oneTBB community to find out more as this develops.

Using oneTBB and TBB Together

Migrating to oneTBB ensures access to the latest features and bug fixes. Therefore, migrating is strongly recommended. It is however possible to use both the oneTBB and TBB runtime libraries from different components in the same application.

Explaining why it is possible to use both libraries in the same application requires diving into implementation details, and we won't go into those in depth here. But, at a higher level, the open source implementations of oneTBB and TBB carefully use namespaces to ensure that symbols that are exported from the shared libraries have unique names. These symbols will not conflict when linking against both libraries. The components of our applications that are compiled against the TBB headers will use the symbols exported by the TBB shared library, and the components of our application compiled against the oneTBB headers will use the symbols exported by the oneTBB shared library.

However, as described in detail in Chapter 10, one of the primary advantages of using TBB is its composability. When we mix TBB and oneTBB together, the result is two distinct global thread pools. These pools and their associated task arenas will be unaware of each other, and so using both TBB and oneTBB together can lead to oversubscription. Even so, TBB is designed to be a good citizen when mixed with other runtimes, so the oversubscription will be limited. Each library will create, by default, P-1 worker threads, where P is the number of hardware threads. So, on a system with P cores, the combined libraries will create 2x(P-1) worker threads.

Summary

In this chapter, we explored the essential considerations and steps for migrating from the original TBB to today's TBB (oneTBB). Emphasizing the alignment with contemporary C++ standards, particularly C++11 and later, we highlighted the key changes, including the adoption of standard atomic interfaces and the removal of outdated classes like task_scheduler_init. These updates not only enhance usability but also ensure that developers can take advantage of the latest features and security improvements available in today's TBB and modern C++.

Together, we are all evolving with modern C++ and focused on making the most of parallel computing.

APPENDIX A

History and Inspiration

In this appendix, we have perspectives on the history of TBB: first, some comments on the transition of TBB to today's "oneTBB," then a look at TBB's first ten years, and then a look at what preceded and inspired TBB. You could consider the three sections as views from 2025, 2016, and 2006 – each relating key history that allows a deeper understanding of TBB for those interested. We hope you enjoy these and that they deepen your understanding of *why TBB*.

Transforming into Today's TBB

After more than a decade of widespread adoption and success, the core of TBB remained valuable, but the project also had some legacy features that were no longer needed as a result of the modernization of C++ to support key basics for parallelism.

Around 2019, the TBB project decided to transform TBB to rely on C++11 features and shed historically important support in TBB that was no longer needed when C++11 is used as a basis for programming. The project was named "oneTBB" at a time when many Intel projects adopted the "one" as they transformed projects for a variety of reasons, many of them in support of oneAPI. The use of "one" for TBB was solely due to the transformation to utilize the new basic parallelism support in C++.

We quickly embarked on an effort to revise our book. Many TBB engineers were in Russia, and events in 2022 delayed our efforts. The project was able to resume by 2024 sufficiently for us to finish this book.

C++ will continue to evolve, but we do not expect that C++ changes will affect TBB as much. This is simply because C++11 and beyond have the basics for parallelism now, which libraries like TBB can sit upon without having to supply and port low-level interfaces to hardware (such as atomics and locks in the original TBB).

© Michael J. Voss, James R. Reinders 2025
M. J. Voss and J. R. Reinders, *Today's TBB*, https://doi.org/10.1007/979-8-8688-1270-5

Today's TBB continues to be valuable for the same reasons as it was from the start in 2006, but with a stronger C++ underneath it. That is a great combination.

The rest of this appendix relates more of the earlier details of the origin of TBB and some credit to the shoulders of giants that TBB started out by climbing upon.

A Decade of "Hatchling to Soaring"

This first part of the appendix is adapted from a piece that James Reinders wrote on the tenth anniversary of TBB (mid-2016). The story of TBB echoes many important decisions past and future that challenge great technical works, so its story can be educational. What follows is an adaptation of James' ramblings with mildly interesting anecdotes that are all completely unimportant to know to simply use TBB.

#1 TBB's Revolution Inside Intel

TBB was our first commercially successful software product to embrace open source, and with continued leadership TBB has more recently moved to Apache licensing.

We knew we wanted to open-source TBB from the start, but we were not ready when we launched in 2006. Open source projects were new to our small team and to Intel. We focused first on creating a strong TBB and launching it as a product in mid-2006. After launching, we shifted our attention to revising our build system, cleaning up code (commenting!), and a dozen other things that would help us invite others who would want to understand and contribute to our source code. We had a goal to be open source in mid-2007. A new problem arose – TBB became an immediate hit with customers. We were not secret with our customers about our desire to open-source, and this only intensified their interest in TBB. Our success quickly became a problem inside Intel as some of our management asked the question, "Why give away the source code to such a successful product?" Armed with facts and figures from our team, James Reinders boldly presented a multitude of reasons we should open up. That was a mistake, and James failed to get the needed permissions before 2006 ended. He licked his wounds, and we eventually realized we only needed to prove one thing: TBB would have far greater adoption if we open-sourced it than if we did not. After all, developers bet the very future of their code when they adopt a programming model. Perhaps openness matters more for programming models than it does for most other software. While we understood this point, we had failed to articulate to our management that this was all that really mattered – and that it was all we needed to know to understand that we must open-source TBB. Armed with this perspective, James surprised our senior VP who had to approve our proposal. He surprised her by showing up with only a single piece of paper with a simple graph on it, which offered a comparison of projected TBB adoption with and without open sourcing. We predicted that TBB would vanish and be replaced within five years if we did not offer this critical programming model via open source. We predicted great success if we did open-source (we actually far underestimated the success, as it turns out). Senior Vice President Renee James listened to his two-minute pitch, looked at him, and asked, "Why didn't you say this the first time? Of course, we should do this." He could have pointed out it was exactly slide 7 of the original way-too-long 20-slide presentation that he had presented two months earlier. Instead, he settled on "Thank you" and the rest is history. We choose the most popular open source licensing at the time: GPL v2 with classpath exception (important for C++ template libraries). Ten years later, we moved TBB to the Apache license. We have received a great deal of feedback from the community of users and contributors that this is the right license to use for TBB in our times.

#2 TBB's First Revolution of Parallelism

The first revolution of parallelism offered by TBB was to fully embrace the task-stealing abstraction while giving full C++ support with full composability.

OpenMP is incredibly important, but it is not composable. This is a mistake of epic proportions with long-reaching ramifications, and it cannot be changed because OpenMP is so important and committed to compatibility. James often says he was complicit in the OpenMP mistake along with everyone else who helped pull it together, review it, and promote it starting in 1997. We all overlooked the importance nested parallelism would have as the amount of hardware parallelism grew. It simply was not a concern in 1997.

Being composable is the most amazing feature of TBB. We cannot overstate the importance of never worrying about oversubscription, nested parallelism, and so on. TBB is gradually revolutionizing certain communities of developers that demand composability for their applications. The Intel Math Kernel Library (MKL), which has long been based on OpenMP, offers a version built on top of TBB for exactly this reason. And the much newer, and open source, Intel Data Analytics Library always uses TBB and the TBB-powered MKL. In fact, TBB is finding use in some versions of Python too.

Of course, the task-stealing scheduler at the heart of TBB is the real magic. While HPC customers worry about squeezing out the ultimate performance while running an application on dedicated cores, TBB tackles a problem that HPC users never worry about: how can you make parallelism work well when you share the cores that you run upon? Imagine running on eight cores, but a virus checker happens to run on one core during your application's run. That would never happen on a supercomputer, but it happens all the time on workstations and laptops! Without the dynamic nature of the TBB task-stealing scheduler, such a program would simply be delayed by the full time that the virus checker stole …because it would effectively delay every thread in the application. When using TBB on eight cores, an interruption, of duration TIME on one core, may delay the application by as little as TIME/8. This real-world flexibility matters a lot!

Finally, TBB is a C++ template library that fully embraces bringing parallelism to C++. The dedication of TBB to C++ has helped inspire changes to the C++ standard. Perhaps our biggest dream of all is that TBB will one day only be the scheduler and the algorithms that use it. The many other things in TBB to help parallelize parts of STL, create truly portable locks and atomics, address shortcomings in memory allocations, and other features to bring parallelism to C++ can and should be part of the standard language eventually. Maybe even more of TBB? Time will tell.

#3 TBB's Second Revolution of Parallelism

The second revolution of parallelism offered by TBB was to offer superior alternatives from bulk synchronous programming.

As much as we can praise the task-stealing scheduler of TBB, the algorithms most often used in applications are organized with a lot of synchronization happening at runtime. This is a sign of the times in terms of how parallel programming has been done successfully for years. However, as the amount of parallelism has grown, this has become a great obstacle in the pursuit of scaling. A better approach is to express the flow of data and require a much more minimal level of synchronization. The TBB flow graph, in addition to TBB, is a leader in this critical new revolution in parallel programming. This type of thinking is required for any parallel programming model to support the future well.

WILD CANARIES

The original TBB book (2007) was an O'Reilly Nutshell book that included O'Reilly's choice for an animal on the cover: a wild canary. We continued (with a non-infringing take on a wild canary) on t-shirts, websites, and the second book (2019). For today's TBB (2025), we continue this tradition by incorporating a photo of a wild canary.

#4 TBB's Bird

On a quite different note, we do get asked about the birds we have used. Of course, the original TBB book (2007) was an O'Reilly Nutshell book with its iconic design that always features an animal. O'Reilly made it clear to James, as the author, that they would pick the animal (a mysterious process). Undaunted, he did convey some ideas for animals that made sense to us. O'Reilly chose a beautifully drawn canary for the cover, a beautiful bird that was not an animal we had even considered. Everyone can have opinions, but soon, our cry around Intel was "Embrace the bird." We can thank Belinda Adkisson for that reframe and for the popular non-infringing "Chirp" bird that we used on t-shirts, stickers, and websites. A cheery little bird remains our mascot for TBB. We have "embraced the bird," with an actual photo on the cover of this book.

Embrace the Bird!

The colophon in the original book reads:

The animal on the cover of Intel Threading Building Blocks is a wild canary (Serinus canaria), a small songbird in the finch family. It is also known as an island canary or Atlantic canary because it is native to islands off western Europe, particularly Madeira, Azores, and the Canary Islands, for which the bird was named. The name comes from the Latin canaria ("of the dogs"), first used by Pliny the Elder in his Naturalis Historia because of the large dogs roaming the Islands. Canaries live in orchards, farmlands, and copses and make their nests in bushes and trees.

Although the wild canary is darker and slightly larger than the domestic canary, it is otherwise similar in appearance. Its breast is yellow–green, and its back is streaked with brown. Like many species, the male is more vibrantly colored than the female. The male also has a sweeter song. When the Spanish conquered the Islands in the fifteenth century, they domesticated the birds and began to breed them. By the sixteenth century, canaries were prized as pets throughout Europe. (Samuel Pepys writes about his "canary birds" in a 1661 diary entry.) Five hundred years of selective breeding have produced many canary varieties, including the bright-yellow type common today. The small birds are popular pets because they can live up to ten years, require little special attention, and are considered to have the most melodious song of all birds.

As late as the 1980s, coal miners used canaries as a warning system, with two birds in each coal pit. According to the US Bureau of Mines, canaries were preferred to mice because they are more sensitive to fumes and more visibly show distress in the presence of gas. A canary in a mine would chirp all day, but if the carbon monoxide level rose, it would stop singing and sway on its perch before falling dead – warning the miners to get out fast.

James wrote the first TBB book (*Intel Threading Building Blocks*) in the spring of 2007 with a great deal of help from the TBB team. James was joined by Michael and Professor Rafa first to do a tutorial on TBB together in 2017 and then to collaborate on the second book (*Pro TBB*) with much more educational material. Michael and James updated that work, particularly due to the move by the TBB project to streamline against the latest C++ standards, to produce this book (*Today's TBB*). We dedicate this book to the memory of our friend and colleague, Professor Rafa.

This section was adapted from a piece James wrote for the tenth-anniversary special edition of Intel's *Parallel Universe* magazine. Issues are available free online at https://software.intel.com/parallel-universe-magazine. You can read more about the history of TBB in the article "The Genesis and Evolution of Intel Threading Building Blocks" as related by its original architect in the same issue – including his two "regrets" in the initial TBB 1.0 design. Many interesting articles about TBB have been published in the *Parallel Universe* magazine over the years.

Ten years of TBB – special issue of Intel's *Parallel Universe* magazine

Inspiration for TBB

This final part of the appendix is adapted from the historical notes that James produced for the first TBB book (2007) when TBB was only one year old. This is a look at what preceded and inspired TBB.

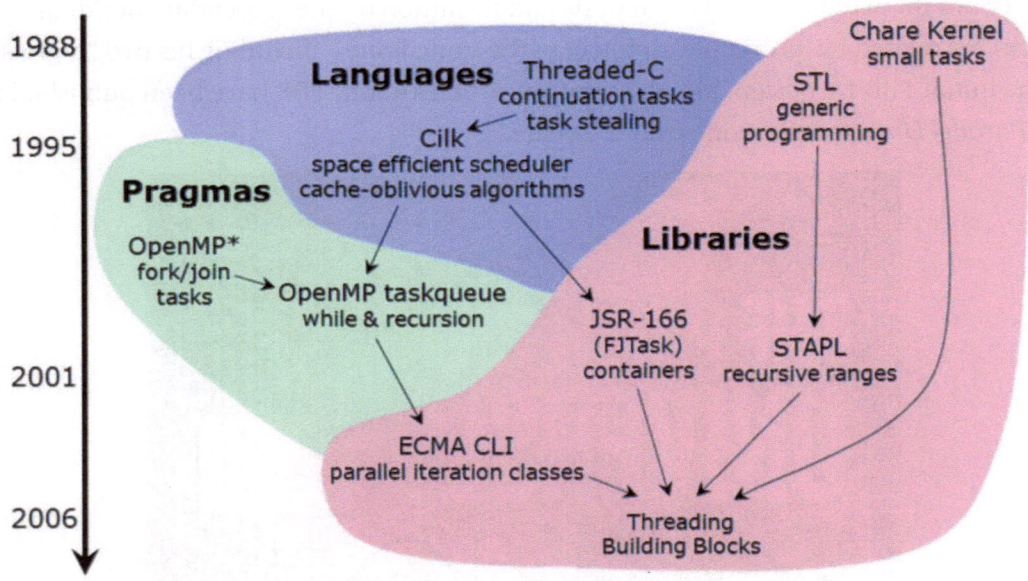

Figure A-1. *Key influences on the design of Threading Building Blocks*

Threading Building Blocks draws from a great many sources. Figure A-1 highlights the key influences of the past decade or so. The influences were in the form of inspiration and, other than McRT-Malloc, they have no actual source code connection. Influences prior to 1988 are left as an exercise for other historians.

1988, Chare Kernel, University of Illinois at Urbana-Champaign

In 1988, it was simply a C library. The key notion was to break a program into small bits of work, called chares, and the scheduler would take care of packing these efficiently (in both space and time) onto processors. Mapping tasks onto threads instead of programming threads directly is an important concept. The Chare Kernel was later extended with some features for marshaling to address distributed memory machines, becoming Charm++.

1993, Standard Template Library (STL) for C++, Hewlett-Packard

STL was presented in November 1993 to the ANSI/ISO C++ committee, and HP made it freely available in 1994. It was adopted into the C++ standard. Arch Robison related: "I once heard Stepanov give a great talk on generic programming, where he went through how to write a really generic greatest-common-factor algorithm. [The paper is similar to that talk, but with more mathematical emphasis.] In its full glory, generic programming is not just parametric types, but programming with concepts." Works by Stepanov on STL and generic programming are listed later in this chapter. *Note: Alexander Stepanov kindly wrote the foreword for the original book, which included praise for the embracing of generic programming in TBB's design.*

1999, Java Specification Request #166 (JSR-166), Doug Lea

It was actually not standardized until later, but 1999 was the year Lea first introduced it. FJTask was an attempt to put Cilk-style parallelism into the stock Java library. It was proposed for JSR-166, but it did not make it into that standard.

2001, Standard Template Adaptive Parallel Library (STAPL), Texas A&M

STAPL introduced the notion of recursive parallel ranges ("pRanges") and the concept of using these ranges instead of iterators to bind parallel generic algorithms to parallel containers. STL lacks a recursive range. STAPL is more complex than TBB because it encompasses distributed memory architectures typical of High-Performance Computing (HPC). Furthermore, STAPL supports the specification of arbitrary execution order for parallel task graphs. This allows the use of multiple scheduling policies to optimize execution time.

2004, ECMA CLI Parallel Profile, Intel

This ECMA spec for the .NET virtual machine has classes for parallel iteration, designed by Arch Robison.

2006, McRT-Malloc, Intel Research

A scalable transactional memory allocator, McRT, forms the basis of the scalable memory allocator supplied with Threading Building Blocks. Sections 3 and 3.1 of a 2006 paper by Hudson, Saha, Adl-Tabatabai, and Hertzberg (http://doi.acm.org/10.1145/1133956.1133967) describe the basis for the scalable memory allocator in TBB, which was excellent for smaller (under 8K) objects. The scalable memory allocator has been greatly enhanced in the years since.

Influential Languages

1994, Threaded-C, Massachusetts Institute of Technology

The Parallel Continuation Machine (PCM) was the runtime support for Threaded-C. It was a C-based package that provided continuation-passing-style threads on Thinking Machines Corporation's Connection Machine Model CM-5 Supercomputer and used work stealing as a general scheduling policy to improve the load balance and locality of the computation. This language is not to be confused with the Threaded-C for EARTH from McGill University and the University of Delaware. PCM was briefly mentioned on page 2 of the original Cilk manual.

1995, Cilk, Massachusetts Institute of Technology

The first implementation of Cilk was a direct descendent of PCM/Threaded-C. Cilk fixed the difficulty of programming continuation tasks and produced methods to tailor task allocation to caches without knowing the size of the caches with cache-oblivious algorithms. Cilk is an extension of C that supports very efficient fork/join parallelism. Its space efficiency is discussed in http://supertech.csail.mit.edu/papers/cilkjpdc96.pdf. FFTW (www.fftw.org) is an example of a cache-oblivious algorithm.

Influential Pragmas

1997, OpenMP, by a Consortium of Major Computer Hardware and Software Vendors

OpenMP supports multiplatform, shared memory parallel programming in C and Fortran, offering a standard set of compiler directives, library routines, and environment variables. Prior to OpenMP, many vendors had proprietary compiler directives with similar intent, but they lacked portability. OpenMP embodies a fork/join philosophy. See www.openmp.org.

1998, OpenMP Task Queue, Kuck & Associates (KAI)

Proposed extensions for OpenMP to move beyond loops. A refinement of this proposal was adopted and added to OpenMP in 2008 (a year after our book) as of OpenMP 3.0.

Summary

TBB was developed at an ideal time, leveraging prior research to make informed design choices. A team of parallel tooling experts created a foundational robust library to address the emerging need for multicore parallelism. The significant interest in TBB, driven by the appearance of multicore processors, helped refine its implementation, and making it open source facilitated widespread adoption. Experience with TBB played an important role as C++ embraced parallelism.

Parallelism is permanently a part of all computing today. Parallelism in computers is no longer new news. C++ support for parallelism is no longer new news. The use of accelerators to augment computers with a profound amount of specialized parallel processing is not new news. At the heart of any parallel system is the need for robust and dependable controls to orchestrate the parallelism of the entire system.

Today's TBB solves that need for C++ programmers. On top of firm foundation possible with TBB, we can also address more specific needs of vectorization and other accelerations with tools like pragma SIMD, OpenMP, CUDA, SYCL, OpenCL, and more. Under it all, TBB helps us ensure we do our best to achieve maximum parallelism in the quest to minimize the negative effects of Amdahl's Law.

Further Reading

Acar, U., G. Blelloch, and R. Blumofe (2000). "The Data Locality of Work Stealing." *Proceedings of the Twelfth Annual ACM Symposium on Parallel Algorithms and Architectures*, 1–12.

Amdahl, G. M. (1967, April). "Validity of the single-processor approach to achieving large scale computing capabilities." *AFIP Conference Proceedings*, 30. Reston, VA: AFIPS Press, 483–485.

An, P., A. Jula, et al. (2003). "STAPL: An Adaptive, Generic Parallel C++ Library." Workshop on Language and Compilers for Parallel Computing, 2001. Lecture Notes in Computer Science 2624, 193–208.

Austern, M. H., R. A. Towle, and A. A. Stepanov (1996). "Range partition adaptors: a mechanism for parallelizing STL." *ACM SIGAPP Applied Computing Review*, 4, 1, 5–6.

Blumofe, R. D., and D. Papadopoulos (1998). "Hood: A User-Level Threads Library for Multiprogrammed Multiprocessors."

Blumofe, R. D., C. F. Joerg, et al. (1996). "Cilk: An Efficient Multithreaded Runtime System." *Proceedings of the 5th ACM SIGPLAN Symposium on Principles and Practice of Parallel Programming*, 207–216.

Boehm, H. (2006, June). "An Atomic Operations Library for C++." C++ standards committee document N2047.

Butenhof, D. R. (1997). *Programming with POSIX Threads*. Reading, MA: Addison Wesley.

Flynn, M. J. (1972, September). "Some Computer Organizations and Their Effectiveness." *IEEE Transactions on Computers*, C-21, 9, 948-960.

Garcia, R., J. Järvi, et al. (2003, October). "A Comparative Study of Language Support for Generic Programming." *Proceedings of the 2003 ACM SIGPLAN Conference on Object-Oriented Programming, Systems, Languages, and Applications*.

Gustafson, J. L. (1988). "Reevaluating Amdahl's Law." *Communications of the ACM*, 31(5), 532–533.

Halbherr, M., Y. Zhou, and C. F. Joerg (1994, March). "MIMD-Style Parallel Programming Based on Continuation-Passing Threads." Computation Structures Group Memo 355.

Halbherr, M., Y. Zhou, and C. F. Joerg (1994, September). "MIMD-style parallel programming with continuation-passing threads." *Proceedings of the 2nd International Workshop on Massive Parallelism: Hardware, Software, and Applications*, Capri, Italy.

Hansen, B. (1973). "Concurrent Programming Concepts." *ACM Computing Surveys*, 5, 4.

Hoare, C. A. R. (1974). "Monitors: An Operating System Structuring Concept." *Communications of the ACM*, 17, 10, 549–557.

Hudson, R. L., B. Saha, et al. (2006, June). "McRT-Malloc: a scalable transactional memory allocator." *Proceedings of the 2006 International Symposium on Memory Management*. New York: ACM Press, 74–83.

Intel Threading Building Blocks 1.0 for Windows, Linux, and Mac OS – Intel Software Network (1996).

"A Formal Specification of Intel Itanium Processor Family Memory Ordering" (2002, October).

ISO/IEC 14882:1998(E) International Standard (1998). Programming languages – C++. ISO/IEC, 1998.

ISO/IEC 9899:1999 International Standard (1999). Programming languages – C. ISO/IEC, 1999.

Järvi, J., and B. Stroustrup (2004, September). "Decltype and auto (revision 4)." C++ standards committee document N1705=04-0145.

Kapur, D., D. R. Musser, and A.A. Stepanov (1981). "Operators and Algebraic Structures." *Proceedings of the 1981 Conference on Functional Programming Languages and Computer Architecture*, 59–63.

MacDonald, S., D. Szafron, and J. Schaeffer (2004). "Rethinking the Pipeline as Object-Oriented States with Transformations." Ninth International Workshop on High-Level Parallel Programming Models and Supportive Environments.

Mahmoud, Q. H. (2005, March). "Concurrent Programming with J2SE 5.0." Sun Developer Network.

Massingill, B. L., T. G. Mattson, and B. A. Sanders (2005). "Reengineering for Parallelism: An Entry Point for PLPP (Pattern Language for Parallel Programming) for Legacy Applications." *Proceedings of the Twelfth Pattern Languages of Programs Workshop*.

Mattson, T. G., B. A. Sanders, and B. L. Massingill (2004). *Patterns for Parallel Programming*. Reading, MA: Addison Wesley.

McDowell, C. E., and D. P. Helmbold (1989). "Debugging Concurrent Programs." *Communications of the ACM*, 21, 2.

Meyers, S. (1998). *Effective C++*, Second Edition. Reading, MA: Addison Wesley.

Musser, D. R., and A. A. Stepanov (1994). "Algorithm-Oriented Generic Libraries." *Software – Practice and Experience*, 24(7), 623–642.

Musser, D. R., G. J. Derge, and A. Saini, with foreword by Alexander Stepanov (2001). *STL Tutorial and Reference Guide: C++ Programming with the Standard Template Library*, Second Edition. Boston, MA: Addison Wesley.

Narlikar, G., and G. Blelloch (1999). "Space-Efficient Scheduling of Nested Parallelism." *ACM Transactions on Programming Languages and Systems*, 21, 1, 138–173.

OpenMP C and C++ Application Program Interface, Version 2.5 (2005, May).

Ottosen, T. (2006, September). "Range Library Core." C++ standards committee document N2068.

Plauger, P. J., M. Lee, et al. (2000). *C++ Standard Template Library*. Prentice Hall.

Rauchwerger, L., F. Arzu, and K. Ouchi (1998, May). "Standard Templates Adaptive Parallel Library." *Proceedings of the 4th International Workshop on Languages, Compilers, and Run-Time Systems for Scalable Computers (LCR)*, Pittsburgh, PA. Also Lecture Notes in Computer Science, 1511, Springer-Verlag, 1998, 402–410.

Robison, A. D. (2006). "A Proposal to Add Parallel Iteration to the Standard Library."

Robison, A. (2003, April). "Memory Consistency & .NET." Dr. Dobb's Journal.

Samko, V. (2006, February). "A proposal to add lambda functions to the C++ standard." C++ standards committee document N1958=06-028.

Schmidt, D. C., and I. Pyarali (1998). Strategies for Implementing POSIX Condition Variables on Win32. Department of Computer Science, Washington University, St. Louis, MO.

Schmidt, D. C., M. Stal, et al. (2000). Patterns for Concurrent and Networked Objects. Pattern-Oriented Architecture, 2.

Shah, S., G. Haab, et al. (1999). "Flexible Control Structures for Parallelism in OpenMP." *Proceedings of the First European Workshop on OpenMP*.

Siek, J., D. Gregor, et al. (2005). "Concepts for C++0x."

Stepanov, A. A., and M. Lee (1995). "The Standard Template Library." HP Laboratories Technical Report 95-11(R.1).

Stepanov, A. A. (1999). "Greatest Common Measure: The Last 2500 Years."

Stroustrup, B. (1994). *The Design and Evolution of C++*, also known as D&E. Reading, MA: Addison Wesley.

Stroustrup, B. (2000). *The C++ Programming Language*, Special Edition. Reading, MA: Addison Wesley.

Stroustrup, B., and G. Dos Reis (2005, April). "A Concept Design (rev.1)." Technical Report N1782=05-0042, ISO/IEC SC22/JTC1/WG21.

Stroustrup, B., and G. Dos Reis (2005, October). "Specifying C++ concepts." Technical Report N1886=05-0146, ISO/IEC SC22/JTC1/WG21.

Su, E., X. Tian, et al. (2002, September). "Compiler Support of the Workqueuing Execution Model for Intel SMP Architectures." Fourth European Workshop on OpenMP, Rome.

Sutter, H. (2005, January). "The Concurrency Revolution." Dr. Dobb's Journal.

Sutter, H. (2005, March). "The Free Lunch Is Over: A Fundamental Turn Towards Concurrency in Software." Dr. Dobb's Journal.

Voss, M. (2006, December). "Enable Safe, Scalable Parallelism with Intel Threading Building Blocks' Concurrent Containers."

Voss, M. (2006, October). "Demystify Scalable Parallelism with Intel Threading Building Blocks' Generic Parallel Algorithms."

Willcock, J., J. Järvi, et al. (2006). "Lambda Expressions and Closures for C++." N1968-06-0038.

Glossary

Abstraction: In the case of TBB, abstraction serves to separate the work into work appropriate for a programmer and work best left to a runtime. The goal of such an abstraction is to deliver scalable high performance on a variety of multicore and many-core systems, and even heterogeneous platforms, without requiring rewriting of the code. This careful division of responsibilities leaves the programmer to expose opportunities for parallelism and the runtime responsible for mapping the opportunities to the hardware. Code written to the abstraction will be free of parameterization for cache sizes, number of cores, and even consistency of performance from processing unit to processing unit.

Accelerators are specialized hardware created specifically to perform certain types of computation more efficiently than is possible with general-purpose CPUs alone. Massive parallelism is the most common source of their ability to greatly accelerate certain computations.

Affinity: The specification of methods to associate a particular software thread to a particular hardware thread usually with the objective of getting better or more predictable performance. Affinity specifications include the concept of being maximally spread apart to reduce contention (scatter) or packing tightly (compact) to minimize distances for communication. OpenMP supports a rich set of affinity controls at various levels from abstract to full manual control. Fortran 2008 does not specify controls, but Intel reuses the OpenMP controls for "do concurrent." Intel Threading Building Blocks (TBB) provides an abstract loop-to-loop affinity biasing capability.

Amdahl's Law: Speedup is limited by the non-parallelizable serial portion of the work. A program where two-thirds of the program can be run in parallel and one-third of the original nonparallel program cannot be sped up by parallelism will find that speedup can only approach 3× and never exceed it assuming the same work is done. If scaling the problem size places more demands on the parallel portions of the program, then Amdahl's Law is not as bad as it may seem. See **Gustafson's Law**.

M. J. Voss and J. R. Reinders, *Today's TBB*, https://doi.org/10.1007/979-8-8688-1270-5

Arbitrators resolve conflicts between software components when they request overlapping compute resources. TBB uses a priority-aware, proportional arbitrator to fulfill demands from arenas for worker threads. The oneAPI Toolkits provide Thread Composability Manager (TCM), an arbitrator that grants requests for access to CPU compute resources and can be used by TBB, as well as some implementations of OpenMP, OpenCL, and SYCL.

Atomic operation is an operation that is guaranteed to appear as if it occurred indivisibly without interference from other threads. For example, a processor might provide a memory increment operation. This operation needs to read a value from memory, increment it, and write it back to memory. An atomic increment guarantees that the final memory value is the same as would have occurred if no other operations on that memory location were allowed to happen between the read and the write.

Barrier: When a computation is broken into phases, it is often necessary to ensure that all threads complete all the work in one phase before any thread moves onto another phase. A barrier is a form of synchronization that ensures this: threads arriving at a barrier wait there until the last thread arrives, and then all threads continue. A barrier can be implemented using atomic operations. For example, all threads might try to increment a shared variable and then block if the value of that variable does not equal the number of threads that need to synchronize at the barrier. The last thread to arrive can then reset the barrier to zero and release all the blocked threads.

Block can be used in two senses: (1) a state in which a thread is unable to proceed while it waits for some synchronization event or (2) a region of memory. The second meaning is also used in the sense of dividing a loop into a set of parallel tasks of a suitable granularity.

Cache is a part of a memory system that stores copies of data temporarily in a fast memory so that future uses for that data can be handled more quickly than if the request had to be fetched again from a more distant storage. Caches are generally automatic and are designed to enhance programs with temporal locality and/or spatial locality. Caching systems in modern computers are usually multileveled.

Cache-friendly is a characteristic of an application in which performance increases as problem size increases but then levels off as the bandwidth limit is reached.

Cache lines are the units in which data are retrieved and held by a cache, which in order to exploit spatial locality are generally larger than a word. The general trend is for increasing cache line sizes, which are generally large enough to hold at least two double-precision floating-point numbers, but unlikely to hold more than eight on any current design. Larger cache lines allow for more efficient bulk transfers from main memory but worsen certain issues including false sharing, which generally degrades performance.

Cache-oblivious algorithm is any algorithm that performs well, without modification, on multiple machines' memory organizations such as different levels of cache having different sizes. Since such algorithms are carefully designed to exhibit compact memory reuse, it seems like it would have made more sense to call such algorithms cache agnostic. The term *oblivious* is a reference to the fact that such algorithms are not aware of the parameters of the memory subsystem, such as the cache sizes or relative speeds. This is in contrast with earlier efforts to carefully block algorithms for specific cache hardware.

Cache-unfriendly is a characteristic of an application that does not effectively utilize the memory cache, leading to inefficient data access patterns. This can result in increased latency and reduced performance. Issues may include extensive use of random memory access patterns, extremely large data structures, frequent context switching, high memory bandwidth demands, and otherwise inefficient algorithms. Cache-unfriendly applications can significantly degrade performance, especially in systems where memory access speed is critical. Optimizing these applications often involves improving data locality, minimizing random access, and designing algorithms that leverage the cache hierarchy effectively.

Clusters are a set of computers with distributed memory communicating over a high-speed interconnect. The individual computers are often called **nodes**. TBB is used at the node level within a cluster, although multiple nodes are commonly programmed with TBB and then connected (usually with MPI).

Communication: Any exchange of data or **synchronization** between software tasks or threads. Understanding that communication costs are often a limiting factor in scaling is a critical concept for parallel programming.

Composability: The ability to use two components in concert with each other without causing failure or unreasonable conflict (ideally no conflict). Limitations on composability, if they exist, are best when completely diagnosed at build time instead of requiring any testing. Composability problems that manifest only at runtime are the biggest problem with non-composable systems. Can refer to system features, programming models, or software components.

Concurrent means that things are logically happening simultaneously. Two tasks that are both logically active at some point in time are considered to be concurrent. Contrast with **parallel**.

Core: A separate sub-processor on a multicore processor. A core should be able to support (at least one) separate and divergent flow of control from other cores on the same processor.

CUDA is a proprietary parallel computing platform developed by Nvidia that is targeted at Nvidia accelerators.

Data parallelism is an approach to parallelism that attempts to be oriented around data rather than tasks. However, in reality, successful strategies in parallel algorithm development tend to focus on exploiting the parallelism in data, because data decomposition (generating tasks for different units of data) scales, but functional decomposition (generation of heterogeneous tasks for different functions) does not. See Amdahl's Law and Gustafson–Barsis' Law.

Deadlock is a programming error. Deadlock occurs when at least two tasks wait for each other and each will not resume until the other task proceeds. This happens easily when code requires locking multiple mutexes. For example, each task can be holding a mutex required by the other task.

Deterministic refers to a deterministic algorithm, which is an algorithm that behaves predictably. Given a particular input, a deterministic algorithm will always produce the same output. The definition of what is the "same" may be important due to limited precision in mathematical operations and the likelihood that optimizations including parallelization will rearrange the order of operations. These are often referred to as "rounding" differences, which result when the order of mathematical operations to compute the answer differs between the original program and the final concurrent program. Concurrency is not the only factor that can lead to **nondeterministic** algorithms, but in practice it is often the cause. Use of programming models with sequential semantics and eliminating data races with proper access controls will generally eliminate the major effects of concurrency other than the "rounding" differences.

Distributed memory is memory that is physically located in separate computers. An indirect interface, such as message passing, is required to access memory on remote computers, while local memory can be accessed directly. Distributed memory is typically supported by clusters that, for purposes of this definition, we are considering to be a collection of computers. Since the memory on attached coprocessors also cannot typically be addressed directly from the host, it can be considered, for functional purposes, to be a form of distributed memory.

DSP (Digital Signal Processor), a computing device designed specifically for digital signal processing tasks such as those associated with radio communications including filters, FFTs, and analog-to-digital conversions. The computational capabilities of DSPs alongside CPUs gave rise to some of the earliest examples of heterogeneous platforms and various programming language extensions to control and interact with a DSP. OpenCL is a programming model that can help harness the compute aspects of DSPs. See also **heterogeneous platforms**.

emacs is the best text editor in the world (according to James), and it is open source. Compare to the vi editor. "emacs" is the first package James installs on any computer that he uses.

Embarrassing parallelism is a description of an algorithm if it can be decomposed into a large number of independent tasks with little or no synchronization or communication required.

ExaFLOP/s = 10^18 double-precision (64-bit) floating-point operations per second.

ExaFLOPs = 10^18 double-precision (64-bit) floating-point operations.

ExaOP/s = 10^18 mathematical operations per second.

ExaOPs = 10^18 mathematical operations.

False sharing: Two separate tasks in two separate cores may write to separate locations in memory, but if those memory locations happened to be allocated in the same cache line, the cache coherence hardware would attempt to keep the cache lines coherent, resulting in extra interprocessor communication and reduced performance, even though the tasks are not actually sharing data.

Far memory: In a NUMA system, memory that has longer access times than the near memory. The view of which parts of memory are near vs. far depends on the process from which code is running. We also refer to this memory as non-local memory (in contrast to local memory) in Chapter 11.

Floating-point number is a format for numbers in computers characterized by trading a higher range for the numbers for a reduced precision by using the bits available for a number (mantissa) and a shift count (exponent) that places the point to the left or right of a fixed position. In contrast, fixed-point representations lack an explicit exponent, thereby allowing all bits to be used for number (mantissa).

Floating-point operations include add, multiply, subtract, and more, done to floating-point numbers.

FLOP/s = Double-precision (64-bit) floating-point operations per second.

FLOPs = Double-precision (64-bit) floating-point operations.

Forward scaling is the concept of having a program or algorithm scalable already in threads and/or vectors so as to be ready to take advantage of growth of parallelism in future hardware with a simple recompile with a new compiler or relink to a new library. Using the right abstractions to express parallelism is normally a key to enabling forward scaling when writing a parallel program.

FPGA (Field Programmable Array), a device that integrates a large number of gates (and often higher-level constructs such as DSPs, floating-point units, or network controllers) that remain unconnected to each other until the device is programmed. Programming was originally a whole chip process that was intended to be done once when a system was started, but modern FPGAs support partial reconfigurability and are often dynamically loaded with new programs as a matter of course. Traditionally, FPGAs were viewed as a way to consolidate a large number of discrete chips in a design into a single FPGA – usually saving board space, power, and overall cost. As such, FPGAs were programmed using tools similar to those used to design circuitry at a board or chip level – called high-level description languages (e.g., VHDL or Verilog). More recent usage to harness FPGAs as compute engines has used the OpenCL programming model.

Future-proofed: A computer program written in a manner so it will survive future computer architecture changes without requiring significant changes to the program itself. Generally, the more abstract a programming method is, the more **future-proofed** that program is. Lower-level programming methods that in some way mirror computer architectural details will be less able to survive the future without change. Writing in an abstract, more **future-proofed** fashion may involve trade-offs in efficiency, however.

GigaFLOP/s = 10^9 double-precision (64-bit) floating-point operations per second.

GigaFLOPs = 10^9 double-precision (64-bit) floating-point operations.

GPU (Graphic Processing Unit), a computing device designed to reform calculations associated with graphics such as lighting, transformations, clipping, and rendering. The computational capabilities of GPUs were originally designed solely for use in a "graphical pipeline" sitting between a general-purpose compute device (CPU) and displays. The emergence of programming support for using the computation without sending results to the display and subsequent extensions to the designs of the GPU lead to a more generalized compute capability being associated with many GPUs. OpenCL and CUDA are two popular programming models utilized to harness the compute aspects of GPUs. See also **heterogeneous platforms**.

Grain, as in *coarse-grained parallelism* or *fine-grained parallelism*, or *grainsize*, refers to the concept of "how much work" gets done before moving to a new task and/ or potentially synchronizing. Programs scale best when grains are as large as possible

428

(so threads can run independently) but small enough to keep every compute resource fully busy (load balancing). These two factors operate somewhat at odds with each other, which creates the need to consider grainsize. TBB works to automate partitioning, but there is never a perfect world in which a programmer cannot help tune for the best performance based on knowledge of their algorithms.

Gustafson-Barsis' Law is a different view on **Amdahl's Law** that factors in the fact that as problem sizes grow, the serial portion of computations tends to shrink as a percentage of the total work to be done.

Hardware thread is a hardware implementation of a thread with a separate flow of control. Multiple hardware threads can be implemented using multiple cores or can run concurrently or simultaneously on one core in order to hide latency using methods such as hyperthreading of a processor core. In the latter case (hyperthreading or simultaneous multithreading (SMT)), it is said that a physical core features several logical cores (or hardware threads).

Heterogeneous platforms consist of a mixture of compute devices instead of a homogeneous collection of only CPUs. Heterogeneous computing is usually employed to provide specific acceleration via an attached device, such as a GPU, DSP, FPGA, etc. See also **OpenCL**.

High-Performance Computing (HPC) refers to the highest-performance computing available at a point in time, which today generally means at least a petaFLOP/s of computational capability. The term HPC is occasionally used as a synonym for supercomputing, although supercomputing is probably more specific to even higher-performance systems. While the use of HPC is spreading to more industries, it is generally associated with helping solve the most challenging problems in science and engineering. High-performance data analytics workloads, often using artificial intelligence (AI) and machine learning (ML) techniques, qualify as HPC workloads in their larger instantiations and often combine well with long-standing (traditional) HPC workloads.

Hyperthreading refers to multithreading on a single processor core with the purpose of more fully utilizing the functional units in an out-of-order core by bringing together more instructions than executable by one software thread. With hyperthreading, multiple hardware threads may run on one core and share resources, but some benefit is still obtained from parallelism or concurrency. Typically, each hyperthread has, at least, its own register file and program counter, so that switching between hyperthreads is relatively lightweight. Hyperthreading is associated with Intel. See also **simultaneous multithreading**.

Latency is the time it takes to complete a task, that is, the time between when the task begins and when it ends. Latency has units of time. The scale can be anywhere from nanoseconds to days. Lower latency is better in general.

Latency hiding schedules computations on a processing element while other tasks using that core are waiting for long-latency operations to complete, such as memory or disk transfers. The latency is not actually hidden, since each task still takes the same time to complete, but more tasks can be completed in a given time since resources are shared more efficiently, so throughput is improved.

Load balancing assigns tasks to resources while handling uneven sizes of tasks. Optimally the goal of load balancing is to keep all compute devices busy with minimal waste due to overhead.

Load imbalance is an uneven distribution of work to compute resources. A load imbalance may result in inefficient use of resources and longer application execution times since some compute resources will not be fully utilized.

Locality refers to utilizing memory locations that are closer, rather than further apart. This will maximize reuse of cache lines, memory pages, and so on. Maintaining a high degree of locality of reference is a key to scaling.

Lock is a mechanism for implementing **mutual exclusion**. Before entering a mutual exclusion region, a thread must first try to acquire a lock on that region. If the lock has already been acquired by another thread, the current thread must **block**, which it may do by either suspending operation or spinning. When the lock is released, then the current thread is free to acquire it. Locks can be implemented using **atomic operations**, which are themselves a form of mutual exclusion on basic operations, implemented in hardware.

Loop-carried dependence: If the same data item (e.g., element [3] of an array) is written in one iteration of a loop and is read in a different iteration of a loop, there is said to be a loop-carried dependence. If there are no loop-carried dependencies, a loop can be vectorized or parallelized. If there is a loop-carried dependence, the direction (prior iteration vs. future iteration, also known as backward or forward) and the distance (the number of iterations separating the read and write) must be considered.

Many-core processor is a **multicore** processor with so many cores that in practice we do not enumerate them; there are just "lots." The term has been generally used with processors with 32 or more cores, but there is no precise definition.

Megahertz era is a historical period of time during which processors doubled clock rates at a rate similar to the doubling of transistors in a design, roughly every two years. Such rapid rise in processor clock speeds ceased at just under 4GHz (4,000 megahertz) in 2004. Designs shifted toward adding more cores marking the shift to the **multicore era**.

Moore's Law is an observation that, over the history of semiconductors, the number of transistors in a dense integrated circuit has doubled approximately every two years.

Message Passing Interface (MPI) is an industry-standard message passing system designed to exchange data on a wide variety of parallel computers.

Multicore is a processor with multiple sub-processors, each sub-processor (known as a **core**) supporting at least one hardware thread.

Multicore era is the time after which processor designs shifted away from rapidly rising clock rates and shifted toward adding more cores. This era began roughly in 2005.

Node (in a cluster) refers to a shared memory computer, often on a single board with multiple processors, which is connected with other nodes to form a **cluster** computer or supercomputer.

Nondeterministic: Exhibiting a lack of deterministic behavior, so results can vary from run to run of an algorithm. Concurrency is not the only factor that can lead to nondeterministic algorithms, but in practice it is often the cause. See more in the definition for **deterministic**.

Non-uniform Memory Access (NUMA): Used to categorize memory design characteristics in a shared memory architecture. NUMA = memory access latency is different for different memories. UMA = memory access latency is the same for all memory. Compare with **UMA**. See Chapter 11.

Offload: Placing part of a computation on an attached device such as an FPGA, GPU, or another accelerator.

OpenCL (Open Computing Language) is a framework for writing programs that execute across heterogeneous platforms. OpenCL provides host APIs for controlling offloading and attached devices and extensions to C/C++ to express code to run on the attached accelerator (GPUs, DSPs, FPGAs, etc.) with the ability to use the CPU as a fallback if the attached device is not present or available at runtime.

oneAPI is an open standard for heterogeneous programming of devices, such as CPUs, GPUs, AI accelerators, and FPGAs.

oneDPL is a PSTL implementation as part of the oneAPI project.

oneTBB: The new official name for the long-standing TBB project, renamed to align with other naming for projects grouped into the oneAPI effort. The project benefits from community management under the auspices of the UXL (Unified Acceleration) Foundation as part of the greater Linux Foundation.

OpenMP is an API that supports multiplatform shared memory multiprocessing programming in C, C++, and Fortran, on most processor architectures and operating systems. It is made up of a set of compiler directives, library routines, and environment variables that influence runtime behavior. OpenMP is managed by the nonprofit technology consortium OpenMP Architecture Review Board and is jointly defined by a group of major computer hardware and software vendors (`http://openmp.org`).

Oversubscription: When more than one software thread must be scheduled onto the same hardware thread. Since the threads cannot occupy the same hardware thread simultaneously, they occupy it during different time slices that are managed by the operating system. Oversubscription can improve performance in some scenarios, but for many compute-intense parallel applications, it adds OS scheduling overheads without improving performance.

Parallel means actually happening simultaneously. Two tasks that are both actually doing work at some point in time are considered to be operating in parallel. When a distinction is made between concurrent and parallel, the key is whether work can ever be done simultaneously. Multiplexing of a single processor core, by multitasking operating systems, has allowed concurrency for decades even when simultaneous execution was impossible because there was only one processing core.

Parallelism is doing more than one thing at a time. Attempts to classify types of parallelism are numerous.

Parallelization is the act of transforming code to enable simultaneous activities. The parallelization of a program allows at least parts of it to execute in parallel.

PetaFLOP/s = 10^{15} double-precision (64-bit) floating-point operations per second.

PetaFLOPs = 10^{15} double-precision (64-bit) floating-point operations.

PSTL (Parallel Standard Template Library) refers to implementations of STL with parallel capabilities.

Race conditions are nondeterministic behaviors in a parallel program that are generally a programming error. A race condition occurs when concurrent tasks perform operations on the same memory location without proper synchronization and one of the memory operations is a write. Code with a race may operate correctly sometimes and fail other times.

Recursion is the act of a function being reentered while an instance of the function is still active in the same thread of execution. In the simplest and most common case, a function directly calls itself, although recursion can also occur between multiple functions. Recursion is supported by storing the state for the continuations of partially completed functions in dynamically allocated memory, such as on a stack, although if higher-order functions are supported, a more complex memory allocation scheme may be required. Bounding the amount of recursion can be important to prevent excessive use of memory.

Scalability is a measure of the increase in performance as a function of the availability of more hardware to use in parallel.

Scalable: An application is **scalable** if its performance increases when additional parallel hardware resources are added. The term **strong scaling** refers to scaling that occurs while a problem size does not need to be changed as more compute is available in order to achieve scaling. **Weak scaling** refers to scaling that occurs only when a problem size is scaled up when additional compute is available. See **scalability**.

Serial means neither concurrent nor parallel.

Serialization occurs when the tasks in a potentially parallel algorithm are executed in a specific serial order, typically due to resource constraints. The opposite of parallelization.

Shared memory: When two units of parallel work can access data in the same location. Normally doing this safely requires synchronization. The units of parallel work, processes, threads, and tasks can all share data this way, if the physical memory system allows it. However, processes do not share memory by default, and special calls to the operating system are required to set it up.

SIMD: Single Instruction Multiple Data referring to the ability to process multiple pieces of data (such as elements of an array) with all the same operation. SIMD is a computer architecture within a widely used classification system known as Flynn's taxonomy, first proposed in 1966.

Simultaneous multithreading refers to multithreading on a single processor core. See also **hyperthreading**.

Software thread is a virtual hardware thread – in other words, a single flow of execution in software intended to map one for one to a hardware thread. An operating system typically enables many more software threads to exist than there are actual hardware threads, by mapping software threads to hardware threads, as necessary. Having more software threads than hardware threads is known as **oversubscription**.

Spatial locality: Nearby when measured in terms of distance (in memory address). Compare with temporal locality. Spatial locality refers to a program behavior where the use of one data element indicates that data nearby, often the next data element, will probably be used soon. Algorithms exhibiting good spatial locality in data usage can benefit from cache line structures and prefetching hardware, both common components in modern computers.

Speedup is the ratio between the latency for solving a problem with one processing unit vs. the latency for solving the same problem with multiple processing units in parallel.

SPMD: Single Program Multiple Data refers to the ability to process multiple pieces of data (such as elements of an array) with the same program, in contrast with a more restrictive SIMD architecture. SPMD most often refers to message passing programming on distributed memory computer architectures. SPMD is a subcategory of MIMD computer architectures within a widely used classification system known as Flynn's taxonomy, first proposed in 1966.

STL (Standard Template Library) is a part of the C++ standard.

Strangled scaling refers to a programming error in which the performance of parallel code is poor due to high contention or overhead, so much so that it may underperform the nonparallel (serial) code.

Symmetric Multiprocessor (SMP) is a multiprocessor system with shared memory and running a single operating system.

SYCL is an open, cross-platform programming abstraction for heterogeneous computing that is governed by the Khronos Group.

Synchronization: The coordination of tasks or threads, in order to obtain the desired runtime order. Commonly used to avoid undesired race conditions.

Task: A lightweight unit of potential parallelism with its own control flow, generally implemented at a user level as opposed to OS-managed threads. Unlike threads, tasks are usually serialized on a single core and run to completion. Threads are a mechanism for executing tasks in parallel, while tasks are units of work that merely provide the *opportunity* for parallel execution; tasks are not themselves a mechanism of parallel execution.

Task parallelism: An attempt to classify parallelism as more oriented around tasks than data.

TBB: See **Threading Building Blocks (TBB)**.

TCM: See **Thread Composability Manager (TCM)**.

Temporal locality means nearby when measured in terms of time. Compare with spatial locality. Temporal locality refers to a program behavior in which data is likely to be reused relatively soon. Algorithms exhibiting good temporal locality in data usage can benefit from data caching, which is common in modern computers. It is not unusual to be able to achieve both temporal and spatial locality in data usage. Computer systems are generally more likely to achieve optimal performance when both are achieved, hence the interest in algorithm design to do so.

Thread could refer to a *software* or *hardware* thread. In general, a "software thread" is any software unit of parallel work with an independent flow of control, and a "hardware thread" is any hardware unit capable of executing a single flow of control (in particular, a hardware unit that maintains a single program counter).

Thread Composability Manager (TCM) is a shared arbitrator that is included in the oneAPI Toolkits for improving composability between TBB, OpenMP, OpenCL, and SYCL when executing on CPUs.

Thread parallelism is a mechanism for implementing parallelism in hardware using a separate flow of control for each task.

Thread-local storage refers to data that is purposefully allocated with the intent to only access from a single thread, at least during concurrent computations. The goal is to avoid need for synchronization during the most intense computational moments in an algorithm. A classic example of thread-local storage is creating partial sums when working toward adding all numbers in a large array, by first adding sub-regions in parallel into local partial sums (also known as privatized variables) that, by nature of being local/private, require no global synchronization to sum into.

Threading Building Blocks (TBB) is the most popular abstract solution for parallel programming in C++. TBB is an open source project initially created by Intel that has been ported to a very wide range of operating systems and processors from many vendors. TBB is now under the governance of the UXL Foundation.

Throughput is defined as the rate at which those tasks are completed, given a set of tasks to be performed. Throughput measures the rate of computation, and it is given in units of tasks per unit time. See **bandwidth** and **latency**.

TFLOP/s (teraFLOP/s) = 10^12 double-precision (64-bit) floating-point operations per second.

TFLOPs (teraFLOPs) = 10^12 double-precision (64-bit) floating-point operations.

Tiling is when you divide a loop into a set of parallel tasks of a suitable granularity. In general, tiling consists of applying multiple steps on a smaller part of a problem instead of running each step on the whole problem one after the other. The purpose of tiling is to increase reuse of data in caches. Tiling can lead to dramatic performance increases when a whole problem does not fit in cache. We prefer the term "tiling" instead of "blocking" and "tile" instead of "block." Tiling and tile have become the more common terms in recent times.

TLB is an abbreviation for Translation Lookaside Buffer. A TLB is a specialized cache that is used to hold translations of virtual to physical page addresses. The number of elements in the TLB determines how many pages of memory can be accessed simultaneously with good efficiency. Accessing a page not in the TLB will cause a TLB miss. A TLB miss typically causes a trap to the operating system so that the page table can be referenced and the TLB updated.

Trip count is the number of times a given loop will execute ("trip"), same thing as *iteration count*.

Unified Acceleration (UXL) Foundation is a project driving the development of an open standard accelerator software ecosystem. TBB is governed by the UXL Foundation.

Uniform Memory Access (UMA): Used to categorize memory design characteristics in a shared memory architecture. UMA = memory access latency is the same for all memory. NUMA = memory access latency is different for different memories. Compare with **NUMA**. See Chapter 11.

UXL: See **Unified Acceleration (UXL) Foundation**.

Vector operations are low-level operations that act on multiple data elements at once in SIMD fashion.

Vector parallelism is a mechanism for implementing parallelism in hardware using the same flow of control on multiple data elements.

Vectorization is the act of transforming code to enable simultaneous computations using vector hardware. Multiprocessor instructions such as MMX, SSE, AVX, AVX2, and AVX-512 instructions utilize vector hardware, but vector hardware outside of CPUs may come in other forms that are also targeted by vectorization. The vectorization of code tends to enhance performance because more data is processed per instruction than would be done otherwise. See also **vectorize**.

Vectorize refers to converting a program from a scalar implementation to a vectorized implementation to utilize vector hardware such as SIMD instructions (e.g., MMX, SSE, AVX, AVX2, AVX-512). Vectorization is a specialized form of parallelism.

vi is a text-based editor that was shipped with most UNIX and BSD systems written by Bill Joy, popular only to those who have yet to discover emacs (according to James). Yes, it is open source. Compares unfavorably to emacs and Atom. Yes, Ron, James did look at the "vi" Nutshell book you gave to him … He still insists on using vi just long enough to get emacs downloaded and installed.

Virtual memory decouples the address used by software from the physical addresses of real memory. The translation from virtual addresses to physical addresses is done in hardware that is initialized and controlled by the operating system.

ZettaFLOP/s = 10^{21} double-precision (64-bit) floating-point operations per second.

ZettaFLOPs = 10^{21} double-precision (64-bit) floating-point operations.

ZettaOP/s = 10^{21} mathematical operations per second.

ZettaOPs = 10^{21} mathematical operations.

Index

© Michael J. Voss, James R. Reinders 2025
M. J. Voss and J. R. Reinders, *Today's TBB*, https://doi.org/10.1007/979-8-8688-1270-5